P.G. WODEHOUSE

P.G. WODEHOUSE

Man and Myth

BARRY PHELPS

CONSTABLE · LONDON

First published in Great Britain 1992
by Constable and Company Limited
3 The Lanchesters, 162 Fulham Palace Road
London W6 9ER
Copyright © Barry Phelps 1992
The right of Barry Phelps to be
identified as the author of this book
has been asserted by him in accordance
with the Copyright, Designs and Patents Act 1988
ISBN 0 09 471620 X
Set in Linotron Ehrhardt 11pt by
Servis Filmsetting Ltd, Manchester
Printed in Great Britain by
St Edmundsbury Press Ltd
Bury St Edmunds, Suffolk

A CIP catalogue record for this book
is available from the British Library

Also by Barry Phelps

The Inflation Fighter's Handbook
Power and the Party: The Carlton Club 1831–1981

CONTENTS

ILLUSTRATIONS

THOSE WITHOUT WHOM ...
DEDICATION AND
ACKNOWLEDGEMENTS

Back at the turn of the century I and the rest of the boys
would as soon have gone out without our spats as allowed
a novel of ours to go out practically naked, as you might
say. The dedication was the thing.

Bertie Wooster Sees It Through

Every biography is no more the creation of one person than the music of a
symphony orchestra. Many people – friends and strangers – have helped
me with this book. While I take the criticism, the credit and the royalties,
they must make do with my gratitude and the dedication of this book to
each and all of them.

Academy of Motion Picture Arts and Sciences, Beverly Hills, California:
Margaret Herrick Library staff. Gaye Bennett for additional research in
Washington DC. Beverly Hills Library staff, California. Lavender Briggs,
who typed the manuscript of this book with heavenly efficiency. British
Film Institute, London library staff. British Library staff, Bloomsbury,
especially David Maggs, and at Colindale and Blackfriars. Valerie Burgess
for further research at the Wodehouse Library, Dulwich College. Burns
& Oates for permission to quote from Robert Speight's *Hilaire Belloc*.
Columbia University, New York, Butler Library staff. David Cartwright of
Dulwich College for permission to quote the letter to him from the late
John Griffith. Sir Edward Cazalet, Wodehouse's grandson, who read my
draft manuscript, corrected me on several points and made valuable
suggestions but takes no responsibility for my views, many of which he
does not share. Chelsea Library staff, Chelsea Old Town Hall Branch.
Noel Clarke for support, encouragement and correcting my French. Toni
Clarke for annihilating the first draft of chapter 1 (it was rotten) without
annihilating my ego. Sir Colin Cole, KCVO TD, Garter King of Arms
who generously gave of his expertise although he takes no responsibility

9

for my views on the Wodehouse pedigree. Catherine Cooke of the Marylebone Library for providing material from *The Strand*. David Cooper, my
friend and solicitor, for advice on legal matters within this book. *Daily
Mail*, London, library staff and my former boss, the Editor Sir David
English, for allowing me to use those archives. David Damant, for reading
my draft manuscript and making valuable suggestions. Anne Dewe, my
literary agent. Frances Donaldson, author of *P.G. Wodehouse: The Authorized Biography* for permission to quote from that book. James B. Dufficy,
for so many reasons and especially for his invaluable help in professionally
carrying out further researches for me in New York and Washington DC,
and for numerous constructive suggestions. The Master and Governors of
Dulwich College for allowing me to use the Wodehouse Library and
facilities, and to quote from and reproduce their copyright material. *The
Economist* Research Department for providing figures (which I have
rounded off) on the falling value of the US dollar and pound over
Wodehouse's lifetime. Owen Dudley Edwards for permission to quote
from his literary biography, *P.G. Wodehouse*. Her Majesty Queen Elizabeth The Queen Mother for gracious permission to reprint her telegram
to the Wodehouse Centenary celebrants in New York. Mrs Joan Fairlie
for permission to quote from *With Prejudice*, the memoirs of her late
husband, Gerard Fairlie. Christopher Fildes for wit and the fine example
of his writing when I worked for him at the *Daily Mail*. John Fletcher,
Wodehouse scholar of gentle wit who read my entire manuscript, picked
out many errors and made many valuable suggestions. Charles E. Gould
Jr for friendship and inspiration. Benny Green for permission to quote
from his *P.G. Wodehouse: A Literary Biography* and for vetting my chapter
'The Trio Of Musical Fame'. Jonathan Green, lexicographer extraordinary, who advised me 'Bung a lot of Wodehouse quotes into the thing
and no one will notice what a rotten book it is'. The late John Griffith of
Jesus College Oxford for permission to quote his letter to David Cartwright and for additional information. Guildhall Library staff, City Of
London Corporation. Austin Hall, librarian, The Wodehouse Library,
Dulwich College. G.W. Harrison, assistant clerk, Merchant Taylors'
Company for help on the Revd J.B. Deane's association with the company. Martin Harvey, secretary of The Garrick Club, for details of Wodehouse's membership and sponsors. James H. Heineman, Wodehouse
expert, enthusiast and publisher for much help and wise advice including
a firm suggestion not to call this book *Phelps On Wodehouse*. Mrs Alex
Cheeseman of the Hong Kong & Shanghai Bank for further details about
Wodehouse's time there as a clerk. Lady Hornby, Wodehouse's granddaughter Sheran, who read my draft manuscript, corrected me on several
points and made various helpful suggestions but takes no responsibility for

my views, many of which she does not share. Paul Hosefros of the *New York Times* for help with material from that great paper. Dr Louis Hughes, oenophile and friend for advice on the medical matters in this book. India Office Library staff at Blackfriars. Richard Ingrams for permission to quote from his essay 'Much Obliged Mr Wodehouse'. David A. Jasen, author of the first biography *P.G. Wodehouse: A Portrait Of A Master* (and the first Wodehouse bibliography) for permission to quote from that exemplary work and for blazing the trail. Alan Kennard, who gave me space in his office where I wrote most of this book and was a cornucopia of helpful advice and information culled from his own extensive knowledge and outstanding reference library. Jean Kennedy, BA, county archivist, Norfolk Record Office for help in researching the Wodehouse family. Mark Le Fanu, general secretary of the Society of Authors, for directing me to the Society's papers at the British Library and for permission to quote the unpublished Council statement of c. 1 August 1941. Bernard Levin for permission to quote from his obituary in *The Times* of P.G. Wodehouse. Victor Lewis for help in researching the Hollywood Cricket Club. Library of Congress staff, Washington, DC. The Little Church Around The Corner, New York. The Revd Norman J. Catir Jr., rector, and the Revd Charles S. Temple, curate. David Lloyd, scriptwriter for *Cheers*, *Taxi* and *Amen* among others; for valuably reviewing my chapters on the role of scriptwriters today, on the theatre and on Hollywood. Kenneth A. Lohf, librarian for rare books and manuscripts at the Butler Library, Columbia University, New York for access to their Reynolds Collection. Los Angeles Public Library, South Spring Street. Eileen McIlvaine, for producing her comprehensive and scholarly Wodehouse bibliography and for answering my further questions. Katrina McQuillan, assistant librarian of the United Grand Lodge of England for details of Wodehouse's membership of the Freemasons. Barry Mann, Hon. Archivist, The Savage Club, for details of Wodehouse's membership. Lady Moncrieffe of that Ilk for permission to quote from the writings of her husband, the late Sir Iain Moncreiffe of that Ilk, Bart. David Morgan for details of the Jerusalem Lodge of the Freemasons to which Wodehouse belonged. Jan Morris for permission to quote from her book *Pax Britannica*. Norman (N.T.P.) Murphy, soldier, scholar, author, engraver, friend, polymath and author of *In Search of Blandings* for permission to quote from that book. National Army Museum London, library staff. New York City, Department of Records and Information. New York City Library staff at 42nd Street, the Mid-Manhattan branch, the Lincoln Centre branch and the 43rd Street Annexe. The Oppenheim-John Downes Memorial Trust for permission to quote from E. Philips Oppenheim's *The Pool Of Memory*. Revd Cannon David Painter for advice on the ecclesiastical elements in Wodehouse. Dr Jan Piggott, Head of Archives at Dulwich College, for much help willingly given. Dr David Pyke for help on medical matters in this book. Tony Ring, who is writing a book on the saga of P.G. Wodehouse's tax battles, for his technical vetting of my own work on that aspect of Wodehouse's life. Cecily Roberts, my daughter, who revealed an invaluable talent for constructive critical reading. It is due to her that the structure of this book is far better and the prose leaner than it would otherwise have been. Mark Roberts, my son-in-law, for essential help with the software of my word-processor. Robson Books for permission to quote from Michael Freedland's *Jerome Kern: A Biography*. Revd David Rye, vicar of the parish of Barnham Broom, Norfolk, which embraces Kimberley House. Mrs P.M. Schute, secretary of the Royal Society of Literature. The editor of the *Scunthorpe Evening News* for permission to quote John Hatton's article from his paper. Sir Patrick Sergeant, longtime City editor of the Daily Mail, for teaching me the disciplines of writing. Linda Shaw of Nottingham University for researching Leonard Rowley's period there. J.A. Simpson, co-editor, the *Oxford English Dictionary*, for providing me with details of all Wodehouse citations in the *OED*. Barbara Sinclair, one of England's leading graphologists, who proved to me that graphology can enhance our understanding of people and who analysed Wodehouse's youthful writing for this book. D.J. Skipper, MA, headmaster, The Merchant Taylors' School for help with the Revd J.B. Deane's association with the school. Margaret Slythe, Head of Library 1981–91, The Wodehouse Library, Dulwich College, London, for unstinted help. This included not only providing me with much new and valuable information about Wodehouse when at the college but also reading my entire draft manuscript and making many wise and valuable suggestions. Also for friendship. John Snuggs, my bank manager, for support while working on this book. Iain Sproat, author of *Wodehouse At War*, for permission to quote from that book and for friendship and shrewd advice. Theatre Museum, London, library staff. Ralph Thompson, Regimental Museum, 15th/21st King's Royal Hussars for help with the career of Colonel Philip Wodehouse. Richard Usborne, not only for inspiration but for much personal kindness, wise advice and permission to quote from his books and essays on P.G. Wodehouse. Auberon Waugh for permission to quote his father, Evelyn Waugh, and from his own works. Westminster Central Reference Library staff. Wetherbys and Mrs Loraine Moran for providing details of Ethel Wodehouse as a racehorse owner and of her horse, Front Line.

WODEHOUSE AND ME: INTRODUCTION

'Tell me were you always like this or did it come on suddenly?'

'Sir?'

'The brain. The grey matter. Were you an outstandingly brilliant boy?'

'My mother thought me intelligent, sir.'

'You can't go by that. My mother thought *me* intelligent.'

'Episode Of The Dog McIntosh'
from *Very Good Jeeves*

M Y mother feared I was mentally retarded. She could read fluently at the age of three; my sister could do so at four, but I couldn't until I was five. The wait was worth it for then a new world opened up to me.

One day when I was five and a half I went into the library and took down a book in green cloth. I had just read *Simple Heraldry Cheerfully Illustrated* and thought that a book called *The Code Of The Woosters* by someone named P.G. Wodehouse would complement my new found knowledge of heraldry with expertise on chivalry. So it did, for no character in fiction is more chivalrous than Bertie Wooster. With *The Code Of The Woosters* I entered that magical English Eden which never has and never will exist this side of Paradise but surely does on the other. It has remained with me ever since as a happy haven whenever I need a respite from the storms and squalls of the real world.

Although this book began as yet another act of homage to Wodehouse I was already convinced that we did not know the real man. Ten years spent as an antiquarian bookdealer specializing in Wodehouse material enabled me to see more comment on Wodehouse, especially rare early profiles in periodicals and memoirs, than most enthusiasts – while a decade as a

13

Fleet Street journalist developed my sense for a suspect story. My original synopsis for this book, the harvest of fifteen years planning and research, included many of the accepted Wodehouse nostrums: one by one they turned out to be either downright wrong or merely a misleading part of the whole truth. My conviction was proved a certainty. The Wodehouse we know is only the Wodehouse he wanted us to know, far different from the real man. He is a lord of language and, *ipso facto*, a master communicator.

Discovering the real Wodehouse required checking where possible every story he told about himself and, if plagiarism is stealing from one source and research from many, this is a well researched book. Apart from Wodehouse's own 'autobiographical' books plus the biographies by David Jasen and Frances Donaldson I have found the following volumes of literary criticism and research invaluable, inspiring or both.

Richard Usborne's *Wodehouse At Work To The End* is the definitive analysis of Wodehouse as a writer, *tout court*. Usborne has become recognized as a Wodehouse expert but that underestimates him. He is as fine and perceptive an analyst of English writing as we have. Since he first wrote *Wodehouse At Work* much has been written about Wodehouse's prose. Those who have trodden in Usborne's footsteps and then walked a little further have written perceptively; those who have not have not. Usborne, like Wodehouse, is a classicist.

Sadly Geoffrey Jaggard was taken from the Wodehouse world (or to it) before he could complete his planned *Wodehouse Concordance* but he did leave us extracts as two books: *Wooster's World* and *Blandings The Blest*. They are pure delight. Jaggard makes no attempt to emulate Wodehouse's style but his own is in perfect harmony with it.

> GISH, Lillian: for love of whom, Bonzo Travers' prime of youth is but a frost of cares, his feast of joy a dish of pain.[1]

A remarkable work of literary detection and scholarship is Norman Murphy's *In Search Of Blandings*. He tracked down the original sources of people, places and events that occur in the Wodehouse canon and proved that the genius of Wodehouse did not lie in creating them – he never did – but in the way he adapted them from real life and the unique and perfect prose with which he made them his own. As Wodehouse said of another playwright 'The treatment is everything'. Murphy's book is comparable to A.J.A. Symons' *The Quest For Corvo* but Frederick Rolf, self-styled Baron Corvo, was not only one of our finest writers but also a cheat, a liar, a sponger and a psychological mess who died destitute. Far better copy than Wodehouse who liked to think of himself as he described his father: 'Normal as rice pudding', which is strictly accurate – like calling Mozart 'a normal composer' or the *Mona Lisa* 'a normal painting'.

In referring to Wodehouse's books I have used the first publication title, whether US or UK, with the transatlantic title (where different) following in brackets. Titles of his books either side of the Atlantic often varied from as early as 1915 when *Something Fresh* in the UK became *Something New* in the US. These first editions accord with the McIlvaine-Heineman bibliography of Wodehouse, a work of outstanding scholarship and as definitive as any ever will be. It is essential for any serious collector.

I have also made use of hundreds of other sources, listed among the acknowledgements at the front of the book and in the References (see Appendix 1). There are no anecdotal gems hidden in the numbered references which relate only to sources, while the footnotes are minimal. This is a gesture to Wodehouse who disliked footnotes as interfering with the flow of the prose and so with the readers' pleasure. The Foreword to *Over Seventy*, with twenty footnotes in five pages, makes the point.

It is high time,[5] in my opinion, that this nuisance was abated and biographers and essayists restrained from strewing these unsightly blemishes[6] through their pages.

5. Greenwich Mean or, in America, Eastern Standard.
6. Footnotes.

So my reference notes can be safely ignored by all except Wodehouse fanatics anxious to prove me wrong on some arcane point and those who wish to read the original sources.

Over Wodehouse's long life the purchasing power of the British pound fell horribly and that of the US dollar steadily. A rule-of-thumb to calculate the 1991 value of earlier sums of money is to multiply 1900 pounds by forty, 1930 pounds by thirty and 1960 pounds by ten. For dollars the same calculations are; multiply 1900 dollars by sixteen, 1930 dollars by eight and 1960 dollars by five. Such is inflation.[2] (Younger readers, and those outside the UK, may be unfamiliar with the old British currency in which Wodehouse was paid, in England, for most of his working life. Twelve pennies made one shilling, twenty shillings made one pound. However professional people were often paid in guineas; a guinea was twenty-one shillings, half a guinea ten shillings and sixpence.)

Writing this book required me to reread, once more, the entire Wodehouse opus: an abiding pleasure. (The UK version of *The Prince And Betty* is the only Wodehouse book I find unreadable.) However in commenting upon or quoting from his writings I have concentrated on his books, largely leaving aside the huge numbers of early stories where he was teaching himself his craft. (Selecting from these it is possible to prove any thesis about Wodehouse-the-writer you care to propound.) Writing to Usborne in old age Wodehouse relates how annoyed he was when picking up Leslie Charteris's *Saint Detective Magazine* to find in it a detective story – he thought it lousy juvenilia and no credit to him – which he had sold to *Pearson's Magazine* somewhere around 1910. (It was '*The Harmonica Player*', actually sold to New York's *All-Story Cavalier Weekly* in 1915.)

Such stories showed the greatness to come and the beauty and cadence of his English but they were largely experimental, often alien to the writer who became beloved the world over and thin fare compared with the rich treats to follow. In many of them the influence of O'Henry comes out strongly but the American's sentimentality was to be refined out of Wodehouse's own style.

Owners of copyrights quoted by me beyond that allowed by law are thanked in the acknowledgements, except where they have charged a fee and are, instead, credited in my reference notes. I have tried to trace the owners of all such copyrights and illustrations and in the few instances where I have failed I apologize and would like to hear from the persons concerned via my publishers.

Lastly I must make clear that many of the P.G. Wodehouse quotations in this book are the copyright of the Trustees of the Estate of P.G. Wodehouse. Where I have quoted Wodehouse without further attribution those quotations are the copyright of the Trustees used by me as allowed by law which permits fair dealing for purposes of criticism or review.

In this biography there is a great deal of new information and a much different perception of the man to that he allowed us to see but it cannot hurt him now and I believe he deserves to be seen for the complex and fascinating person he actually was. He had nothing to hide but his genius.

BARRY PHELPS

London, New York, Los Angeles, Valley Fields
1992

— I —

THE MYTH

The world knows him only as he wishes to be known.[1]

David Jasen

P G. WODEHOUSE worked hard to create the image of himself we have today – the amiable and unworldly recluse, the simple man with a lucky ability to write sparkling humour who claimed he was about as pronounced an oaf as ever went around with his lower jaw drooping and a glassy look in his eyes.[2]

The cause of this myth-making is clear. Pelham Grenville Wodehouse (pronounced Woodhouse) – creator of such greatly loved immortals as Bertie Wooster and Jeeves, a phalanx of aunts, Lord Emsworth, Psmith, Ukridge, Uncle Fred and a host of lesser stars in the galaxy of English literature – unwisely gave a series of five innocuous broadcasts from Germany to neutral America whilst a civilian internee during the Second World War. The hysterical abuse heaped on him as a result devastated him, although he never let this show. Thereafter he retreated firstly to New York, then to Remsenburg (an out of the way hamlet on Long Island) and rarely ever again said or wrote anything for publication that was not ortho-dox or anodyne or complimentary and usually all three. Then he set to work creating an image he thought would protect him against the world.

He was never a boastful man and seemed to find some pleasure in portraying himself as slow witted due, he claimed, to having been dropped on the head as a baby and, as a result, not what one would call bright[3] and writing of himself at his first job as the worst bungler ever to have entered the portals of the Hong Kong & Shanghai Bank. He pictured the managers in conversation arguing about the shortcoming of a new recruit to the bank who ought to have been chloroformed at birth, with the old hands reminiscing that, compared with Wodehouse, the lad was in the top tier of the intelligentsia. And for good measure he added that he was just a plain dumb brick.[4]

17

Almost all the published biographical material we have on Wodehouse comes directly from him and it comes from 1953 onwards with the UK publication of *Performing Flea*, a selection of his letters to his lifelong friend from their schooldays together, William Townend, with a few asides from Townend back to him. (Originally this was to be called *Thirty Years of P.G. Wodehouse* by William Townend, but that wouldn't have sold so well.) The book was a carefully constructed image-building project. All those letters, especially Townend's, were edited or rewritten by Wodehouse to reinforce the impression of a humorous writer who knows all about his craft and not much about anything else. When that book came out later in America those same letters had been further edited and rewritten, often with whole chunks added verbatim from his novels. The US title, *Author! Author!*, is much less fun than the working title using the *New York Times*' description of him 'The Burbling Pixie'.[5] *Performing Flea* has great value as a treatise on the art of writing fiction and some value as a biographical source but it must be treated with caution: *Author! Author!* is almost a novel in letters in the same form as A.G. Macdonell's *Flight From A Lady*.

That same year, in America, Wodehouse gave us *Bring On The Girls* 'co-written' with another lifelong friend, Guy Bolton with whom he collaborated on many musicals and plays, about their times together as book and lyric writers on Broadway. Every droll New York theatrical anecdote of the period is given as happening to them. It was mostly written by Wodehouse and vintage Wodehouse it is, but it too was aimed at creating the image Wodehouse wanted us to have of him. It is as much fiction as fact, presenting Wodehouse and Bolton as two very ordinary Joes, ping-pong balls buffeted by kindly and unkindly fates. *America I Like You* (1956) is loosely autobiographical, a light and freestyle book which, again, portrays an amiable old buffer who just happens to write well. It is significantly different from the UK version, *Over Seventy*. Both those books reinforced the image of Wodehouse presented to the world in *Performing Flea/Author! Author!*.

The first biography of Wodehouse from another pen is David A. Jasen's *P.G. Wodehouse: A Portriat Of A Master*, published in 1974 in New York and 1975 in London. A beguiling book, it carries the reader along with its enthusiasm. Jasen, a devotee of Wodehouse's writing, invited himself to Remsenburg. 'I went off to seek him out. Arriving in the afternoon I introduced myself'. He was a frequent visitor thereafter. Derek Grimsdick, then Wodehouse's publisher in the UK, met the young biographer and told Wodehouse that Jasen talked about him with the same sort of reverence that Aileen Peavey showed towards Psmith when he was masquerading as Ralston McTodd in *Leave It to Psmith*.[6] Wodehouse, while gently mocking his own work in public, knew himself to be a great writer and realized he would inevitably be subject to biography. So, typically, saying he only did it to please his wife Ethel, he put up with Jasen's incessant trips and gave way to the young man's desire to write his life story (and compile the first serious Wodehouse bibliography).[7] From these visits Jasen garnered a wealth of information about Wodehouse, his life and work; most of it fact, some of it not, but all of it presented with Wodehouse's own gloss. Every subsequent book on Wodehouse has had to make substantial use of Jasen's. That means that everyone has had to use material Wodehouse supplied to Jasen, all of it structured to give the world the idea of Wodehouse he wanted us to have. He was wise: co-operation gave him effective control over both the content and the approach of the text. He also hoped, too modestly, that the Jasen biography would deter any other author from repeating the task. Jasen, a clever man, knew just what was happening and accepted the unspoken, unwritten terms upon which Wodehouse co-operated. Thus he took down facts, checked them whenever he could and set down Wodehouse's life story, but he did not write any assessment of Wodehouse himself, except briefly in his introduction where he posted a coded signal to show he knew more than he wrote. 'The world only knows him as he wishes to be known'. He also described both *Performing Flea* and *Bring On The Girls* as 'almost true stories'.

The authorized biography of Wodehouse is Frances Donaldson's, *P.G. Wodehouse* published in 1982. In private life she is Lady Donaldson of Kingsbridge and was a close friend from their schooldays of Wodehouse's adopted daughter Leonora; her husband Jack played golf with Wodehouse before the Second World War and her father was one of Wodehouse's friends. She remains close to Wodehouse's step-grandchildren, Lady (Sheran) Hornby and Sir Edward Cazalet who gave Lady Donaldson access to his substantial treasury of Wodehouse's private papers. Her most important new material was Wodehouse's internment diary and related post-war papers and, naturally, she focuses on these, which take up nearly half her book. A safe pair of hands.

There are two other biographical studies. Herbert Warren Wind wrote *The World of P.G. Wodehouse* (1972), based on many interviews with him at Remsenburg, for a *New Yorker* profile. (In 1952 Wodehouse said all the profiles were about dull people one had never heard of!)[8] It is an enjoyable book, mellifluously written by one gentleman about another, but Wodehouse also had control of this book as the content was, again, based almost entirely on what he said. Joseph Connolly's short *P.G. Wodehouse: An Illustrated Biography*, written in a style imitative of Wodehouse, provides an introduction to his subject but does not attempt any new assessment of the man, his life or his work. All the other books about Wodehouse are literary criticism concentrating on his writing, although Benny Green's *P.G. Wodehouse: A Literary Biography*, the best assessment there is of the theatrical side of his work, includes a brisk canter through his life.

The most valuable book of Wodehouse's writings is the posthumous selection of his letters, *Yours Plum*, edited by Frances Donaldson and not by Wodehouse. For the first time those with eyes to see can perceive just a few hints of the real man. Much more of the real man emerges from the hundreds of letters he exchanged with Guy Bolton; William Townend; his much loved Leonora; friend and writer Denis Mackail; with his American agents for thirty years, Paul R. Reynolds and Son and his publishers Derek Grimsdick in London and (post-World War Two) Peter Schwed in New York. The letters not only show aspects of Wodehouse never revealed to his public but aspects totally incompatible with that public persona he created. Post-war memories of pre-war Wodehouse are of scant use, invariably being coloured by his later image building. They support the myth. Pre-war pen-portraits of Wodehouse do not.

Aiding and abetting the fabrication of the myth were Wodehouse's legion of loyal fans and the literary critics. They were reluctant to think that their idol coloured the truth, which is odd. One should not expect a genius whose field was fiction to do anything else. Christopher Isherwood may have been a camera, Wodehouse was not. He could not come across any story or event without seeing how it could be made more amusing and interesting with a little judicious tinkering and polishing. And so judiciously tinkered with and polished they were. Thus anything he said or wrote about himself for publication has to be treated as a suspect source. It's no wonder that different commentators give different 'facts' about the same events. Discussing *Bring On The Girls*, Wodehouse told Bolton that they should let the truth go to the wall if it interfered with entertainment, even if they had to invent everything.[9] Typically he changed the order of their Broadway shows for sound, artistic reasons. Too long a run of successes would have become boring for the reader so the flops were brought forward. Later in life Wodehouse admitted to Usborne that quite a lot of the stories in *Bring On The Girls* were fathered on him by Guy Bolton and he approved as it knitted the book together so well. But, typically, he didn't see why Usborne shouldn't continue to use those stories as having happened to him as they made good copy.[10] For example there is a fine story of Wodehouse throwing letters into the street from the window of his London apartment, confident that some kind and honest passer-by would post them, or even deliver them. That story is true – apart from the fact that Wodehouse's friend and theatrical collaborator,

Fred Thompson, was the man with that optimistic quirk. As Wodehouse might have said to Bolton, 'That's another fine myth you've got me into.' The same approach was adopted with *Performing Flea*. He told Townend that he felt they must fake much of the letters and add a lot of anecdotes about celebrities, the sort of thing people would want to read about.[11]

That artist's approach made *Performing Flea* a highly enjoyable book, contributing to making the Wodehouse myth a seamless whole as befits a master craftsman. It is plausible and convincing, skilfully showing us just part of the man during part of his life; the post-war Wodehouse, a modest recluse who liked to be left alone to write. It portrayed an innocent abroad in a real world which he did not understand; a person with little interest in or understanding of money; a man with no ability to deal with people; a happily henpecked and devoted husband whose wife handled all their finances and kept him short of money; an anodyne, kindly man without strong emotions or feelings, except towards dogs, and with only one close friend.

That cardboard caricature has been accepted by the world which likes the famous and the infamous to be two dimensional: the icons of unblemished purity, the villains of irredeemable villainy. But we shall see there was nothing two-dimensional about Wodehouse. Had he not made those foolish broadcasts, nor suffered the resulting opprobrium, he might have let us see the real man, the one we glimpse in pre-war memoirs. 'Just writing one book after another, that's my life' is what he told David Jasen[12] but that was less than the full story of an interesting and long life which divides into two distinct main periods: prior to 1941, which covered the first two-thirds of his life including his formative years – and post-1945. The tragically early death of his beloved Leonara in 1944 also contributed to the change; when she died a part of him died too. Wodehouse, like most human beings, evolved and 'The Master' who died at Remsenburg was a very different character from the thrusting tyro journalist of the 1900s, the successful lyricist and dramatist of the 1910s and the world famous author of the twenties and thirties. Friends and family who only knew Wodehouse after the Second World War find this hard to accept. Several of them have told me, 'You're wrong to say he was gregarious. I knew him well at Remsenburg and he really was a shy man' but they did not know him prior to his internment and the pre-war records tell a different tale.

The success of Wodehouse's image-making was also abetted by all those who loved him, including his readers, fastening on the excuse he gave them for making those broadcasts. His unworldliness. Later we shall see that he scarcely needed an excuse and that the entire myth-making operation should have been unnecessary. That success is very evident

from his obituaries and the wave of press comment and books about his
work that has flooded out ever since. 'The most innocent and unworldly
of men. He was not an intellectual.' 'A not very complex man.' 'In all
important ways he never thought about money.' 'His claim to greatness lay
in masterly exploitation of his limitations. The chief of these was an
inability to cope with the real world.' 'He was a solitary man.' 'There is
little to say about his life. He did little except write. He had few friends
and was unhappy in society unless it was the closed society of the boys'
school. He was like the three wise monkeys put together when it came to
evil.' 'A lack of interest in, or knowledge of, what the workaday world was
up to.' 'P.G. Wodehouse was an innocent.' '. . . the childlike innocence of
Wodehouse. He took little interest in the outside world.' 'His innocence
was total.' 'The lack of awareness of reality that afflicted Bertie and his
butler (*sic*) also marked their creator's life. His genius, after all, was the
ability to present a world totally removed from reality and make it believable. Perhaps he could describe that world so well because he lived in it.'
'Wodehouse had a certain spontaneous simplicity about him. [He] himself
was as gentle as the world he created.' 'I have an overwhelming impression of a genuinely innocent man who is obviously ill-fitted to live in an
age of ideological conflict.' 'A solitary man.'[13]

   That is the myth Wodehouse gave us. While he and his wife were alive
it was right to respect it. Now they are dead and cannot be hurt by
anything written about him he deserves to be seen for the complex, subtle,
paradoxical and phenomenally intelligent intellectual he was. The man
behind the myth is infinitely more interesting and worthwhile than the
image he left us.

— 2 —

THE MAN

No alienist could possibly have guessed him to be the
fanciful, erudite, brilliant and highly intellectual man he
actually was.[1]

Frank Crowninshield

Editor, *Vanity Fair*

T HE Wodehouse of the Wodehouse myth could never have written
as he did, achieved what he did and won the esteem he did.
During his long life from 1881 to 1975 Wodehouse helped trigger
the reorganization of MI5, Britain's counter-espionage service. He was a
major influence on the English public-school story and on the development of the American musical theatre, especially the lyric. He was one of
the very first transatlantic commuters and, as I shall show, the first truly
Anglo-American author. He had a significant impact on the English
language. He was revered by his peers and influenced almost every
subsequent novelist writing in English, whether they realize it or not. He
became caught up in The Hollywood Writers' Wars and was a founder of
the famous Hollywood Cricket Club. He caused a brief furore over his
remarks on the way the great Hollywood studios were run. He was
awarded the Mark Twain Medal in America and an Honorary Doctorate
of Letters by Oxford University. He was one of the highest paid writers in
the world in the nineteen-thirties and met many of the most powerful,
famous, talented and wealthy people of his era. He was interned when the
Germans overran Northern France in 1940 and endured, without com-
plaint, grave hardship as a civilian prisoner of war. He unwisely made
some lighthearted broadcasts from Germany in 1941 and suffered terribly
as a result. He is one of the tiny band of individuals, and one of the tinier
band of non-citizens, to take a case to the United States Supreme Court
and have it heard. He received a knighthood for his services to English

literature. He wrote ninety-eight books (mostly novels but including six-teen volumes of short stories, three of 'autobiography', two of collected articles and one posthumous volume of letters) most of which have remained in print since their first publication; he penned all or part of the book and lyrics for thirty-one produced musicals; wrote or co-authored seventeen staged plays and poured out a vast amount of journalism in his early years. That is not the record of an ordinary man.

The real Wodehouse is a subtle personality full of complex contradic-tions. He loved his wife Ethel and let her boss him on all the many things which did not bother him, but was immovable on those few that did. He was totally honest in private but for all his published writing the truth was a malleable raw material. He was sharp and shrewd in his many financial dealings and obsessively interested in money. He was both mean and generous, a team player and also a loner. He had simple tastes but a far from simple character. He was well able to deal with the outside world but mostly chose not to. He was in early life a gregarious man leading an active social life who later became less gregarious and while he loved very few people he inspired love and admiration in all those who got to know him. He was a kind man yet capable of a caustic wit when annoyed. He had impeccable manners but preferred writing to socializing. He was extraordinarily perceptive about people and events that interested him but unpleasant people and events were often totally expunged from his mind. He had great courage and tried to avoid the need for it. He was pro-digiously intelligent but portrayed himself as suffering from a less than average intellect. He was a pleasant conversationalist and gave superb radio interviews but eventually preferred to communicate in writing, even with close friends. He was modest in many ways but had total self-assurance and in private was objectively immodest about his own work. He was highly sensitive but never allowed this to show.

The one true element of the Wodehouse myth is that he preferred to spend his time in writing rather than anything else – but that attitude was far more extreme than anything he allowed us to see. Like many another genius he had tunnel-vision and focused intently on his work – in later life to the exclusion of everything else. Nothing at all was allowed to get in the way of his writing and the sensibilities of other people were nugatory by comparison. Much as he loved his wife Ethel he sacrificed her to his *daemon* and, to a lesser extent, Leonora as well. It was that driving force, as acute as any extreme psychiatric disorder, that refusal to be distracted by the world, that allowed him to make those Berlin broadcasts. It was why he liked meeting people individually when he could discuss writing rather than several at a time when he couldn't. His later preference for corresponding with friends to meeting them was a preference for writing rather than conversation. (The critic Cecily Roberts suggests this is why descriptive passages in his novels are often even better than the dialogue.[2]) All these qualities were contained within a courteous, kindly man, what in his young days would have been called a gentleman.

Wodehouse was not an anti-social man. A writer needs people to help create characters and generate ideas. The number of social events he attended without demur – just those mentioned in *Yours Plum*, *Performing Flea* and *Bring On The Girls* – rebuts the idea. The hundreds of social functions mentioned in his unpublished letters confirm that rebuttal beyond argument and show that before his internment he was a gregarious man who had many more friends than the average person, mostly other writers and theatre people. Unknown young authors whose work had impressed him often received a lunch or dinner invitation out of the blue. He frequented the theatre, enjoyed going to occasional race meetings, stayed with friends for country weekends and invited them to stay with him, was for many years a passionate cricketer and later golfer who regularly attended sporting events including rugger and boxing matches but especially anything at his old school, Dulwich College.

He was not a shy man. The theatrical world is one for strong men and resolute women who can fight their corner, say their say and hold their ground. It is no place for kindly weaklings or diffident authors who can only express themselves in writing and lack the ability to thump the table, at least metaphorically, and get their way in production conferences. Wodehouse was highly successful in the theatre.

He was also self-confident. He found no need for the frantic search for masculine re-assurance that drove Ernest Hemingway to big-game hunting and bullfighting, nor for the social self-justification that drove Old Etonian Eric Blair (pen name George Orwell) to messianic soldiering for the Communists in the Spanish Civil War. Not for Wodehouse the restless globetrotting for scenes and characters pursued by W. Somerset Maugham. He knew his work was good and was not driven by the self-doubts that prompted Hugh Walpole's obsequious behaviour to every book reviewer he could hunt down.

That self-confidence also showed in the way he frequently disparaged his abilities – and he always seemed particularly pleased when the gullible believed him. Wodehouse took intense pleasure in such private jokes where only a few people, and often he alone, knew they existed. To pull someone's leg when they did not realize it was being pulled was, for him, acutely funny. Norman Murphy in *In Search Of Blandings* christened these private jokes 'Wodehouse allusions'. As early as 1905 Wodehouse cast the actor-manager Seymour Hicks, whom he had met the year before, as the actor-manager Higgs in *The Head Of Kay's*. Fifty years later in 'Big

Business' (from *A Few Quick Ones*) Reginald Mulliner visits a firm of
London solicitors Watson, Watson, Watson, Watson & Watson: Wodehouse's US attorney at the time was Watson Washburn. Wodehouse
enjoyed such private jokes all his life, long before they were to help him
create the Wodehouse myth. The more fatuous a remark he could get
taken at face value, the happier he was.

In a masterly essay, 'The Toad At Harrow', the American scholar
Charles E. Gould Jr. analyses one phrase of Bertie Wooster's in *Aunts
Aren't Gentlemen* (US *The Catnappers*), that he felt as much like a toad at
Harrow as anybody with an Eton education could. Gould points out those
fifteen words (which would mean nothing in another language) embrace a
pun, a mangled cliche, a simile, a double irony and two synthesized
images.

> It's a crazy statement, but it has meaning and it has meaning fast. It has
> meaning so fast, in fact, that our sweaty haste that makes the night
> joint-laborer with the day and does not divide the Sunday from the
> week could never *teach* it fast enough to make it worth the teaching.[3]

No simple soul wrote those fifteen words.

In revealing the real P.G. Wodehouse we shall examine not only the
facts of his life – as distinct from his gloss on them – and contemporary
pre-war memoirs, newspaper and periodical profiles of the time, but
particularly his unpublished letters. Together they uncover a very different character to the image he bequeathed us; a man from, and formed by,
one of the oldest, great landed families of England; the Wodehouses of
Kimberley House, Wymondham in the county of Norfolk.

GENEALOGY, GENES AND GENIUS

Long before many of the proudest houses in England
were known to fame, Wodehouses of knightly fame were
found fighting side-by-side with the warrior Kings.[1]

Our Old Nobility

WHEN Wodehouse wrote of earls, barons and baronets, of stately
homes and servants, of priests and prelates he did so from
personal knowledge. The Wodehouses were not of the *haute
bourgeousie* but of the landed gentry and, from 1797, the aristocracy. You
won't find much hint of this in his correspondence – far from boasting
about such connections a gentleman does not mention them – but Wodehouse was quietly proud of his lineage and it imbued his writing, and that
of his best loved 'hero', Bertram Wilberforce Wooster, whose mess jacket
was very near to his heart and for which he fully intended to fight with all
the vim of grand old Sieur de Wooster at the Battle of Agincourt.[2] John
Wodehouse fought with distinction at Agincourt;[3] he was P.G. Wodehouse's direct forebear sixteen generations back. An early seventeenth-
century rhyming pedigree of the Wodehouse family tells of Sir John's
exploits. The Woosters are very largely the Wodehouses who have taken
part in English and later British national affairs for at least 700 years.
Bertie tells us the Woosters came over with the Conqueror and were
extremely pally with him.[4] The Wodehouses did not although their pedigree (see Appendix 3) traces them back to the Conquest. Blomefield, the
eighteenth-century Norfolk historian, dismisses the idea of Norman
ancestry stating, 'The pedigrees indeed of this family (I may say, all that I
have seen) deduced them from Bertram of Wodehouse Tower in York-
shire, who 'tis said compounded with the Conqueror and enjoyed his
lands and inheritance, but this is supported by no evidence'.[5]

Panting for breath, his Murrian in his hand
Woodhouse comes in, as back the English beare

My Lords (quoth he) what now inforced to stand
When smiling Fortune off'reth us so faire.
The French lie yonder, like the Wreakes of sand
And you by this our Glory but impair
On now, or never your first fight maintaine
Chatillyon and The Constable are slaine
Hand over Head, Pell Mell upon them runne
If you will prove the Master's of the Day
Ferrers and Greystock have so bravely done
That I excise their Glory, and dare say
From all the English, they the Gole have wonne
Either let's share, or they'll beare all away
This spoke, his axe about his Head he flings
And hasts away, as though his Heeles had Wings
The Incitation of this youthful Knight
Besides amends for this Retrayte to make
Doth re-enforce their Courage with their Might
A second charge, with speed to undertake
Never before were they so mad to fight.[6]

From the Wodehouse Rhyming Pedigree c. 1640

Wodehouse certainly knew of one Bertram de Wodehouse (there were two), the Knight who fought gallantly for Edward I in his wars against the Scots between 1277 and 1283. That Sir Bertram is the literary godfather of Bertram Wooster who was so proud of his fighting ancestors. 'I think that in about another half jiffy I should have been snorting, if not actually shouting, the ancient battle cry of the Woosters. . . . There comes a moment when [a fellow] has to remember his ancestors did dashed well at the Battle of Crecy and put his foot down'.[7]

Sir Bertram's younger son, Robert, occupies a whole page of *The Dictionary of National Biography* as Baron of the Exchequer from 1318 and a favourite of three Kings, Edward I, Edward II and Edward III. Sir Bertram's elder son, Sir William, was ancestor of John Wodehouse who was made Constable of Castle Rising in Norfolk in 1402, Steward of the Duchy of Lancaster in 1414 and was Esquire to the Body and Groom To The Chamber of Henry V between 1413 and 1422. He was a Commissioner of Array for Norfolk responsible for raising troops for the French campaign and later an executor of King Henry's will. He is the John Wodehouse who fought at Agincourt and in honour of whose gallantry his descendants assumed 'Agincourt' as their motto (as well as *Frappe fort* – strike hard). The supporters of the family's arms are two 'Wodehouses', the heraldic term for wild men of the woods – the usual sort of heraldic pun.

When Wodehouse, through Bertie, talked of his fighting ancestors he wasn't just thinking of Sir Bertram and John at Agincourt. Thomas Wodehouse, MP, Standard Bearer for Lord Protector Somerset's army, was killed at the battle of Musselburgh (or Pinkie) in 1547 fighting against the Scots. Sir Philip Wodehouse was knighted on the field of battle by the Earl of Essex for his valour at the capture of Cadiz in 1596 and in 1611 'purchased, compulsorily or freely'[8] the new title of baronet (effectively an hereditary knighthood) from England's new King, James VI of Scotland. During the Civil War Sir Thomas Wodehouse, living in staunchly Parliamentarian East Anglia, kept a low profile – a sensible attitude in keeping with his descendant's approach to the nastier aspects of life.

No other warrior appears among Wodehouse's ancestors until Colonel Philip Wodehouse, Pelham's grandfather. He was appointed an ensign in August 1806, reached full colonel in January 1837 and 'retired by the sale of his commission on 27 December the same year' to marry an heiress, Lydia Lee. In between he fought under Wellington at Waterloo as a captain in the 15th Light Dragoons.[9] Thus, 170 years later, Wodehouse was possibly the last man alive whose grandfather fought at that great battle.

Through the centuries a Wodehouse was usually one of the two Members of Parliament for the County of Norfolk or one of the East Anglian boroughs. Wodehouse numbered seven MPs just among his direct Wodehouse forebears. One of them, Sir Roger Wodehouse, was knighted by Queen Elizabeth I in 1578. Later in the same year she honoured him with a visit to Kimberley during her snipe-like migrations around the country.

A useful characteristic of the Wodehouse line was its habit of marrying heiresses. Money helps in social advancement; a lot of money helps a lot. One hundred and eighty-six years after Sir Philip was made a baronet his great-great-great-great grandson, Sir John Wodehouse, MP, Recorder of Falmouth, was elevated to the peerage in 1797 as Baron Wodehouse of Kimberley in the county of Norfolk. The Wodehouse family had entered the nobility.

In 1866 Sir John's great-grandson, John 3rd Baron Wodehouse, became the first Earl of Kimberley.

'What makes them haughty?' asked Lord Ickenham warmly.
  'Are they Earls?'
  'No, they aren't Earls.'

'Then why the devil' said Lord Ickenham warmly 'are they haughty? Only Earls have the right to be haughty. Earls are hot stuff.'[10]

Kimberley was not lacking in hauteur or family pride. Upon his promotion in the peerage he tried hard to be created Earl of Agincourt[11] which, for a politician whose primary interest was foreign affairs, would hardly have been thought diplomatic by the French. He was thwarted by the College of Heralds and had to settle for Kimberley instead. He was one of the great, aristocratic, Whig politicians of the nineteenth century, holding government office almost continuously from 1852 to 1895 when he retired as Gladstone's Foreign Secretary. Among other honours he became a Knight of the Garter, Chancellor of London University and High Steward of Norwich Cathedral. Lord Kilbracken reminisced:[12]

> He was himself well aware of his own failing. Lord Burghclere told me that Lord Kimberley, getting on to the subject of an ancestor of his who had fought at Agincourt, and of whom Burghclere had spoken with interest, held forth for an hour – literally an hour – without pause. At the end of that time he looked at the clock, stopped suddenly, and said with a laugh 'You brought it on yourself.'*

That great genealogist, Sir Iain Moncreiffe of that Ilk, looked further into the Wodehouse family tree.

> Through grand marriages the Wodehouse baronets brought to our late beloved writer much romantic blood. Sir Philip Wodehouse, the third baronet, married a grand-daughter of Lord William Howard, son of the fourth duke of Norfolk (axed for having designs on Mary Queen of Scots), himself son of the equally beheaded poet Lord Surrey whose father was the victor of Flodden Field, Scotland's greatest military disaster. Through these Howards, long the premier noble house of England, P.G. Wodehouse descended from many strange folk: devious Byzantine emperors and hard-riding Magyar and hot-tempered Plantagenet kings and grim Russian grand princes. From the Cid and blue-blooded de Veres and Harry Hotspur, also (by way of the sinister

---

* The Norfolk antiquarian, Walter Rye (1843–1929), argued vehemently and frequently that John Wodehouse did not fight at Agincourt but was one of the civil servants left behind in London by the King. He made pejorative remarks about the Wodehouse coat-of-arms, sneered at Sir Roger Wodehouse's courageous attempt to talk the leaders of Ket's Rebellion (1549) out of their folly and derided Sir Thomas Wodehouse for keeping his head during the Civil War, but he is remarkably offhand about Sir Philip Wodehouses's well documented valour at the Capture of Cadiz and about the achievements of John Wodehouse, first Earl of Kimberley. One gets the impression he did not like the Wodehouses.[13]

Orsini, hence Popes for uncles) from Simon de Montfort. Tragic Lady Jane Grey, headless too, sovereign Queen of England for a few reluctant days, was his ancestral first cousin; St Thomas Aquinas his ancestral uncle.

There were writers among his forebears too: such as Geoffrey de Villehardouin (died c. 1213) 'the first vernacular historian of France and perhaps of modern Europe, who possessed literary merit', the chronicler of the Fourth Crusade in which he himself had taken part. A remoter forefather of PGW was King Alfred the Great (born 849 and still going strong in folk cake-lore), 'eminently a national writer' who translated books into Anglo-Saxon and to whom we owe it 'that the habit of writing in English never died out'. And also through the Dukes of Norfolk (if, as I believe, the Arden-Whalesborough-Moleyns connection is incorrect) he was the ancestral fifth cousin of Shakespeare.[14]

Thanks to marrying heiresses and to primogeniture (where the eldest son or heir scoops all the family estates) Kimberley enjoyed the means to live as earls should. Cockayne says:

KIMBERLEY. Family Estates. These, in 1883, consisted of 10,805 acres in Norfolk worth £15,195 a year; and of 342 acres in Cornwall (overstated as) worth £9,805 a year. Total 11,147 acres worth £25,000 a year.[15]

Allowing for any exaggeration that was a substantial estate, even then. It also included the patronage or advowson – the right to appoint the priest – of eleven parishes.

They have not neglected to turn them to their own advantage. I find that of the sons and descendants of Sir Armine Wodehouse no less than sixteen have been in Holy Orders. As a sample there was the Hon and Rev Armine Wodehouse, son of the first Lord, who held Barnham Broom, Bixton, Kimberley, West Lexham and Litcham, Norfolk, livings procured for or presented to him by his father, whose united present value is £1,510 with a house attached to each.[16]

That lordly disposal of church livings was well known to Wodehouse. For example Lord Emsworth appoints the Revd Rupert 'Beefy' Bingham, that most irritating and clumsy curate, to the living of Much Matchingham just to make life difficult for Sir Gregory Parsloe-Parsloe, Bt., his rival in the Fat Pigs handicap, who lives in the parish. Stiffy Byng eloquently urges her guardian Sir Watkyn Basset to give her fiancé, the sainted Harold

'Stinker' Pinker a parish so they can get married. Like several Wodehouse heroines she argues her man has no scope as a curate but, if slipped a vicarage, will prove hot stuff. She spoke 'wriggling from base to apex with girlish enthusiasm. But there was no girlish enthusiasm in old Bassett's demeanour'.[17]

Sir Armine's lands had been even more extensive than those of Kimberley who, in 1864, wrote to his uncle, Raikes Currie, 'Without your aid and advice the Estate must have been sold at a ruinous loss. Now everyone has been paid and I have a good prospect of future profit from what remains'.[18]

Like Lord Emsworth he had a wayward son, writing in 1873 of 'My eldest son's infatuated folly and extravagance'. A chorus girl? The first earl also wrote his memoirs *A Journal Of Events During The Gladstone Ministry 1868–1874*, but not for publication. So of course they were published – as were those of his fellow Norfolk peer, Reginald John Peter Swithin, third Earl of Havershot of Biddlecombe Castle in that county and entitled *Laughing Gas*.

The fourth Earl of Kimberley was one who, like Elmer Chinnery the American fish-glue millionaire, married young and kept on marrying, springing from blonde to blonde like a chamois of the Alps leaping from crag to crag. By 1974, when *Bachelors Anonymous* was published, he had matched Chinnery's five wives and by 1982 equalled Henry VIII's record of six and seemed content to stop there.

Eldest sons hold primogeniture in high regard. Younger sons have their doubts about the idea for they must go out into the world to earn a living, or at any rate make one. They officered the armed forces; they enabled the Church of England 'to provide a resident gentleman in every parish' and largely monopolized the learned professions from which most writers come.

Wodehouse was descended from the fifth baronet, Sir Armine Wodehouse, through his younger son the Revd Philip Wodehouse, father of Colonel Philip. His son was Ernest Wodehouse (his first name was Henry, which he never used), Pelham's father. So Wodehouse or any of his three brothers could, in theory, have inherited the baronetcy. Sir Pelham Wodehouse, Bt., has a pleasing ring to it. Jaggard thought Wodehouse could also have inherited the barony of Wodehouse and the earldom of Kimberley.

'No chance of Bill Bailey becoming an earl, I suppose?'
'Not unless he murders about fifty-seven uncles and cousins.'
'Which, being a curate, of course, he would hesitate to do.'[19]

Pelham, Earl of Kimberley, has an even better ring to it but it could never be as he was not descended from the first holders of either of these titles. The first baron was his great-great uncle and the first earl his third cousin. 'Mark you, when I say I'm the third Earl of Havershot, I don't mean that I was always that. . . . But you know how it is. Uncles call it a day. Cousins hand in their spades and buckets. And little by little and bit by bit, before you know where you are – why, there you are, don't you know.'[20] A little wistfulness and a lot of Wodehouse there. He put much of himself into Reggie Havershot. Both were former amateur boxers who still followed the sport and both visited Hollywood. Like any blue-blooded Englishman, Wodehouse would have loved to inherit an earldom.

His father, Ernest Wodehouse, after education at Repton, passed his Indian Civil Service exams and went to Hong Kong in 1867 to assume his fraction of the White Man's Burden bringing the law to lesser breeds without it as a magistrate. Another Hong Kong civil servant at the time was Walter Meredith Deane who, starting as an interpreter in 1862, rose to become Colonial Secretary in 1881. In between he was second-in-command of the Hong Kong police force, as was George Emerson in *Something Fresh* and, coincidentally, Wodehouse's eldest brother Philip some years later. Walter Deane's sister, Eleanor, went out to Hong Kong 'to visit her brother' on one of those husband-hunting trips so common for young ladies of the period who had failed to find a suitable husband at home. She succeeded in Hong Kong, marrying Ernest Wodehouse on 3 February 1877.

Eleanor's sister, Mary Bathurst Deane, completed a family genealogy begun by their father, the Revd John Bathurst Deane: *The Book of Dene, Deane, Adeane*, to which Ernest Wodehouse was a late subscriber.[21] The shield of Wodehouse of Kimberley appears among the laid-in, hand-tinted, armorial plates but the connection is not mentioned in the text. The book lists distinguished people of those names but cannot link the different branches of the family to each other or to a common ancestor. So such notables as Henry Dene, Archbishop of Canterbury 1501–1503, are only a little more likely to be Wodehouse's relatives than Henry Psmith, Brown or Jones. Mary traces her own, and thus Wodehouse's, Deane line only back as far as Christopher Deane, born in 1636 the son of Aaron Deane and admitted a barrister of the Middle Temple in 1660.

Unlike Grandfather Wodehouse, who left few tracks in the sands of time and died thirty-five years before his famous grandson was born, Grandfather Deane merits closer study. He was a clergyman who had fourteen children, (of which Eleanor was the fifth), three boys and eleven girls[22] and Jasen writes, having had the story from Wodehouse:

He married and bought a house, Chyne Court, in Bath. As a gift his parents bought him the parish of St Helen's Bishopsgate. But he continued to live in Bath and hired a curate to take charge of St Helen's which he visited only once a month in order to give a sermon. Throughout his life the Reverend Deane drew a stipend of £1,000 a year [worth £40,000 in today's pounds] from his parish, despite the fact that during his last fifteen years he was blind and never went near the place.[23]

It's a good story. It could have been true in those days of institutionalized simony. It is not. While more amusing than the truth, it tells us much less about Wodehouse's genetic inheritance. The records show the Reverend Deane was a hardworking and talented man far different from the caricature above. He was born in 1797 at the Cape of Good Hope, the son of Captain Charles Meredith Deane of the 24th Light Dragoons who died on duty in India in 1815. After education at the Merchant Taylors' School and Pembroke College, Cambridge, he took Holy Orders in 1823.[24] That year he became a curate at St Benetfinck at £100 a year and later at St Michael, Wood Street, both in the City of London. After those posts he was, for nineteen years from 1836, head mathematical and second classical master at his old school, then as now funded by the eponymous City livery company.[25] In 1855, as a form of pension for loyal service, the company gave him the Parish of St Martin-Outwich, which was in their gift.[26] In 1873, when he was seventy-eight, St Martin merged with St Helen's Bishopsgate and he became rector of the new parish. The vestry minutes show that, while he never attended its meetings, as late as April 1886, a year before his death at ninety, he was writing a lucid, concerned and detailed letter to the parish council about a restoration fund for St Helen's.[27] His house in Bath was Sion Hill, Cheyne Court (not Chyne) near Box being the Wiltshire home of his widow and four unmarried daughters.

He was the author of numerous articles in learned journals and of four books: *The Church And The Chapters*, *The Campaign of 1708 In Flanders*, *The Life of Richard Deane, Major General and General at Sea in the Service of the Commonwealth* and *The Worship of The Serpent, Traced Throughout the World and its Traditions Referred to in the Events in Paradise Proving The Temptation and Fall of Man by the Instrumentality of a Serpent Tempter*.[28] A goodly title, narrowly winning on points over: '*Hypnotism As A Device To Uncover The Unconscious Drives And Mechanism In An Effort To Analyse The Functions Involved Which Give Rise To Emotional Conflicts In The Waking State* but the title's going to be changed to *Sleepy Time*. Popgood thinks it snappier.'[29]

If genes matter Wodehouse owes a debt to grandfather Deane whose writing, although Victorian, is of elegance and clarity. This extract from the peroration of his life of Richard Deane also shows a Wodehousian generosity of spirit.

> Doubtless there were some who took up arms only to prosecute their own private interests, but by far the greater number were personally disinterested: they fought for a cause. All were not tyrants who stood up for the King; all were not Regicides who fought against him.[30]

By and large the Deanes were solidly middle class and cannot compare in lineage with the Wodehouses, landed gentry for centuries. The Deanes were provincial mayors, brewers, lawyers and academics but while not great landowners they were often rich – sometimes very rich. Great-great-great-great-grandfather, John Deane, 'lost about £100,000 in the South Sea Bubble [1720], after which he took Holy Orders and became Rector of Willersley of which he had the advowson'.[31] Ukridge would have admired so stylish a response to adversity.

The Victorians were great genealogists especially Wodehouse's formidable aunt Mary Deane. With her and his other aunts certain, in Jeeves' phrase, to be, like the page-boy Harold, '. . . acutely aware of the existence of class distinctions, sir' they would have made sure that Wodehouse was well acquainted with his illustrious forebears and the story of the gallant hero of Agincourt. Yet while Wodehouse seemed to pay scant attention to them they crop up time and again in the opus, but rarely elsewhere. He would write to his beloved Leonora lightly mentioning his descent from Anne Boleyn's sister, Lady Mary,[32] yet, during sixty years close friendship with Guy Bolton, 'He never mentioned that Cardinal Newman was his great uncle.'[33] (Actually he was first cousin once removed.) Newman's fine likeness in the National Portrait Gallery in London is by aunt Emmeline Deane and shows his strong family resemblance to his cousin Eleanor.

Critics who imagine that Wodehouse took no interest in his lineage because he didn't boast about it would, presumably, boast about their own distinguished ancestors if they had any. Wodehouse was better bred and did not even though, during his formative years, *Who's Who* was littered with relatives in important and powerful positions, including, in a minor role, Wodehouse's father Ernest. In Parliament were the first Earl of Kimberley, KG, Gladstone's Foreign Secretary, his elder son, Lord Wodehouse, younger son, the Hon. Armine Wodehouse, Liberal MP for Saffron Waldon and the Rt. Hon. Robert Wodehouse, Privy Councillor and MP for Bath. In the armed forces there were Colonel Sir Philip

Wodehouse, GCSI, KCB, Governor of Bombay, Lt. General Sir Josce-
line Heneage Wodehouse, KCB, CMG, Vice-Admiral George Wode-
house and Rear Admiral Capel Wodehouse. In government, either at
home or ruling the Empire, were Sir Edwin Wodehouse, KCB, KCVO,
Assistant Commissioner of the Metropolitan (that is London) Police and
Edmond Wodehouse, CB, Commissioner of the Inland Revenue. Walter
Meredith Deane, CMG, was Colonial Secretary of Hong Kong and
author of *Letters on Whist* published in 1894 and Wodehouse's father,
Ernest, was a Hong Kong magistrate. In the law were the Rt. Hon. Sir
James Parker Deane, DCL, QC, Vicar General to the Archbishop of
Canterbury and the eminent High Court judge, the Rt. Hon. Sir Henry
Bargrave Deane, QC, with whom the young Wodehouse stayed and who
was dedicatee of the Newnes edition of *Love Among The Chickens*.

There were many other relations, less close and not quite so important
but still from the aristocracy and upper classes who ran Victorian England.
Wodehouse was a gentleman by birth and breeding, a scion of an ancient
family and thus at ease in the most exalted circles. Yet he was also one of
nature's gentlemen equally at home in the servants' hall or chatting to
cabbies. This ability to be at ease with people across the entire range of
society helped greatly in creating a full range of characters to people his
stories.

Sharing that background with Pelham were his two older brothers. The
eldest, Philip Peveril John, arrived on 26 September 1877 and, as the first
English child born in the Peak district of Hong Kong, was given his
second name as an echo of Sir Walter Scott's *Peveril Of The Peak*. Ernest
Armine, always known as Armine and so referred to in this book, was
born in 1879, two years before Wodehouse, and as an afterthought a
fourth brother, Richard Lancelot Deane, appeared eleven years later in
1892.

> 'His name's not Lemuel?'
> 'I fear so, sir.'
> 'Couldn't he use his second name?'
> 'His second name is Gengulphus.'
> 'Golly, Jeeves,' I said, thinking of old Uncle Tom Portarlington,
> 'there's some raw work pulled at the font from time to time, is there
> not?'[34]

Pelham Grenville Wodehouse himself was born on 15 October 1881 at
1 Vale Place, 50 Epsom Road, Guildford, Surrey, when Eleanor was on
home leave from Hong Kong and visiting one of her sisters. So he had an
aunt about him the moment he was born. He was not overly impressed

with the names given him, writing that, if asked if he liked the Pelham Grenville, he would frankly confess that he did not and that in his dark moods they seemed to him about as low as one could get. He thought he was given them after a godfather and said he had nothing to show for it except a small silver mug he lost in 1897.[35]

That godfather, who later took part in the Nile Expedition of 1894–95 and ended his career as a colonel, was Lieutenant Pelham George von Donop of the Royal Engineers.[36] But George was too tame a name to please Eleanor and Ernest so their third son was christened Pelham Grenville. His early attempts to say his own name came out as 'Plum' and so as 'Plum' or 'Plummy' he was always known to his family and close friends. In this book we shall not presume to call him 'Plum' until we know him better.

−4−

A SURGING SEA OF AUNTS

What is home without a mother?[1]

Alice Hawthorne

P.G. WODEHOUSE was, for all practical purposes, an orphan. Between the ages of two and a half and fifteen he saw his parents for scarcely six months. This was fundamental in forming his character.

It was common in the late nineteenth century for the civil servants of the Empire to send their children home for a British education. While we must not copy liberal historians – judging earlier eras and people by the standards of radical *chic* in the late twentieth century – the lack of maternal instinct in Eleanor Wodehouse was extreme, even by the standards of the time. In 1883 she took Peveril age six, Armine age four and tiny Pelham, not yet three, back to England. There she rented a house in Bath, hired a Miss Roper (hitherto unknown to her) as governess to her three children and returned to Hong Kong.

'God could not be everywhere, therefore he invented mothers', but not in the case of the Wodehouse boys. The bond between mother and child is probably the deepest and most entrenched of all human emotions: the child taken away from a drunken mother who beats it will scream to go back to her. Great is the love of many foster mothers, some of them aunts, but it is not the same – least of all on a roster basis by Victorian ladies who would not have been demonstrative of whatever affection they felt.

In 1886 Ernest, with Eleanor, returned to England to be invested by Queen Victoria as a Companion of the Order of St Michael and St George for his work as Hon. Secretary and Special Commissioner for Hong Kong for the Colonial and Indian Exposition in London the same year. Then, before returning to the Crown colony, the couple moved their three boys to a dame school in Croydon run by the Misses Prince, Florrie and Cissie. They were ladies of the most excruciating gentility, as found only in the lower middle classes trying to ape their betters.

To impress the neighbours and encourage their charges to behave like little gentlemen, the sisters forced them to spend their weekly pocket money of three pence each on biscuits for the local crossing sweepers who, in those days, were unpaid and relied on tips. A more counter-productive idea is hard to imagine.

Once Pelham and Armine went to play in the drawing room, which was out of bounds to the boys, when one of the Misses Prince came in with her young gentleman, a Mr Scott. The boys hid rapidly beneath the sofa while Mr Scott explained, at length, that his sentiments were deeper and warmer than those of ordinary friendship, proposed marriage, and was accepted. That is why the sofa motif recurs throughout the canon. 'My eye had been caught by a substantial sofa in the corner of the room, and I could have wished no more admirable cover. I was behind it with perhaps two seconds to spare.'[2]

Economy was another characteristic of the school. Each of the boys had one boiled egg once a week – but whoever's turn it was for the egg that day had to share it with the others! After three years living *en prince* the trio were sent to Elizabeth College, a small public school in Guernsey. Two years later Armine went to Dulwich College and Pelham to Malvern House, a preparatory school in Kent which specialized in preparing boys for the Royal Naval College, Dartmouth. Ernest's ambition for his third son to enter the Senior Service was myopic since, even then, it was obvious that Pelham's eyesight unfitted him for any military service. During his school holidays Pelham visited Armine at Dulwich and fell in love with the place at first sight. His father understood: it was through seeing the college from a train that he had decided to send Armine there (a nice example of serendipity) and so he readily agreed to Pelham's entreaties to go there too, starting in the summer term of 1894.

During those eleven years between 1883 and 1894 the three Wode-house brothers led a peripatetic existence. Wodehouse told Jasen: 'You know, they sort of shoved us off on to various uncles for the holidays. I never knew any of them at all. But we were very happy and I had a very happy childhood.' Whether any child deprived of its parents in those stern Victorian times and shuttled around various relatives could truly be happy is doubtful but dwelling on unhappiness is a guarantee of its continuation. When the boys were not at school it was the aunts, not the uncles, who had to look after them and those ladies were another major influence in forming young Pelham's character.

An unduly large number of authors have been orphaned by death or geography in their early years. Kenneth Grahame, W. Somerset Maug-ham, George Orwell, W.M. Thackeray and Edgar Wallace spring to mind, but the two orphaned by the Far Eastern countries of the British

Empire, 'Saki' (Hector Hugh Munro) and Rudyard Kipling, respectively eleven and sixteen years older than Wodehouse, yield the closest comparison.

Saki, whose mother died when he was two, was also looked after by aunts while his father served in the Burma police.

> Mrs De Ropp would never, in her honestest moments, have confessed to herself that she disliked Conradin, though she might have been dimly aware that thwarting him 'for his good' was a duty which she did not find particularly irksome.[3]

Lacking the inalienable kindness of Wodehouse, Saki takes his revenge by having that aunt, whom Conradin thought of as 'The Woman', killed by a polecat-ferret. Wodehouse would not have written such a finale but he might have marooned an aunt in an old water tank (dry) all afternoon, as did Saki. Saki's *The Lull* and Wodehouse's *Mr Potter Takes A Rest Cure* demonstrate two vastly different humorous treatments of the same theme.

Kipling, too, called the stranger who looked after him for six terrible years in Southsea 'The Woman' and where they lived 'The House of Desolation' but 'He used up so much hatred on her he had none for others in his life'.[4] Maybe. In *The Village That Voted The Earth Was Flat*, to my mind comparable with Wodehouse at his funniest, the humiliation of Sir Thomas Ingell, Bt., MP, is as merciless and savage as anything Saki wrote. Oddly Wodehouse didn't think anything of the tale, telling Townend that, if anyone had ever written a worse story, he had never met him.[5] The scene in *Stalky & Co* where Stalky, Beetle (Kipling) and M'Turk torture Sefton and Campbell (two school bullies) is equally savage. In Kipling's highly autobiographical story 'Baa Baa Black Sheep' (about his six years separation from his mother when the veriest child) the horror of his maltreatment expunges the latent sentimentality from the reader's mind – but the misery and pain were clearly inextinguishable from Kipling's mind.

In both Saki and Kipling there is a fierce rage at the pain and impotence of childhood. In Wodehouse there is none. He was more fortunate a child than Saki or Kipling, his aunts treated him well, and he was far wiser. While Little Hector became the man in the ironic mask, little Pelham began the lifelong habit of ignoring the nastinesses of life where he could, simply shutting such things right out of his mind. Later he was an admirer of Charles Dickens but, Usborne tells us, simply could not read the parts where people were unkind to children.[6] Where he could not ignore nastiness he repressed it, clothing it in humour to make it painless. Early on he taught himself the great truth that most things really do not matter.

These formative years provided some of the basic types for Wodehouse's stock of characters (greater than the 1,200 created by Dickens): the peers, servants, clergymen, and aunts. However young Pelham's first literary creation was about pets, more or less.

O ah, that sorryful day

When on the battlefield

The pets did lay

In sorryful disgrace

With red blood streaming fast

Their life was passing fast

And in the camp there lay

Thousands of dead men.

P.G. Wodehouse

This is a bit of

poetry I made up.[7]

At five Pelham's spelling was not yet perfect but while the content is childishly simple what is extraordinary is that, by laying out the poem as I have done on the right of the facsimile, you can see it has a musical rhythm and balance that many adults would envy. For another view I asked one of England's leading graphologists, Barbara Sinclair, to look at the handwriting. (She knew he became a great humorous writer but nothing more about him.) Cursing a goodish bit at the lack of both the original writing and a fee she tells me:

Children cannot produce neat handwriting until the will power is stronger than the emotions. In the case of this five-year-old boy whose emotions were intense, the amount of self-discipline was unusually mature, even taking into account the rigidity and repression of children's upbringing in the Victorian era. There are some signs of strain, inhibitions and lack of self-confidence, making it apparent that the high standards he achieved were a result of dogged determination and did not come easily to him. The originality and suppleness of the sample are the product of a phenomenal intellect which probably provided him with an escape from external pressures, as he appears to have been an introverted child who could express himself more easily on paper than with people.

What Pelham had been doing before he wrote that piece he couldn't remember, admitting that he may have loafed up to the age of five, which was when he began writing, but after that he had stuck to the old typewriter pretty closely. In his seventies Wodehouse lets the dunce's mask slip, confessing that at the age of six he read the whole of Pope's *Iliad*, but he recovers rapidly by inviting the reader not to believe him.[8] In those early years the fauna theme predominated. Jasen gives us a story written when Wodehouse was seven, once thought to be his earliest surviving work.

> About five years ago in a wood there was a Thrush, who built her nest in a Poplar tree. and sang so beautifully that all the worms came up from their holes and the ants laid down their burdens. and the crickets stopped their mirth. and moths settled all in a row to hear her. she sang a song as if she were in heaven – going higher and higher as she sang.
>> at last the song was done and the bird came down
>> panting.
> Thank you said all the creatures.
> Now my story is ended.
>> Pelham G. Wodehouse[9]

Already, at that tender age, we can see the balance, the poetic feel applied to prose, the musicality of his English which was to be summed up by Bernard Levin of *The Times* in the finest of all the obituaries to Wodehouse. Discussing Bertie's phrase about Pauline Stoker sitting up in his bed 'In my heliotrope pyjamas with the old gold stripe' he writes:

> You cannot replace any syllable of that phrase by another without disturbing the rhythm to its detriment. More: you can scarcely change a letter. Suppose that the colour referred to was not 'heliotrope' but

'heliobright': say it aloud both ways, and see whether there is not a tiny but discernible loss in the second version.[10]

That feeling for English was a gift from God but the background of the Wodehouse world came from his early experiences. The Wodehouse boys would often be taken by the aunt-of-the-moment on social calls but, sometimes, the hostess would suggest that the boys might be happier having tea in the Servants' Hall. They were and Pelham listened, observed and remembered all that happened there. From them he would draw the host of butlers, cooks, valets, footmen and others of his *dramatis personae* who were to delight the world. *Something New* shows an insider's knowledge of the intricate hierarchy and below stairs etiquette, mimicking that above stairs, in the great houses before the First World War with the upper servants living in some state, waited upon by the lower. He notes those upper servants assembling in the housekeeper's room before dinner while awaiting the arrival of the butler, Beach, later immortalized as 'A solemn procession of one'; the kitchen-maid, with all the appearance of one who has been straining at the leash and has at last managed to get free, opening the door with the announcement, 'Mr Beach, if you please, dinner is served'; the butler extending a crooked elbow towards the housekeeper and leading the way high and disposedly down the passage, followed in order of rank by the rest of the company in couples, to the steward's room. Young Pelham also noted such idiosyncrasies as the way a personal servant would refer to his master by Christian name or nick-name but the other servants would always refer to him by his formal style and title.

Similarly the aunts would visit the local vicar, but here there was valuable material closer to hand. Murphy found that of Pelham's fifteen uncles by blood or marriage four were clergymen: all of them, of course, in The Church of England As By Law Established, not a Dissenter among them.

For all young gentlemen of the period church attendance each Sunday was compulsory, the services sticking rigorously to Cranmer's Book of Common Prayer and the King James authorized translation of the Bible. The poetic beauty of their English made a deep impression in the retentive mind of young Pelham, which can clearly be seen throughout his writing.

Of aunts Murphy disinterred no less than twenty! Quite enough for a surging sea of them and while, no doubt, one was deaf and one was dotty, some of them must have been fit for human consumption – and some not. 'There are dozens of aunts you've not heard of yet – far-flung aunts scattered all over England, and each the leading blister of her particular county.'[11] The eldest of the Deane aunts was amiable Louisa of whom Wodehouse was very fond and who, Jasen tells us, was 'the blueprint for Bertie Wooster's kind hearted aunt Dahlia'. The most important of them was Mary who was 'something of a tyrant and her demeanour made an indelible impression on her young nephew that was to manifest itself in Bertie's unsympathetic aunt Agatha'.

We might note that Bertie's kind hearted Aunt Dahlia bullies him into stealing cow-creamers, Fothergill Venuses and amber statuettes; is quite ready to let him go to jail so that she can keep her chef Anatole; browbeats him into singing *Sonny Boy* at Beefy Bingham's clean bright entertainment in Bottleton East; forces him to ride eighteen miles at night on an uncomfortable bicycle without lights; knocks him unconscious with a gong-stick and makes him an accessory to assault, blackmail, theft and catnapping (that is, stealing cats, not catching *traumatic symplegia* from Augustus, the Brinkley cat). She also uses moral blackmail to force him to play Santa Claus at the Brinkley Court children's Christmas party. Faced with Bertie's forebodings she had the cheerful courage of the non-combatant telling him the worst the kids could do, as tribal custom ordained, would be to rub chocolate eclairs in his whiskers, or strawberry jam.

On the other hand his unsympathetic aunt Agatha – the one he suspects wears barbed wire next to the skin, kills rats with her bare teeth and conducts human sacrifices by the light of the full moon – only wants Bertie to marry a suitable girl, get a job, cut down on his smoking and drinking, take his share of family responsibilities and make something of his life.

Wodehouse, both in his own life and in his books, seemed to like those who bullied with style and humour but disparaged bullying by do-gooders. Perhaps that was the effect of aunt Mary, a professional writer, who published twelve books. Her last, appearing in 1921, was *A Book of Verse*. The following poem by aunt Mary could easily have been written by Bertie's friend Rockmetteller Todd.[12]

So the night covers us
   and our white souls
Grow dark
   Even thy pale endeavour
Of sympathetic minds
Touches us not
And the wind blows
   Listlessly.[13]

Mostly Mary's poetry rhymes, scans and makes sense; albeit sometimes in the sloppy, sentimental style of Wodehouse's Madeline Bassett.

Tread softly where the flowers grow
So primitive and wild
For if you crush a single bud
You kill a fairy child.

Madeline, who believed that every time a fairy hiccups a wee baby is born and that the stars are God's daisy chain, first appears in *Right Ho, Jeeves* (US *Brinkley Manor*) in 1934. Murphy shows there is a varying gestation period between Wodehouse getting a new inspiration and it appearing in print; Aunt Mary, that tough old biddy, is thus the improbable inspiration for the Bassett. She was certainly the sort of lady who either gave nephews copies of her books or, more likely, expected them to buy copies. The whimsy of that extract does not reflect the quality of Mary's poetry, most of which is very fine, especially her love poems. While discreet they are passionate, anguished and not inspired by men. By 1921 when they were published – seven years before Radclyffe Hall's *The Well of Loneliness* – Mary was seventy-six and too old to be bothered by any gossip they might arouse. The Deanes, like the Wodehouses, were a long-lived family: Mary died in 1940, aged ninety-five.

Her prose is competent without the elegant purity of her father's writing. Her most successful book, which ran through three editions, was *Seen In An Old Mirror*,[14] an historical romance set in eighteenth-century Bath. It is Jane Austen without the genius, Georgette Heyer without the verve and Barbara Cartland without the pace. Yet her nephew possibly learned one trait from her: diligent, hard work at the author's desk. Twelve books may not sound much set beside Wodehouse's total of ninety-eight but it is eleven more than most authors write in a lifetime.

The highlight of the boys' year was their annual visit to Grandma Wodehouse at Ham House, overlooking the River Teme in Powick. For the rest of the time Mary and Louisa led the roster of surrogate parents, none of whom, jointly or severally, could be an adequate substitute for the missing Ernest and Eleanor, the only remarkable thing about whom was the effect of their absenteeism upon their third son. One of the many remarkable things about him is the way he coped with that parental vacuum. Writing in *Over Seventy* he pointed out that the three essentials for an autobiography are that its compiler should have had an eccentric father, a miserable misunderstood childhood and a hell of a time at public school, and that he had none of those 'advantages'. He described his

father as 'Normal as rice pudding' adding that his childhood went like a
breeze from start to finish, with everybody he met understanding him
perfectly.

There is no mention of his mother in that paragraph. Throughout his
life Wodehouse strove to put his mother out of his mind. In later years he
would urge his daughter Leonora dutifully to visit her 'grandmother' –
unaccompanied by him. From her widowhood in 1929 until her death in
1941 Eleanor Wodehouse lived with Nella, Armine's wife (and, from
1936, widow). Nella told Frances Donaldson that during all the years that
her mother-in-law lived with her, Wodehouse only visited her once. Just
once in a decade! Throughout his life Wodehouse never said a bad word
about his mother – nor a good one.

Yet, despite maternal deprivation, he seems to have been a happy child
even in his early years. With innocent wisdom he persuaded himself he
was happy and the myth became the reality. No wonder that the young
Wodehouse became an observer, blending in with his background. He
looked, he listened and he stored up all he saw and heard. The world had
hurt Wodehouse by giving him a travesty of a mother, which was worse
than none at all. How much safer to treat the world with cordial neutrality,
ignoring it all (as far as possible) except those aspects which appeal to you.

Aunt Dahlia and her son Bonzo appear in the same stories, as do aunt
Agatha and her son Thomas and the Dowager Lady Chuffnell and her
son Seabury but Wodehouse never writes any scene where mother and
son appear together and there is no dialogue between them at all. There is
the Marchioness of Malvern who treats her son, Lord Pershore, abomina-
bly but their conversations are noticeably one-sided. Mrs Ponsford Botts
talks to her son, Irwin, but his total contribution to the dialogue is 'wah,
wah, wah'. The only significant mother and son dialogue in all the millions of words Wodehouse wrote is between Nesta Ford and young
Ogden, the most repulsive of all his repulsive children. The scene in *The
Little Nugget* where Ogden, kidnapped from paternal custody by his
mother's agent, meets her again for the first time in months should be
heartrending. It is in fact a cruelly vicious sketch masked as farce by a
master wordsmith. Cutting out as much as one can of the camouflage we
get:

> Mrs Ford roused herself from her fascinated contemplation of Ogden.
> She swooped. She descended in a swirl of expensive millinery, and
> clasped him to her.
>   'My Boy!'
> It is not given to everybody to glide neatly into a scene of tense
> emotion. Ogden failed to do so. He wriggled roughly from the embrace.

'Got a cigarette?' he said.

Even Mrs Ford was momentarily chilled. She laughed shakily.

'How very matter of fact you are darling!'

She broke off. 'Come near me, my little son.' He lurched towards her sullenly.

'Don't muss a fellow now,' he stipulated, before allowing himself to be enfolded in the outstretched arms.

'Ogden, darling,' observed Mrs Ford, 'don't go away. I want you *near* me.'

'Oh, all right.'

'Then stay by me, angel-face.'

'Oh, slush!' muttered angel-face beneath his breath. 'Say, I'm darned hungry,' he added.

'My poor child! Of course you must have some lunch. Ring the bell, Cynthia.'

'I think it would be better if Ogden had his downstairs in the restaurant,' said Cynthia.

'Want to talk scandal, eh?'

'Ogden, *dearest*!' said Mrs Ford. 'Very well, Cynthia. Go, Ogden. You will order yourself something substantial, marvel-child?'

'Bet your life,' said the son and heir tersely.

Note the devastating effect of the redundant 'Swirl of expensive millinery'. Observe the use of 'The' rather than 'Her' outstretched arms, let alone 'His mother's outstretched arms' and the power of the adverb 'Even'. The use of italics also furthers the author's hidden agenda. When Ogden is taken back to school by his father's agent he shows total indifference to leaving his mother. Wodehouse could take his revenge as well as Kipling and Saki, and less crudely.

Another candidate for the Sore Thumb Award is Molly McEachern's assertion to her dogs, in *The Intrusion of Jimmy* (UK *A Gentleman Of Leisure*), that they nearly burst themselves with joy 'Because auntie had come back from England.' Auntie! Auntie? When ladies anthropomorphize their relationships with their dogs it is always on a mother and child basis. That extract was written before Wodehouse was married with a daughter of his own. Later, as his happy relationship with her dulled the remembrance of his own mother's neglect, he allowed Beatrice, Mrs Chavender, in *Quick Service*, to call herself mother to her Peke, Patricia, but that was when Eleanor was eighty-seven. The aunts in Wodehouse may be mothers as well, but they are always primarily aunts. Later in life Wodehouse said it would be wrong (and uncommercial) to cast a mother in a villainous role but this sounds like rationalization.

Of the fifty-three members of the Drones Club listed by Jaggard in
Wooster's World not one of them is given an extant mother. A few of the
boys in Wodehouse's public-school stories have mothers in the background, such as Rupert Ronald Eustace Psmith who, in *Mike*, requires
one for a parody of a period cliche. 'What would my mother say if she
could see her Rupert in the midst of these reckless youths!' By the time
he became a member of The Drones in *Leave It To Psmith* he is as
motherless as Bertie Wooster.

There are also remarkably few father and son relationships in the
Wodehouse canon and most of those are purely comic, such as the doting
Pop Blumenfield who relies on Junior's judgement on backing new plays
('He reasons logically that what appeals to the mentality of a child of eight
must infallibly win the approval of the average modern audience.'[15]) or
Lord Emsworth and his son Freddie Threepwood. Instead, most of the
fond relationships in the stories are between uncles and their nieces and,
to a lesser extent, nephews while most of the antagonistic relationships are
between aunts and nephews. The Duke of Dunstable is an exception who
tests the rule. A.P. Ryan, literary editor of *The Times*, argued that every
authority figure in Wodehouse such as Jeeves (or His Grace of Dunstable)
is an aunt in disguise.[16]

The lack of parent-child relationships in Wodehouse should not be
taken as implying he was lacking in feelings – rather the opposite, but they
were deeply suppressed. In 'Lord Emsworth And The Girlfriend' from
Blandings Castle And Elsewhere there is as beautiful and feeling an adult-
and-child relationship as you can find but, here again, the sentiment is
lightly masked by the prose of a master humorist.

> The spectacle of [McAllister] charging vengefully down on him with
> gleaming eyes and bristling whiskers made him feel like a nervous
> English infantryman at the Battle of Bannockburn. His knees shook and
> the soul within him quivered.
>
> And then something happened, and the whole aspect of the situation
> changed.
>
> It was, in itself, quite a trivial thing, but it had an astoundingly
> stimulating effect on Lord Emsworth's morale. What happened was
> that Gladys, seeking further protection, slipped at this moment a small,
> hot hand into his.
>
> It was a mute vote of confidence, and Lord Emsworth intended to be
> worthy of it.

Rudyard Kipling told Ian Hay that 'Lord Emsworth And The Girl Friend'
was 'One of the most perfect short stories I have ever read'.[17]

In *Their Mutual Child* Ruth and Kirk disagree on how to bring up their son Bill (the only child ever born within the time-span covered by a Wodehouse novel). This has all the potential for a tear-jerking mother-and-child relationship, indeed the plot cries out for it, but it just doesn't appear. The original dustwrapper for the English edition (*The Coming of Bill*) has a golden-haired child tugged one way by a male hand and the other way by a female hand but it was changed in later editions for a comic picture of Mrs Lora Delane Porter (the 'heavy') looking disapprovingly at a man she has just run over with her car. Mrs Porter is a Wodehouse oddity, a genuinely unpleasant character (whose faults stem from arrogant good intentions) and the only really bad aunt in the canon.

At last, in 1969, we get one expression of normal maternal feeling from Wodehouse in *A Pelican At Blandings* (US *No Nudes Is Good Nudes*) where Vanessa Polk comes across a sleeping Wilbur Trout. 'She stood watching him, and was surprised at the wave of maternal tenderness that surged over her.' That is all and it took almost three decades from Eleanor's death for it to come from Wodehouse's pen. He dedicated *The Head Of Kay's* 'To My Father' but *Tales Of St Austin's* is dedicated *Ad Matrem* which could mean either 'To My Mother' or 'To my school'.

His lack of relationship with his mother – and his deeply buried hurt at the fact – was set, remaining unaltered after his parents came home to retire. (Jasen and *Burke's Peerage* give the date as 1895, Donaldson as 1896 and *Who Was Who* as 1898: such is the biographer's lot. I believe he came home on health grounds in 1895 and went on the retired list in 1898.) Ernest Wodehouse had taken part in a walking race, or accepted a wager that he could not walk around the coast of Hong Kong Island in one day. Either way he suffered so badly from sunstroke as a result that he retired prematurely, drawing a pension for over three decades until his death in 1929. He, at least, was able to establish a comradely relationship with his third son – but it was not especially close for by then Wodehouse had found his first true love – Dulwich College.

ALMA MATER
WODEHOUSE AT DULWICH

Genius turned out by people dedicated to stamping out
genius is necessarily a strange one, and Wodehouse,
squirming around Parnassus with his hands in his pockets,
must be at least the strangest since Jane Austen.[1]

Wilfrid Sheed

Alma Mater means literally bounteous mother and colloquially, one's old
school. For Wodehouse, Dulwich College was both and it was an abiding
love on both sides. When he was temporarily in disgrace during the
Second World War the College did not remove his name from their
honour boards – it simply put them into store. Later they went up again
with Wodehouse's name there, just as before. Today the school takes
pride in the library, *The Wodehouse Library* and its unique archive of
Wodehouse material. The library includes a reconstruction of Wodehouse's study at Remsenburg with his books, Royal typewriter, furniture
and other personal items received from his widow, Ethel, Lady Wodehouse. (Prophetically the *Strand* writer, Augustus Muir, said back in 1927
that the Wodehouse typewriter would end up in 'The Wodehouse
museum of the future'.)[2]

Dulwich was founded by Edward Alleyn in 1619 in what was then a
rural Surrey manor five miles from London. To the cynic it is pleasing
that Alleyn, an actor, a friend of Shakespeare and man of many talents,
made part of his huge fortune through his Bankside brothels, *The Barge*,
The Bell and *The Cock* (*sic*).[3] In those days fear of eternal damnation often
bothered ageing malefactors. To that we owe the great school which is
still properly called 'Alleyn's College of God's Gift' and which retains
some of the rural charm it has enjoyed for centuries. The main college
building is a pleasing Victorian complex of red brick, terracotta and stone.
It must still have looked pretty garish when Wodehouse minor was there,
only fourteen years after its completion in 1870, but it has mellowed into

beauty and is an excellent example of the work of Charles Barry Jr. (whose father built the new Palace of Westminster). It won him the Gold Medal of the Royal Institute of British Architects in 1877.

It was not just the beauty of the college that attracted Ernest. As an ancient and well endowed foundation it had, and has, many scholarships to distribute. Unlike many of Britain's public schools (which in America would be called private schools) Dulwich still gives the best possible education to many boys whose parents cannot afford to pay for it. Both Armine and Pelham won scholarships and, while the awards seem small today, they were respectable sums in 1894. The scholarships were by competitive examinations – the size of the awards reflecting the ability of the candidates. Armine won £15 a year for three years while Pelham won £20 a year, also for three years. The school fees were then £7.10s a term for day-boys so those awards went a long way towards paying for Pelham and Armine's eduction.[4]

Pelham entered the college on 2 May 1884 as Wodehouse minor. Armine, already there, immediately became Wodehouse major. (Had all four Wodehouse boys been at Dulwich at the same time they would have been Wodehouses major, minor, tertius and minimus.) This nomenclature was needed because, in those days, you could pass your entire time at an English public-school without learning the first names of any but your closest friends.

It was an extraordinary time to be a British schoolboy of the upper middle classes. The British were then masters of a quarter of the earth while the Royal Navy ruled the high seas – all of them. It was the greatest Empire the world had ever known and the British, well aware of the fact, were determined everybody else should be too. During the last decades of Queen Victoria's reign the attitude of the average Briton towards the rest of the world makes that of the divine Emperors of the Middle Kingdom, China, pale into modesty by comparison.

That vast Empire owed much to the disciples of Dr Thomas Arnold, the great headmaster of Rugby School. He was a pioneer in educational reform, introducing the study of modern languages and mathematics alongside team sports, Christian principles and discipline, whilst continuing to stress the importance of studying the classics. Sadly he died in 1842 aged only forty-seven leaving his followers zealously corrupting his broad vision and ideals. They dominated the British public school system, concentrating on the discipline, the Christianity and the team sports. They lacked Arnold's balance, compassion and greatness. Instead they substituted certainty: the certainty that breeds intolerance, closed minds and, in this instance, an arrogant belief in the superiority of the British race in general and the English upper classes in particular. It produced the stereotypes who did so much to expand the Empire – and so much to lose it when the world changed and they did not.

In earlier centuries the British aristocracy had financed privateers (licensed pirates), drained the Fens, opened coal mines, dredged docks, funded tin mines, established waterworks, built canals, carried out speculative building on their urban estates and much more. Under Arnold's disciples they and their sons were not to soil their hands with trade but to be healthy, sporting, Christian (that is, Church of England) classicists working only in the professions – the church, the law, the navy, the army, government, teaching, medicine – and fully aware that:

> The rich man in his castle
> The poor man at his gate.
> God made them high and lowly
> And ordered their estate.

Their doctrine created a tunnel-visioned upper class, largely unable to adapt to the changes brought about by the march of democracy or profit from the new forms of wealth creation that made nineteenth-century Britain so rich. (For example the Kimberley estates are almost all lost to the family.) They showed extraordinary valour in war and the service of their ideals but the business sense – essential for class survival – was educated out of them as it was from the sons of the tough, able, entrepreneurs who built up Victorian industry. The latter were turned into gentlemen, almost indistinguishable from the real thing. To be British was undeniably to be the noblest creation of God with rights and privileges taken for granted as His will.

The jingoism inculcated into the public school youth of late Victorian vintage such as Wodehouse, was extreme, well reflected in G.W. Hunt's showstopping song, first sung in 1878.

> We don't want to fight
> But by jingo if we do
> We've got the men, we've got the ships
> We've got the money too.

The writing was already on the wall, but nobody read it. In the First Boer War (1880–81) the British were defeated by a motley collection of Afrikaner farmers who, unsportingly, didn't play by the old (British) rules but invented their own. That was conveniently forgotten and was to be 'corrected' with a British victory in the Second Boer War (1899–1901). Jingoism was particularly virulent then and the pacific but amenable

Wodehouse minor got his only taste of the military life with compulsory membership of the college OTC (Officer Training Corps) under the martinet's eye of Sergeant-Major Beale. The Empire, the public-school system that staffed it and the symbiotic ethos of both were vividly encapsulated in a moving poem by Sir Henry Newbolt, 'Vitai Lampada' published in 1892.

There's a breathless hush in the Close to-night –
  Ten to make and the match to win –
A bumping pitch and a blinding light,
  An hour to play and the last man in.
And it's not for the sake of a ribboned coat,
  Or the selfish hope of a season's fame,
But his Captain's hand on his shoulder smote –
  'Play up! play up! and play the game!'

The sand of the desert is sodden red –
  Red with the wreck of a square that broke; –
The Gattling's jammed and the Colonel dead,
  And the regiment blind with dust and smoke.
The river of death has brimmed his banks,
  And England's far, and Honour a name,
But the voice of a schoolboy rallies the ranks:
  'Play up! play up! and play the game!'

This is the word that year by year
  While in her place the School is set,
Every one of her sons must hear,
  And none that hears it dare forget.
This they all with joyful mind
  Bear through life like a torch in flame,
And falling fling to the host behind –
  'Play up! play up! and play the game!'

As James Morris wrote in his panoramic celebration of the British Empire, *Pax Britannica*:

They were children of a unique culture, that of the English public schools, with its celibate discipline, its classical loyalties, its emphasis on self reliance, team spirit, delegated responsibility, Christian duty and stoic control. . . . At his worst the public school man was a snobbish hearty; at his best he combined authority with Christian kindness and what he would have called grit: the rarest of his virtues was human sympathy, the rarest of his vices cowardice. And the most irritating of his traits, at least in the imperial context, seems to have been smugness.

While Eustace H. Miles, one-time tennis champion of the world, wrote in all seriousness, in a comment that was treated seriously:

> It would be terrible to think what would happen to us if our public school system were swept away, or if – and this comes to very much the same thing – from our public school system were swept away our Athletics and our Games.[5]

Most boys would have accepted the propaganda of their formative years, a few would have rejected it all. Yet the extraordinary young Wodehouse was imbued with all the admirable aspects of the system, honesty, loyalty, courage, and largely unaffected by its arrogance, intolerance and other vices. How any such youngster, especially one as obliging and outwardly conventional as he was, could be so selective towards such an all-pervading formative influence defies any explanation except that genius does not abide by the rules that shackle the rest of us. Part of the reason was, as Wodehouse said, that to be a humorist one must see the world out-of-focus, be slightly cock-eyed,[6] but most of the reason is that the humorist has to see clearly the absurdities of things that other people take seriously – which, maybe, is the same thing. Whatever the reason, go through the Wodehouse canon to find those period attitudes of Empire. You will fail.

The Empire offended Wodehouse's sense of tolerance. He wanted to be left alone to do as he wished, to write, and he felt other people should be left alone too. The idea of going, uninvited, to the uttermost ends of the earth to conquer foreign lands and open them up to British trade clearly struck him as bad manners. In later life he felt that Britain should not interfere in the Italian-Abyssinian war (1936) on the same principle.[7] His comments on those who ruled the British Empire go from the gentle mockery of a romantic novelist's hero – 'One of those strong, curt, Empire-building kind of Englishmen with sad unfathomable eyes, lean sensitive hands and riding boots' – to pure farce and merciless leg-pulling with the characterization of Bwana Biggar – Captain Cuthbert Gervase Brabazon Biggar – in *Ring For Jeeves* (US *The Return of Jeeves*), although kindly Wodehouse allows even him to end up marrying the rich widow he loves.

Yet the Empire did give Wodehouse one great benefit. His English was enriched by the flow of new words from British possessions around the globe, not only the more obvious ones like Bwana, coolie (as in Tiger's breakfast), Raj, purdah and veld but uncommon ones like the dazzling parasang or the ornamental chi-yicking, tofah, Oolong and Bohea. Wodehouse takes full advantage of these and, even where they have fallen into disuse, they still enrich his prose, their meaning clear from the context.

Although rejecting so much of the teaching of the public-school system and its glorification of Empire young Wodehouse took for granted that public-school ethos of 'honesty, loyalty, service, courage'. It was bred in the bone and Dulwich reinforced it.

He spent his first term at the college living at the East Dulwich home of an assistant master, H.V. Doulton, but in September he became a boarder in Escott's. Dulwich houses were named after the housemasters, in this case the Revd E.H. Sweet-Escott, not after the building which was Ivyholme.[8] Unlike St Austin's, Eton or Wrykyn, the boarders were in a minority at Dulwich but they also looked down upon the day-boys. 'Being a miserable day-boy he had had no experience of the inner life of a boarding house, which is the real life of a Public School.'[9]

As a boarder Wodehouse felt truly part of the college and after only five months had his first article, on third form cricket, printed in *The Alleynian*.[10] Later he wrote of his time there as six years of unbroken bliss. They were, in fact, broken when Ernest and Eleanor came home from Hong Kong and took a house, 62 Croxted Road, in Dulwich.[11] He became a day-boy again and discovered he rather liked the stranger who was his father. Of Eleanor, says Jasen, 'Plum found no reason to amend his earlier impressions of his mother'. Was that scene between Nesta Ford and her son Ogden based on the reunion between Eleanor and Pelham? As Murphy shows, Wodehouse would have got the basis of that scene from real life — somewhere — and adapted it to his purpose.

However the demotion to mere day boy was not to last long. Soon Ernest and Eleanor decided to move to the country. They inspected a number of houses including the Old House, Stableford, Shropshire. Jasen tells of Ernest, after a peremptory look, leaving Eleanor to continue her detailed inspection of the property. By the time he returned to collect her for their homeward journey, Eleanor had come to the conclusion that this was the least desirable of all the houses they had visited and told her husband she was glad they had seen the last of that house. Ernest stopped in his tracks and, possibly paling a fraction, told her he had just taken a lease on it for six years.

Unlike the anecdote about Grandfather Deane it is impossible to check up how much Wodehousian tinkering and polishing there is in that story. Be that as it may, Stableford became Pelham's holiday retreat (Dulwich remained his 'home') and the surrounding Shropshire countryside the basis of his Blandings Eden. It was here that he had the first of his many dogs upon which he 'Lavished a love which might have been better bestowed on a nephew' as Bertie noted of Aunt Agatha and the Dog McIntosh.[12]

With his parents safely in Shropshire Pelham became a boarder again but this time at Treadgold's – the building was Elm Lawn. E.C. Tread-gold was a dreaded disciplinarian. The headmaster once asked him how the classical Vth form were doing. Came the reply 'If they get one wrong they get "0". If they get all right they get "10". At present they are all equal bottom with "0".'

There he met William Townend, establishing the first great friendship of his life, even though Townend was only at the College for fourteen months from May 1898 to July 1899. The two shared a study and slept in the same small dormitory. Townend noted that, even then, Wodehouse was an omnivorous reader, as happy with popular trash as with the Greek poets (in Greek). Most of all the pair looked forward to the appearance of *The Strand* each month, eagerly waiting at West Dulwich station for its arrival with Conan Doyle's latest Sherlock Holmes story.

Wodehouse minor had all the qualities required for popularity at a public-school: he was reserved without being paranoid about it, enthusiastic about and good at games and not only highly intelligent but sufficiently so to pretend he wasn't. His school nickname was 'Podge', a comfortingly unimaginative derivation by his peers from 'PG' reflecting someone swimming safely in the mainstream of school life. To the twelve and a half year old boy the college represented certainty, security, a base and a reassuring position in an enclosed, structured, society. As Margaret Slythe comments, 'School is a "game" with rules and opportunities. Wodehouse understood this immediately.' He thrived.

With his background and abilities he was put on the classical side of the school (the other sides were the modern, the science and the engineering) learning Latin and Greek as well as French. Later he became a member of the classics VI form at Dulwich to which boys were not admitted unless among the brightest of the crop. He told Jasen, 'I went automatically on the classical side and, as it turned out, it was the best form of education I could have as a writer'. He was dextrous in written Greek and Latin and, of course, magically fluent in English, cheerfully translating from any of those three languages into any other. Townend told Jasen, 'He worked, if he worked at all, supremely fast, writing Latin and Greek verse as rapidly as he wrote English.' Usborne makes the point neatly.

. . . only a writer who was himself a scholar and had had his face ground into Latin and Greek (especially Thucydides) as a boy, would dare to embark on such a sentence as:

'With the feeling, which was his constant companion nowadays, for the wedding was fixed for the fifth of July and it was already the tenth of June, that if anybody cared to describe him as some wild thing taken in a trap, which sees the trapper coming through the woods, it would be all right with him, he threw a moody banana skin at the loudest of the sparrows, and went back into the room.'
And would emerge so triumphantly.

Dulwich also gave him a competent working knowledge of French, which the hero of *The Luck Of The Bodkins* lacked.

Into the face of the young man who sat on the terrace of the Hotel Magnifique at Cannes there had crept a look of furtive shame, the shifty hangdog look which announces that an Englishman is about to talk French.

. . . which Godfrey Smith, the *Sunday Times*' Renaissance Man in residence, has strongly championed as a candidate for the finest opening sentence of any English novel.

Later in life Wodehouse, who frequently visited France and lived there for a total of some nine years, wrote from Aribeau in 1932 to Townend that all his favourite authors had let him down and that he had to fall back on the French, telling him he had read everything by Colette he could get hold of including her autobiography *Mes Apprentissages*.[13] The first edition in English was not published for another thirty-five years. A couple of years on he was enthusing over *Les Demi-Soldes* by Desparbes. 'It's thrilling.'[14]

Those are the remarks of a man for whom French holds few terrors. Wodehouse occasionally writes of problems, for example telling his friend, the author Sir Compton Mackenzie, that he simply couldn't master the French language,[15] but for a classical scholar of some modesty 'master' is both a relative and subjective word. When Wodehouse took lessons in 1934 to polish his French conversation he was pleased with himself: 'I'm getting darned good'.[16] The grounding Dulwich gave him in the classics and French taught Wodehouse about the English language. He learned of its roots and of the tributaries that watered them, its form, its construction, its development and its secrets. Other writers of the period had the same advantages but few of them possessed genius as well.

That ability with languages owes much to Wodehouse studying under Arthur Herman Gilkes, Dulwich's Master (as the headmaster is called) from 1885 to 1914. He ran the college in an enlightened manner (which the boys, including Wodehouse, looked upon as weakness) and, unlike most other schools of the time, did not try to force ability into too standard a mould. '[He] . . . hated this worship of sport and actively worked against this stereotype'[17] but not with much success. Wodehouse told Jasen that Gilkes was a man with a long white beard who stood six-foot-six in his stockinged feet and had a deep musical voice. 'I can still remember how he thrilled me when he read us that bit from Carlyle's *Sator Resartus* which ends "But I, mine Wether, am above it all". It was terrific. But he also always scared the pants off me.'

There is some of Gilkes in the first headmaster portrayed by Wodehouse; the Revd Mr Perceval of St Austin's in *The Pothunters*. Any boy – especially one prodded, as most boys are, by a grubby conscience – might write of a headmaster being a good judge of character who thought he could tell when a boy was speaking the truth and when he was not. Yet Wodehouse, who completed writing that book only eighteen months after leaving school, paints a highly adult picture of Perceval agonizing over whether or not his judgement, over Jim Thomson, a boy accused of theft, was right or not.

> The Head also passed a bad night. He was not easy in his mind about Jim. He thought the matter over for a time, and then, finding himself unable to sleep, got up and wrote an article . . . on the Doxology. . . . The article was subsequently rejected – which proves that Providence is not altogether incapable of a kindly action – but it served its purpose by sending its author to sleep.

The masterly touch is starting to show through with that aside on the Doxology while the years of saying little and observing everything were paying dividends remarkably soon in his writing life. That writing began to blossom in the school magazine, *The Alleynian* of which Wodehouse became an editor, as Armine had been before him.

He continued to write for it for decades – usually reporting the school's football (that is Rugby football, not soccer) matches which he saw whenever he was in London. Between 1920 and 1939 he wrote reports of twenty rugger and four cricket matches. Sports were his great passion after writing and he was good at them. All his life he was a daily and prodigious walker, as was his father. He was in the school's first football XV and cricket XI and boxed for the college until barred from the sport by poor eyesight. In the inter-house sports of the Lent Term 1900 he won the High Jump and came second in Putting The Weight.[18] As Townend told Jasen:

Plum was an established figure in the school, a noted athlete, a fine footballer and cricketer, a boxer; he was a school Prefect, in the Classical Sixth, he had a fine voice and sang at the school concerts, he edited *The Alleynian*: he was, in fact, one of the most important boys in the school.

He also wrote 'A series of plays after the pattern of the Greek tragedies, outrageously funny, dealing with boys and Masters. I would give a good deal to have those plays in my possession now'. Wouldn't we all?

The Alleynian listed his prowess on the sportsfield. He won his college first cricket XI colours in the summer of 1899 and his first XV colours for rugger on 11 November that year.

P.G. Wodehouse

First XV (1899–1900) 12st 6lb. A heavy forward. Has improved greatly, but still inclined to slack in the scrum. Always up to take a pass. Good with his feet. Still too much inclined to tackle high.

First XI (1899) Bowled well against Tonbridge, but did nothing else. Does not use his head at all. A poor bat and a very slack field. (1900) A fast right-hand bowler with good swing, though he does not use his head enough. As a bat he has very much improved, and he gets extraordinarily well to the pitch of the ball. Has wonderfully improved in the field, though rather hampered by his sight.[19]

Tact, it seemed, was an effete luxury in those robust days at the college, or maybe not. Those three items have been quoted before, but what was not known is that the second criticism of Wodehouse minor was written by none other than Wodehouse minor[20] (and possibly the others too). As an eighteen year old he could already see his strengths and weaknesses and write a balanced assessment of them for his peers to read. Most people take another decade or two to achieve that objectivity and many writers never do so at all.

Wodehouse won a better write-up in *The Alleynian* for his performance at the school concert in July 1899 when he was the star of the show, taking the top slot as the last act before the school song, 'God Save The Queen' and 'Auld Lang Syne' ended the entertainment and the school year. He sang 'Hybrias the Cretan' with great brio.[21] The next year on Founder's Day, 23 June 1900, the extrovert young Wodehouse won a rave review for playing Guildenstern in W.S. Gilbert's *Rosencranz And Guildenstern* with *The Alleynian* reporting:

The chief part of the acting fell upon Hamlet, Rosencranz and Guildenstern, who all played their parts very well. The most amusing scene
in the play is that between the trio, where at the Queen's pathetic
request they prevent Hamlet from soliloquizing. . . . Guildenstern's
accompanying dance (exact species unknown) was very striking and the
masterly way in which he twirled round the chambers of the revolver to
shew Hamlet that it would really work was a very effective piece of
by-play.[22]

Wodehouse clearly enjoyed the theatre, in which he was later to play an
historic role, and had no qualms about performing in the Great Hall at
Dulwich in front of several hundred of his peers and their parents. Nor,
even then, did he mind telling the world how good he was. At that time he
was an editor of *The Alleynian* and if he didn't write that review of the play
it was certainly edited by him.

While Wodehouse is the greatest writer to be nurtured by Dulwich he
is not alone. Apart from his friend William Townend, a writer of adventure yarns, mainly about travel and the sea, there are other notable Old
Alleynian authors of the period. Hugh de Selincourt, at Dulwich between
1890 and 1896, wrote cricketing novels. A.E.W. Mason was at the college
1878 to 1884; his best known and oft filmed book is *The Four Feathers*.
He, like Wodehouse, co-wrote a play with Ian Hay – in his case *A Present
From Margate* produced in 1933.[23]

C.S. Forester, creator of the immortal naval hero Horatio Hornblower,
and newspaper correspondent in Spain during the Spanish Civil War, was
at Dulwich from 1915 to 1917, having previously been at a sister establishment, Alleyn's School. He recalled, some forty years later:

> In the Buttery at the eleven o'clock break the lordly ones would lounge
> against the counter admired by all beholders. The ideal refreshment at
> eleven o'clock (but sometimes even the lordly ones could not afford it)
> was a hot bun, fresh from the oven, into which were stuck two sticks of
> milk chocolate. The fiery interior of the bun reduced the chocolate to a
> desirable viscosity, and then this delectable combination of warm bun
> and melting chocolate was washed down with lemonade with a straw-
> berry ice in it. But this called for ample pocket money; our funds always
> used to give way before our digestions did.[24]

Like all the boys of that time Forester was much influenced by the school
ikon, Sir Ernest Shackleton, an Old Alleynian, or OA, as former students
of the college are known. His quiet authority and charisma played a major
part in the creation of Hornblower.

Raymond Chandler, creator of the antiheroic Los Angeles detective, Philip Marlowe, went to Dulwich in the Autumn of 1900 missing Wodehouse by one term. He too appreciated the college. 'A classical education saves you from being fooled by pretentiousness. If I hadn't grown up on Latin and Greek, I doubt I would know so well how to draw the line between what I call a vernacular style and what I should call an illiterate or *faux naif* style.'[25] Another author (whom Dulwich does not boast about) is Denis Wheatley, once a best-seller but little read these days and only remembered for his black magic books. He was at Dulwich for two and a half terms in 1909 and about the kindest thing he says about it in a vituperative piece of self justification is 'God, how I hated that rotten school!'[26] He was expelled by Gilkes for theft and truancy.

'Podge', however, loved that excellent school in spite of a rotten form placing, twenty-third out of twenty-five in the summer of 1899, and a somewhat schizoid report from Gilkes which must have puzzled his stolid father.

He has done just fairly in the summer examinations, but no more. I fear he has spent too much thought upon his cricket and the winning of colours. He is a most impractical boy – continually he does badly at examinations from lack of the proper books: he is often forgetful: *he finds difficulties in the most simple things and asks absurd questions, whereas he understands the more difficult things.* [Author's italics.]

He has the most distorted ideas about wit and humour; he draws over his books and examination papers in the most distressing way, and writes foolish rhymes in other people's books. Notwithstanding, he has a genuine interest in literature, and can often talk with much enthusiasm and good sense about it. He does some things at times astonishingly well and writes good Latin verse.

He is a very useful boy in the school and in the VI form and one is obliged to like him in spite of his vagaries. We wish him all success and if he perseveres he will certainly succeed.[27]

Another of those who liked him was William Beach Thomas. He taught at Dulwich for the academic year 1897–98. Like Wodehouse he was a classicist and a sportsman – he won his Oxford Blue for athletics.

Gilkes' reference to writing in books included the schoolboy habit of putting matchstick figures on the margins of the pages of his textbooks. When flicked over rapidly these give the crude impression of a moving man. One day in class Gilkes asked Wodehouse to lend him his *Euripides* but handed it back with a shudder. 'No thank you. This book has got a man in it' which, Townend told Usborne, made its owner laugh for about a year.[28]

Regardless of that mixed report Wodehouse had been earmarked for a classics scholarship to Oxford – then the most prized of all scholastic achievements for a boy leaving public school. Armine won such a scholarship and went on to gain a first class degree, the Newdigate Prize for poetry, the Chancellor's Essay Prize and was later to write elegant verse for *The Times of India* as 'Senex'. Pelham worked hard and wrote in eager anticipation to his friend 'Jeames' (Old Alleynian, Eric George, the author and artist) in September 1899 that he had been working hard for a scholarship at Oriel, which he thought he was certain to get, and said how ripping it would be if the two of them were together at the same College.[29]

Then disaster. In another undated letter to Jeames a little later he writes: 'Friend of me boyhood, here some dread news for you. My people have not got enough of what are vulgarly but forcibly called 'Stamps' to send me to Varsity. Damn [illegible]. Oh! money, money, thy name is money! (a most lucid remark)'. He adds that he is going into the Hong Kong & Shanghai Bank for two years so that he will have that time in which to establish himself on a pinnacle of fame as a writer.[29] What made the blow ever worse was being withdrawn from the scholarship exam at the last moment. In the face he showed the world young Wodehouse accepted the decision with good grace and clothed it in humour writing of the rupee – in which Ernest's pension was paid – jumping up and down and throwing fits. 'Watch the rupee' was, he claimed, the cry in the Wodehouse household and expenditure had to be regulated in the light of what mood it happened to be in at any moment.[30] Later Ernest investigated exchanging his uncertain rupee pension for one smaller but fixed in re-assuringly sound pounds and probably took that option.[31]

Inside himself Wodehouse felt devastated. (Later in life rich Uncle Plum never felt obliged to assist Armine, the modestly paid head of the Theosophical College in Benares, with such things as the school fees for Armine's son. There is a forced reiteration in what Wodehouse told Jasen of how fond he was of Armine which sounds as much like Wodehouse trying to convince himself as Jasen or the reader; to thrust from his mind the very human resentment of his brother that he must have felt but of which he felt ashamed.)

This shortage of 'stamps' was probably a major factor in developing the obsessive interest in money Wodehouse was to show throughout his life.

Ernest's pension was worth some £900 a year and would not stretch to two sons at university. John Buchan, later the first Lord Tweedsmuir, creator of Richard Hannay and author of *The Thirty-Nine Steps* and other best-sellers, paid his own way through Oxford by scholarships and writing, entering *Who's Who* while still an undergraduate.[32] Wodehouse could more easily have trod the same path. All Dulwich boys going to Oxford or Cambridge received a payment from the college governors which in Pelham's case could have been £30 a year.[33] So with only a modest sum from Ernest and a little more from Wodehouse writing it would have been possible for the family to finance a second son at Oxford. At that time an assistant master at Dulwich only earned £150 a year. But that mildly risky approach either never occurred to Ernest, or was rejected.

So it was to be another forty years before Wodehouse (P.G.) finally got his Oxford degree. It also left Wodehouse scholars with a perpetual debate. What effect would three years at Oxford have had on his writing? Would he still have been so great a writer and if so in what way would his prose be different? Would university have stifled his burgeoning talent or not? The author and playwright Cosmo Hamilton wrote 'He came into the world with a silver spoon in his mouth and ought to thank his lucky stars that it fell out in his youth. If he had gone on from school to Oxford and conformed thus to the traditions of an admirable family he might have followed in their footsteps into Parliament and a title and the subsequent obscurity of all patriotic men.'[34] Or perhaps graduate Wodehouse would have been as great a writer and not so different a one. His habit of observing quietly from the sidelines was already too firmly part of his character to be affected, even by Oxford.

It would be hard to overestimate the significance of Dulwich to Wodehouse. He remained the most devoted of Old Alleynians all his life and he loved the college as much as he loved anything or anybody. Those who wish to can slot every Wodehouse story into the setting of an English public school with the permanent skirmishing between authority, the aunts or masters, and those set under it, the eggs, beans and crumpets or boys, yet all within a framework of duties, responsibilities and a common code shared by everyone. At the college the worst sin in the schoolboy lexicon was 'putting on side' or boasting. Temperamentally Wodehouse was unlikely to do so anyway, he was a gentleman, but this deeply imbued attitude meant his habitual denial of any ability, understanding or intelligence came easily to him. Dulwich was also his first real home and perhaps his only one. The parental vacuum of those early years and his time at Dulwich were the two most important influences on his life. The college gave him not only happiness and security but also the education to exploit his genius to the full. No wonder he was grateful. In *Mike* he writes of Adair having that passionate fondness for his school that every boy is supposed to have, but which is really implanted in about one in every thousand. 'To Adair, Sedleigh was almost a religion. . . . The average public schoolboy *likes* his school. He hopes it will lick Bedford at footer and Malvern at cricket, but he rather bets it won't.' That passage has been oft quoted by critics as an example of the superior realism of the Wodehouse schoolstories. It is more, for Wodehouse was that one boy in a thousand and he put much of himself into Adair. 'Both his parents were dead [!] . . . and the only really pleasant times Adair had had, as far back as he could remember, he owed to Sedleigh'. Wodehouse's innate sense of the ridiculous prevented him from expressing those views personally but his undiminishing love for Dulwich was as Adair's for Sedleigh. It harmed nobody and meant a great deal to him.

Those years at Dulwich gave Wodehouse the experience to create some of the finest public-school stories in the English language (and they were not written in any other) and of his urban Blandings, Valley Fields.

> It was worth the sun's while to take a little trouble over Valley Fields, for there are few more pleasant spots on the outskirts of England's metropolis. One of its residents, a Major Flood-Smith, in the course of a letter to the *South London Argus* exposing the hellhounds of the local Rates and Taxes Department, once alluded to it as 'a fragrant oasis'. He gave the letter to his cook to mail, and she forgot it and found it three weeks later in a drawer and burned it, and the editor would never have printed it, anyway, being diametrically opposed to the policy for which the *Argus* had always fearlessly stood, but – and this is the point we would stress – in using the words 'fragrant oasis' the Major was dead right. He had rung the bell, hit the nail on the head and put the thing in a nutshell.[35]

You could fill an entire doctoral thesis analysing that one paragraph and several pages writing down all that is implied about the major, the cook, local papers and their editors, let alone the suburbs. It could not have been written by 'a not very complex man'. Wodehouse, even when only on the threshold of manhood, was already a complex individual as he left the protective womb of Dulwich.

—6—

MONEY IN THE BANK

Tho' never nurtured in the lap
  Of luxury, yet I admonish you
I am an intellectual chap
  And think of things that would astonish you.[1]

W.S. Gilbert

THERE was no Serpent Tempter to drive Wodehouse from his Dulwich Eden. Just 'the new and dread, necessity of earning bread'. He had already made a start by winning a competition run by *The Public School Magazine* with an essay on 'Some Aspects of Game Captaincy' published in February 1900, six months before he left Dulwich, and for which he won ten shillings and sixpence, or half a guinea. In those days it would have bought twenty-one large ice-creams (and they would have been made from cream) in 'The Butt', Dulwich's school shop. Today it would buy one. That half guinea was the first entry in a notebook of his literary earnings which he kept from February 1900 to February 1908. The above quotation was aptly on page one of that cashbook under the heading 'Motto'.

Writing was all he wanted to do when he left Dulwich in July 1900 but, reasonably, his father insisted he get a job, and using his old Hong Kong contacts gained his son a London clerkship with the Hong Kong & Shanghai Bank. Their Lombard Street office acted as a training ground for the (British) management of the bank's Far Eastern branches, which did most of its business. Such trainee clerkships – there were only twenty-four that year[2] – were prized as the bank's managers in the Far East lived in great style. Ernest could congratulate himself on making amends for the lack of funds for that Oxford scholarship by securing a prosperous future for young Pelham. Young Pelham, as he began work in the postage room of the Bank that September, was less enthused. He was paid £80 a year, to which his father added another £80 from his own limited means.

That made £3.3s.10d a week; an adequate income for a young man in those days – whole lower-middle-class families survived respectably on less. Two more factors now reinforced the young clerk's obsession with money. One was the reverence for money induced in modestly paid wage-slaves working with huge sums belonging to other people. The second was the desperate race to earn enough money from writing to leave the bank before he was sent to the Far East. Literally every penny mattered for in those days there were still hundreds of things that could be bought for a farthing, one quarter of an old penny. Later in life money acquired another important quality – he looked upon the prices paid for his work as the yardstick for judging his status as an author both in relation to his peers and as an indication of his rising reputation.

Wodehouse's own reports suggest a touch of 'The young genius starving in a garret'. He wrote that from now on all he would be able to afford in the way of lunch would be a roll and butter and a cup of coffee[3] and told Jasen, of his room in Markham Square, that he had horrible lodgings in the Chelsea neighbourhood off the King's Road and that right through his two years at the bank he never had the slightest inkling of what banking was. This, perhaps, struck him as artistically right, sharpening, by contrast, his later success. Yet sixty-seven years later in his *Do Butlers Burgle Banks?* Wodehouse displayed a competent working knowledge of the private banks of nineteenth-century England. That expertise predates his stint with the bank and came from his observant visits to aunt Lucy Wodehouse who had married the Revd Edward Isaac, whose family owned the Worcester Old Bank.[4]

In Wodehouse's book *Psmith In The City*, which is closely based on his time at the bank, the mournful descriptions of Mike's desolation at his servitude within the New Asiatic Bank have been treated as simply auto-biographical, applying to all Wodehouse's time there. That fails to allow for his toughness, adaptability and calculated policy of seeing the brighter side of life. Decades before Norman Vincent Peale wrote *The Power Of Positive Thinking* Wodehouse was practising it. He rapidly overcame his unhappiness at the bank: he was too wise not to and it would have done no one but him any harm. But he didn't waste the emotions of those early days, he never wasted any material that might be used in an article or book. Soon he was enjoying life at the bank, playing for both its cricket and rugby football teams and in a photograph of the latter team for a match against the London and Westminster Bank in 1900 he shows no evidence of undernourishment or despondency. He liked the people he worked with, and they liked him – with the possible exception of Sir Ewen Cameron, the London manager of the Bank who appears in that photograph as president of the team. He bears such a close resemblance to the unpleasant Mr Bickersdyke, the London manager of the New Asiatic Bank in *Psmith In The City* as illustrated by T.R.M. Whitwell, that the artist must have been briefed by the author. Wodehouse was not unhappy at the bank but he was bored with it – on the simple grounds that it was not writing. Townend told Jasen, 'From the first time I met him, he had decided to write. He never swerved.'

J.R.D. Jones collected notes for a history of the Bank[5] (which he did not live to write) including some on Wodehouse. One Greyburn wrote 'Will the Bank ever have three such comedians in one department as Nicola, P.G.W. and Rodolph?' H.E. Nixon wrote 'I can just remember P.G. Wodehouse in London and the moments stolen from odd slack periods in the Inward Bills Dept for the composition of his brilliant little paragraphs for the By The Way column of the London *Globe* newspaper. He was a good cricketer and used to bring a team of journalists to play the Bank team at New Beckenham.' One Melhuish wrote 'I took over the Postage Desk from P.G. Wodehouse. The Bank Inspector would have lifted his eyebrows at the happy go lucky method of keeping his book on that job.' Those letters were written between September 1941 and January 1957. Clearly his old colleagues remembered Wodehouse affectionately and the man who organizes a cricket team of journalists – notoriously an individualistic breed – to play his old employers would not have been an introvert who hated his time there.

Wodehouse himself wrote to Jones 'I enjoyed my two years in the bank enormously' and the evidence, notwithstanding *Psmith In The City*, is that he did. To the end of his days he maintained an account at the bank into which he paid all small cheques – in 1936, he told the *Daily Express*, those for less than fifteen guineas (£15.75p) – to be used for little extras for Townend or Leonora 'Without telling Mummy'.[6]

As often as he could Wodehouse visited the Shropshire countryside he loved, and his parents. It was here that he spent three weeks in June 1901 getting over an extremely severe case of mumps – about the worst minor disease a young man can contract. Bad attacks often lead to sterility and sometimes impotence as well and this was almost certainly the effect on Wodehouse and, in turn, this had an important influence on his writing and the asexuality of his heroes and heroines. The mumps also affected his eyesight badly, hence the strong glasses he wore for the rest of his life. Of course he used his convalescence to write. At Stableford, Ernest Wodehouse, CMG, servant of the Empire and cousin of the Earl of Kimberley would, with his wife, have been accepted by the county families as one of their own and so the young Wodehouse, when staying with his parents in Shropshire, was naturally included in invitations they received. His own story of one such visit[7] is typical, showing again that he met the test of having a sense of humour: the ability to laugh at himself.

He tells of a county lady who, hearing of the Wodehouse boy's social graces, invited his mother to bring her son to tea and was appalled to discover she was landed with graceless Pelham, rather than graceful Armine. The story reflects well on Pelham's modesty, lack of side and ability to tell a good story, but not on his accuracy. It is not credible that the friend of a woman with four sons would be unaware of such a fact: the Edwardians took class distinctions to a new high (or low, depending on your viewpoint) and routinely checked up on new acquaintances in Burke or Debrett's peerage. (Wodehouse continued to visit his parents whenever he could until late 1902 when they moved to 3, Wolseley Terrace, Cheltenham, a town he disliked.) Wodehouse The Social Bumbler is as much a work of fiction as everything else he wrote. All the stories about his social gaffs come from Wodehouse himself, none from people who knew him. This casts doubt on another classic Wodehouse story.

Dining at Grim's Dyke, the home of Sir William Schwenk Gilbert, one of his early heroes and a great influence on his own poetry and lyric writing, Wodehouse was listening to a story by his host (and, of course 'Tucked away inside my brother Armine's frock coat and my cousin George's trousers'). It was one of those very long, very dull, shaggy-dog stories where everything falls hilariously into place with a punch line which more than makes up for the tedious build-up. Wodehouse didn't think it a very funny story but he thought that it must be because W.S. Gilbert was telling it. So when Gilbert paused, just before the punch line, Wodehouse laughed, thinking that was the end of the story. He claimed that in those days he possessed rather an individual laugh, something like the explosion of one of those gas mains that slays six. The other guests were a little puzzled, as if they had expected something better from the author of *The Mikado*. Then as they all laughed politely and conversation became general, Wodehouse caught the full baleful glare of his host's eye.[8] Given Wodehouse's habit of appropriating any good story going when writing his 'autobiographical' works it is more likely than not that the anecdote was borrowed and he was not the dunderhead in question.

During this period he was writing every evening when he got home from work. Like many struggling young writers he was inspired by J.M. Barrie's *When A Man's Single*, a thinly veiled autobiography of JMB's early years as a journalist after arriving in London from Scotland.

You beginners seem able to write nothing but your views on politics, and your reflections on art, and your theories of life, which you sometimes even think original. Editors won't have that, because their readers don't want it. Every paper has its regular staff of leader-writers, and what is wanted from the outside is freshness. An editor tosses aside your column-and-a-half on evolution but is glad to have a paragraph saying that you saw Herbert Spencer the day before yesterday gazing solemnly for ten minutes in a milliner's window.

Wodehouse followed that advice, as did H.G. Wells among others, and it enabled him to earn enough on which to live while teaching himself his craft. He became 'a slanter', a writer who studies what editors want, reading the magazines carefully and turning out stories as similar to the ones they published as he can manage without actual plagiarism.[9] It was not, as he later thought, a waste of time before he turned to his true *metier*, for the humorist, like the comedy actor or cartoonist, is as much as anything else a parodist. You cannot parody that which you do not understand. The trainee Wodehouse learned to write to order whether it was sentimental slush, thrilling adventure stories or non-fiction features, and that training enhanced all the humorous writing that followed.

During those two years he had eighty pieces published including his first overtly humorous piece, 'Men Who Missed Their Own Weddings' in *Tit-Bits* in November 1900 and with Townend he wrote, for a short while, the *Answers To Correspondents* column in that paper. He had the good fortune of starting his writing career during an explosion in the demand for printed entertainment following compulsory education and the resulting stampede (since reversed) towards universal adult literacy. When Wodehouse was establishing himself in the first decade of this century there were scores of 'pulps' in London that would take humorous pieces and Wodehouse sent unsolicited articles to most of them. Between 1900 and 1960, when he was at his most prolific, an author wrote largely to please himself and what he thought would please his market – the editors.

Publishers might advise their writers and Wodehouse was grateful for any suggestions they gave him but he had, largely, to find his own way. The modern role of authors' editor, with its concomitant power, did not exist. So he could, and did, develop as he saw fit.

On 17 September 1902 he first appeared in *Punch*, then the undisputed national humour magazine, with 'An Unfinished Collection', drawing himself to the attention of Owen Seaman, a cricketing classicist with a first class Oxford degree. Seaman, who worked on the magazine for thirty-five years (the last twenty-six as editor) retiring with a baronetcy in 1932, took the young writer under his wing and on to the *Punch* cricket XI. This important friendship gave Wodehouse a reliable, albeit small, income. In February 1906, when Seaman became editor, Wodehouse wrote to congratulate him, saying, 'You were so good to me when I started writing. I shall never forget how patient you were with my stuff'.[10] Seaman appointed the young Alan Milne as assistant editor, although his new deputy was rankled at not becoming a member of the Punch Table until 1910. Milne's appointment would have introduced him and Wodehouse. Seaman also introduced his socially and professionally acceptable prodigy to other writers, among them J.M. Barrie.

Soon the young journalist became a member of Barrie's cricket team, the *Allahakbarries* – from 'Allah Akbar' or 'God help us'.[11] As a member of the team Wodehouse got to know 'JMB' quite well, especially as on his daily walks between home in Chelsea and *The Globe* in Bouverie Street, he passed close by Barrie's Adelphi flat every day.

As an *Allahakbarrie* Wodehouse played with many of the great authors of the day including another of his heroes, Sir Arthur Conan Doyle. Through this connection he was able to interview the great man. 'Grit. A Talk With Sir Arthur Conan Doyle' appeared in the *V.C. Journal Of The Brighter Side Of Life*, for which the editor, Harold Begbie, paid him two guineas. The young journalist described Doyle as 'Immensely powerful in build, and the keenest of sportsmen, he is the very embodiment of the Man of the Field. There is strength behind everything he does. Whether he is riding straight on the hunting field, or going in in a bad light to stop the rot, or bowling to break up a long stand at cricket, he does it with the air of a man who gets there.'[12] Doyle confided to Wodehouse that he would like to learn to parachute as he thought the man who first tried coming down in one was the pluckiest man on earth and added that he would like to try it just for the sake of the one great experience. The two men, already friends, became close. Wodehouse was usually invited to the cricketing weekends Doyle held at his country house, Windlesham, near Crowborough in Sussex and in the evenings after a big dinner they would have long discussions together on literature and also on spiritualism,[13] one of Doyle's passions; the ordinary world was too limited for his extraordinary mind.

Wodehouse gained the impression that Doyle held Sherlock Holmes in no great affection and so threw the odd custard pie at the great detective most notably in his 'From A Detective's Notebook'.[14] Adrian Mulliner, the detective, unmasks Sherlock Holmes, now better known as the fiend of Baker Street, as, in fact, Moriarty. There is no disproof of this as Dr John Watson never saw Moriarty and relied totally on what Holmes told him about the master criminal.

In *Punch* in 1903, just after Doyle killed off Holmes at the Reichenbach Falls, Wodehouse wrote a story, narrated by 'John Waddus', of 'Dudley Jones – Borehunter' who leaned too far over the crater atop of Mount Vesuvius and, when recovered, was 'a good deal charred and, to be brief, of very little use to anybody'.[15] When Holmes was resurrected Wodehouse celebrated the event with a poem, 'Back to His Native Strand'.[16] In *The Prodigal*[17] Wodehouse actually uses Dr Watson as the narrator who tells of meeting a thoroughly Americanized Holmes in the Strand, in London, which shows how close his friendship with Doyle must have been. In the March and April 1902 issues of *Sandows Magazine* Wodehouse wrote 'The Pugilist In Fiction' which singles out Doyle's *Rodney Stone* and Bernard Shaw's *Cashel Byron's Profession* as two novels in the library of pugilistic fiction which stand alone. His 'Wrestling In The Halls' in the same publication gives what is probably his first mention in print of Sherlock Holmes when he likens a referee to Holmes as depicted by Wiliam Gillette in the play *Sherlock Holmes*. Sherlockians and Holmesians* – many are also Wodehousians – have counted hundreds of allusions to Holmes in Wodehouse's work and had great fun in drawing Holmes-Watson, Psmith-Mike and Jeeves-Bertie analogies; in analysing the effect of Doyle on Wodehouse[18] and proving that Jeeves must be the son of Sherlock Holmes.[19] Wodehouse topped all the analysts when he had the fictional Jeeves loftily refer to Holmes as 'Sir Arthur Conan Doyle's fictional detective, Sherlock Holmes . . .'[20] Doyle was a laconic correspondent. He once sent a note to Wodehouse, who forgot to answer it, and in a few days received this reminder on a post card. '? A.C.D.'.[21] The influence of Doyle, particularly the Holmes stories, permeates the Wodehouse canon.

Under Doyle's captaincy Wodehouse played at Lords, the home of cricket, for the Authors against the Publishers in August 1910, watched by the young Alec Waugh, brother of Evelyn. Wodehouse went in first wicket down and scored an impressive sixty runs but 'It was a sound, straightforward performance, unmarked by brilliance or eccentricity of style'.[22] But life wasn't all cricket, it was, as it always remained, mostly writing. During these early years Wodehouse's principal market was two magazines for boys. *The Public School Magazine*, started in 1898, was edited by P.G. Witson and later taken over by A. and C. Black, while *The Captain*, its great rival, was set up by George Newnes in April 1899 under the inspired editorship of R.S. Warren Bell. He was a former teacher whose own schoolboy sense of humour provided exactly what his readers discovered they wanted. The athletics editor of *The Captain* was that great all-round sportsman, C.B. Fry, capped for England in both cricket and association football, who thought that Wodehouse should have been called 'humour editor' of the magazine.[23] *The Captain* was a more generous

---

* There is a vital difference between Sherlockians and Holmesians but it is not for ordinary mortals to probe such mysteries.

paymaster than *Punch*, becoming the bedrock of the Wodehouse bank balance from his first article for them, a St Austin's school story in October 1901, to his last, on the public-schools boxing at Aldershot in September 1913. (It ceased publication in March 1925 due, Fry suggested, to an inability to persuade advertisers that schoolboys bought soap.) From April to September 1900, *The Captain* ran a story called 'Acton's Feud' by Fred Swainson. Wodehouse was so impressed that it prompted him to write fiction, initially short stories. The first of these was 'The Prize Poem', a St Austin's school story, which appeared in *The Public School Magazine* in July 1901. From as early as December 1900 he was writing Under The Flail, a column in the same periodical, and *The Pothunters* was serialized in it from January 1902 until it was halted in mid-flow in March when Black closed the magazine, *The Captain* having pushed its older rival into losses. However Black promised to complete *The Pothunters* by publishing it as a book. In the *Public School Magazine* in March 1901 Wodehouse wrote 'Concerning Relatives', dealing with their visits to boys at school. 'Fathers stand in the same relationship to their sons as Consols [a British Government stock] do to investors. The income derived from them is safe, even if in many cases regrettably small.' A neat analogy showing a familiarity with risk-return-ratios which again contradicts the Wodehouse claim that he never understood anything that went on at the bank outside the postage room. The article mentions fathers, brothers, sisters, aunts and uncles but not, of course, mothers.

A stroke of luck occurred when his old schoolmaster, William Beach Thomas, having left teaching for journalism, became the assistant editor of the By The Way column on *The Globe*, a staunchly conservative London evening paper then owned by George Armstrong (later the second baronet). The columnar editor was Harold Begbie. Wodehouse asked Beach Thomas for work and he, remembering the quality of those pieces in *The Alleynian*, suggested Wodehouse stand in when he or Begbie wanted a day off. So on 16 August 1901 Wodehouse played truant from the bank for his first taste of life as a newspaper journalist: he was paid another half guinea. Other days followed, working on both the By The Way and Men And Matters columns, and a whole week, from 2–7 April 1902, when he feigned non-existent attacks of neuralgia. Destiny was doing its stuff which was all right by Wodehouse and, he modestly suggested later, a good thing for the Hong Kong & Shanghai Bank as well.

In *Over Seventy* he implies he was finally sacked for writing a story on the white, gleaming, front page of a virgin ledger. It was a richly comic description of the celebrations and rejoicings marking the Formal Opening of The New Ledger including a bit about Wodehouse being presented to his Gracious Majesty The King (who, of course, attended the function) which, Wodehouse assures us, would have the reader gasping with mirth. To avoid discovery Wodehouse cut the page from the ledger, which caused the Chief Cashier, a Mr Moore, to summon his old foe, the Head Stationer. In a sparkling piece of dialogue between the two Wodehouse portrays himself as an imbecile and, for good measure, weak in the head as well. It was, he reported, immediately after this that he found himself at liberty to embark on the life literary.

That miniature masterpiece is so much better than the merely prosaic facts, although not until old age did Wodehouse admit that while the story, as he told it, always ended with him being sacked he was, in fact, forgiven. Wodehouse resigned from the bank on 9 September 1902 for four sensible reasons. Beach Thomas was taking his annual five week holiday at that time and asked Wodehouse if he would stand in for him for the entire period. Wodehouse was ready to resign anyway as he felt his imminent posting overseas – to which most of his colleagues eagerly looked forward – was incompatible with his becoming a professional writer. Also he had saved £50 from his writing and was, by then, earning more money from spare time journalism than he was paid in salary. Finally *The Pothunters* was to be published on the 18th of that month. The bank had been kind to him, turning a blind eye to his articles in numerous papers and periodicals (many of them written in the bank's time, in the bank's premises using the bank's writing paper and other facilities), but nursing a fully-fledged author to their bosom would have been foreign to their policy.

Thus September 1902 was the pivotal month in Wodehouse's career. Not yet twenty-one he had a hardback book issued by a major publishing house; his first article printed in *Punch*; a staff job on a London newspaper (albeit a temporary one) and a record of adequate if uncertain earnings as a freelance writer. For the next seventy-two years he devoted himself full time to authorship.

The Globe was London's oldest evening paper publishing five editions a day on light pink paper. Newsprint, when made then, was pale pink and had to be bleached, so unbleached paper was cheaper. Wodehouse learned a great deal from Begbie and Beach Thomas, both journalists' journalists. That is, professionals who turn out articles at short notice to required length, style and deadline on any subject at all. On an evening paper like *The Globe*, with five editions daily, pressures on journalists are most acute. Beach Thomas wrote 'His speed was fantastic and he could write verse very nearly as quickly as he could write prose.'[24] He might easily have been describing Wodehouse or himself but was actually referring to Begbie whose books range from the lightweight and amusing *Strewelpeter* series to his heavyweight two-volume *Life Of*

William Booth: Founder Of The Salvation Army.

All too soon those five weeks were over, Beach Thomas returned and Wodehouse was truly alone in the real world. He earned £16.4s.od that September from writing and for the four months to December that year £65.6s.7d, including his ten per cent royalty on *The Pothunters* which had sold 396 copies at 3s 6d grossing £69.6s.7d and netting him £6.18s.8d.[25] It was enough on which to live providing he worked hard and sent a plethora of articles, stories and poems to a wide range of publications. He did but it was hard work as he noted in his cashbook in February 1903: 'Rather a bad time to start with, especially with *Fun* who refused ten contributions running.' He persevered and in the first decade of the century his work appeared in at least forty-two UK publications: *Answers, Books of Today And Tomorrow, The Captain, Cassell's, Chums, The Daily Chronicle, The Daily Express, The Daily Mail, The Evening News, The Evening Standard, Fun, The Globe, The Grand, Ideas, Illustrated Sporting & Dramatic News, John Bull Year Book, Land And Water, Little Folks, London Echo, London Opinion, Nash's Magazine, The Novel Magazine, Onlooker, Pearson's, The Public School Magazine, Punch, Royal, St James's Gazette, Sandow's Physical Culture Magazine, Scraps, The Sportsman, Stage And Sport, The Strand Magazine, The Sunday Magazine, Tit-Bits, Today, Vanity Fair* (UK), *V.C., Weekly Telegraph, Wheel Of Fortune, The Windsor Magazine, The World*[26] and others not yet unearthed plus American periodicals. The total will never be known as in his early days Wodehouse also wrote under pseudonyms which even he could not recall.

By early 1903 Wodehouse could afford to move to better lodgings, again in Chelsea, at 23 Walpole Street where he had the top-floor, front room. It was perhaps a lucky house for writers. Apart from Wodehouse at least three other recognized authors lived there in later years:[27] Mrs Maxtone-Grahame who wrote as Jan Struther and Mrs Miniver; author and critic Douglas West and novelist, biographer and Peke fancier Denis Mackail who with his wife Diana were to become among Wodehouse's close friends.

Shortly after moving into Walpole Street Wodehouse was visited by one Herbert W. Westbrook, a teacher with literary ambitions and a letter of introduction from a mutual friend from the Hong Kong Bank, Frank Kendall. Westbrook was a would-be writer and typically Wodehouse stopped work on a poem for *Punch* and 'Plum gave me good advice and, more than that, sincere encouragement'.[28] As a result Westbrook invited Wodehouse to visit him at the small preparatory school where he taught, Emsworth House near Portsmouth, owned and run by Baldwin King-Hall, inevitably known to the boys as 'Baldie' and to his friends as 'Bud' or 'Buddie'. He and Wodehouse took to each other immediately: both were cricket fanatics and both had escaped naval careers because of weak eyesight. In January 1903 Wodehouse took up residence in a room above the school stables, only going up to London when required to do a stint on *The Globe*. Soon thereafter he rented Threepwood Cottage, Emsworth, later immortalizing both names in English literature. Lord King-Hall, Baldie's nephew (who also wrote plays with Ian Hay) recalls the school: 'All I can remember about Emsworth is that we sat round my uncle's bed at ten every morning whilst he ate his breakfast and conducted what I suppose might be called a seminar on life in general and that Mr P.G. Wodehouse was a member of the staff.'[29] Wodehouse took an active part in the life of the school, playing cricket with the masters and boys and helping King-Hall's sister, Ella, organize plays, but he was never on the staff.

Wodehouse and Westbrook were to work closely together for nearly ten years and for the tolerant, hardworking Wodehouse it was a time packed with incident. Murphy is the only author to research Westbrook properly, writing to and interviewing surviving relatives. He reveals a man of great charm, a Greek and Latin scholar with a beautiful voice: a man fascinating to women and disliked by many men; a man generous when he had money but with elastic ethics. He would borrow money from friends, never repaying it nor intending to, and took a similarly communal attitude to their property. On one occasion Wodehouse got back to Threepwood to discover that Westbrook had, without asking, borrowed his evening clothes.

This forced Wodehouse to go to dinner at a nearby stately home wearing a primitive suit of soup-and-fish bequeathed to him by his Uncle Hugh (Major Hugh Pollexfen Deane) who stood six feet four and weighed in the neighbourhood of fifteen stone, as a result of which, through dinner, the trousers rose inexorably higher and higher until, per Wodehouse (six feet tall himself), they rose to the level of his tie: possibly an exaggeration. The facts, suitably clothed, went into Wodehouse's Ukridge story, *First Aid For Dora*.

On another occasion Wodehouse took up playing the banjolele, as did Bertie. 'Those who know Bertram Wooster best are aware that he is a man of sudden, strong enthusiasms and that, when in the grip of one of these, he becomes a remorseless machine – tense, absorbed, single minded.'[30] Bertie's banjo era ended when his instrument was burnt, along with his cottage, by Jeeves's stand-in, Brinkley, that Apostle of the Revolution who wants to see the gutters of Park Lane running red with blood – although in Bertie's case it would, of course, have been blue. The Wodehouse banjo era ended when Westbrook pawned the instrument and lost the ticket. Wodehouse's rural idyll ended too when in August 1903 Beach

Thomas left *The Globe* for the *Outlook*. (He was later knighted for out-standing reporting as a war correspondent in 1914–1918 on behalf of the *Daily Mail*.) 'When I left I bestowed my mantle on a Dulwich boy, who has since become a national hero, worshipped by boys and approved even by Lord Balfour, no less a person than P.G. Wodehouse.'[31] The hours were short, in theory only 10 a.m. to noon, but frantic and he worked a six-day week. The By The Way column required humorous, even facetious, comments on the news of the day and, always, a similarly topical set of verses. Such newspaper editorial offices are always noisy, chaotic and no place for the shy or faint-hearted. Christopher Fildes, the *Spectator* columnist, notes 'Journalists work best in a deep-litter system', an apt agricultural analogy. The experience of producing copy against such a background was valuable training and in later life Wodehouse would prove able to write almost anywhere – on ships, trains, cattle trucks and internment camps.

When Wodehouse felt the need for a day off Westbrook stood in for him. In August 1904 Begbie quit *The Globe* to join the *Daily Mail*, handing his column over to his deputy who saw his salary increase to the large sum of £5.5s a week. Bill Townend became the holiday-relief while Westbrook became Wodehouse's deputy. The pair worked well together although over the years Wodehouse became less and less tolerant of Westbrook's unenthusiastic approach to work. Wodehouse's *The Gold Bat* is dedicated, perhaps as a tactful hint, to Westbrook as 'That Prince of Slackers'. Westbrook was also the dedicatee of the first, Alston Rivers, UK edition of Wodehouse's *A Gentleman Of Leisure* (but not the US book, *The Intrusion of Jimmy*). It says 'To Herbert Westbrook without whose never failing advice, help and encouragement this book would have been finished in half the time'. That dedication became famous when it was given to Leonora in Wodehouse's second book of golf stories, *The Heart Of A Goof* (US *Divots*).

It was probably Westbrook's idea that he and Wodehouse should produce their column from Threepwood. That worked well until the day when the train failed to get their copy to London in time and the editor insisted the job be done from the paper's offices.

In 1908 *The Globe* was sold by the Armstrongs to Hildebrand Harms-worth (later the first baronet) and brother of Alfred, Lord Northcliffe, the unstable genius who revolutionized the British newspaper industry. His Lordship inspired Wodehouse to create that Napoleonic Press baron, Viscount Tilbury. The new owner of *The Globe*, aping his brother, began an intense promotional campaign. One idea was publicizing the By The Way column with a book of Wodehouse-Westbrook extracts to be called *The Globe By The Way Book*. It was a cheaply produced compilation, priced at one shilling and sub-titled 'A Literary Quick Lunch for People Who Have Only Got Five Minutes' and is by far Wodehouse's worst book. Even his incipient genius glitters only occasionally through the jokes which are either so dated and topical as to be unintelligible or so eternal as to be uninteresting. Today less than ten first editions are known to exist outside the UK copyright libraries and at auction even a poor copy is likely to fetch at least £4,000. There is also a facsimile edition published by the noted collector, James H. Heineman, in New York in 1985 in a limited edition of 500 and worth about £40.

Wodehouse and Westbrook also co-authored two theatrical sketches, a play and, in 1906, another scarce and valuable book *Not George Washington* which was placed with Cassell by Wodehouse's first literary agent, James B. Pinker.[32] It is not a good novel but it has strong autobiographical elements with the hero, James Orlebar Cloyster, working on a London evening paper called *The Orb* and a column called On Your Way – he even lived at Wodehouse's address, 23 Walpole Street, Chelsea. Wodehouse did most of the work but, with typical generosity, let Westbrook appear first on the title page. At that time Wodehouse was the author of eight published books but the only 'book' Westbrook had to his name was a paper-wrapped advertising pamphlet, *The Cause Of Catesby*,[33] in the form of a humorous story, commissioned by a firm of cork-lino (flooring) manufacturers in London's Tottenham Court Road. It has the undeserved distinction of being the first of at least seventeen books to be dedicated 'To That Brilliant Humorist P.G. Wodehouse'. Wodehouse sometimes wrote articles under Westbrook's name and the first time he did so, 'More Mind Readers' for *Books Of Today* in 1907, he notes this as 'A clever move' in his cashbook but doesn't note why. Perhaps the editor had said there was not enough space for more Wodehouse material in any one issue.

One sketch on which they collaborated was *The Bandit's Daughter*, produced at the Bedford Music Hall in Camden with music by Ella King-Hall. She married Westbrook in 1911, 'eloping' due to the opposition of her family. Wodehouse was fond of Ella and always remained loyal to her. When she set up a literary agency the year after her marriage he appointed her to act for him in the UK (in place of Pinker) which she did until she retired in 1935 shortly before her death.[34] This was also an act of loyalty to Westbrook, almost a way of pensioning-off their friendship, as he, after being commissioned and then wounded in the First World War, was no more successful than before, *faute de mieux* joining Ella in her agency. However loyalty and Wodehouse's hard-headed professionalism had to compromise and so Ella accepted an agent's commission of five per cent instead of the usual ten.

The other sketch was *After The Show*, only notable for the Hon. Aubrey Forde-Rasche who lives in Albany and has a manservant, Barlow, who is pretty sharp with his master over some of 'our cravats' of which he disapproves. Barlow has hints of Jeeves who was yet to come.

The play was *Brother Alfred*, produced by and starring Lawrence Grossmith, son of George and nephew of Weedon, the authors of *The Diary Of A Nobody*. It ran for only fourteen performances at the Savoy Theatre, London, in April 1913. Lawrence's brother George, called 'The Younger', was to become a firm friend and theatrical collaborator of Wodehouse.

That play marked the end of Wodehouse's collaboration with Westbrook but the latter lives on in English literature, though not by his own pen. His personality and peccadilloes are a major ingredient in the character of the first of Wodehouse's immortals, Stanley (pronounced Stanley) Featherstonehaugh (pronounced Fanshaw) Ukridge (pronounced Yukeridge) who dominates Wodehouse's first adult novel, *Love Among The Chickens*, and everyone in it. The idea for the book came when Townend wrote to Wodehouse about an acquaintance, Carrington Craxton, who with a friend had set up as a chicken farmer in Devonshire. Neither of them knew anything about chickens and every possible disaster hit the farm. Craxton used one amoral or fraudulent expedient after another to keep going until the creditors arrived like vultures at a carcass and the venture, amid tumult and shouting, died. Ukridge is mostly Westbrook with a generous dash of Craxton and a little of Townend thrown in for seasoning. He had a book of short stories to himself, *Ukridge* (US *He Rather Enjoyed It*) and Wodehouse continued to write about him occasionally until the last story 'Ukridge Opens A Bank Account' in *Plum Pie* 1966.

Townend contributed Ukridge's seafaring past for, failing to make a living as a black-and-white illustrator, he felt he needed a new source of material and so, financed by Wodehouse, set sail on a tramp steamer.

I went for my voyage, to Sulina in Roumania, and returned after three months with a broken nose and no hat, with no pictures, but with note-books filled with stories I had heard on board my tramp, scraps of fo'c'sle and engine room gossip, local colour, details of every-day routine, anecdotes and so on, which I jotted down more or less idly with no thought in my mind that in years to come they might be of use to me. Later when I had finally decided I should never earn a living as an artist, I unearthed these note-books, read through them, much as I have read through Plum Wodehouse's letters, and set to work to write a sea story, *The Tramp*, the first of thirty-nine books which I have had published in the last thirty years.[35]

It was dedicated, of course, to Wodehouse. Townend also worked his way across America, including a job in California as a lemon sorter – which had an inordinate fascination for his grub-staker. While no lemon sorter features as a Wodehouse character some of his Townend types have done the job and the profession frequently crops up in his non-fiction pieces.[36] Wodehouse – who could not imagine himself sailing in the fo'c'sle of a tramp steamer nor working as a lemon sorter – admired the doer in Townend and gained vicarious pleasure from his friend's adventures. All those Wodehouse heroes who have a cauliflower ear, are good at stopping dog fights and travel on tramp steamers – Sam Shotter in *Sam The Sudden* (US *Sam In the Suburbs*) for example – are based mainly on Townend, Ukridge only partly so. *Sam The Sudden* remained one of Wodehouse's favourites among his work and first introduced us to that South London paradise, Valley Fields.

Ukridge is an amoral rogue and not even a stylish one. He wears a dirty macintosh and pince-nez held on by ginger-beer bottle wire. He uses false names as 'an ordinary business precaution' and is a cheat, a liar, a blackmailer and a sponger – yet servants fawn on him. The only virtue he possesses is that his depredations exclude women whom he treats with respect (except his Aunt Julia who inspires fear as a substitute). It is a tribute to the author that Ukridge is as well liked as he is. Even so Ukridge remains the only major Wodehouse character about whom his fans strongly disagree. They will argue whether or not the Bertie-Jeeves cycle is superior to the Blandings saga whilst loving them both. Only the Ukridge stories provoke strong liking and dislike.

The Hon. Theodora Benson (Lord Charnwood's daughter), like me no fan of Ukridge's but one of Wodehouse's, wrote of her first meeting with Wodehouse in 1922:

I gave him an immense lecture on the works of Mr P.G. Wodehouse. I was only about sixteen, and it is not surprising that he was much too nice to resent it. What surprises me is that on finding out there was nothing else I wanted to talk about he took the trouble to talk about his work with intelligence and interest. He defended Ukridge against my attacks quite eagerly and yet impersonally. 'Yes I know there is that school of thought but I really do think that it is wrong.' And I was able to let my admiration flow without blushing for it afterwards.[37]

Typically Wodehouse, out of a first royalty cheque of £31.5s.8d, gave
Townend £10 for the idea of *Love Among The Chickens* and continued to
use it as a pretext for giving him money to the end of their days.

Westbrook and Wodehouse collaborated, in close rapport, from 1903 to
1913 or so but as early as 3 March 1905 Wodehouse was finding Slacker
Westbrook irritating. Writing to Townend he damned Westbrook for
attempting to steal the idea of Craxton and the chicken farm; said that a
whole regiment of Westbrooks, each slacker than the last, wouldn't deter
him, Wodehouse; wrote that Townend was not to bring 'Westy' to Walpole Street as he was fed up with him; mentioned he had locked-up the
manuscript in case of a raid by Westbrook; instructed Townend not to
give Westbrook any more information about Craxton but concluded
cheerfully by noting that, despite Westbrook's intention of rushing
through a book, he doubted that Slacker would ever get beyond chapter
two.[38] Strong stuff about a friend from an easy-going, unbelligerent man.

With Ella working for Wodehouse, he and Westbrook probably met
after 1913 but there is no record of such meetings nor of continued
intimacy although he was writing to Westbrook on matters to do with
handling his books until Ella retired. In 1924 came Westbrook's, *The
Booby Prize*[39] – one of only two books (plus *Catesby*) written on his own –
with the wan dedication 'To P.G. Wodehouse I dedicate this book at the
risk of impairing our ancient friendship'. Wodehouse's original dedication
of *A Gentleman Of Leisure* to Westbrook was removed in the 1921 reissue
by Herbert Jenkins and was replaced with 'To Douglas Fairbanks'.
Wodehouse owed Westbrook nothing and Westbrook owed him a great
deal – so the chance to compliment Fairbanks, the star of the play based
on the book, was seized without compunction about Westbrook's feelings.
However Wodehouse was replying to Westbrook's letters as late as 1954,
five years before the latter's death. From his mention of these to Townend[40] it is clear he would have been happy to let the link die, but he was
too kind to kill it off himself.

One major milestone was Wodehouse's first story in *The Strand* magazine whose regular authors, such as Conan Doyle, inspired the same sort
of following as stars in television soap operas enjoy today. Wodehouse was
to be mainstay of *The Strand* for thirty-five years. 'The Wirepullers'
appeared in the July 1905 issue and is written in first-person girl. 'It is a
splendid thing to be seventeen and have one's hair up and feel that one
cannot be kissed indiscriminately any more by sticky boys and horrid old
gentlemen . . .' (Wodehouse tried this device in another story, 'Against
The Clock', which appeared in *Pearson's Magazine* in June 1909 and for
the first three chapters of *Not George Washington* in 1907 but thereafter
wisely dropped the ploy. Gender transfer in first-person writing is a bit of

a drag. On the other hand 'The Mixer', written in first-person-dog, is highly effective.)

Between 1903 and May 1909 Wodehouse enjoyed the security of his salaried job on *The Globe* but also worked equally hard at freelance jobs. For 1903, his first full year as a professional writer, he earned £215.18s.1d and 1907, the last full year of his cash-book, he earned £527.17.1d, a very large sum for a twenty-six year old at that time.[41] The scope of his work is shown by his writing paper which also proves how aggressively he marketed himself.[42] There was nothing shy or modest about that writing paper. In bright red print it has his name across the paper in half-inch high letters and the top half of the page is taken up with four columns listing his books, articles and lyrics plus publications which had carried his work. Wodehouse was already developing the range of his activities but was then best known as the author of public-school stories.

TALES OF ST AUSTIN'S
AND ELSEWHERE

In the flat landscape of the school story it is right to recognise P.G. Wodehouse's *Mike And Psmith* as eminences, though only foothills in his own literary *massif*.[1]

Arthur Calder Marshall

T HE Wodehouse public-school stories have been rightly praised, but for the wrong reasons. Critics admire their superior realism and lack of moralizing. There is as much unreality and moralizing in Wodehouse as in, say, that classic so alien to contemporary adult taste and to schoolboys of any period, *Eric Or Little By Little*. (Eric is assured of eternal damnation from the moment he innocently uses the word 'devil' with the inevitable series of downward steps that stem from so grievous a sin.) The difference is that Dean Farrer was no genius and the unreality and moralizing in Wodehouse are unobtrusively woven into the stories. The key to the Wodehouse public-school stories is that they portray the wish-fulfilment of their readers, as does F. Anstey's *Vice Versa: A Lesson To Fathers* where, due to the magical Garuda Stone, father and son swap bodies and Bultitude senior has to attend Bultitude junior's school. Most other writers of the genre prior to Wodehouse portray schools as foolish parents imagine they are and as more foolish pedagogues think they should be.

When Wodehouse set out to write, the only background he knew well was his own public-school. So he wrote stories about public schools. They were all *based* on Dulwich but represent it no more faithfully than a holiday brochure represents a foreign tourist resort. The school stories form a distinct sub-sector of the Wodehouse *oeuvre*. All the full-length books appeared in serial form (which dictated the episodic nature of the chapters) and all in *The Captain* except for some short stories and *The Pothunters*. That book was dedicated to three little girls, Joan, Effie and Ernestine Bowes-Lyon, granddaughters of the twelfth Earl of Strathmore and Kinghorne and thus first cousins of Queen Elizabeth the Queen Mother. Wodehouse used to take tea with the trio at their London home, 22 Ovington Square, and also stayed with them at their country home at Lyme Regis where he set *Love Among The Chickens*: indicative of the milieu from which Wodehouse came and within which he fitted naturally.

All the books of Wodehouse's school stories were published by A.C. Black who also own, now as then, the UK *Who's Who* in which he first appeared in 1908, his entry no doubt facilitated by his association with the firm.

After *The Pothunters* came *A Prefect's Uncle*, *Tales of St Austin's* (short stories), *The Gold Bat*, *The Head of Kay's*, *The White Feather* (with illustrations by William Townend, and pretty wooden they are too) and, as a glorious finale, *Mike* in 1909. Brian Doyle in his *Who's Who of Children's Literature* called *Mike* 'Probably one of the best and most entertaining school stories ever written'.[2] Wodehouse wrote one other boys' book, almost entirely forgotten, and the only one with the story set in a preparatory school (based on Emsworth House), *The Eighteen Carat Kid*, which was serialized in *The Captain* in the first three months of 1913. Later Wodehouse expanded the book, adding a love interest, and republished it as an adult novel, *The Little Nugget*, which has been in print ever since. The original story was finally published in book form, in New York, in 1980. It remains hard to obtain, but is well worth the effort. Wodehouse also published a number of stories about Wrykyn school in *The Captain*. These were intended to form a book, *Tales of Wrykyn*, but never did so and there probably remain some school stories in other magazines of the period waiting to be unearthed by the diligent enthusiast. Jacynth Hope-Simpson, in *Tales In School* expressed the consensus, 'The most stylish writer in this field was P.G. Wodehouse'.[3]

While the unreality of most public-school stories lies in what is put into them, the unreality of the Wodehouse books lies mainly in what is left out. We have a good description of what Dulwich was really like from Forester who was also at the College during Gilkes' reign. In *Life Before Forty* where, curiously, he never mentions Dulwich by name, he wrote:

The first month after I arrived was marked by the explosion of a frightful scandal; two day-girls at a neighbouring school were suddenly found to be pregnant and were being put through a ferocious cross-examination by parents and mistresses and clergymen and police. I believe they maintained silence very pluckily indeed for a few days, but remorseless questioning broke them down by degrees. Every day or so some fresh names would be dragged from them. Then more girls would hurriedly be called from their classes and put through the same ordeal, and the circle widened steadily, so that every morning a fresh bulletin arrived at my school, and the school porter would appear in the form rooms with a message to the effect that the Master would like to see Mr So-and-so and Mr So-and-so at once in his study. They would go, without alacrity, stuffing caps into the seats of their trousers in case it might be of some avail; some of them we never saw again – they were expelled. It was a time of dreadful agony of mind for a good many of the older boys, who moped about all day long wondering whether or not their names would appear in the affair, and what their lot would be if they did. The business was one of those scandals that crop up regularly in schools and apparently shake them to their foundations, and are marked by half a dozen expulsions, much wild gossip, a guarded paragraph or two in the newspapers, and then silence and oblivion.

I missed the full savour of it because, as a newcomer, I did not realise the almost godlike divinity of the boys involved, captains of this and captains of that (what girl with any knowledge of the school hierarchy would give her favours to anyone below the Second Fifteen?).[4]

From reading Wodehouse you would think that all schoolboys – and he was writing for and about teenage boys – are as asexual as the dummies in a draper's shop window. His approach was right. Boys at that age do not want to read about those disturbing adolescent feelings. Least of all do they want to read school love-stories such as H.O. Sturgis' *Tim* or Horace Annersley Vachell's *The Hill*, in each of which one of the boys dies to resolve the unmentioned danger of physical consummation of their love. Most physical relationships were, as Forester relates, more basic.

Violence ruled in a way which astonished me on my arrival. I was quite used to seeing small boys dragged away from the Buttery counter by big ones anxious to be served, and by seeing small boys kicked or their heads smacked merely because they had happened to be within kicking or smacking distance. And the thing that amazed me more than anything else was to find that the boys beat each other, and with what frequency. Everyone seemed to be beaten at some time or other; one kind of offence called for the use of a cane, another an OTC swagger stick. Small boys beat each other, big boys beat small boys, and big boys beat each other as well, and the masters joined in when necessary. Any offence, from cutting football practice to acting in a sidey manner, called for this form of punishment. What I found hardest to understand about it was the casual way in which it was regarded.[5]

In later life Wodehouse claimed he could not remember any bullying at Dulwich. He was telling the truth as he recalled it for his memory was as excellent at filtering out unpleasantness as his pen was at editing it out of his public-school stories, where beating and bullying get barely a passing mention, all being sublimated into milder forms of violence, such as study rags. Boys who have been beaten and bullied at school may enjoy getting their own back by dishing out to juniors the same punishment they once suffered themselves but the memory of their own beatings tends to be too green to make them relish reading about it. It seems likely that Wodehouse minor, already an intelligent observer of his peers and circumstances, avoided most bullying and punishments. He was neither cheeky nor extrovert while boxers were rarely at risk and he had accustomed himself, when visiting his numerous aunts, to adapt quietly to the different rules of different households. Forester continued:

> There was a fool of a chaplain who was positively imbecile – on one occasion when my guard had been pierced boxing and my late opponent was assisting me groaning from the ring after hitting me severely in the stomach he came up and clapped him on the shoulder and said, 'That's right, always help your enemies' which I think is quite the most idiotic remark I have heard from human lips.[6]

In Wodehouse schools the chaplains put in only brief appearances and God is on leave. Apart from omitting the sex, bullying and religion Wodehouse's public-school stories give his boys an enviable degree of freedom, not only from authority but from the senior boys as well. Psmith and Mike would never have been allowed to bag Spiller's study at Sedleigh, nor would participation in cricket and games practices have been optional. As Forester wrote:

> Many of the school rules were enforced not by Authority, but by the boys themselves, and it was the boys who decided whether other rules should be observed at all. Soon after my arrival [in 1915] the Master issued a decree that in future boys might wear soft collars – mounting laundry costs and a shortage of starch had done their work. But in all the time I was there I never saw a soft collar worn. Public opinion had decided against soft collars and public opinion saw to it that they were not worn.[7]

Similarly every schoolboy would like to patronize an objectionable master as Psmith did Mr Downing in *Mainly About Boots*, a classic chapter in *Mike*.

'Do you intend to disobey me, Smith?' Mr Downing's voice was steely.

'Yes, sir.' . . .

'What!' . . .

Psmith waved a hand deprecatingly.

'If you will let me explain sir.'[8]

. . . and explain he does, without interruption, for another page. It's not quite Wodehouse at his best, our willing suspension of disbelief has to work overtime, but his schoolboy readers must have revelled in it. They could forget that, in real life, every school has the equivalent of the Army rule 'Acting in a manner prejudicial to the good name of Her Majesty's Forces' under which any boy can be punished for anything from impertinence – saying anything – to dumb-insolence – saying nothing. Every school, that is, except Sedleigh with Psmith in residence.

The moralizing in Wodehouse is for the schoolboy's own code of honour, not for the hearty Christian code enjoined by J.I. Welldon and most writers of the genre. Unlike them Wodehouse puts over his message by an apparently unconscious assumption in what he writes, and in the behaviour of his heroes, that the code is fair, right and something of which an Englishman should be proud – without ever saying so. The Wodehouse schoolboy works hard at sports, hardly ever gets caught out in his escapades, and does little schoolwork but seems to absorb enough Greek and Latin – presumably by some form of osmosis – to get adequate marks in exams. But he is, above all, loyal: loyal to his word, his friends, his school, his family, his class and his responsibilities. Any boy who abided by the Wodehouse Code would keep every one of the Ten Commandments except possibly the sixth ('Remember the Sabbath day, to keep it Holy'). He would also score pretty highly on the moral precepts of all the other major religions.

Throughout the Wodehouse public-school stories there is a light, barely noticeable, irony at the crasser absurdities of the public school, both in reality and in fiction. Every tyro journalist is taught 'Never use irony. You'll be taken literally' but from the age of twenty-one Wodehouse was of the elite, an author who could use irony effectively – which requires as nice a judgement as the amount of paprika in a Hungarian goulash. Here is the meeting of titans at Sedleigh.

'Are you the Bully, the Pride of the School, or the Boy who is Led Astray and takes to Drink in Chapter Sixteen?'

'The last, for choice,' said Mike, 'but I've only just arrived, so I don't know.'[9]

Psmith was a very long, thin youth, with solemn face and immaculate clothes, who used a monocle and adopted a weary and patronizing tone with the entire world. Mark Psmith well. Appearing in only three and a half books, he is nearly as well known as Bertie Wooster and Lord Emsworth. Psmith is one of the few characters that Wodehouse found ready made. He told Jasen:

> Psmith was to a certain extent drawn from life. A cousin of mine who had been at the public-school Winchester with Rupert D'Oyly Carte, son of the Savoy Opera's D'Oyly Carte, was telling me one day about his eccentricities – how he was very long and lean, immaculately dressed, wore a monocle, and talked kindly but not patronisingly to the headmaster. When one of the masters asked him 'How are you, Carte?' he replied, 'Sir, I get thinnah and thinnah.' It gave me enough to build the character on.

(Dame Bridget D'Oyly Carte said that the description of Psmith much better fitted her Uncle Lucas, who died young, rather than her father, Rupert.)[10]

Psmith's entrance heralds the end of Wodehouse as a writer of stories for boys. In *Mike* Psmith and Jackson masquerade as adults in a schoolboys' world. In *Psmith In The City* and *Psmith Journalist* they are schoolboys in a grown-up world but in *Leave It To Psmith* they blossom as adults. Although a few Wodehouse characters such as Tuppy Glossop went to St Austin's and Ukridge and Jeremy Garnet went to Wrykyn, Mike and Psmith alone are central characters in both adult and public-school stories.

I use the term 'public-school stories' deliberately. The Wodehouse school stories are written for public-school boys such as he had been. Many of the jokes were those of the sept, unintelligible to most outsiders. At the time there were also many writers producing stories set in public-schools – not at all the same thing. These appealed to boys at local grammar and board schools, the sons of the Mr Pooters of the age, who enjoyed them because of their own unfulfilled yearnings to go to such schools and the implausible adventures engaged in by the heroes of those stories.

Wodehouse could write such exciting trash as well as anyone 'at the rustle of a cheque', in Usborne's fine phrase. Under the pen-name Basil Windham he, with some assistance from Townend, wrote a series in *Chums* called *The Luck Stone*. It uses all the well tried staples of the penny-dreadfuls: a silenced air gun with poisoned pellets, the Maharajah's talisman stone, a mysterious sunburnt stranger from India, cricketing centuries gloriously scored and a suspicious new master waiting to be maltreated at the *finale* of the serial. If you are lucky enough to come across those old volumes of *Chums* (from 16 September 1908 to 20 January 1909) suspend your disbelief and enjoy the free-flowing prose of an apprentice genius at work.

Wodehouse influenced all later writers for boys, inspiring Huge Walpole to try his hand at the genre. The result was three mushy but popular books, *Jeremy*, *Jeremy And Hamlet* and *Jeremy At Crail*, and his one great book by which he may be remembered, *Mr Perrin and Mr Traill*. None of them have anything in common with the Wodehouse school stories, which were also a strong influence on Charles Hamilton, best known as Frank Richards (one of his pen-names, he had at least twenty-six)[11] the creator of the immortal Billy Bunter, Tom Merry, Greyfriars, St Jim's and more. He too was a professional, carefully studying his market and his competitors. He began writing school fiction five years after Wodehouse, to whom his debt is obvious: the same schoolboy wish-fulfilment, light tone, lack of sex and religion and, victim Bunter apart, not much bullying. Richards was careful never to mention Wodehouse, but well read copies of Plum's public-school stories were on his shelves![12]

Wodehouse wrote one children's book, *William Tell Told Again*, a witty re-telling of the classic Swiss legend with colour illustrations by Philip Dadd and a set of verses by John W. Houghton. Like many Wodehouse fans I thought he must have written the verses as well but Houghton's lyrics for songs in, for example, the Burnette and Newte musical drama, *Queen Of Hearts*,[13] confirm that those in *William Tell* are Houghton's work too. In Houghton as well as Wodehouse the influence of W.S. Gilbert is readily apparent.

The tale is worth reading for one wonderful mixed metaphor alone. 'Gentlemen,' continued Tell, 'the flood-gates of revolution have been opened. From this day they will stalk through the land burning to ashes the slough of oppression which our tyrant governor has erected in our midst.' There are many more nuggets equally as good.

The book poses a mystery. Counting the Earl of Oxford and Asquith as one, forty-three people are dedicatees in fifty-three Wodehouse books, often with different dedications on different sides of the Atlantic. Miss Biddie O'Sullivan, dedicatee of *William Tell*, is the only one remaining untraced.[14]

Evelyn Waugh wrote, 'Collectors prize as bibliographical rarities such early works as *Williami Tell Told Again* and *Swoop*, but it is impossible to discern in them any promise of what was to come.'[15] That contentious view is widely held, though not by me. Both books are early Wodehouse, writing rapidly for cash rather than art, giving them an exuberant, uninhibited freshness. He clearly enjoyed writing them and they are a marker for what is to come.

It is impossible to categorize Wodehouse's *The Swoop! Or How Clarence Saved England*. Unique in English literature, it is only 22,000 words long and was written in just five days specifically for the railway-bookshop market – light reading for train journeys. It tells of the invasion of England. 'England was not merely beneath the heel of the invader. It was beneath the heels of nine invaders. There was barely room to stand.'

These are the Russians under the Grand Duke Vodkakoff, the Germans under Prince Otto of Saxe-Pfennig, the Chinese under Prince Ping Pong Pang (who land at Lllgxtplll in Wales), the Swiss Navy, the Moroccans, the Monegasques, the Young Turks, a Mad Mullah from Somaliland and the Bollygollans in war canoes led by their king. As Wodehouse remarks, 'It was inevitable in the height of the Silly Season that such a topic should be seized upon by the Press.'

The English, however, are far too bothered about their prospects of defeating the Australians in the forthcoming cricket test matches to pay any attention to such minor matters. Until, that is, cricket pitches are trampled down and in many cases even golf greens dented by the iron heel of the invader, who rarely, if ever, replaced the divot. 'Deep down in his heart the genuine Englishman has a rugged distaste for seeing his country invaded by foreign powers.'

Eventually, the minor invaders having left, Clarence Chugwater, leading Britain's boy scouts, saves England with a simple ruse: he makes both the Russian and German commanders jealous of the fee the other receives for appearing on the stage of a rival music hall.

There is no jollier book in the Wodehouse canon. In it he makes fun of generals, politicians, the English, foreigners, boy scouts, diplomats, publishers, music hall impresarios, newspaper proprietors, journalists, golfers, cricketers, judges, life assurance salesmen, the Albert Hall, London's statues and, for good measure, himself.

The Swoop is far more than just a piece of period fun; one could argue that it is Wodehouse's most serious book, which I shall now do. In the late nineteenth century and early 1900s there was much anti-German war-scare literature. The most prophetic was H.G. Wells' *The War In The Air*, the most famous Erskine Childers' *The Riddle Of The Sands* which had the merit of being finely written, and the most infamous William Le Queux's *The Invasion Of 1910*, published in 1906. That book was concocted by Field Marshal Lord Roberts, financed by Lord Northcliffe, owner of the *Daily Mail*, and written by Le Queux in a style of numbing banality penning every possible cliché with an air of earnest discovery. With more recent memories of Britain's unpreparedness for war in 1939 some students have assumed Le Queux and his ilk were prescient patriots. They were not. It was a blatantly dishonest piece of work serving Le Queux's avarice, Roberts' paranoia and Northcliffe's circulation. Twelve years earlier Le Queux had written *The Great War In England In 1897* when the invaders had been Russian and French but with Northcliffe's gold on offer – Le Queux had £3,000 from the *Daily Mail* in research expenses alone – he found no moral dilemma in a change of invader. At least Guy du Maurier, then a serving officer, was sincere in his concern when he wrote a war-scare play, *An Englishman's Home*, produced by his brother Gerald in 1909. But if James Blyth was sincere he must have lacked all sense of the absurd when, in early 1909, he wrote *The Swoop Of The Vulture* which set the German invasion in 1918 and laid all the blame on the Cabinet and the Navy.

Yet, unlike the late 1930s, there was no danger of a German invasion in 1909, let alone 1906. Such books didn't help prevent war, rather the reverse. They soured Britain's relations with Germany and hindered attempts to halt the Anglo-German armaments race. A Liberal MP, Sir John Barlow, asked the Secretary of State for War, Richard Haldane, whether he was aware that there were 66,000 trained German soldiers in England. Lord Roberts said there were '80,000 Germans in the United Kingdom, almost all of them trained soldiers'. A Captain Daniel Driscoll claimed '350,000 living in our midst' – which would have meant that over half the German peacetime army was clandestinely stationed in England.[16] All of these scaremongering effusions were targets for Wodehouse's political satire.

Wodehouse thus managed to include in his satire not only the fiction of invasion but also the related activities of Baden-Powell [the Boy Scouts' leader], and to be funny and sensible about the mood of the time.

Humour and good sense may have had a temporary effect; at any rate the number of invasion stories declined sharply after 1909.[17]

The Swoop was the only anti-war-scare book and publishing it in 1909 showed courage on Wodehouse's part for *The Globe* was by then owned by the brother of the intolerant and unforgiving Lord Northcliffe. The book effectively deflated the pretensions of Northcliffe's hack, Le Queux, of Blyth and the others and inspired a series of Heath Robinson cartoons in the *Sketch* and also Harry Graham's successful 1910 music-hall song.

I was playing golf the day
   That the Germans landed.

All our troops had run away
   All our ships were stranded
And the thought of England's shame
   Nearly put me off my game.

Not to be outdone *Punch* happily published a piece which imagined Le Queux sent off to invade Berlin, blow up the Kiel Canal and then the German High Seas Fleet.[18]

The Swoop has proved a good investment. Published at one shilling (today five new pence) as a paperback it now fetches in average (well-used) condition at least £2,000 – a gain of 39,900 per cent over eighty years comfortably beating inflation and giving an annual compound-interest rate of 14 per cent.

There was an historic sequel to all this. In 1909 the Prime Minister, H.H. Asquith, set up a subcommittee of the Committee of Imperial Defence to examine the Official Secrets Act of 1889 in the light of the claims of Roberts and Le Queux that the country was riddled with German spies. The committee, chaired by Haldane, examined all the invasion-scare literature and, according to leaks from members, while Le Queux and Blyth made them angry, *The Swoop* made them apoplectic. So they recommended reorganizing Britain's espionage services with Military Operations 5 (today Military Intelligence 5 or MI5) under a Captain Vernon Kell, to handle internal counter-espionage. Decades later Wodehouse was to have dealings with MI5, in whose formation he played a minor role.

When the German danger became a reality there was a burst of serious literature warning against such an invasion, most notably Saki's *When William Came*, held up by production delays so it did not appear until December 1913 (although dated 1914).

The Swoop proves that, when he wished to, Wodehouse could turn his perceptive gaze on the political as well as the social scene. Every one of his targets, with the possible exception of the Albert Hall, had a purpose: for example Baden Powell was sold a bogus invasion plan by an enterprising group of forgers in Belgium and continued vehemently to believe in it even after it was proved fraudulent.[19] It is curious how Wodehouse's fans reiterate that he was no satirist. Even so perceptive a critic as Auberon Waugh writes, 'He could not by any stretch of the imagination be described as a satirist'[20] and then goes on to describe him satirizing a pretentious poet, John Hall Wheelcock, using that skill learned at *The Globe* half a century before. Wodehouse relates that on reading in the *New York Sunday Times* the line 'Sir, I take issue with Walter S. Swisher' he was inspired to poesy. In part it goes:

The day, I recall, was a Spring one,
Not hot and oppressive, though warm,
The sort of a day apt to bring one
Right up to the peak of one's form.
So when a kind friend and well-wisher
Said 'Don't just sit dreaming there, kid.
Take issue with Walter S. Swisher,'
I replied 'Yes, I will' and I did.[21]

Wodehouse meets the criteria for a satirist. *The Oxford English Dictionary* requires ridicule while my Fowler's *Modern English Usage* (1930 edition!) says the motive of satire is the amendment of perceptions in the field of morals and manners by means of accentuation and targeting the self-satisfied. So satire does not have to be hurtful, except in so far as ridicule may be hurtful.

Wodehouse's satire was all the more effective for being gentle – as in Psmith's neat definition of socialism which remains valid eight decades later. 'I've just become a Socialist. It's a great scheme. . . . You work for the equal distribution of property and start by collaring all you can and sitting on it.'[22]

Mike is the last public-school story Wodehouse wrote and after it he aimed to leave the genre behind him. On 16 November 1909 Wodehouse replied to his friend Leslie H. Bradshaw's offer to help sell the school stories in America – strongly declining the proposal. He explained that, far from wanting to get those stories published in America he looked upon them as part of his guilty past and aimed to start in New York with a clean sheet as a writer of adult stories. He looked back on his *Captain* books as all right of their kind but thought their point of view immature. He worried that they might kill his chances of doing anything big in America. So he didn't want US editors to know him as a writer of school stories but wished to break into the big league. His ambition was for the Americans to say he was a better man than O'Henry rather than better than Andrew House, a local writer of school stories. Wodehouse's public-school stories had served their purpose and he didn't want them bobbing up when he was trying to do bigger work. He concluded, 'I have given up boys' stories absolutely.'[23] Bradshaw was then living in New York, as was Wodehouse who loved the city from the first day of his first visit there four years earlier.

Henry Wodehouse CMG. 'He found he rather liked the stranger who was his father'

Eleanor Wodehouse. 'He never said a bad word about his mother – nor a good one'

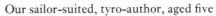
Our sailor-suited, tyro-author, aged five

Three brothers, Pelham, Peverill and Armine Wodehouse.
Richard was an afterthought

The demon bowler of Dulwich in 1899

Final House Match
Treadgold v Rendall.
From the "Wykehamist":

This match was played toward the end of the term, & resulted in a win for Treadgold by 82 runs after an interesting match. Treadgold won the toss, and secured the respectable total of 165, chiefly by aid of Knabbe (29), Toward (46) — a really good innings, and Rutley Ricketts (21). Ripley was by far the most destructive of the Rendallian bowlers, obtaining 7 wickets. On Rendall going in first, they knocked up 47, Ripley (33) & Toward (22) being the chief contributors, while Taylor obtained a hard-hit 7. Ripley was fairly caught at the wicket by C. Whittaker. Wodehouse and Ricketts bowled best, each obtaining four wickets. Treadgold then batted a second time, & wickets fell fairly rapidly. Matters might have gone badly with them had not Wodehouse come to the rescue with a sterling 57, while Rawling-Adams and C. Whittaker made an exceedingly useful stand for the last wicket. Total 167, leaving Rendall 210 to win. Ripley and Knatley made a gallant effort & actually put on 50 before they were separated. But after this wickets fell rapidly, thanks to the efforts of Hitchins, who bowled very well and secured 5 wickets for 63 in splendid style. to run the trouble Ripley Wodehouse also (Toward) well, securing 4 wickets & in the first innings. He innings closed for 118. Ripley's batting & bowling for the losers made

match far clearer than it would otherwise have been, as Knatley scored far stronger all through.
Treadgold:- C.P. Knabbe (captain), P.G. Wodehouse, H.J. Ricketts, C. Whittaker, A. Jackson, W. Toward, P.A.J. Hitchins, C.P. Knabbe, H.L. Whittaker, C. Work, H. Rawling-Adams.

Additional Cricket Notes.

In the Bradshaw v School, Wodehouse (24), Jackson (28) & Ricketts (17 retd.) were outplaying in the batting. Wodehouse took 2 wickets & Ricketts 4.7 one; the latter caught three catches at point. The School won by some twenty runs. Toward and Hitchins also played in this match.

From the Cricket Characters of the 1st XI

C.P. Knabbe - He made an admirable captain, & that the XI was not successful was certainly due to the fault of his (Pour?) excellent judgment in the management of this team in the field. He did not quite come up to expectations as a batsman, probably owing to over-anxiety. Worked very hard at the school cricket & the games & practice were worth more kindly than before. Was awarded the fielding prize which he really deserved.

P.G. Wodehouse. - bowls well against Tonbridge but did nothing else. Too uncertain. He had at all. A far too fiery slack field.

P.G. Wodehouse was 2nd in the 1st bowling averages with 16 wickets at 14 runs apiece.
H.J. Ricketts head by the far the best average in the 2nd XI

The Anglo–American author in 1904 when he was hair apparent

'To my daughter Leonora, without whose never failing sympathy and encouragement this book would have been finished in half the time'

Wodehouse told Bill Townend in 1920 that he drove his own car in New York and was 'very hot stuff in all sorts of traffic

Wodehouse, Guy
Bolton, Ray Comstock
and Jerome Kern

Family man at Le
Touquet 1926

'I met and was completely fascinated by Leonora, who seemed to me
to be the most brilliant young woman I have ever known'
Sir Compton Mackenzie

−8−

AMERICA I LIKE YOU

... from my earliest years ... America ... was always to
me the land of romance[1]

P.G. Wodehouse

P.G. WODEHOUSE spent half his life in America. Calling the original US version of *Over Seventy* by the different title, *America I Like You*, after a popular song by Bert Kalmar and Harry Ruby, was not a marketing ploy but an expression of real feeling. Like most Englishmen he never felt Americans were foreign but cousins whose departure from British rule in 1776 should be looked upon as a regrettable but harmless eccentricity. Wodehouse always thought of himself as an Englishman and never lost his English accent or cast of mind, but equally he thought of himself as American: it just depended which side of the Atlantic he was on. He felt American in America and English in England but he became homesick for America if he was away from it too long, just as he did for England. With strong family ties to the Far East Wodehouse wondered why he never felt the call of the Orient. 'Ship me somewhere East of Suez where the best is like the worst, and there aren't no Ten Commandments and a man can raise a thirst'[2] found no echo within him. Instead he felt the call of America which offered hundreds of publishers, thousands of publications and millions of readers who bought books in English: the East offered no such allure.

Wodehouse first visited America in 1904 – just as soon as he had saved enough money for the trip. With five weeks holiday a year from *The Globe* and passenger liners then taking nine days each way across the Atlantic, he could spend seventeen days in New York. On 16 April he sailed second class on the *St Louis* arriving in America on the 25th.

While there he enjoyed himself enormously, staying with a friend from his banking days, Nesbitt Kemp, who had a cheap apartment at the then unfashionable Washington Square end of Fifth Avenue. From there

Wodehouse sallied out to meet an English journalist on the *New York World*, Norman Thwaites, to whom he had a letter of introduction. Thwaites provided Wodehouse, whose interest in boxing had not dimmed, with the highlight of his trip – a visit to the White Plains training camp of 'Kid' McCoy, the middleweight boxing champion of the world, then preparing for his title fight with 'Philadelphia' Jack O'Brien. In his cash-book Wodehouse noted the trip would be worth many guineas in the future in spite of it causing a sharp fall in his April earnings.

All too soon he had to sail home to London and *The Globe*, enriched by the experience. Before the days of mass travel his brief trip lent him stature as an authority on all things American. Bertie Wooster's unbidden visitor to his New York apartment, Lady Malvern – who fitted into his biggest armchair as if built round her by someone who knew they were wearing armchairs tight about the hips that season – reckoned that a one month visit to America would be ample for her to write *America And The Americans*, since her friend, Sir Roger Cremorne, had written his *America From Within* after a stay of only two weeks.

Wodehouse found he could now charge correspondingly more for articles about the land of the brave and the free, such as 'Society Whispers From The States' for *Punch* that August. He found a ready market for other stories and features with an American setting and also made his first sale to America. A series of Kid Brady stories in *Pearson's* magazine of New York commenced in September 1905, a landmark in his career. He was paid $50 or £10 an episode while those same stories in *Pearson's* in London earned him only £2.2s each. This strengthened his love affair with America, setting him off down the road to becoming an Anglo-American author aiming to sell all he wrote to both UK and US publishers. Thus he had sent the manuscript of *Love Among The Chickens* to Norman Thwaites who replied, 'I am giving it to A.E. Baerman,'[3] a literary agent. Baerman was good – he sold the magazine rights to *The Circle* and the book rights to its sister company, Circle Publishing, for a total of $1,000. He also obtained a favourable review, six column inches, in the *New York Times* which concluded:

> Whoever wants an entertaining story for a railway journey or for an idle Summer afternoon will be hard to please if he does not find P.G. Wodehouse's *Love Among The Chickens* an ideal book for the occasion. . . . It is a merry tale, cleverly told and never lacking in good taste.[4]

That was a rare accolade for a young foreign author's 'first' novel. One small problem marred Wodehouse's enjoyment of his success. Baerman took the word 'give' literally and not only did Wodehouse have great trouble getting his money but the book appeared with 'Copyright A.E. Baerman' on the title page. Later Wodehouse had to pay him $250 to release the movie rights. However it was the first book Wodehouse had published in America and this event, on 11 May 1909, plus the chance to tax Abe Baerman with his malversation, provided an eagerly seized excuse for a second visit to the USA.

Wodehouse was staying at the Hotel Earle at 103 Waverley Place in Greenwich Village. (In old-age when talking to Jasen he remembered it as the Hotel Duke!) There he met Seth Moyle who promptly sold 'The Good Angel' to *Cosmopolitan* for $200 and 'Deep Waters' to *Collier's Weekly* for $300. On the strength of this Wodehouse wired his resignation to *The Globe*. Moyle – drinking companion, friend and first biographer of O'Henry – briefly became Wodehouse's New York agent. He wasn't much more reliable than Baerman.

In Wodehouse's 'The First Time I Went To New York'[5] there is a description of Baerman, with a dash of Moyle thrown in. Typically it ignores the line between fact and fiction to produce another good story. The agent's name is given as Jake Skolsky and the events moved to Wodehouse's first New York trip rather than his second and more import-ant visit. The only time one of his authors ever got the better of Baerman was when Charlie Sommerville prised a cheque for $150 out of him. It bounced, coming back marked 'insufficient funds'. Sommerville, using his reporter's guile, found out that Baerman had $115 in his account and so paid another $35 into it and represented the cheque which was cleared. Baerman was deeply hurt that an old friend could stoop so low.[6] Archie Fitzmaurice in *America I Like You* is another Baerman-Moyle portrait.

Wodehouse spent some of the funds actually received via Moyle on a second-hand Monarch typewriter which was to remain a faithful com-panion for a quarter of a century and might almost have been a character in a Wodehouse novel. Later it became extremely temperamental and led a pampered life. The company that made it became defunct and it was so much repaired, cost was no object, that by the twenties there was hardly a single original part of it left. Novelist Tom Sharpe told me that Wode-house bought a second, identical, Monarch but in due course one had to be cannibalized to feed spare parts to the other. Leonora thought it (they) managed to hang together somehow so as not to disappoint her Plummy.[7] If it was used too regularly it broke down, and if it wasn't used regularly enough the keys stiffened. No stranger was allowed to touch it and it went everywhere with him, occupying its own first-class seat on railway jour-neys. Porters were never allowed to carry it and, at journey's end, it was usually met by a typewriter mechanic for a little cosseting since travelling always seemed to give it mechanical colly-wobbles. Wodehouse had five other typewriters at different times, bought in despair when his beloved Monarch had been pronounced dead, but the new ones were always given to Leonora or cast aside.

It still had many masterpieces to write when, in the autumn of 1909, Bradshaw, an adult 'Captainite', as readers of *The Captain* grotesquely called each other, went to see Wodehouse at the Earle and wrote a 1,500 word pen-portrait of him, the earliest there is, which appeared in the March 1910 issue of the magazine.

He is just what I imagined: tall, big and strong; a young man, with dark hair, rather light blue eyes, a healthy colour and the most friendly, genial, likeable manner in the world. He has a big hand and shakes with you vigorously. When conversing his manner is quiet and rather thoughtful. It makes you feel that he is very carefully considering what you are saying. He has a very cheery laugh. His deep set eyes put you at your ease. There is something singularly cool and genial about them. You feel that they see the humour of things and that their owner is a person who likes most people and whom most people like.

He is unusually well-read and well informed. But, after all, this is only to be expected when we recall the calibre of his writing. There are a number of American journalists at the same hotel and one of them told me that Mr Wodehouse has made a small reputation at the game of German bowls. Although playing it for the first time, he easily defeated their champion by a substantial majority. His victories are attributed to subtle manipulations of the ball, resembling the break in cricket, which his opponents are unable to duplicate. The same man told me that P.G. has been nicknamed 'Chickens' among the writing fraternity. This is from his book *Love Among The Chickens* which ran serially in a magazine here, came out in book form later, and was the first thing to bring him to the notice of American editors.

He has already made a big reputation here as an original humorist of the first water. The best magazines such as *Cosmopolitan, Collier's Weekly* etc are printing his stories. The former called him 'a second O'Henry'. (O'Henry is considered to be the greatest short-story writer in America today.)

I had an awfully hard job to tear myself away. I finally did so but first he gave me a cheery promise to look me up at my home a few days later. Since then I have seen him frequently and have been the recipient of much kindness from him. Great as his stories are, their author is greater. He is a fine specimen of the public school man at his best. As I have discovered since meeting him for the first time, the keynote of his character is generosity. You can't imagine how kind he is. No wonder he has made friends amongst the American magazine men so quickly.[8]

The two men became friends and when Wodehouse gave up writing public-school stories, he presented Bradshaw his notebooks with the caveat 'Use any public-school stuff but don't swipe any of my other notes'.[9] Bradshaw, a professional author too, wrote only one school story: it was called *The Right Sort* and dedicated simply 'To P.G. Wodehouse, The Right Sort'.

Wodehouse, that unworldly innocent, also got Bradshaw to help in promoting his work, writing in late April or early May 1910 to ask him to put in a bit of underhand work by showing a story, 'Peaches', to Brubaker, an editor at *Success*. Wodehouse asked Bradshaw to tell Brubaker that everybody who had read it said it was his star story and then let slip casually that he, Wodehouse, wanted $600 for it. Alas Brubaker didn't bite and while Wodehouse continued to earn a reasonable living, America was not the cornucopia of dollars he had expected from his early successes. He worked as hard as ever but failed to establish with any US periodicals the reliable links he enjoyed in England with *The Strand* and *The Captain* which accepted his work on a regular basis. In early 1910 he returned to England and bought Threepwood for £200, furnishing it with all his simple tastes required: one bed, one chair, one table and his typewriter. Soon afterwards he resumed work at *The Globe*, with Westbrook, but he stayed there for less than a year before returning to New York.

Thereafter he moved regularly between America and England as his business commitments demanded. With the second-class fare only £10 each way he could afford to do so. By 1913 he could also afford to leave the Earle and trade up to the, still modest, Algonquin Hotel on West 44th Street. Between his first US publication in 1905 and 1916 his work appeared in at least twenty US publications: *All-Story Cavalier Weekly*, *Ainslee's*, *Century*, *The Circle*, *Collier's*, *Cosmopolitan*, *Delineator*, *Everybody's*, *Hampton's*, *Illustrated Sunday Magazine*, *Ladies Home Journal*, *McLure's*, *Munsey's*, *The New York Times*, *Pearson's*, the *Pictorial Review*, the *Red Book*, the *Saturday Evening Post*, *Vanity Fair* and the *Woman's Home Companion*.[10] *Munsey's* was a poor paymaster but had one great advantage in its editor, Bob Davis, who if he liked authors would give them ideas and plots and then buy the resulting story from them. It was Davis who gave Wodehouse the unwodehousian plot for *Their Mutual Child* and then bought the serialization rights of the book for $2,000. Wodehouse also enjoyed a close relationship with George Lorrimer of the *Saturday Evening Post*, although in later years if Lorrimer did not pay Wodehouse top prices the latter's loyalty went on vacation.[11]

What Wodehouse needed was a good literary agent in America. Baerman was a crook and Seth Moyle was as likely to turn up for an important meeting sozzled as sober. Bradshaw had acted as Plum's *ad hoc* US agent for a few years and then, for a short while, a Mrs Wilkening, 'a hopeless incompetent'.[12] Unsurprisingly Wodehouse (and other artists) became wary of her when she sued a client, Mary Pickford, who later became his friend, for extra commission payments. Then in January 1915 he appointed Paul Revere Reynolds who was to become his friend and remain his US literary agent for nearly thirty years, a mutually profitable arrangement. Reynolds looked after many top writers including Jack London, Upton Sinclair and Winston Churchill (the novelist, not the politician). Reynolds was, like Wodehouse, a gentleman who belonged to decent clubs. Meeting at one of them Reynolds introduced Wodehouse to Scribner, the publisher, and his new client was properly impressed.[13] Reynolds immediately proved his worth by selling *Something New* to the *Saturday Evening Post* for $3,500, the sort of money Wodehouse knew existed but thought he would never see himself.

His Anglo-American credentials were confirmed with the publication of *The Intrusion of Jimmy*, a Blandings novel in all but name. It was his first book published in New York before London. It is also the first in which Wodehouse puts Americans into an English setting – although the similarities with Henry James end there. That book shows a curious amorality. One of the central characters, a retired New York police captain called McEchearn, has become rich by taking bribes and buying promotion – a good investment; it meant he got bigger bribes and could afford further promotion. McEchearn ends up not with retribution but fulfilling his dearest wish by having '. . . butted into [English] society so deep that it would take an excavating party with dynamite to get him out of it'. This shows an important side of Wodehouse; not so much the lack of censoriousness nor the understanding of the pressures on such a man, but the attitude that the rules of the group transcend the laws of the land. In an unforgiving environment McEchearn had played the game by the rules *de facto* (but definitely not by the rules *de jure*) and won. Wodehouse respected him for it.

At the same time Wodehouse was planning another milestone, his first book set mostly in America. *The Prince And Betty*, published in New York, is a nice blend of thrills and romance with the apprentice not yet allowing the humour to dominate the book. It has a complicated bibliographical relationship with the London book of the same title, published in the same year, and *Psmith Journalist*, a sequel to *Psmith In The City*. All three have overlapping characters and plot and are largely different books but they show that, somehow, Wodehouse had gained a deeper knowledge of the

New York underworld of the time than would have been garnered by mere reading and research. Did Wodehouse, I wonder, ever wander into Hell's Kitchen and get robbed or have his hat shot off? The UK *Prince And Betty* is a standard Mills and Boon romance written to their exact formula and requirements for what in those days was called 'the shop-girl market'.

From now on Wodehouse's writing would be carefully crafted to appeal to both American and English readers. His long absences from England also helped his calculated development of the Wodehouse world into one as beguiling to American readers as to the English. He had got beyond the simple stage of editing one story so that it became 'The Pitcher And The Plutocrat' for *Colliers* in America and 'The Goal-Keeper And The Plutocrat' for *The Strand* in England. At the superficial level he mixed American and English characters and added many American words and expressions to his prose while also modifying some details – Brinkley Court in his English stories became Brinkley Manor in America for example – but there was much more to it than that. Wodehouse took full advantage of the vigorous growth and vivid imagery of American English to give further zest to his vocabulary, even if many of his American heroes speak as if they'd been to Dulwich College. The first known literary use of the American slang term 'crust' for impudence is in a 1923 Wodehouse novel. Other examples are 'Put on the dog', 'Give someone the elbow', 'Lallapaloosa', 'Hornswoggle', 'Lulu', 'Hoosegow', 'Calaboose' and 'Oil out'. Along with such unlikely bedfellows as The Beatles and Elvis Presley he contributed to keeping standard and American English within hailing distance of each other. That transatlantic cross-fertilization of our language is no new thing. A typically British phrase used by Wodehouse is 'A stiff upper lip', as in his novel *Stiff Upper Lip, Jeeves*. His scholarly friend, the lyric writer Ira Gershwin, traced its earliest known use back to the *Massachusetts Spy* of 1815 and noted that Partridge, the English philologist, says it was only used in England from 1880.[14]

Those dual demands helped Wodehouse create his unique world, based on, but remote from, those golden days of Edwardian England. His success is shown by his sales in both countries – a feat only equalled (for different reasons) by another of his fans and pen-friends, Dame Agatha Christie, who dedicated her *Hallowe'en Party*: 'To P.G. Wodehouse, whose books and stories have brightened my life for many years. Also, to show my pleasure in his having been kind enough to tell me that he enjoys *my* books'.

Wodehouse is the first truly Anglo-American author. Before Wodehouse, when travel was more difficult, Mark Twain sold well in England as an American humorist and Dickens sold well in America as an English writer. After Wodehouse there have been many Anglo-American authors but he was the first to craft his books to appeal simultaneously to both markets, to sell well in both of them, to publish almost all he wrote in both of them and to live for over a third of a century in both of them. Back in 1936 *The Saturday Review* called him:

> The only Englishman who can make an American laugh at a joke about America. Most British jokes about America have been sour ever since Oscar Wilde and Bernard Shaw. They are either too clever, and therefore fraudulent, or too stupid, and therefore fraudulent. They either pretend to know more than they know, or palpably know nothing. But with Wodehouse it is different. He clearly has caught the drift. This may be due to the amount of time he had spent here and the amount of money he has taken away. Both doubtless have something to do with it. Yet the secret of his success in making jokes about America is that he really likes Americans.[15]

J.B. Priestley, reviewing Wodehouse's *Mr Mulliner Speaking*, said, 'In the matter of wildly metaphorical slang he has beaten the Americans at their own game. Meet a New York crook of Mr Wodehouse's invention and you will find that he talks not as such crooks actually do talk, but as they would like to talk.'[16] Perhaps not. A real New York crook, Edward Osterman who called himself Monk Eastman, is quoted as saying 'I like the kits and the boids and I'll beat up any guy dat gets gay wit a kit or a boid in my next of the woods.'[17] Put those words into the mouth of Mr Bat Jarvis of *Psmith Journalist* and you wouldn't be able to find the join.

Another Eastman, Max, in one of those straightfaced tomes analysing humour, wrote:

> Wodehouse belongs conspicuously to the period of Anglo-American re-union through the moving picture and the radio – the period, so to speak, of the hook-up. He is, I believe, the only man living who can speak with equal fluency the English and American languages.[18]

On the other hand Wodehouse gained much pleasure from an American critic's condemnation of the American dialogue in his novel *Barmy In Wonderland* (US *Angel Cake*) which was based on George S. Kaufman's play, *The Butter And Egg Man*. 'After all these years Mr Wodehouse has not learned to imitate colloquial American. His Broadway characters talk like Aaron Slick of Punkin Creek, which rather tends to spoil the effect.'[19] Every single line of Broadway dialogue was by that recognized master of vernacular American, George S. Kaufman, with whom Wodehouse split the royalties of the book fifty-fifty.[20]

Wodehouse was also one of the very first transatlantic commuters with his friends often uncertain if, at any moment, he was living in London, Threepwood or New York. In the summer of 1914 he was writing a series about the actor John Barrymore for Cameron Mackenzie's *McLure's Magazine* in New York (unpublished unless under a pseudonym somewhere). This required him to travel with Barrymore on a German ship which left England on 27 July and arrived without incident in New York on 2 August. War broke out two days later.

Wodehouse promptly did the right thing registering with the British authorities in New York – it would have been unthinkable for a man of his background not to do so – but he joked with Townend claiming he registered as aged sixty-three, blind and the sole support of a wife and nine children.[21] He was rejected for service because of his poor eyesight and probably felt a tinge of shame at letting down half a millennium of family tradition – but a far stronger feeling was one of extreme relief. With his pacific nature, tolerance and desire above all to get on with his writing, war was contrary to his nature. Most people were expecting the war to be over by Christmas that same year so it seemed unimportant anyway.

Marooned in America by German submarines and the shortage of liner berths for non-essential personnel, Wodehouse spent the war there, working hard as always. He did not shut his mind to events in Europe but, inevitably, viewed them from his own professional viewpoint. He wrote a long and serious article in the *New York Times Magazine* (in the form of an interview with reporter Joyce Kilmer,[22] who won recognition as a poet with 'Trees' which was later set to music and became a global success). It is a masterly *tour d'horizon* about the effect of the war on English humour and American humour and humorists and the differences between them – particularly the class-based approach of the English. Prophetically he expects those class barriers in English humour to be broken down by the war and so 'The years that follow the war will afford a great opportunity for the new English humorist who works on the American plan'.

Wodehouse was the English humorist, more than any other, who recognized that opportunity and seized it – but the war was to have another equally important and profound influence on him. The First World War was the most traumatic event to affect Europe since the Black Death 570 years before. It was the first total war and remains the bloodiest ever. Public hysteria was extreme: white feathers were handed out indiscriminately to men not in uniform, anyone with a German sounding name was immediately suspected of being a German spy. The British royal family had to change its name from Saxe-Coburg-Gotha to Windsor and 'patriots' even stoned dachshunds in the streets for the crime of being 'German' dogs. A horrifying proportion of Wodehouse's class and generation was to perish on the fields of Flanders, the hills of Gallipoli or beneath the high seas. Those who fought were to resent those who did not and many of those who lost sons, husbands, fathers and brothers were bitter about the non-combatants. Wodehouse felt this at first hand when one of the partners in A. & C. Black, who had lost his son in the war, was harshly offensive about Wodehouse spending the war in America – which is why *Tales of Wrykyn* never appeared as a book of public-school stories. When the world of literature suffered so grievously with the loss of Wilfred Owen, Saki, Rupert Brooke and many more whose talent never had the time to flower, such as Premier Asquith's brilliant son Raymond, we can be grateful that we did not lose Wodehouse. His absence from the battlefield was to be remembered during the Second World War. It also shows in his writing. Tom Chase, of the Royal Navy, in *Love Among The Chickens* is the only serving officer in the canon although there are lots of retired officers such as the euphoniously named whip-fetishist, Major-General Sir Masterman Petherick-Soames. Silly ass Archie Moffam (pronounced Moom) from *Indiscretions of Archie* stands out, uniquely among Wodehouse's young heroes, as having a gallant war record. Bertie's friend, William Egerton Bamfylde Ossingham Belfry, ninth Earl of Rowcester, was in the commandos during the Second World War but we know nothing of his war record. Jeeves admits to having dabbled in the First World War 'to a certain extent'[23] but he does not confide to what use his giant brain was put.

Many who did not fight in that holocaust felt guilty for the rest of their days at not having squandered their lives in Field Marshal Earl Haig's blinkered offensives, and perhaps Wodehouse did too. At any event it had one crucial effect on him. While fighting in the Great War prompted many, such as the young Grenadier Guards Captain Harold Macmillan, to turn their attention to politics, not fighting caused Wodehouse to turn his attention away from politics. That dazzling intelligence, illuminating any subject to which it was directed, never again focused on war. Indeed war became one of those matters he consciously shut out of his mind – a point that cannot be overemphasised. No one dwells on unpleasantness and they thrust the recollection of it to the backs of their minds, as Wodehouse did with World War I and all wars, to his later cost. It was this that caused so highly intelligent a man as Wodehouse to behave so foolishly in the Second World War. The writer Gerard Fairlie later quoted Wodehouse as telling him, 'I take no interest in wars.'[24] That remark has been ignored by scholars out of respect for Mr Fairlie's powers of imagination but while Wodehouse would never have used such flat and pompous phrasing the sentiment is true to the man.

Meanwhile two unmemorable, indeed best forgotten, collections of short stories were published. *The Man Upstairs* is one of Wodehouse's twelve books published in the UK but not in the US. *The Man With Two Left Feet* has the modest distinction of introducing Jeeves and Bertie to the world. In 'Extricating Young Gussie' Jeeves has just two lines, only later allowing Wodehouse to chronicle his machinations in detail. That began in *My Man Jeeves* which had four stories about Reggie Pepper, a Bertie prototype, and four proper Bertie stories. Five of the eight were later tidied up and appeared in *Carry On Jeeves*. In 1922 came a classic: the golf stories of *The Clicking Of Cuthbert* which are a joy to read regardless of whether or not one has ever hit a golf-ball in anger.

There are six further books, not yet mentioned, of Wodehouse's apprenticeship which fail to meet the high standards he led us to expect of him, but which are impressive by any other criteria: *Uneasy Money*, *A Damsel In Distress*, *The Little Warrior* (UK *Jill The Reckless*), *Three Men And A Maid* (UK *The Girl On The Boat*), *The Adventures of Sally* (US *Mostly Sally*) and *Piccadilly Jim*. That last book was the first of seventy-one titles Herbert Jenkins published for Wodehouse over half a century and their successor companies continue to publish his UK editions to this day.

In his introduction to a posthumous volume of stories by Herbert Jenkins, *The Bindle Omnibus*, Wodehouse wrote of his friend who died in 1923 (to be succeeded at the firm by John Grimsdick) that during all the years he had known him, his little office in York Street, St James's had been a repairing station for the self-esteem of writers who needed encouragement. They entered it drooping and came out revived. After five minutes with Jenkins, even when their latest story had bogged hopelessly in the middle of chapter ten, they came out infected with his confidence and gaiety. Until Jenkins had come into Wodehouse's life, he claimed, it had not occurred to him that one of his books could actually sell.[25]

That last remark hints that Ella King-Hall was not the most effective of literary agents as does the comment of Paul R. Reynolds Jr., the son of Wodehouse's American agent. 'He had a great loyalty to his friends. For years he used an agent in England, a woman with almost no other clients. Wodehouse was devoted to her, and stayed with her until she retired.'[26] Ironically, Iain Sproat in *Wodehouse At War* made an almost identical remark about Reynolds junior twenty years later.

While Ella retained Wodehouse's loyalty, any affection he may have felt for her evaporated when, at a theatrical party in New York the day war broke out, he met Ethel Wayman, the woman who had his total commitment until the day he died.

$-9-$

THE MATING SEASON

A mixture of Mistress Quickly and Florence Nightingale
with a touch of Lady Macbeth thrown in – I grew to love
her.[1]

Malcolm Muggeridge

ETHEL Wodehouse was an extraordinary woman who deserves far
more attention than she has been given. She enjoyed a double dose
of personality, overcame with panache an appalling early life and
was the only constant influence on her husband throughout their lifelong
marriage. The world owes her an enormous debt. For over sixty years she
provided her Plummie with an environment in which he could spend most
of his time writing the novels and stories that gave, and continue to give,
so much happiness to so many millions of people around the globe. She
managed his household, his travel arrangements, his dogs and other pets
and assisted him with some of his business affairs but very rarely those
concerning agents and publishers. She protected him from the outside
world to the extent that he wished her to. In later years she led an
uncongenial, not to say miserable, life to enable her husband to carry on
doing the only thing that kept him happy: writing. Yet she gets no
acknowledgement for such service from the majority of commentators on
Wodehouse and little from the rest. She was too strong a personality to
inspire sympathy; a few people who got to know her well, like Malcolm
Muggeridge, adored her but many people disliked her. Ethel has had, I
think, an undeservedly bad press, both in what was said about her – and
what wasn't.

The film star Maureen O'Sullivan (today we would call her a megastar)
relates that when she first met the Wodehouses, in Hollywood, 'Ethel
soon invited me to their house and gave me some blunt and sensible
advice on a stormy romance'. Miss O'Sullivan was big enough to appreciate it, many were not. Ethel volunteered advice to those who hadn't

asked for it but it sprang from (damning phrase) good intentions. She also told Miss O'Sullivan – then at the start of her career, hard up and wearing the costume jewellery which was all she had – 'Darling, never wear jewellery unless it's real. It's better to wear nothing.'[2] She then gave the star one of her own expensive bracelets. That characteristic generosity was less well known than her unrequested advice to the love-lorn and her strength of personality.

In Iain Sproat's book, *Wodehouse At War*, he tells a story that has the authentic Ethel ring to it. She and Plum were living in the Adlon Hotel in Berlin while interned during the Second World War.

A man in the uniform of a naval officer was telling the hotel receptionist that he was there on behalf of Admiral Doenitz, head of the German Navy. Doenitz would be arriving the next day and would require two rooms: in one of them he would be keeping his pet Alsatian dog. The receptionist threw up his hands in horror: it was not possible to have a dog in the hotel: it was against the rules which were strictly kept. But the naval officer said, this was for the great Admiral Doenitz.

The receptionist said it made no difference. The naval officer persisted. A heated argument followed. While this argument was in progress, Ethel Wodehouse appeared, walking down the main staircase with her Pekinese, Wonder, on a lead. The naval officer pointed out furiously that apparently dogs were allowed in the Adlon. 'Ah, well, yes,' replied the receptionist, 'but you must understand that that is Mrs Wodehouse.' Doenitz was not allowed to bring his dog.[3]

She told novelist Tom Sharpe of meeting Dr Paul Schmidt, Hitler's interpreter, in Berlin and saying to him, 'How can you possibly work for that dreadful man?' To which came the reply, 'Mrs Wodehouse, I have nothing to say.' Ethel had the courage of the totally confident and unselfconscious.

She was born Ethel Newton on 23 May 1885 in Norfolk, the Wodehouse county, the daughter of a King's Lynn milliner, Anne Newton. The birth was registered by 'Mary Wilson in charge of the child'[4] so Ethel was probably put into care at an early age. At her first wedding, she was 'Ethel Walker otherwise Ethel Newton'. She claimed, plausibly, to have had an unhappy childhood and that she disliked her mother who, she said, was an alcoholic.[5]

Ethel was a feisty lass, early on succumbing to the charms of one Joseph Arthur Leonard Rowley, known as Leonard. (Possessing three Christian names, surely, 'inspires confidence, even in tradesmen'?) Ethel said he came of a good family who lived at Dee Bank in Cheshire and came originally from Lancaster. Leonard, whose father had independent means, was a fine golfer and his grandson owns two silver-mounted, cut-glass claret jugs which he won in tournaments. Leonard was almost certainly studying mining-engineering at Nottingham University's Department of Mining but, if so, either did not sit or did not pass his final exams. The couple were married in 1903 at the local register office when Ethel was eighteen and her groom twenty-four. Their daughter was born on 12 March 1904 in Nottingham and named Leonora for her father.

Rowley obtained a post as assistant engineer at the Ooregaum Gold Mining Company of India Ltd.'s mine at Kolar, near Mysore and in 1905 took his young family out to India. He was promoted to chief engineer in 1909 and died the next year. His death was not registered either in England or India and the only records we have are those at the Probate Registry at Somerset House in London. The ledgers state Rowley died on 8 June 1910; that probate was granted in London on 12 December that year to Ethel as sole executrix; that his estate was valued at £1,837 2s.7d. The will, of the most basic nature, was not signed by Rowley as, it says, he was paralysed and could only make his mark, which was witnessed by two local, British, doctors. It was dated 7 June 1910, the day before that given for his death.[6] Jasen was told that Rowley died in 1910 'through drinking infected water'.

Ethel's mourning was brief. On 28 January 1911 she married twenty-seven years old John Wayman at the St George's Register Office, in Hanover Square, London. He seems to have been a Jack-the-lad. Born the son of a coachsmith and his illiterate wife in Tyer Street, Vauxhall, a poor suburb of South London, he described himself as a company director and gave his address as 47 Chester Terrace, Eaton Square – then an apartment house in a fashionable and expensive street now called Chester Row – when he married Ethel. She recorded a father on this wedding certificate, 'John Newton (deceased), Gentleman Farmer'. Only eighteen months later Wayman was declared bankrupt (with no trade or profession given) from 49 Old Bond Street.[7] After his initial success and high ambitions he was shattered at the prospects of returning, bankrupt, to the stews of Vauxhall and died. Ethel never mentioned him but Wodehouse knew of him. While the British volumes of *Who's Who* say he married 'Ethel May Rowley', his entries in the American edition record him as marrying 'Ethel Rowley Wayman' (and from 1924 to 1970 record him as having worked on the By The Way column of *The London Glove*!).

The young English widow Mrs Wayman was in New York in 1914 and was asked on 3 August to make up a fourth with two men, one of whom had only arrived from England the day before: it was, of course, Wodehouse. He was struck by *un coup de foudre* although he did not then know

what a godsend she would be to him for the rest of his life. Theirs was a
curious courtship, apparently consisting entirely of swimming trips to
Long Beach, Long Island and one important car trip. Wodehouse had to
be driven to New York from Long Island with raging toothache and
during the two-hour journey the talkative Ethel made no attempt to talk to
him. He proposed to her within days and less than two months after they
first met they were married on 30 September at The Little Church
Around the Corner on East 29th Street, New York which gave a special
welcome to theatre folk, not then admitted to 'respectable' society. The
service was conducted by the Vicar, the Revd George Houghton, who,
Wodehouse said, arrived late and elated because he had just made a large
sum playing the stock market. The witnesses were Edith Allen and
Richard Upjohn, whose name stuck in Plum's mind. The bride listed her
mother as 'Anne Green (deceased)' and exercised a lady's prerogative by
dropping a year off her age. Wodehouse later wrote one of his most
delightful and free flowing lyrics in celebration.

Dear little, dear little Church Round The Corner,
    Where so many lives have begun,
Where folks without money see nothing that's funny
    In two living cheaper than one.
Our hearts to each other we've trusted:
    We're busted, but what do we care?
        For a moderate price
    You can start dodging rice
        At the Church Round The Corner,
        It's just round the corner,
        The corner of Madison Square.[8]

What Plum saw in Ethel was a woman of striking looks and strong
personality; a reassuring combination of aunt, nanny and wife; a sense of
security. It must have been obvious to him, even on so short an acquaintance, that a man married to Ethel would not have to deal with the boring
and time-consuming matters of everyday life that keep a man away from
his typewriter. If the outside world came knocking on the door wanting to
get at Plum when he was writing, Ethel would clearly send it away with a
flea in its collective ear. Only Hitler's Panzer Divisions foiled her in this
task. Right up until extreme old age Ethel looked years younger than she
was, remained a stylish dresser and maintained a restless energy, yet Plum
found her restful.

What Ethel saw in Plum was the kindness and strength of the man. A
perceptive woman, she probably saw his acute intelligence too, which

many of his friends underestimated. After two short-lived marriages she finally met the right man. Then for richer for poorer, for better for worse and for as long as they both did live she had a doting and devoted husband giving her, until their last years, the happiness she had never known before.

Their grandson, Edward Cazalet, told me, 'One of the most remarkable things about Plum's and Ethel's relationship was the absence of discord between them. I have no recall of ever having heard them have a serious argument. I have no doubt that one reason for this was because Plum had resolved not to allow this to happen. But although the picture is painted of Ethel as being dictatorial, she gave way to Plum more often than she is given credit for.'

Malcolm Muggeridge, the author and broadcaster whose comments are always uncannily perceptive, later wrote of Ethel, in a description that also tells us as much about Wodehouse, 'A high spirited and energetic lady trying as hard to be worldly wise as Wodehouse himself to be innocent'.[9] Not everyone was taken in by the Wodehouse myth-making.

From their first meeting the young couple had struck up an extraordinarily close rapport that lasted without faltering for the entire sixty years of their marriage. Most successful marriages evolve from initial passion into a deep friendship based on converging habits, shared experiences and a community of interests but the Wodehouse marriage started that way. In a revealing letter to his friend Bradshaw less than two weeks later Wodehouse wrote that the question of a successful marriage was, he thought, not so much in whether a couple were in love but a shared communion of tastes that enabled them to live with each other harmoniously.[10]

One such bond was their sharing an indiscriminate love of animals. They always owned dogs, usually a cat or two as well, at least one parrot and a varied assortment of strays to which they gave refuge. Their favourite dogs were Pekes and they owned many including Bimmy, Boo, Loopy, Mrs Miffen, Squeaky, Miss Winks (also called Winkie) and Wonder as well as bulldogs, mongrels, a foxhound, a boxer and at least one dachshund. They also owned an Aberdeen terrier called Angus, the only dog they ever failed to love beyond all reason. Wodehouse found him so austere and Presbyterian that it was impossible not to feel ill at ease in his presence and noted that Angus looked at him like a Scottish preacher about to rebuke the sins of his congregation. Eventually Wodehouse gave him away 'To a better man than myself'[11] – but he remains immortalized as that censorious Calvinist, Stiffy Byng's hound Bartholomew. The Wodehouses also liked attending boxing tourneys and, later when funds allowed, gambling together. Plum enjoyed social functions almost as much as Ethel.

Less than a month after his marriage Wodehouse was writing to Bradshaw that Ethel had come out very strongly with three fine plots on which he was then working. He thought that if she could keep that up the maintainance of the home would be a cinch, adding that he never appreciated married life so much as when he came home the previous night, tired and hungry after walking from Patchogue and having had nothing to eat for hours. He was met at home by Ethel who had a fine dinner and a blazing fire waiting for him and then fussed over her appreciative husband. 'It was perfectly ripping.'[12] The letter was signed 'Yours ever, Chickens'.

Ethel could have done nothing better to cement Plum's love for her than come up with ideas for plots. They were always a problem. While he never ran out of plots he always feared he would do so, carefully hoarding those he had to hand while his friends were expected to provide him with new ones, or ideas for them. Sometimes he even bought plots from other authors for reworking, for example instructing his New York agents to pay $500 for the use of the plot of Clifford Grey's story 'Fate'.[13] If, as some claim, there are only seven basic story plots in the world then so prolific a writer as Wodehouse was bound to face a plot famine, but what he did to other people's plots, made each reworking of them unique too. *Spring Fever* and *The Old Reliable* have the same plot and similar casts – the former set in Sussex and the latter in Hollywood – but unless read consecutively this is unnoticeable.

The strength of that marriage was not based on conjugal passion, due to those mumps at nineteen. Ethel and Plum had separate bedrooms from at least 1920[14] and probably all their married life. When they were over from France staying at London's Dorchester Hotel for Leonora's wedding they didn't just have separate bedrooms but separate suites on different floors.[15] And when they got a flat in Paris in April 1945 Ethel still kept on her room at the Hotel Lincoln where they had been living. Wodehouse's letters to Townend, Bolton, Mackail and other friends are full of regrets that Ethel is away and of the forty-four to Leonora in *Yours Plum*, no less than twelve of them mention Ethel's absence and him missing her. Phrases on the theme 'This bachelor life is no good for me' and 'I'm missing Ethel dreadfully' recur throughout his unpublished letters too.

In *Wodehouse On Wodehouse*, combining his three 'autobiographical' books and published after his death, the four-times married Bolton added a story implying Wodehouse had an affair with a chorus girl. Like all ladies' men, Bolton felt he was giving his friend a boost with that story, as well as taking a swipe at Ethel, but it rings untrue. Unlike Plum, who was utterly truthful outside his writing, Guy's confusion of fact and fiction applied as much to his private life as to his writing. So, despite his great charm, he was always an unreliable testator.

The asexuality of Wodehouse's writing is one of its most striking and pleasing features. His own sense of good taste stopped him ever including anything salacious in his writing, but it's unlikely that he ever had any salacious thoughts to exclude. Indeed the serious love scenes in his earlier stories read perilously like the young Wodehouse parodying the old. All of which results in a refreshing absence of prurience throughout his prose. You will find more mention of sex in St Paul's first epistle to the Corinthians than in the entire Wodehouse canon. All his characters have orthodox and uneventful love-lives and for all of them only within wedlock. (Except for one very early story: Peggy Norton of 'In Alcala' is the mistress of an actor she does not love and so faces an un-Wodehousian and morally conventional future of unhappiness.) Usborne remarked, 'There is no suggestion that either clubman or girl would recognize a double bed except as so much extra sweat to make an apple pie [or short-sheeted] bed of' and quotes from *The Little Warrior* as the nearest Wodehouse ever gets to genuine sexual emotion. Wodehouse describes Jill's feelings about her fiance, Sir Derek Underhill, Bart, MP: 'The touch of his body against hers always gave her a thrill, half pleasurable, half frightening. She had never met anybody who affected her this way as Derek did. She moved a little closer and felt for his hand.' Naturally, being a baronet and a Member of Parliament, Underhill turns out to be a rotter. Wodehouse punishes him by giving him not the usual aunt but, unusually, a mother who is, of course, a nasty, domineering snob. Jill, a trouper who goes into the theatre when her trustee loses all her money, is rewarded by becoming engaged to Wally Mason, a Bill Townend-Guy Bolton hybrid.

There are just two more oblique references to illict sex in the Wodehouse canon. In *Heavy Weather* Lady Constance asks her bachelor brother Galahad if Sue Brown, daughter of Dolly Henderson, is his daughter too, which is coldly denied, and in *Doctor Sally* the eponym is setting out to embarrass the lovesick hero, Bill, for summoning her with a feigned malady:

> 'Now tell me about your sex life,' said Sally. . . .
> Bill recoiled. 'Don't you know the meaning of the word "reticence"?' he asked.
> 'Of course not, I'm a doctor.'
> Bill took a turn up and down the room.
> 'Well, naturally,' he said with dignity, halting once more, 'I have had – er – experiences – like other men.'
> Sally was at the stethoscope again.

'Um-hum,' she said.
'I admit it. There *have* been women in my life.'
'Say ninety-nine.'
'Not half as many as that!' cried Bill starting.

That uncharacteristic extract is probably a hang-over from the original
text of Ladislaus Fodor's Hungarian play upon which Wodehouse based
his own play, *Good Morning Bill*, and from which, in turn, he wrote the
novel *Doctor Sally* (only published in America in shorter form as *The
Medicine Girl*). Wodehouse thought Fodor's script was far too dirty and so
'I cleaned it up thoroughly'.[16] That puritan streak didn't stop him selling
stories to *Playboy*, the 'soft-porn' magazine, in his post-war years. He took
the Josh Billings' view that 'The only sort of tainted money is money tha'
taint mine'. He wrote to Bolton, after selling *Playboy* the US first serial
rights to *Biffen's Millions*, that, at any moment, it was likely to be scooped
in by the police as an indecent publication[17] but that didn't bother him –
he was only concerned about the wholesomeness of his own writing. Thus
divorce, death, coition and even birth are all unthinkable in Wodehouse
stories. Where they occur it is never described, barely mentioned and
always (except in *Their Mutual Child*) before a story starts, although in
later books the divorce rule was relaxed for Lord Tidmouth, Ivor Llewel-
lyn and Elmer Chinnery. Wodehouse admitted that he couldn't handle
'sex scenes' properly and speculated that his large sales in Sweden, where
all sorts of pornography are on rampant sale, were because his books were
not dirty.[18] The nearest Wodehouse ever got to joking about sex was 'I'm
all for incest and tortured souls in moderation, but a good laugh from time
to time never hurt anybody'.[19] Even the gigolos in Wodehouse abide by
his code. Adrian Peake, in *Summer Moonshine*, is improbably engaged to
his formidable Sugar Mommie, Heloise, Princess von und zu Dwornitzchek, and it is quite clear the hanky-panky will come after, not before, the
wedding day.

On the other hand Ethel had a number of men friends after her
marriage who escorted her to the dances and formal dinner-dances she
loved and Plum did not, particularly R.T.B. 'Bobby' Denby. Wodehouse
dedicated the US *Golf Without Tears* partly to Denby and wrote to Leonora urging her to write to Bobby as he had written a long letter to her
and would be feeling blue all alone at Dinard.[20] Whatever the role of
Bobby and Ethel's many other men friends such as Gerard Fairlie, they
never caused Wodehouse concern and had no effect on the strength of his
relationship with Ethel. Wodehouse was generous to Denby, allowing him
to live with his family for some years and to act as an *ad hoc* agent, but only
within limits. Denby got a very sharp telegram when he sold a story for

$7,500 instead of the expected $5,500 and pocketed the extra as 'additional commission' thinking that Wodehouse would never find out.[21] About as unlikely as expecting a kerbside umbrella salesman not to notice it was raining.

The great bonus Ethel brought to the marriage was a ready made daughter for Plum in Leonora, then aged ten. I never met Wodehouse, sharing the view of Charles Gould, 'It has been to me a secret source of pleasure and self-congratulation that I never on a summer's day, from noon to dewy eve, drove the easy drive to Remsenburg to drape myself, like Lord Emsworth over the Empress's sty, over Wodehouse's front fence'.[22] One should not impose oneself on an old man who has given one so much pleasure, knowing he wished to be undisturbed. But I regret never having met Ethel and, even more, not meeting Leonora.

She too was extraordinary, but in sharp contrast to her mother. Everyone who met her loved her. Nobody ever had a bad word to say about her but went out of their way to say good words about her. Miss O'Sullivan said, 'There was something magical about Leonora – whenever I pick up a book of reminiscences of that period, I am apt to find accounts of her captivating the author with her gentle wit and strange beauty.'[23] Frances Donaldson, not a sentimental woman, writes simply and movingly of Leonora's essential qualities of loyalty and kindliness adding, 'She died more than thirty years ago. I still think of her and miss her.'[24] Sir Compton Mackenzie wrote, 'I met and was completely fascinated by Leonora, who seemed to me to be the most brilliant young woman I had ever known.'[25] Godfrey Winn wrote, 'She succeeded in making anyone with whom she came into contact, even to exchange a few words, feel that they were the only person in the world of any importance at that moment.'[26] Denis Mackail, in an obituary, wrote, 'She was wise as well as deliciously witty – that kind, brave generous creature, with the charming voice. . . . So gay, so quick, so amusing; but with depths in her too. . . . She was unique.'[27]

No wonder Leonora's biggest fan was Plum. To start with he called her Nora[28] but later 'Snorkles' or 'Snorkie' from her schoolfriends' corruption of Nora, 'Poots'[29] or exuberant names like 'Precious Angel' and dedicated the US edition of Piccadilly Jim 'To my step-daughter Lenora (sic), conservatively speaking the most wonderful child on earth'. This appears only in the earliest editions and was then dropped. Perhaps Leonora found it a tiny bit overstated? His letters to her are written in his most relaxed and happy style. Plum's love was reciprocated and later he adopted her. Leonora also became a writer, usually under the pen-name Loel Yeo. The April 1932 issue of The Strand led off with the Wodehouse story 'Open House' but also included Loel Yeo's 'Inquest'.[30] Plum gained more pleasure from Leonora's successes than from his own. When she submitted a story, anonymously, to *The American* he wrote to Denis Mackail, bursting with pride, of enthusiastic reviews from four editors, the purchase of the story for $300 and the request for more stories from her, adding 'She really can write like blazes'.[31] He also came to place great trust in her judgement of his work sending her drafts of his stories to read and writing that he could make any changes she wanted.[32] Over the years the Wodehouse heroine was to become more and more like Leonora – outgoing in personality, intelligent, perky but ultimately the boss half of the partnership with their overt and covert fiances. Joan Valentine is the heroine of *Something Fresh* written just before Plum met Leonora.

How perfectly splendid. I was terrified lest I might have made you change your mind. I had to say all I did, to preserve my self-respect after proposing to you. Yes, I did. But strange it is that men never seem to understand a woman, however plainly she talks. You don't think I was really worrying because I had lost Aline, do you? I thought I was going to lose you, and it made me miserable. You couldn't expect me to say so in so many words, but I thought you guessed. I practically said it.

Wodehouse told Leonora that he thought he had captured her so well as Flick Sheridan in *Bill The Conqueror* that 'The *cognoscenti* cannot but be charmed'.

Seven years ago . . . she had been a leggy, scraggy, tousle-haired, freckled thing . . . And now the sight of her suggested . . . a Hamadryad or some shepherdess strayed out of an Idyll of Theocritus. A slim, fair-haired girl with a trim figure delightfully arrayed. Her eyes were very blue and seemed unusually large.

Nobby Hopwood in *Joy In The Morning* is, I think, an even better picture of Leonora.

Her voice was soft and tender, like that of a hen crooning over its egg. . . .
    'Boko leaves for Hollywood next month. I don't know how you feel about this dream man of mine but to me, and I have studied his character with loving care, he doesn't seem the sort of person to be allowed to go to Hollywood without a wife at his side to distract his attention from the local fauna.'

She had one other odd effect. In Wodehouse books you will often find girls with different names to their father's with no reason given. In *Fish Preferred* and *Heavy Weather* Sue Brown is the daughter of Dolly Henderson and Jack Cotterleigh of the Irish Guards, but there is never any mention of a Mr Brown. Thus, in the Wodehouse world where illegitimacy does not exist, she could only be a step-daughter. The Wodehouse scholar John Fletcher gives a more detailed example.

> Did Wodehouse make mistakes? I do not think so. Take one example, Miss Mabel Murgatroyd from 'The Word In Season' in *A Few Quick Ones* and 'Bingo Bans The Bomb' in *Plum Pie*. She is given in the second story a father, the Earl of Ippleton. If he were her real father, she would be Lady Mabel Murgatroyd. She is not called that. In both stories she is Miss Mabel Murgatroyd; repeatedly in the second, and she is also called once in a *Daily Mirror* caption 'The Hon Mabel Murgatroyd'. It is clear that the *Mirror* journalists are not above giving a title to someone who might not have one. But why was she not Lady Mabel but a mere Miss? The answer is that she was not Lord Ippleton's daughter but his step-daughter. Her name is Murgatroyd. His full name, given twice in case we missed it, is George Francis Augustus Delamere, fifth Earl of Ippleton. Not a trace of a Murgatroyd. Why then do she and he claim to be father and daughter? There is a book to be written on the closeness of step-fathers and daughters in works written by novelists who were themselves loving step-fathers of loving step-daughters.[33]

Wodehouse, as you would expect of an English gentleman of a landed family, knew and used correct forms of address as unconsciously as he breathed. The differences between, say, Cecily Lady Roberts, Lady Cecily Roberts, Lady Roberts and the Hon. Cecily Roberts held no mystery for him. It was another of his private jokes that characters in his books occasionally get these things wrong, as do real people from less elevated stations in life. Peter Burns, the schoolmaster narrator of *The Little Nugget*, refers to one of his charges as 'Lord Beckford' and also as 'the Hon. Augustus Beckford' – which are incompatible. Wodehouse the narrator never makes such errors.

'Aunts' with second husbands and a child by a former marriage are legion, such as Myrtle, Dowager Lady Churfnell, with her son Seabury in *Thank You Jeeves*. She has overtones of Ethel who makes no obvious appearance in the canon but 'the Wodehouse aunt' only began after his marriage – with Lady Ann Warblington in *Something New* in 1915. There is much of Ethel in all of the Wodehouse aunts: more than there is of Aunt Mary Deane.

However before the good times came there were more mundane matters to deal with as the newly-weds settled down at Bellport, Long Island, so Plum could get writing the next lyric, play, short story or novel to pay for such things as school fees, three square meals a day, pet food and rent for their home. Money was certainly not among the factors that attracted Ethel and Plum to each other. According to Wodehouse the happy couple had only $70 between them when they married.[34] That seems a bit improbable for the thrifty, hardworking author with twelve of his sixteen books in print and earning royalties – and in fact the careful Wodehouse had excluded his 'London savings' from that figure. By mid-October he was writing to Bradshaw that he had $425 in the bank.[35] In those early years of the First World War Wodehouse claimed he was having a Dickens of a job keeping the wolf from the door with no one buying his short stories and that if it hadn't been for Frank Crownin-shield, editor of *Vanity Fair* in New York, liking his work and taking all he was offered he, Wodehouse, would have been very much up against it.[36]

Crowninshield, editor of *Vanity Fair* from its relaunch in March 1914 (previously it was *Dress & Vanity Fair*) until it merged with *Vogue* in February 1936, was a gentleman. Once, discussing someone with a col-league, he said, 'How can we get in touch with him? He's not in the Social Register.'[37] Robert Benchley, one of his assistant editors, wrote of him in 1920:

> He believes that the hope of a revival in Good Taste lies in those men and women who are college graduates, have some money, who know porcelains, and Verlaine, and Italian art, who love Grolier bindings, Spanish brocades and French literature. . . . Any writer who writes entertainingly [may] say practically anything he wants, so long as he says it in evening clothes.[38]

Crowninshield was saved from being a snob by his dry sense of humour. When Robert Sherwood produced an issue of the Harvard Lampoon as a burlesque of *Vanity Fair* it so amused him that he offered the tyro editor a job.[39] General Kurt von Hammerstein would have approved of Crownin-shield as his ideal of the lazy intelligent man.* Crowninshield's passion was conjuring and often work in the *Vanity Fair* office would come to a

---

* 'I divide officers into four classes; the lazy, the stupid, the clever and the industrious. Each officer possesses at least two of these qualities. Those who are clever and industrious are fitted for high staff appointments. Use can be made of those who are stupid and lazy. The man who is clever and lazy is fit for the very highest command. He has the temperament and the requisite nerves to deal with all situations. But whoever is stupid and industrious must be removed immediately.' c 1933[40]

halt while he demonstrated his newest trick. No wonder he usually found himself short of copy as the magazine's monthly deadline approached.

It was Wodehouse's ability to produce reams of good copy at short notice that appealed to Crowninshield as much as his breeding and good manners. The young journalist became the contributing editor of *Vanity Fair*, turning his hand to anything that needed doing and writing articles under his own name and a host of pre-deadline fillers under pen-names including Pelham Grenville, P. Brooke Haven, C.P. West, J. William Walker, J. Plum and, I suspect from reading 'A Hindu At The Polo Grounds To His Brother In India', also Mahatma Sri Paramananda Guru Swamiji. The paper's fashion artist, Ethel Plummer, really was Ethel Plummer and not, alas, Plum's wife Ethel.[41]

Crowninshield is probably without peer among all the editors of twentieth-century magazines for the talent he discovered and nurtured. In late 1918 he had not only Wodehouse but Robert Benchley and Dorothy Parker working for him at the same time – arguably three of the funniest writers of the period. Other staff members included Sherwood, later to make his name as a dramatist, and the critic Edmund Wilson, while Stephen Leacock was a regular contributor who entered the magazine's 'Hall of Fame' in the same August 1915 issue as Wodehouse, whose citation read:

> Because in *The Little Nugget* he has written a farce that is sure to take Broadway by storm. [No. It was never staged.] Because he has (in his current serial *Something New*) introduced the restrained, or English, type of humor into the pages of *The Saturday Evening Post*. Because in writing he strives to satisfy his conscience as an artist, and finally because he and Stephen Leacock are the star boarder-humorists at *Vanity Fair's* monthly banquets.[42]

Wodehouse and Leacock became friends; both wrote humour of a gentle and kindly form. Wodehouse visited Leacock at his home in Montreal on his way back from Hollywood in 1931,[43] and probably on other occasions. For any Wodehousian who has read *Sunshine Sketches Of A Little Town* or any of Leacock's humorous works it is no surprise that Wodehouse called him 'A kindred spirit'. The admiration was mutual. In his *Humour and Humanity* Leacock begins, 'Humour may be defined as the kindly contemplation of the incongruities of life, and the artistic expression thereof.' The essence of the definition lies in the word 'kindly', there are no more kindly writers than Plum.

A host of other contributors were also launched onto great literary careers by Crowninshield including John Peale Bishop, Clare Booth, Carl

Carmer, David Cort, Nancy Hall, Margaret Case Harriman, Edna St Vincent Millay, Richard Sherman, Allene Talmey, Frank Tuttle and Elinor Wylie. Other contributors ranged from Noel Coward and Jean Cocteau to Carl Sandburg and Aldous Huxley.[44]

The first Wodehouse piece for *Vanity Fair* was in the May 1914 issue. Entitled 'The Physical Culture Peril' it gently satirized keep-fit enthusiasts.

I meet some great philosopher, and, instead of looking with reverence at his nobbly forehead, I merely feel, that if he tried to touch his toes thirty times without bending his knees he would be in hospital for a week. An eminent divine is to me simply a man who would have a pretty thin time if he tried to lie on his back and wave his legs in the air fifteen times without stopping.[45]

The private joke is that every morning from his late twenties to the end of his days Wodehouse did fifteen minutes of serious exercises, based on a 1919 article in *Colliers* by Walter Camp. This, and his daily habit of extended afternoon walks, contributed to his long life with hardly any illnesses, except those of old age.

From March 1915 Wodehouse was also *Vanity Fair's* drama critic and his first review, hardly about the theatre at all, shows the satirist, with the fervent belief in tolerance, very much in existence. In 'Boy: Page Mr Comstock' he discusses a Mr Anthony Comstock, self-styled 'Roundsman Of The Lord' and for forty-three years founder and secretary of the New York Society For The Suppression of Vice. This righteous Christian gentleman boasted not only of the 160 tons of 'obscene' literature he had destroyed and the 3,600 'pornographers' he caused to be imprisoned but also of the fifteen 'sinners' he had driven to suicide.[46] Libertarians were seriously outraged by Comstock but Wodehouse's gentle satire of this evil man was probably far more effective. Noting Mr Comstock had failed to attack several innocent Broadway musicals, Wodehouse wrote:

Did you hear what Mr Billy Sunday [the revivalist preacher] has been saying about us? Here are his exact words: 'There's rotten, stinking, corroding, corrupt, hell-ridden, God-defying, devil-ridden New York. God will get it in His own good time.' It must have been the theatres which gave Mr Sunday that idea. There is not a bit of harm in New York, but the place is getting a bad name simply because these powerful dramatists try to make out that all men are villains and all women are either villainesses, or Women Who Have Been Wronged.

Mr Comstock must act, and at once.

There is still time. In this morning's papers there was a headline:

BILLY SUNDAY CANNOT SAVE NEW YORK
UNTIL THE FALL

That gives us a few months more in which to put our house in order, but every moment is precious. We must rout out Mr Comstock at once. Boy: page Mr Comstock.[47]

No wonder Crowninshield treasured Wodehouse and gave him a free hand to use the *Vanity Fair* offices on 44th Street as his New York base, which he did from 1914 until 1923. There was no objection to all his other writing and he was free to take unpaid leave when he wanted to go to England, with his job as the magazine's drama critic always waiting for him when he got back. Crowninshield remembered him in those days.

> Judged by exterior appearances only, he seemed merely a stodgy and colourless Englishman; silent, careful with his money, self-effacing, slow witted and matter-of-fact. . . . In all those years – at dinners, at his cottage in the country, on the golf-links, at the Coffee House Club, over a week-end, at the theatre – I never heard him utter a clever, let alone brilliant, remark. No alienist could possibly have guessed him to be the fanciful, erudite, brilliant and highly intellectual man he actually was.[48]

He was far different from his colleagues at the time. For Dorothy Parker, Robert Benchley and Robert Sherwood conversation and audiences were the breath of life. Writing seemed merely the means of financing their lives and those all-afternoon lunches of the Round Table at Wodehouse's old home-from-home, the Algonquin Hotel. *Bring On The Girls* shows that Wodehouse and Guy Bolton attended one or two of those lunches (they only pinched stories that mocked themselves) however neither cared for them. So while his colleagues lunched and talked Wodehouse worked. To help him do so he developed an almost Jeevesian ability to leave a room, especially one with a party going on in it, without anyone noticing he had gone. As Bertie said, 'He seemed to flicker and wasn't there any more.'[49] This became known as 'The Wodehouse Glide' and helped him to escape from importuning friends such as the Algonquin set. As he later remarked to Usborne, 'All those three hour lunches. . . . when did those slackers ever get any work done?'[50] He never became close to Sherwood as he did with most colleagues and his distaste for Miss Parker was so intense that, in spite of having worked in the offices of the same

magazine with her from the autumn of 1917 until April 1918,[51] he
obliterated her from his mind and in later life claimed, 'I never actually
met her. I don't think I'd have liked her, would you? Those prepared *bons
mots*. And she was a slacker too, any excuse not to work'.[52] Like any other
man, he came across people he disliked but he never said so in public,
although his letters contain plenty of acerbic comments about them. In
Miss Parker's case that blind spot was effectively applied. He hated the
hurtfulness of her bitter humour while still admiring her writing,
especially *Laments For The Living*. While she said that if all the girls who
attended the Yale Prom were laid end-to-end she wouldn't be surprised,[53] Wodehouse took the idea and told us that if all the girls Freddie
Widgeon had wooed and lost were placed end-to-end they would reach
from Piccadilly Circus to Hyde Park Corner. Further than that, probably,
because some of them were pretty tall. The gentle, witty Benchley was
unlike his two colleagues and he and Wodehouse became and remained
friends. They lunched together when their paths crossed and both were
pleased when Benchley was one of the stars of the film of *A Damsel In
Distress* based on Wodehouse's novel of the same name.[54]

For Wodehouse writing, not conversation, was the breath of life and
Vanity Fair was financing the lives of himself and his new family. He was
still getting rejection slips from other papers but he never had one from
his editor. Such missives were highly prized. Dickson Hartwell said:

> Mr Crowninshield's letters of rejection were so complimentary that
> they usually had to be read twice to discover whether he was making a
> nomination for a Pulitzer Prize or expressing regret. Once he sent back
> a manuscript to Paul Gallico. 'My Dear Boy, This is superb! A little
> masterpiece! What colour! What life! How beautifully you have phrased
> it all! A veritable gem! Why don't you take it round to *Harper's
> Bazaar*?'[55]

Wodehouse's active days with *Vanity Fair* came gently to an end with
more lucrative work flowing his way. In 1921 he was doing so well that
Ethel, attending a selling-race, impulsively bought a racehorse, Front
Line by Fugleman out of Hackline, from a Mr J.P. Walen. When she
returned home her husband was in the bath and she shouted up to him
that she had bought a horse. There was a silence. Then 'Is it downstairs?'
Ethel's racing colours were scarlet crossbands and black cap. Front Line,
a steeplechaser, had three wins out of four races in 1921, was unplaced in
four races in 1922 and had two wins from eleven races in 1923, after
which Ethel sold the animal to a Mr Mosley.[56] (Front Line was eventually
sold to a Belgian and probably ended up in cans as dog food.) It must have

been deeply satisfying for the little girl from an anonymous, working-class, provincial background to join in the sport of kings, aristocrats and millionaires and to lead her own horse into the winner's enclosure. Her husband was equally enthusiastic, especially when Front Line won at Hurst Park in 1924 at odds of thirty-three to one. Racing takes a deep pocket and while Wodehouse was making a lot of money from his short stories and novels the means to pay for this little extravagance of Ethel's came mostly from Wodehouse's new-found success in the Broadway musical theatre and another chapter in his life.

10

THE TRIO OF MUSICAL FAME

Wodehouse may well be considered the first truly great
lyricist of the American musical stage, his easy, colloquially flowing rhythms deftly interwoven with a sunny wit.[1]

The Concise Oxford Companion to The American Theatre

I F Wodehouse had never written a single short story, novel or magazine
article he would still be remembered as one of the greatest and most
innovative lyricists of the American musical stage. Lyrics for musical
comedy are, perhaps, the trickiest of the theatrical crafts. While most
practitioners write the words for which the composer produces the
melody, Wodehouse preferred to work the other way round. He told
Jasen:

Jerry [Kern] generally did the melody first and I put the words in. W.S.
Gilbert always said that a lyricist can't do decent stuff that way, but I
don't agree with him – not as far as I'm concerned anyway. If I write a
lyric without having to fit it to a tune, I always make it too much like a
set of light verse, much too regular in metre. I think you get the best
results by giving the composer his head and having the lyricist follow
him. For instance the refrain of one of the songs in *Oh Boy* began: 'If
every day you bring her diamonds and pearls on a string'. I couldn't
have thought of that, if I had done the lyric first, in a million years.
Why, dash it, it doesn't scan. But Jerry's melody started off with a lot of
little twiddly notes, the first thing emphasized being the 'di' of
diamonds and I just tagged along after him. Another thing is that when
you have the melody, you can see which are the musical high spots in it
and in fact fit the high spots of the lyric to them. Anyway, that's how I
like working and to hell with anyone who says I oughtn't to.

W.S. Gilbert was a major influence on Wodehouse as he was to be on his
own successors. Some of the early poems are admiring copies, such as his

paean to the actor-manager Mr H. Beerbohm Tree to the tune of the
Major-General song from *The Pirates of Penzance*.

> If I'm asked to tell the reason for his
>   well-earned popularity,
> His acting's always funny while avoiding all vulgarity;
> As Hamlet, when he had his conversation
>   with the phantom, I'm
> Not certain that he didn't beat the leading lights
>   of pantomime.[2]

. . . but Wodehouse comic poems and lyrics developed to become
uniquely his own.

His career as a lyricist began in London in early December 1904. The
actor-manager-playwright Owen Hall asked Wodehouse to write a lyric for
his new musical, *Sergeant Brue*, the principal lyricist being the improbably
named J. Hickory Wood. The show opened on the 10th at London's
Strand Theatre. Wodehouse also wrote the words for 'Put Me In My
Little Cell', to be sung by the three crooks in the show. It was a great
success and the first of at least 210 lyrics he was to write. It prompted
Cosmo Hamilton, the author and playwright, to ask Wodehouse to write
lyrics for his next show, *The Beauty Of Bath*, written by Hamilton and
Seymour Hicks, actor-manager at the Aldwych Theatre. Hicks invited
Wodehouse to join him and his wife, the actress Ellaline Terriss, as the
resident (part-time) lyricist for the show. Wodehouse's job was to com-
pose topical lyrics, sometimes changed daily, for certain songs in the
show, very much doing his By The Way job to music and working with an
American composer, Jerome Kern, then only twenty-one. Kern got on
well with Wodehouse – everybody did – and asked him for lyrics for a new
melody and to revise two mediocre lyrics which F. Clifford Harris had
written, 'The Frolic Of A Breeze' and 'Oh, Mr Chamberlain!'.[3] The
latter was a song satirizing the former apostle of Free Trade, the Rt. Hon.
Joseph Chamberlain, MP, then campaigning for restrictive tariffs on
imports under the politically more beguiling name of tariff reform. Wodehouse gave him some unexpected leisure pursuits.

> He plays for Aston Villa by way of keeping fit
> He runs the mile in four fifteen and wrestles Hackenschmidt
> He sleeps a couple of hours a week and works right round the clock
> He wrote *The Master Christian* and *Stop yer ticklin', Jock*.[4]

It was the biggest hit of a successful show – apart from the black cat. This walked across the stage on the first night just as the curtain went up at eight o'clock, guaranteeing good luck in England (and bad luck in America). Which goes to show that luck is 90-per cent hard work. Hicks had trained that cat, feeding it centre front stage at eight p.m. sharp, every evening, for the preceding fortnight.[5] The new melody was dropped before the show opened and so one of Wodehouse's first original, professional lyrics is lost to us. He spent the following Christmas with the Hickses and in her 1928 memoirs, *By Herself,* Terriss recalls:

> P.G. Wodehouse was also a struggler at this time, writing on the now defunct *Globe* newspaper. We knew him well and today, although in his busy and superlatively successful life we seldom meet, when we do he has the same unspoiled boyish nature as he had when he stayed with us and was christened 'The Hermit' because he would insist on doing his writing hidden away in a plantation near our house.

And being a professional she recycled that story in her 1955 memoirs *A Little Bit Of String,*[6] adding, 'He was always a rather large boy with an open and happy nature. Seymour was very fond of him.' The next Hicks play, *The Gay Gordons* at the Aldwych, was also a success and had additional lyrics by Wodehouse and Charles H. Bovill, another colleague from his days at *The Globe.*

In November 1906 Wodehouse bought Hicks' car, a Darracq. He told Jasen that he paid £450 for it, all his savings and a lot of money in those days. With no drivers' licences or tests then required he took one cursory lesson from Hicks and drove off for Emsworth. All was going well but just before he reached journey's end he crashed the car into a hedge, abandoned it, caught a train back to London and never drove again. Another nicely rounded story. Wodehouse was not so foolish as to drive until he felt he had an adequate grasp of the art and he drove the first seventy-five miles without mishap. Furthermore it is highly improbable that Wodehouse, always careful with money in his early days, was as foolish as he claimed and spent all his savings on it. Fourteen years after the Darracq incident he was telling Townend that he drove his own car in America and was very hot stuff in all sorts of traffic.[7] Two years later he mentions that, during one of Ethel's absences, he took himself on a motoring trip which included Stonehenge and ended up at Emsworth for the school's sports.[8] He probably gave up driving not long after that as his eyesight and the traffic got worse but he continued to list 'motoring' among his interests in *Who's Who* (UK and US) to the last entry.

Towards the end of the following year he left Hicks to become resident

lyricist at the Gaiety. Although the theatre reference books of the period
fail to give him credit for a single lyric for any of the shows put on at the
theatre at that time his writing paper recorded the lyrics for 'Our Little
Way' from *The Girls From Guttenberg* (*sic*) among 'Some recent song
successes'. Even then Wodehouse's talents clearly merited a bigger role in
the theatre. That began when, towards the end of 1910, the producer
William A. Brady suggested *A Gentleman Of Leisure* would make a good
play and Wodehouse agreed to dramatize it with the help of John Stapleton. The premier was at The Playhouse Theatre, New York, on 24
August 1911 and it ran for a respectable seventy-six performances. It gave
a boost to the careers of two rising young actors: Douglas Fairbanks, Sr.,
and John Barrymore who starred in the Chicago production retitled *A
Thief For A Night*. Wodehouse never saw the Broadway production but did
see Fairbanks play the role in Baltimore.

Back in England in October 1913 Wodehouse renewed his friendship
with Bovill who invited his friend to leave his hotel and stay with him and
his family in their flat overlooking Battersea Park. Together the two wrote
the biggest flop of Wodehouse's theatrical career, *Nuts And Wine*, set
vaguely in the future under a new order. Typically the editor of the *New
News* actually creates the news – for example the office boy is sent out to
commit murder when the paper wants to write about one – so efficient,
cutting out the uncertainty of relying on the amateur murderer. At least it
got reviewed by *The Times* (which had merely 'noticed' *Brother Alfred*) in a
lukewarm article '. . . but for a lack of wit in the treatment some of the
best things misfire'.[9] The show ran for just seven performances at London's Empire Theatre in January 1914. Bovill and Wodehouse collaborated on a much more successful project, *A Man Of Means*, about the
adventures of a young man after he comes into a lot of money. Bovill
provided the plots and ideas while Wodehouse wrote them up. They are
splendid stories, early Wodehouse at his best cheerfully writing hack work
at speed, and were serialized in *The Strand* from April to September 1914
in the UK and in the *Delineator* in the US. The stories came to an abrupt
halt when Bovill joined the Army on the outbreak of the First World War
while Wodehouse was stranded in America.

His career as a New York journalist was making good progress and it
was as the drama critic of *Vanity Fair* that Wodehouse went to the
Princess Theatre on 23 December 1915 to see the first night of *Very Good
Eddie*. A young stage-struck millionaire, Philip Bartholomae, wrote the
original libretto (based on his own farce *Over Night*) which had to be
polished into workable form by Guy Bolton; Schuyler Green wrote the
lyrics to Jerome Kern's music and there were interpolations by Clare
Kummer. From 1916 Bolton, Wodehouse and Kern worked together,

becoming the most famous trio in the history of the American musical and upon which they had a profound effect. Those are the facts. How Wodehouse first met the greatest friend of his life – in old age, when Townend was dead, he was to say 'A man only needs one friend' and his was Bolton – has been a mystery.

The story offered in *Bring On The Girls* is that after the final curtain call for *Very Good Eddie* Wodehouse met Kern again for the first time since London and, at a cast party after the show at Kern's apartment, was introduced to Bolton, who claims the following diary entry.

> *Eddie* opened. Excellent reception. All say hit. To Kern's for supper. Talked with P.G. Wodehouse, apparently known as Plum. Never heard of him, but Jerry says he writes lyrics, so, being slightly tight, suggested we team up. W so overcome couldn't answer for a minute, then grabbed my hand and stammered out his thanks.[10]

Contrariwise the Wodehouse diary records:

> To opening of *Very Good Eddie*. Enjoyed it in spite of lamentable lyrics. Bolton, evidently conscious of this weakness, offered partnership. Tried to hold back and weigh the suggestion, but his eagerness so pathetic that consented. Mem: Am I too impulsive? Fight against this tendency.[11]

(*Very Good Eddie* has the distinction of causing Noel Coward to be worsted in repartee. Years later Bolton told Coward, just after the triumph of *Private Lives*, how similar he thought the two plots were. 'Do you think', said Coward, puffing at a cigarette through a long holder, 'that the authors of *Very Good Eddie* could have seen *Private Lives*?' 'No.' said Bolton. 'Because *Very Good Eddie* was written in 1915 and *Private Lives* in 1930.')[12]

Guy Reginald Bolton was born on 23 November 1884 in Broxbourne, Hertfordshire – less than a month after Wodehouse in Guildford and only eighty-five miles away – of American parents, his father being a noted engineer. Bolton himself trained in France as an architect and was part of the design team for the Soldiers' and Sailors' Monument on New York's Riverside Drive. He was a hardworking, short, dapper, man and if he has an *alter ego* in the Wodehouse canon it is George Bevan, the hero and writer of musical plays in *A Damsel In Distress*; and he contributes largely to the Hon. Galahad Threepwood's appearance.

Bolton had turned his hand to writing plays, including one called *The Drone*, but with only middling success until he teamed up with Kern writing the book for the Daniel V. Arthur show, *Ninety In The Shade*. Since the cast set out for rehearsals in Syracuse on 28 December 1914, Bolton and Kern must have got to know each other weeks before that. The show was not a success, running for only forty performances, but the pair also worked together on *Nobody Home*, which opened at the Princess Theatre in New York on 20 April 1915 and ran for a goodly 135 performances.

Meanwhile Wodehouse would not have allowed his friendship with Kern to lie fallow but would have looked him up early on during his second stay in New York, if not his first. He needed every contact and, being a thorough professional, used them all – besides which the two liked each other. There is much supporting evidence for this. Writing in *Vanity Fair* in March 1915 Wodehouse mentioned Bolton and *Ninety In the Shade*, which he had clearly seen and which he reviewed the following month calling it 'thin' and adding:

We spoke above of optimistic managers. If Mr Daniel V. Arthur really expected to set Broadway ablaze with *Ninety In The Shade*, he is the noblest optimist of them all. Our lawyer tells us that, as we did not pay for our seat, an action for damages against the perpetrators of *Ninety In The Shade* will not lie: so we must be content with a strongly worded protest. If Mr Guy Bolton wrote the book as it is being served up to the public at the Knickerbocker, he is to be censured: if, as from a small acquaintance with the inner workings of musical comedy productions we are inclined to suspect, his original book was mangled and disintegrated to suit the purpose of Miss Cahill and Mr Carle, [it was] he is to be commiserated with. Miss Cahill has some good lines which she makes the most of. Mr Carle has an excellent song entitled 'Foolishness'. He had an excellent song entitled 'Foolishness' in *The Doll Girl* and an excellent song entitled 'Foolishness' in *The Girl From Montmartre*.

To use one song in three successive plays on Broadway shows thrift and nerve – both of them excellent qualities.[13]

The lyrics for *Ninety In The Shade* were by Clare Kummer – but there is also a Kern song, 'A Package Of Seeds', with lyrics by Wodehouse![14] It is possible this is the lost melody and lyrics from *The Beauty Of Bath* but more likely a New York renewal of the London partnership. As the *Vanity Fair* drama critic Wodehouse wrote of several shows with which he had some association without mentioning the fact to his readers – a slightly unexpected but very human lapse of good form.

In the September 1915 *Vanity Fair* Wodehouse reviewed *Nobody Home*, the Bolton and Kern musical, writing:

It is impossible not to enjoy *Nobody Home*; it is so cosy and restful and confidential, and Jerome Kern, who has so long song-hitted for others, has at last got the chance to song-hit for himself with the best results.[15]

It is not conceivable that Wodehouse reviewed a Kern musical without meeting his old friend and collaborator. Two pieces in the *Dramatic Mirror* also support the idea of an earlier Bolton-Wodehouse meeting. The first on 8 September 1915 announced two new Kern musicals, one of which was to be 'A new musical farce by P.G. Wodehouse and Mr Kern'. The second was on 27 November, promising a Bolton, Wodehouse and Kern musical called *Funny That*.

Playwright Bolton would obviously have known of the drama critic of *Vanity Fair* and, like everyone in New York show business, would have seen those pieces in the *Dramatic Mirror*. Like any normal person he would have checked up on at least the second of them. It has been suggested that those two items were planted by Miss Bessie Marbury, a public relations agent, to give her clients some useful press exposure. If so, such a professional operator would not have linked the names of people who did not know each other.

Another reason why the *Bring On The Girls* chronology has to be wrong (apart from the authors altering it for dramatic effect as Wodehouse later admitted they did) is that it lists among those present at the Kern party the English cast of *Tonight's The Night* including Wodehouse's old friend Lawrie Grossmith and his brother George who had both sailed back to London in late March 1915. It seems likely that Bolton and Wodehouse swapped the story of their original meeting from the first night of *Tonight's The Night* and the cast party of that show, to that of *Very Good Eddie*, their own show and a much better known one. So it is almost certainly on Christmas Eve 1914, that Bolton and Wodehouse first met, beginning that lifelong friendship that was to last sixty years and to embrace working together on over twenty musicals, four plays, two film scripts and a book plus many unproduced and unpublished works.

To his death Bolton insisted that the *Bring On The Girls* version of his first meeting Wodehouse in December 1915 was correct – but in *Jerome Kern: His Life And Music* (which would be the definitive life of Kern, had it included a bibliography) Gerald Boardman doubted him, writing 'Bolton, whose memories in his middle nineties were relatively clear and complete, insisted that he had absolutely no recollection of anything called *Funny That*'.[16] Those who knew Bolton attest not only to his charm but to the fact that once he had invented an anecdote that pleased him he told it so many times he came to believe it was true.

Be that as it may, once the trio got together they created those Princess shows which changed the course of the American musical theatre. The shows were conceived by Miss Marbury to fill the small and unfashionable Princess Theatre on East 39th Street which she briefly managed with F. Ray Comstock. The theatre was owned by the Shubert brothers – Lee, J.J. and Sam – who, as fire regulations only applied to theatres with a capacity of 300 or more, had thoughtfully arranged for the Princess to seat an audience of just 299. This cost-cutting on safety seemed a commercial error as the Broadway theatre of the time was dominated by spectacular musicals with big casts, huge choruses, large orchestras, outlandish special effects, frequent changes of gorgeous scenery and budgets to match. The Princess was too small either to stage such shows or to seat enough theatregoers to fund them. The Marbury concept was to make a virtue out of necessity. She wrote:

> I became associated with F. Ray Comstock and with Lee Shubert in that form of entertainment which has been so successfully imitated ever since – namely, a comedy with music in which each extra girl became an individual, dressed according to her personality, and was not given a uniform costume. We had only twelve young women, who were especially selected for their charm and distinction.
>
> In fact, musical comedy lost its commonplace atmosphere, and through the joint efforts of my associates and myself it was raised from the ranks into the realms of a different and better form of entertainment. Another thing of which I am justly proud is that Jerome D. Kern's first score, *Nobody Home*, was our opening production. This was followed by *Very Good, Eddie* and *Love of Mike* [a Kern show at the Shubert Theatre] which in turn established a series of successes.
>
> We had put a certain deserted theatre upon the map; we had introduced a novelty and had popularised a composer. We had brought Guy Bolton, P.G. Wodehouse and Philip Bartholomae together on our librettos. We had proved that a small, intimate, clean musical comedy, devoid of all vulgarity and coarseness, could be made financially successful.[17]

These shows had only two changes of scenery, an orchestra of just eleven and a small cast. Overall the first two shows, *Nobody Home* and *Very Good Eddie* were successful but their weakness was Bolton's. Although a good playwright and librettist he was a weak lyricist. It took the addition of Wodehouse before the Princess shows became pivotal in taking the American musical along a new and invigorating path after the tried and tired formula of Viennese operetta stuck in its Ruritanian rut, which Wodehouse satirized in *Vanity Fair*.

The plot of *Alone At Last* is as follows: An Austrian baron, in order to win the love of an American girl, poses as a Swiss guide. An Austrian count (comic) is being forced by his father to marry the same American girl for her money, although he is really in love with a pretty actress. Which of our native purveyors of tawdry musical comedy would ever have thought of anything so novel and ingenious. Why should we have Viennese opera? We have done nothing to Austria. And now Austria picks on us like this. It isn't right.[18]

The trio helped put that right, creating seven musicals and working together on five more. Of the seven only two were produced at the Princess, *Oh Boy!* and *Oh Lady! Lady!* (Between 1912 and 1919 there were nine Broadway musicals whose title started with the word 'Oh'. Between them Bolton, Wodehouse and Kern were responsible for five of them. As an afterthought the authors called the show they wrote with George Gershwin for Gertrude Lawrence's musical New York debut in 1926, *Oh Kay!*)

What was so new and refreshing about the Princess shows was not only their intimacy, with the audiences drawn into the shows, but Kern's light and fresh music and the Wodehouse lyrics carrying the Bolton story forward in a way not achieved since Gilbert and Sullivan's Savoy operas.

Very Good Eddie, after mixed reviews, turned into a great success running for 341 performances. (A look at the lyrics hints that Wodehouse had improved them from the out-of-town originals, as does the success of the show after lukewarm reviews – but we may never know.) That success meant there was no rush for the new team to write a replacement Princess show. This was lucky as in late 1915 Bolton and Wodehouse were called in by Marc Klaw and Abe Erlanger (who, inappropriately as his first names were Abraham Lincoln, had a Napoleon Bonaparte complex). They then dominated Broadway. Guy and Plum were required to repair the weak book and lyrics of a show called *Pom Pom*, produced by Henry Savage (who was so crooked he could hide at will behind a spiral staircase), ahead of the February New York premier – not something that would happen to a pair of unknowns who had only met each other a few days before. The revised show was a success, perhaps helped by a modest boost from the drama critic of *Vanity Fair*! 'Full of humour. Mizzi Hajos infuses into the performance a brightness and snap that are electrifying'.[19]

Bolton, Wodehouse and Kern wrote only four Princess shows, yet they gave a name to an entire new genre of musical comedy. The four were: *Oh Boy!* (*Oh Joy!* in London) at the Princess; *Leave It To Jane*, a Princess show staged at the Longacre Theatre; *Oh, Lady! Lady!* at the Princess and which Plum turned into a novel *The Small Bachelor*; and *Have A Heart*, properly the first of them, which had been intended for the Princess but was staged at the Liberty Theatre because of the long run of *Very Good Eddie*. The trio also wrote *The Riviera Girl*, a Klaw and Erlanger spectacular, *Miss 1917*, an old style extravaganza (which Bolton and Wodehouse refer to as *The Second Twentieth-Century Show*), *The Rose Of China* which flopped and lastly, in 1924, *Sitting Pretty*. They worked together on *Miss Springtime* and *Sally*, of which theatre historian, Sheridan Morley, says 'It was perhaps *Sally* that could claim to be the first great twenties musical'.[20] At one time the team had five shows running simultaneously on Broadway: *Leave It To Jane*, *The Rose of China*, *The Riviera Girl*, *Miss 1917* and *Oh Boy!*, the last of which ran for a staggering 463 performances (or 475, records vary), cost \$29,262 to produce and made a \$181,641 profit during its New York run. Of its lyrics the critic, Gilbert Seldes, wrote:

> They had the great virtue which Gilbert's lyrics have and which I am told the comic verses of Moliere and Aristophanes also have: they say things as simply as you would say them in common speech, yet they sing perfectly. There is nothing [Wodehouse] wanted to say that he couldn't say to music.[21]

Bolton later said that Wodehouse, although no musician, had a good ear for music and could whistle, accurately, any tune he had ever heard.[22]

Two of the cast of *Oh Boy!*, with their first minor speaking roles, were Marion Davies and Justine Johnstone. Both were very young, very beautiful and very intelligent – but wise enough to look as soft and sweet as candy-floss. Both were so expensively kept that they were above scandal. Miss Johnstone, when told her character was called Polly Andrews promptly asked, 'Is that a play on polyandrous?' Blonde she was but not dumb. Miss Davies was then at the start of her lifelong romance with William Randolph Hearst. Years later, when asked why she didn't join the family at Hearst's funeral, she replied, 'I had him when he was alive. They can have him now he's dead.' Anita Loos based Lorelei and Dorothy of *Gentlemen Prefer Blondes* on them. They became two of Wodehouse's many theatrical friends.

Apart from *The Rose Of China* only *Miss 1917*, (whose rehearsal pianist was a youngster called George Gershwin) with forty-eight performances, ranked as a flop, bankrupting the Century Amusement Corporation in the process.[23] The critics raved about the Bolton, Wodehouse and Kern shows and an anonymous panegyric appeared in the *New York Times* in early February 1918.

> This is the trio of musical fame,
> Bolton and Wodehouse and Kern.
> Better than anyone else I can name,
> Bolton and Wodehouse and Kern.
> Nobody knows what on earth they've been bitten by,
> All I can say is I mean to get lit and buy
> Orchestra seats for the next one that's written by
> Bolton and Wodehouse and Kern.

That has been attributed to George S. Kaufman, Oscar Hammerstein II and to Wodehouse's successor as drama critic of *Vanity Fair*, Dorothy Parker. The magazine's April 1918 issue had two pages of theatre reviews, one by Wodehouse and one by Parker. They both lauded *Oh, Lady! Lady!* (not the performance at Sing Sing with an all-convict cast but the first night on Broadway). Plum wrote:

> And now you will want to hear all about *Oh, Lady! Lady!* at the Princess. Well, it seems pretty nearly all right. Disappointed mobs howl outside the door each night, as they are clubbed away by the police. I wouldn't recommend the piece if I had not a large financial interest in it, but, honestly, you ought to pawn the family jewels and go and see it, if only to reward Guy Bolton and myself for the work we put into it on the road. You wouldn't believe the number of semi-human excrescences who told us during the tour that the show would never 'get over' in New York, and advised us, as friends, to throw away our second act and write an entirely new one.
> And now it is a big success. Well, well! James call up the Rolls Royce offices and order another car for us. Tell them we liked their last one very much.[24]

For Dorothy Parker it was her big chance as the first and only female drama critic in the city. She reviewed five musicals in the pose of a tired businesswoman seeking diversions. Four shows got slammed. She complained that her seat at the Liberty Theatre was practically out in 10th Avenue, reviewed the lady next to her searching for a lost glove, recommended taking your knitting to another show or 'If you don't knit, bring a book' and refused to name the cast at another theatre because 'I'm not going to tell on them'. The fifth show earned her unstinted praise.

Well, Kern, Bolton and Wodehouse have done it again. If you ask me, I will look you fearlessly in the eye and tell you in low, throbbing tones that it has it over any other musical comedy in town. I like the way the action slides casually into the songs. I like the deft rhythms of the song that is always sung in the last act by the two comedians and the comedienne. And oh, how I do like Jerome Kern's music. Every time these three gather together, the Princess Theatre is sold out for months in advance. You can get a seat for *Oh, Lady! Lady!* somewhere around the middle of August for about the price of one on the stock exchange.[25]

That praise was well deserved but there was political calculation in it too. A critic would look silly slamming five shows out of five and boosting *Oh, Lady! Lady!* won approval from both Crowninshield and Wodehouse securing Mrs Parker in that much-coveted job.

Oh, Lady! Lady! was the last Princess show, but the collaboration between Wodehouse and Bolton sealed their friendship for life. Wodehouse, in his introduction to *Gracious Living Limited*, Bolton's only novel, described his friend as never so happy as when seated in front of a typewriter with the telephone switched off and his large collection of animals treading softly as they passed his study door.[26] That might almost have been Bolton writing about Wodehouse, although he actually wrote:

I found working with Plum delightfully easy. I maintained he had a magic typewriter. The story we were writing would run into a road block and we would sit baffled, staring into space.

'We're stuck.'

'No idea?'

'Nary a glimmer.'

'Well, I'll just type out the thing as far as we've got.'

With that he would sit down at his rickety old Royal and his two index fingers would speed over its keys; there, as he pulled out the sheet, would be the solution of the problem which had miraculously come to him as he typed.[27]

Contrariwise, Wodehouse remembers collaborating with Bolton on twenty-one shows, and couldn't recall one of them to which he contributed anything of importance – except a few lyrics. What happened, according to him, was that Bolton would write the thing and he would look in from time to time and say 'How are you getting on?' and Bolton would reply 'All right', Wodehouse would say 'Good. Good.' And 'So little by little the work got done'.[28]

The friendship, unlike that of Gilbert and Sullivan, seldom faltered and lasted until death. As Wodehouse observed, if Guy saw him drowning, he would dive in to the rescue without a moment's hesitation and if he saw Guy drowning he would be the first to call for assistance. Guy's daughter, by his first wife Margaret, was named Pamela (the nearest girls' name to Pelham) in honour of Plum who became her godfather.[29]

Guy Bolton recalled: 'We enjoyed our work together. We planned shows, some of them were written, some went the way of dreams. Those were the days of the gay Kern – Kern at thirty – and the Wodehouse gaiety matched his.'[30] In later life Kern became increasingly arrogant, irascible and egocentric but in the end the partnership faded away for the usual reason – money. Geniuses come in many forms. Wodehouse, built on the large or economy-sized lines, was easy going, cheerful and tolerant. Kern, the neat compact model, jealously guarded his prerogatives of which he took the big, broad view and possessed strong opinions on almost everything. Wodehouse liked money but Kern loved it. When Century Amusement went bust Bolton and Wodehouse were on the creditors' list but one name was missing, Kern's. He had realized too much money had been spent on a show being staged in an unfashionable part of town and that it might not take with the public. So he made sure he got his royalties week by week, but didn't suggest to his friends they do so too. To Kern the obligations of friendship tended to be one-way only.

It was during the successful run of *Oh Boy*, according to Michael Freeland's life of Kern, that Bolton thought the team should be getting more out of the show's success.

'Why don't we get in on these shows,' Guy asked Jerry. 'We should each get at least ten per cent.'

Kern replied, 'I don't know if they'll give it to you. Why not talk to them?'

'No,' said Bolton, 'you talk to them. You're a much better business-man than I am,' and indeed Jerry, who always seemed so self-assured, could not dispute it.

The next day they met again. 'Did you ask him?' Bolton demanded.

'Yes,' Kern replied, 'but they won't do it. They say they can't afford to let thirty per cent out of the show. They've got to give it to the people who are backing them.' As they talked in the empty, dust-sheeted, theatre, the pair were interrupted by the company manager who took Jerry aside and handed him a slip of paper.

'What's that?' Bolton asked the manager.

'Oh, nothing,' he replied. 'Just last night's returns.'

'Why didn't you give them to Plum and me?' asked Bolton, now growing angry. 'I've seen you give them to Jerry twice.'

'Well,' the manager replied, 'Mr Kern has ten per cent of the show. You don't.'[31]

Guy was extremely angry as he and Plum were getting only two and a half per cent of the show each. What hurt most of all was the fact that Kern had kept so quiet about his higher share. Kern then pressured Ray Comstock into giving the authors another two and a half per cent each but his deceitfulness still rankled. Even the pacific Wodehouse told his partner, 'Of course, the bastard's cheated us again'[32] and, led by Guy, the two decided not to work with him any more.

The news devastated Comstock – Bolton, Wodehouse and Kern were the nearest a theatrical producer could get to a guaranteed success. *Leave It To Jane* was already wowing the crowds at the Longacre Theatre and Comstock begged the authors to do another show with Kern. As Wodehouse was not much good at bearing a grudge the three made up and agreed to produce another show together. Guy and Plum left the negotiating to Jerry who secured ten per cent for himself and seven and a half per cent each for the two authors. The result was another hit, *Oh, Lady! Lady!*, from which one song, 'Bill', was dropped during the pre-Broadway tour.

Kern had a habit of saving songs and it was rare for any of his shows not to have something salvaged from earlier days. Later when producer Florenz Zeigfeld heard Ethel Pratt sing 'Bill' at a party on his yacht he wanted it so badly that he talked of building an entire show round it and then of putting it into *Sally*. Wodehouse and Kern were ready to agree but Bolton said 'No' and as he and Wodehouse had an agreement to split their royalties equally on all the books and lyrics produced together, there was no deal. (Zeigfeld was so mean that at his parties, Wodehouse reported, 'The champagne flowed like glue.')[33]

Eventually, ten years later, Kern found just the right vehicle for 'Bill' in perhaps his greatest achievement, *Show Boat*, written with Oscar Hammerstein II, and exactly the right singer in Helen Morgan – who sang it perched on top of a piano. Kern asked Wodehouse if he could use the song in the show and was told he could. The avaricious and venal Kern then told Hammerstein that he, Kern, owned the rights to the whole song. When Bolton and Wodehouse heard what had happened they were furious and, with Bolton handling the lawyers and negotiations, set about getting their dues. It took years. On the copy of a letter from Kern to John Rumsey (Guy and Plum's Hollywood agent) Bolton noted pithily 'As usual several lies'.[34] Finally, in about 1945, Bolton won. Hammerstein's devo-

tees and biographers have been churlish about the lyrics for 'Bill' –
implying their hero had to rewrite Wodehouse's amateur efforts.[35] Hammerstein was not so small a man. Not only did he relinquish all rights to
'Bill' but paid $5,000 in back royalties and wrote in the playbill for the
1946 revival of *Show Boat*:

> I am particularly anxious to point out that the lyric for the song 'Bill'
> was written by P.G. Wodehouse. Although he has always been given
> credit in the program, it has frequently been assumed that since I wrote
> all the other lyrics for *Show Boat*, I also wrote this one, and I have had
> praise for it which belonged to another man.

'Bill' is Wodehouse's most famous lyric, and among the best. As Alec
Wilder wrote:

> The music of the verse does not lead inevitably into the chorus and
> could just as easily have prefaced a different, faster melody. Yet both,
> when combined, have a singularly elusive undercurrent of sadness that
> Wodehouse obviously caught and perpetuated in his lyric. Taken with-
> out the lyric the song is a pleasant minor ballad.[36]

It has always been assumed that the changes to the original lyric of 'Bill'
were by Hammerstein – as in the following example with the original lines
on the left.

But along came Bill,	But along came Bill
Who's quite the opposite	Who's not the type at all
of all the men	You'd meet him in the street
	never notice him.
In story books.	His form and face
In grace and looks	His manly grace
I know that Apollo	Is not the kind that you
Would beat him hollow,	Would find on a statue

However the only evidence that Hammerstein changed the Wodehouse
lyric is one author's assumption that he did so.[37] Benny Green, whose
judgement on popular music is unsurpassed, argues convincingly that
Wodehouse wrote both versions. 'The deft rhyming of "That you" with
"Statue", where the stress is on the first syllable and then following the
logic of the situation and rhyming only the first syllable was something
pioneered by Wodehouse and copied by all the great lyricists who
followed him.'[38]

The last Bolton, Wodehouse and Kern show was *Sitting Pretty*, premiered at New York's Fulton Theatre in April 1924, running for a respectable but unsensational ninety-five performances. But Kern's development also moved them further apart. Benny Green says:

> Kern, for all his originality and erudition, was never quite comfortable with the kind of faster, brighter song which creates the illusion of proceeding of its own volition. Throughout his life he remained preoccupied with the kind of song he could compose best, the romantic ballad which sweeps through two or more tonalities to achieve an almost operatic grandeur. But the bouncing, animated pieces like Gershwin's 'Soon' or Porter's 'Always True To You Baby In My Fashion' or even Donaldson's 'My Baby Just Cares For Me' seem to have been beyond him. And it is precisely these buoyant trifles to which Wodehouse's breezy rhyming mannerisms were best suited. Had Kern not been serving his own apprenticeship in the years of his Wodehouse shows . . . it seems doubtful if he and Wodehouse would have made an effective partnership at all.[39]

Bolton and Kern worked together on one more show, *Brewster's Millions*, but it died on the road before reaching New York. Wodehouse and Bolton also wrote a last Princess show, *Oh My Dear!* with the score by Louis A. Hirsch. His music was so often derivative that it was said 'On a Hirsch first night the audience goes *into* the theatre humming the hits'. *Oh My Dear!* was the first comedy ever to feature a psychiatrist and was a solid hit but it ended an era. The lack of Kern's music was all too obvious. Dorothy Parker wrote: 'The music is so reminiscent that the score rather resembles a medley of last season's popular songs, but it really doesn't make any difference – Mr Wodehouse's lyrics would make anything go.'[40] Just praise. Howard Dietz wrote, 'The lyric writer I most admire [is] P.G. Wodehouse'.[41] Alan Jay Lerner summed up the consensus of all those lyricists for musicals who came after Wodehouse.

> The books [of the Princess Shows] were light and amusing and the music in the popular voice range and Wodehouse wrote lyrics that were appropriate to both: clever graceful and wittily rhymed. Picking up the light verse tradition of W.S. Gilbert, he became the pathfinder for Larry Hart, Cole Porter, Ira Gershwin and everyone else who followed.[42]

Creative artists are not best known for praising their competitors and it indicates the importance of Wodehouse's contribution to the art of the lyric and to his likeability that his successors did so. In a BBC radio interview Ira Gershwin raved about his friend.

Let me tell you about this wonderful, charming man Wodehouse. We collaborated on the lyrics to *Rosalie* for Ziegfeld. We opened in Boston in the big theatre there, I can't think of its name. Anyway, the place was very crowded with Harvard boys, there were a lot of standees and we were overlong in the first act. I'm five feet six or seven and Wodehouse is very tall, and we were watching the show together at the back, but while he could see what was going on I couldn't see anything at all. So he was giving me an account of the proceedings. As I say, we were running overlong, and the first act ended at twenty minutes to eleven and the second act was due to start about ten minutes later. And I felt a tap on my shoulder from Wodehouse. I said 'What is it?' And he reached into his pocket for his Ingersoll watch and said, 'Ira it's eleven o'clock and I must toddle off to bed.' And he left. This is the opening night of his show. Plum was an avid reader, and naturally he wanted to get up early to go to the bookstalls along the Charles River. But I've never heard of anybody leaving his own show on opening night at the start of the second act because he wanted to toddle off to bed.[43]

Toddling off early to bed was not an invariable rule. In 1922 Wodehouse wrote cheerfully to Leonora of the London first night of *The Cabaret Girl* followed by a dinner hosted by novelist E. Phillips Oppenheim and his wife and then a party at the Metropole given by William Boosey. Plum and Ethel didn't get to bed until six in the morning.[44] At the age of sixty-eight Wodehouse took the fiction editor of *Cosmopolitan* to dinner at New York's St Regis hotel, not getting to bed until one in the morning – but all he complained about was the size of the bill. *The Cabaret Girl* was one of two shows on which Wodehouse worked with Kern in the early twenties: the other was *The Beauty Of Bath*. Both were produced by George Grossmith at London's Winter Garden theatre and both were big hits. During the latter show Wodehouse noted the Prince of Wales spending a lot of time hanging around the stage door and thought the press had overdone their boosting of the man, whom he held in low regard long before the rest of the nation.[45]

To the end of his life Wodehouse continued writing lyrics, musicals and comic plays. One of them, *Oh, Kay!*, was based on an adventure of Ethel and Leonora's. When George Grossmith was staying with the Wodehouses at East Hampton, Long Island, he left Plum at home writing and escorted the ladies to a formal dinner at a grand country house. It turned out to be less formal than indicated with all the guests, in full evening dress and ball gowns, helping unload smuggled liquor at Montauk Point – and when his womenfolk told Plum about it he had the bones of the plot for *Oh, Kay!*.[46]

Law abiding Wodehouse had no more use for 'the noble experiment' – Prohibition which lasted in America from 1919 to 1933 – than any other sane person. In later life the evening cocktail became one of the focal points of his day but he was always only a moderate drinker. Throughout the canon there are over a dozen serious and sumptuous menus enthusiastically recalled in detail but apart from Ovens' Home Brewed beer he devotes no loving prose to the matter of drink. Whisky, brandy, champagne, old port and the evening cocktail get walk-on parts but the only starring role is given to the gin which laced Gussie Fink-Nottle's orange juice ahead of the Market Snodsbury Grammar School annual prizegiving. Alec Waugh noted, 'When he lunched with me we shared a bottle of wine. But he did not drink his share of the bottle.' Even so Wodehouse wrote that in Prohibition New York he had to pay the bellhop of the Biltmore Hotel $17 for a bottle of Scotch[47] and his observant satirist's eye caught the hypocrisy of the era perfectly in *Hot Water*. Senator Opal is a rabid supporter of Senator Volstead – he who gave his name to the Act that ushered in Prohibition – and has a million Drys on his voting list but he orders his own private life extremely moistly and is quite ready to fix an ambassadorship for a hopelessly unsuitable man in order to keep his secret.

The theatre-world provided Wodehouse with a host of plots and characters, as did many of the productions with which he was involved. Stories centring on theatrical folk range from Henry Pifield Rice in *Bill The Bloodhound* in 1917 to *Barmy In Wonderland* in 1952 while many of the novels, such as *Jill The Reckless* draw largely on Wodehouse's theatrical experiences.

Novels become plays, *If I Were You* became *Who's Who?* for example, and plays became novels, *Good Morning Bill* becoming *Doctor Sally*. One novel, *Spring Fever*, became a play *Phipps* or *Kilroy Was Here* (written with Bolton but never professionally produced) which then became a different novel, *The Old Reliable!* Starting with writing serials in *The Captain* Wodehouse found the same technique was useful for writing for the theatre – one monthly instalment equals one scene – and he retained it for all his novels even when the demise of *The Strand* and *The Saturday Evening Post* meant that few of his new books were serialized.

Ruth Howard in her biography of her father, the actor Leslie, described Wodehouse simply as 'The plastic surgeon of the theatre'.[48] Wodehouse had a genius for turning other people's turkeys into swans, as he did for Leslie Howard with both *Her Cardboard Lover* and *By Candlelight*. Wodehouse was so confident of his rewriting of *Her Cardboard Lover* that, prior to the first-night, he bought out A.L. Wood's thirty seven and a half per cent of the show for $10,000.[49] A month later he was congratulating himself on his $2,500 a week profit. However Wodehouse appears never to have written a play from scratch. Either he had a co-author, Guy Bolton, George Grossmith, Ian Hay and others, or he used a foreign play, Ferenc Molnar and Ladislas Fodor, or someone else's book or idea. The nearest he got to writing a play himself was *Nothing Serious*, about which little is known as it was not staged in either London or New York, and *The Inside Stand* which was based on his own novel *Hot Water*.

He adapted Molnar's play *The Play's The Thing* from the Hungarian, prompting at least one critic to presume he was fluent in that language. In fact he normally used a bureau translation when working on such plays: all he really needed was their plots.

While Wodehouse was no major playwright, the amount of work he did on straight plays was more than most playwrights get through in a lifetime and the same is true for his lyrics but his short stories and novels, with no co-writers, continued to take up most of his time.

11

SPRING FEVER

I laffed like anything. It was terrific. . . . He's awfully able.
Far abler than any of those highbrows.[1]

Arnold Bennett

THE timelessness of the Wodehouse world makes us forget that
Jeeves first took charge of Bertie over seventy-five years ago in *The
Saturday Evening Post*.[2] Jeeves and Bertie both evolved from the
standard wise servant and foolish master pairing that was a staple of
comedy as far back as the classical age with Virgil writing of Achates and
Aeneas. More recent examples are Sancho Panza and Don Quixote, Sam
Weller and Mr Pickwick, Crichton and the Earl of Loam. In Barrie's case
nature copied art as *The Admirable Crichton* was first staged in 1902 and
then, in 1922, he acquired a new personal servant, Frank Thurston, who
was at ease not only with Latin and Greek but French and Spanish as
well. Lady Cynthia Asquith wrote 'He was puma-footed and nobody ever
heard him leave a room'[3] and called him slightly sinister. Barrie wrote
from Italy, 'The beauty of Venice is almost appalling and so is Thurston's
knowledge of it.'[4] Wodehouse would certainly have met his old cricketing
friend's manservant and so it is probable that Thurston contributed significantly to Jeeves' development. Jeeves had many antecedents but his
name, Wodehouse said, came from the Warwickshire fast-bowler, Percy
Jeeves, who died in Flanders in 1916.

Whereas Aunt Dahlia is simply amoral Jeeves is essentially self-centred.
Bertie's little fads, like the Old Etonian spats, are harmless but the Jeeves
veto always triumphs. Yet the real triumph is Bertie's. He knows that his
enthusiasms – whether for mauve shirts, scarlet cummerbunds or purple
socks – will not last and so he can happily give them up with a false feeling
of noble sacrifice. He enjoys an interesting and varied life. His command
of English is unique, and wonderful. It is Bertie who has kept himself
busy in his free time writing the cycle of books about his adventures.

Jeeves wrote just one story, 'Bertie Changes His Mind',[5] and rightly tried authorship no more. He does not write nearly as well as Bertie who is not the fool popularly supposed. His judgements are invariably shrewd and to the point. Nor is he weak on tactics. Two examples make the point.

Bertie is staying with Mr and Mrs Bingo Little when a ghastly food faddist, Laura Pyke, an old school chum of Mrs Bingo's, arrives for a visit. She sows discord between the Bingeese, Mr and Mrs, by making caustic comments about Bingo's enthusiasm for food. So Jeeves arranges to turn Mrs Bingo against the Pyke by losing the lunch basket at Lakenheath races. He reasons that a lunchless, thus hungry, Mrs Bingo will turn on the Pyke. Foolishly, Jeeves does not consult Bertie in advance and the plan is a wash-out. Bertie points out to Jeeves that women don't mind missing lunch – tea is the meal that matters to them. Having had Bertie's sage advice Jeeves is then able to put the matter right by arranging for Mrs Bingo's car to run out of petrol at tea-time, miles from anywhere. The old school friends duly quarrel and Mr and Mrs Bingo revert to connubial bliss, and hearty meals.[6]

In 'The Inferiority Complex Of Old Sippy' Bertie's friend, Oliver Sipperly, has two problems stemming from a single cause. He lacks the confidence to propose to Miss Gwendoline Moon and to tell his old headmaster to take his tedious articles somewhere other than to his old pupil, now the editor of *The Mayfair Gazette*. Bertie wants to give his chum the confidence to propose to Miss Gwendoline Moon by enabling him to stand up to his bullying old headmaster. Jeeves, however, wants to give Sipperley the confidence to stand up to his old headmaster by enabling him to win Miss Moon. Either plan could equally well succeed. But while Bertie's would involve nothing worse than having the headmaster suffer the mirthful indignity of a flour-bomb, Jeeves' involves knocking Sipperley unconscious with a golf-club and smashing Bertie's new pride and joy, a red Chinese vase which he, Jeeves, dislikes. Fate, in the guise of Mr Wooster's literary agent (as the Sherlockians would say) is, alas, on Jeeves' side, not Bertie's, but Bertie isn't bothered. Although bound by the obligations of a gentleman, he does not wish for adult responsibilities and has shrewdly arranged his life so that he does not have to do so. The *Times Literary Supplement* rightly called him 'That kind, chivalrous and, on the whole, eminently sensible Englishman'.[7] Valid. It was, I think, another private Wodehouse joke that Bertie who passes himself off as an amiable cretin is, in fact, highly intelligent.

The duo had their first book to themselves with *The Inimitable Jeeves* (US *Jeeves*) on 17 May 1923 which is a convenient date from which to begin the glorious springtime of Wodehouse. The years of teaching himself his craft were over. That *annus mirabilis* also saw the publication of one of Wodehouse's finest novels, which we owe to Leonora. She wanted Plum to write another Psmith story and *Leave It To Psmith* was the result with Lord Emsworth, Rupert Baxter and Blandings Castle itself emerging as fully rounded Wodehousian characters. The trouble Wodehouse had – the novel was shortened considerably and there were major changes in the ending between magazine and book publication – is invisible to the reader.

Then for the next half century came a stream of peerless humour. Even his poorer books are only weak compared with his own best and not by comparison with other humorists. In 1921 *The Strand* recognized his status with an unsigned two-page profile in their December issue: 'P.G. wanders happily up and down the world, watching humanity at work and at play, rather like a curious and intelligent boy who has just left school and has not yet had time to lose hope and interest. Where most of us see only gloom and despair and ugliness, P.G. sees humour and laughter and beauty. Hence his popularity.' It was a time of recognition, success and the money that accompanied them.

The next year Gerald Cumberland published a book of pen portraits, *People Worth Talking About*, and described Wodehouse thus.

Foreigners don't – can't – understand our English humour; if they could, Wodehouse's sanity would, no doubt, alleviate the peculiarly crimson madness of the Bolshevists, and sweeten the unpleasant odours made by the ardent disciples of Freud.

He is what the Americans call a 'mixer', hail-fellow-well-met, with barons and bargees, tax collectors and taxi-drivers. His face is kindly and shrewd. When he is amused, the eyes almost vanish in that network of wrinkles possessed by most men who are accustomed to laughter and who lead an open air life. He is devoted to almost all the more violent forms of sport and is specially keen on golfing, swimming and boxing. It is this devotion to sport, a freedom from bookishness, and a liking for the company of quite ordinary people that help to keep him unspoiled. Most successful writing men are marred by a corroding vanity that is only half concealed. Wodehouse is so little aware even of the existence of vanity that he can rarely see it in other people.[8]

Today, people who only knew Wodehouse in old age think describing him as 'a mixer' must be a jest. It is not. Cumberland was a respected critic and journalist, neither a buffoon nor a joker. Calling Wodehouse a hail-fellow-well-met mixer was, then, just factual reporting. Contemporary comments about Wodehouse and his own unedited letters of the period give support to the Cumberland view rather than Wodehouse's post-war image of himself. In all the hundreds of Wodehouse letters I have read I have not found one prior to the publication of *Performing Flea* in 1953 where he expresses real dissatisfaction at going to social functions. For example, when Heather Thatcher came to Hollywood the Wodehouses gave a party for her in their garden at Benedict Canyon. In a letter to Townend in *Performing Flea* Wodehouse said 'I found [it] rather loathsome, as it seemed to pollute our nice garden.' That sentence is not in the original letter of 19 May 1931 which shows that Plum enjoyed the party – even though he did sneak away to his room to get on with his writing. Just once in a while he complains about lunches and dinners at home taking up too much time that could be better devoted to writing, that's all. When he didn't want to go to a function he didn't go. Even Ethel's parties at home in Norfolk Street in London and at Benedict Canyon in Hollywood caused him only mild irritation. He simply made as long or as short an appearance as he wished then retreated to his study and continued writing. Wodehouse had impeccable manners and would rather listen than talk – which is an ideal recipe for social success.

Success, and a wife to look after him and his domestic affairs, meant Wodehouse's writing could take increasingly more of his time. In 1921 at the age of forty his life was settling down to a pattern – if you can call frequent travels across the Atlantic and living in one rented house after another in France, America and England 'settled'.

Wodehouse was usually writing a novel which would be serialized in both UK and US periodicals – normally *The Strand* in the UK and *The Saturday Evening Post*, *Liberty*, *Cosmopolitan* or *Colliers* in the US – and then come out as a book both sides of the Atlantic. At the same time he worked on one or more short stories, which were put through the same publishing formula, and was simultaneously polishing up somebody else's inadequate play and writing the lyrics, and assisting with the book, for a musical.

To fill in the barren hours left by such a lax schedule there was the long daily walk, theatre visits, occasional race meetings, writing letters to friends and family, spending time with Leonora, giving the host of Wodehouse cats and dogs their daily doses of affection, making appearances at Ethel's parties with good grace and trips to watch Dulwich play cricket and rugby. When he went to Dulwich he always declined lunch in the pavilion and went instead to a pub, the Alleyn's Head, on the far side of Alleyn's Park, and for a typically Plummish reason. The Crown and the Greyhound were then opposite each other in Dulwich Village and he could never decide which one to choose.[9] While still a cricket reporter, Wodehouse had given up playing the game for golf.

Plum's unique brand of golf was described by thriller writer E. Phillips Oppenheim in *The Pool of Memory*.

Plum Wodehouse's golf was, and would be still I expect if he had a chance to play, of a curious fashion. He had only one idea in mind when he took up his stance on the tee, and that idea was length. He was almost inattentive when his caddie pointed out the line he ought to take or the actual whereabouts of the next hole, but he went for the ball with one of the most comprehensive and vigorous swings I have ever seen. I am certain that I saw him hit a ball once at Woking which was the longest shot I have ever seen in my life without any trace of a following wind.

'You will never see that again,' I remarked, after my first gasp of astonishment, mingled, I am afraid I must confess, with a certain amount of malevolent pleasure as the ball disappeared in the bosom of a huge clump of gorse.

'I wonder how far it was,' was the wistful reply.

Well, the Wodehouses were spending the week-end, and I noticed after we arrived at the club-house on the conclusion of our round a mysterious conversation going on between P.G. and his caddie. Late in the evening, the caddie was ushered into my garden. He produced a ball and handed it over.

'Found it half an hour ago, I did, sir,' he remarked.

'And did you put the stick in?' P.G. asked eagerly.

'Right where the ball lay to an inch, sir.'

'Got the distance?'

'Three hundred and forty-three yards, sir,' the caddie replied promptly.

There was a glow of happiness in P.G.'s expression. He dragged me down to see where the ball had been found and checked the distance going back. Then he filled a pipe and was very happy.

'Beaten my own record by five yards,' he confided with a grin.

'But listen,' I pointed out, 'how many matches do you win?'

'I never win a match,' was the prompt reply. 'I spend my golfing life out of bounds. I never even count my strokes. I know that I can never beat anyone who putts along down the middle. All the same I get more fun out of my golf than any other man I know when I am hitting my drives.'

'Isn't it a little expensive?' I asked him meaningly.

He produced the pound note we had played for with a smile.

'It's worth it, Opp,' he assured me gently.

A great fellow, P.G.[10]

Again Wodehouse was being unduly modest. In 1938 he had a handicap of only thirteen, rather good for an amateur aged fifty-seven.[11] The golf stories are fine examples of 'Frame stories' (as are those of Mr Mulliner) where the author provides a first-person narrator. The Oldest Member is a talented raconteur and we never pause to wonder why his listeners always try to escape from his glittering eye instead of hanging on his words. All I know of golf comes from reading *The Clicking Of Cuthbert* and *The Heart Of A Goof.* Typically they involve golf as the arena which decides all matters of great moment, whether in affairs of the heart or the enjoyment of prized butlers. Golf is the great purifying force that makes real men out of such dross as poets. Rodney Spelvin would produce a slim volume bound in squashy mauve leather at the drop of a hat, mostly about sunsets and pixies, but through aspiring to the love of a good woman, that is one who is a keen golfer, he turns to writing wholesome blood-and-thunder detective stories, churning out his 2,500 words a day before breakfast to leave himself free for the usual fifty-six holes of golf a day.[12] Most of these stories were written in the 1920s when the athletic Wodehouse had switched from cricket to golf. He was never a great golfer but he did win one trophy, a striped umbrella, at a hotel tournament in Aiken, South Carolina, by going through some of the fattest retired businessmen in America like a devouring flame.[13]

George Grossmith remembers Wodehouse from those days, in his autobiography, *"GG"*. The two friends were travelling to New York on the *SS Aquitania* and working on the book and lyrics of *The Cabaret Girl*, for which Kern, at home in Bronxville, was providing the music.

> Our work proceeded admirably. 'PG' has the faculty of transmitting his fertile humour directly and rapidly to paper by means of a typewriter worked by his own fingers. He allows nothing to distract him.[14]

Grossmith was a great comic actor. 'He is the man to whom Max Beerbohm has conceded his willingness to raise a national monument because "he has raised banality to the sublime".'[15] He made his name playing plausible fools to perfection and in such a way that audiences liked the character, who was usually admirable and came across with unexpected flashes of common sense and perception. No wonder that he and another stage dude, Ralph Lynn, helped Wodehouse evolve Bertie from the rather blah young man of *My Man Jeeves* to the unique and finished character of such masterpieces as *The Code Of The Woosters*. It is Grossmith who reveals that the soloist of 'Hybrias The Cretan' was still prepared, a quarter of a century later, to wow them in the stalls, or to try to, agreeing to give a reading at the *Aquitania* ship's concert.

To the reader had been left the choice of material.

'Give them something short and fitting,' I recommended to him. 'You're the last turn. Make it snappy. The audience want to dance or get back to the smoke-room.'

I thought Plummy looked a little hurt. They had asked for a taste of his work and they should have a mouthful, and like it.

Blushingly he mounted the rostrum to the plaudits of the multitude. A music stand had been supplied on which to place his reading matter. The latter, I fully expected, would bear some battered copy of the *Strand Magazine*, to whose fame he had chiefly contributed since the ultimate demise of Sherlock Holmes. But nothing less heavy did our lecturer produce than a new copy of his latest full-blooded novel of 90,000 words, and solemnly he started at Chapter One. At least so it appeared, for the mumbling commenced immediately he had turned over the left hand cover and two fly-leaves. I couldn't hear very well, being in the second row. But after twenty minutes or so some of the front-row occupants, feeling the need of a little air, crept out less noisily than those at the back and I moved up.

Plummy, quite oblivious to any restlessness amongst his hearers – the word is poorly chosen – was enjoying himself immensely. Although the text proper escaped me, I caught several interjections that the reader made from time to time: mm-m-er-z-z-z- mumble-z-z-mm . . . by jove that's good! I'd no idea . . . mm-z-zzz-mm-mmm . . . devilish funny, I'd forgotten that bit . . . mmm-z-z-mumble.

The National Anthem may have provided an interruption or an obligato. I never learnt, for already I was adding up the first rubber.[16]

Grossmith exaggerated, no memoirs by a creative artist are trustworthy but in essence the story is true. Those many transatlantic crossings were mostly taken up with work, but that included gathering material and ideas. One book, *The Luck Of The Bodkins*, is set almost entirely on the *RMS Atlantic* and is dominated by that fabulous film-star, Miss Lotus Blossom (née Murphy, one of the Hoboken Murphys). Blossom was the name of a prima donna magazine editor whom Wodehouse disliked. Arthur Ransome, author of the well loved *Swallows And Amazons* books named his new boat *Lottie Blossom* after her in 1952. Another character in that book is the doleful steward, Albert Eustace Peasemarsh. The deadpan dedication in William Townend's *The Top Landing* is simply 'To Albert Peasemarsh, Prince among Stewards, with Admiration and Respect. W.T.'. Wodehouse, with his love of private jokes, must have gained particular pleasure from that.

Grossmith and Wodehouse wrote the book of a musical, *The Three*

Musketeers, for Flo Ziegfeld and Plum had also written the lyrics. Ziegfeld then said their script was no good and he was calling in Bill McGuire to write an entirely new book based on Alexander Dumas' out-of-copyright material. McGuire, probably in on the scam, then made some minor changes to the Grossmith-Wodehouse script and Ziegfeld refused to pay the authors anything. Ten months of increasingly bitter correspondence between Grossmith, Wodehouse, Ziegfeld, the Society of Authors in the UK and the American Dramatists Society then followed. Wodehouse wasn't very bothered about the matter for he had done a good deal with Ziegfeld on the lyrics. Eventually, it appears, Grossmith lost his case because, being an actor, he could not guarantee to be present at proposed binding-arbitration hearings. He felt Plum had behaved badly, letting him down, and the two never co-operated again.[17] When Wodehouse felt he had a strong case he would fight to the end for the last cent. When his case was uncertain he cast it from his mind and went on to other, income-earning, projects. Wodehouse, for perhaps the first time in his life, lost a friend but he had many others.

For a man who has been called shy, a recluse, socially inept and every synonym short of misanthropic, Wodehouse had an inconsistently large number of friends. In the 1910s, 1920s and 1930s, these included Robert Benchley, Guy Bolton, Leslie Bradshaw, Nigel Bruce and his wife with whom the Wodehouses spent Christmas in 1936, the Cazalet family, Frank Crowninshield, Bea Davis (also a close friend of Leonora), golfing companion Jack Donaldson, Sir Arthur Conan Doyle, lyricist Ira Gershwin (brother of composer George), Charles Graves, *Strand* editor H. Greenhough Smith, George Grossmith, Ian Hay, the Earl of Ilchester (Chairman of The Royal Literary Fund), and his Countess who contributed much to developing the character of Bertie's Aunt Dahlia. The list continues: Herbert Jenkins, Justine Johnstone and her husband Walter Wagner, playwright George S. Kaufman, Nesbitt Kemp from his banking days, Jerome Kern, Baldwin King-Hall, distant cousins Charles and Bernard Le Strange, playwright Freddy Lonsdale, Denis Mackail, novelist W.B. Maxwell, A.A. Milne, E. Phillips Oppenheim and his wife Elsie, film star Maureen O'Sullivan and her husband John Farrow, Paul R. Reynolds Sr., Sir Owen Seaman, actress Heather Thatcher who appeared in several Wodehouse plays, librettist Fred Thompson, Norman Thwaites, Bill Townend and his wife Rene. Also there was Edgar Wallace who dedicated two of his books – *A King By Night* and *The Gaunt Stranger* – 'To my friend P.G. Wodehouse' – and writer Alec Waugh. There are scores more, mostly unmentioned in books on Wodehouse, who make solo and unexpected appearances, such as Arthur Thompson, a solicitor's clerk in Teignmouth, who first met Wodehouse in Exeter in 1913 and seldom thereafter, yet the two remained firm friends through the post for over forty years. Lord Newborough wrote to *The Daily Telegraph* about Wodehouse in 1941 'As a very old friend' (they met through E. Phillips Oppenheim). The actor Peter Haddon was grateful when 'My old friend Plum' insisted that he play the leading men in a series of Hollywood stories that Wodehouse sold to the BBC for radio in the thirties. In 1944 Wodehouse was pleased at receiving cards of good wishes from many friends in England including 'Slacker' Christison, for forty years Secretary of the OAs, C.T. Rees another OA, Paddy Miller, et cetera. He also had a vast number of business friends from the theatre and writing worlds as well as many friendly acquaintances. One of them was 'Handsome Jack' Lord Wodehouse, his third cousin twice removed, the great polo player and later third Earl of Kimberley (although Wodehouse was not, as sometimes reported, godfather to his only son, the fourth Earl).[18] On one transatlantic liner a lady asked George Grossmith if his friend was the famous Wodehouse to which 'GG' replied he was. 'And has he brought his polo ponies with him?' continued the lady.[19] Wodehouse enjoyed the story but he never told it: one doesn't flaunt one's noble relatives. Instead he gave it a little tinkering and polishing, restaging it at a Hollywood dinner party with the gushing admirer sitting next to him concluding, 'And when I go home tonight and tell them I have actually been sitting at dinner next to Mr Edgar Wallace, I don't know what they will say.'[20] Handsome Jack was, for two years, secretary to a Winston Churchill (a similar fate almost befell Bertie Wooster) and his father, the second Earl, was straight out of a Wodehouse story – or perhaps the other way around.

After his wife's death the second earl became a recluse, locking himself away in Kimberley and allowing no visitors. Eventually he had to go to London to visit a doctor and, arriving at the station just in time to miss his train, hurled a turnip at the station clock, smashing it, and returned to Kimberley. Later, in hospital, regaining consciousness after an operation he saw a pretty nurse, instructed her 'Take your clothes off' and expired. When his executors travelled to Kimberley they found the reason for his secluded life. The house contained a seraglio of mistresses and their offspring, all living together in perfect harmony.[21]

Biographies and memoirs of the period, as well as his own letters, are littered with references to Wodehouse attending lunches and dinners, mainly literary in tone, and entertaining friends at home or going to stay with them. They show that from his time at the bank until the later thirties, when he and Ethel had settled at Le Touquet on the north coast of France, he was a gregarious man. The following are a few incidents from scores. At home in London he entertained Michael Arlen, W.B. Maxwell and H.G. Wells. At Rogate Lodge on just one weekend John

Galsworthy came to lunch while Leslie Howard and Ian Hay were house guests. Wodehouse dined at H.G. Wells' London home meeting Arnold Bennett, Bernard Shaw, John Drinkwater, Augustine Birrell and other writers. He, Ethel and Leonora lunched with his US publisher, George Doran, at the Savoy, meeting a host of other authors. He was on book-swapping terms with W.J. Locke. He and Ethel lunched with the Randolph Churchills in London and the Edward G. Robinsons and Douglas Fairbanks and his wife Mary Pickford in Hollywood. At 'Pickfair' Plum spent most of the evening talking to his hostess and was impressed by her high intelligence. Aunt Mary must have been jealous – one of her most lyrical poems was about Miss Pickford.[22]

Wodehouse was not only a writer but a playwright as well and his long entry in the *Theatrical Who's Who* (1938) lists his numerous theatrical achievements and ends lightly 'Has also written over fifty books'. One of his stage successes, *A Damsel In Distress*, was adapted with Ian Hay from Plum's novel. Hay, A.A. Milne, the theatre management and Wodehouse himself each put up £500 to finance the production and all did well out of it.[23]

Wodehouse met many of his friends at his clubs. The idea has become accepted that Wodehouse hated clubs. 'Friends in England used to put him up for their clubs and other members, thinking "Wodehouse . . . yes . . . he'll keep us in stitches of laughter", supported his candidacy and he was elected; and in weeks rather than months, he would resign politely.' Thus the orthodox litany, but the evidence we have for this is from the usual unreliable source, Wodehouse himself, and a story of Denis Mackail's in his paean to Pekes, *Life With Topsy*. At the London Zoo in Regent's Park, run by the Zoological Society the fellows had their own excellent restaurant. Mackail took Wodehouse there to lunch one day and, as they smoked on the members' lawn afterwards, Plum, fired with enthusiasm, wanted to become a member too. This was arranged and he was elected but he lost his enthusiasm as rapidly as he gained it, never paid his subscription nor answered the secretary's letters – according to Mackail.[24] Undermining that story is the fact that the courteous Wodehouse always replied to letters. However he did make the noxious Percy Pilbeam a Fellow of the Royal (*sic*) Zoological Society in *Summer Lighting*.

Wodehouse in his introduction to *Leather Armchairs*,[25] his friend Charles Graves' book on London's 'Gentlemen's Clubs' (a legal rather than a snobbish term) gently mocked himself with a claimed weakness of character that made him unable to deny friends who wanted to propose him for their clubs and then 'All the weary business of resigning'. That contribution to the Wodehouse myth was written from Remsenburg in 1963.

At least two commentators have been puzzled upon discovering that Wodehouse remained a member of one of his clubs for many years. The answer is that Wodehouse on Wodehouse is fiction. He remained a member of all his clubs, bar one, for decades. Even the Garrick, that conversationalists' club which he later called 'the pest hole', enjoyed his membership for eight years. He was elected on 2 March 1922, proposed by his nearby neighbour in Walton Street, Colonel Vernor Chater and seconded by George Grossmith.[26] In those days he liked the club well enough to use it as his London address for the Society of Authors (who wrote to him there about the Czech royalties on *Jill The Reckless*) and to propose his friend Denis Mackail for membership (seconded by A.A. Milne). He used it for business and friendly lunches with such colleagues as George Grossmith and also ate there when in London on his own. On one such occasion he sat with a fellow member who recorded in his diary, 'I sat next to a man I thought was charming [and] because he was humble I was patronizing. When I left I casually asked the head waiter who the gentleman was I had been sitting next to. "Mr P.G. Wodehouse." I wish I had been nicer.'[27] The diarist was Alfred Duff Cooper who was to have further opportunities to be nicer to Wodehouse twelve years later but instead preferred to be nasty.

Wodehouse became a member of The Savage on the same day as the Garrick.[28] He was proposed by H. Greenhough Smith and seconded by F. Britten Austin the novelist and by Reeve Shaw, an executive with the George Newnes publishing group. The Savage was very much a club for writers and artists, mostly rampant individualists, and the sort of place where throwing bread rolls at a fellow diner would cause no comment other than a return volley. The Savage is the one Wodehouse club which has never been mentioned by those who thought Wodehouse only joined clubs in order to resign from them – and it is the only real club that supports the thesis. On 3 December 1929 he wrote to the secretary: 'I find I have not been in the club since my election several years ago. I think, therefore, that it would be more satisfactory if I were to retire and make way for someone on the waiting list. I should be glad if you would accept my resignation to take effect at the end of the year.'

He also enjoyed the vast, cavernous, anonymity of the Constitutional Club on Northumberland Avenue in London – affectionately putting it into his books as the Senior Conservative Club – and was a member from at least 1908 when he first entered *Who's Who*. He was a member of the Beefsteak from January 1926 – proposed by his friend W.B. Maxwell and seconded by George Grossmith and Ian Hay. Among the dozen other members who signed the book in support of his candidature were Hugh Walpole and Owen Seaman. Wodehouse also ate at the Beefsteak when

Ethel was away. There he met and talked with other writers including one
of his great idols, Kipling. 'Tell me Wodehouse, how do you finish your
stories? I can never think how to end mine.'[29] The reply is not recorded.
Wodehouse also met Kipling at Fairlawne, the Kent house of his friends
William and Molly Cazalet. Kipling and Wodehouse kept up a lively
correspondence and Wodehouse promised Townend to bequeath him
Kipling's letters (which have now disappeared) – a valuable legacy, but
Townend died first.

Wodehouse remained a member of the Beefsteak and the Constitutional until well after the Second World War, resigning only when it was
clear he was unlikely ever to visit London again.

In 1930 he was elected a member of The Other Club and, far from
resigning soon thereafter, remained a member until his death which
indicates that he held it in strong affection and had enjoyed attending its
dinners before the war. The club was founded in May 1911 by that great
lawyer, F.E. Smith (later first Earl of Birkenhead and Lord Chancellor)
and by Winston Churchill as a rival to 'The Club' set up by Dr Samuel
Johnson and Sir Joshua Reynolds in 1764 which was still going strongly
but was apolitical. The Other Club was, and is, a mainly political dining
club for powerful people from what we now call The Establishment.
Membership is limited, highly exclusive and by invitation only, although in
practice the sole qualification for membership at that time was that Smith
or Churchill felt a candidate would be an amusing dinner companion.[30]
As many of Smith's and Churchill's close friends were never invited to
join the only possible conclusion is that Wodehouse, in a milieu he
enjoyed, was an amusing dinner companion. Cooper, the patronizing
diner, was also a member. As with all good clubs new members have to be
well known to both their proposer and seconder. Wodehouse was proposed by Birkenhead and seconded by Sir Anthony Hope Hawkins – as
Anthony Hope the author of that prim and witty masterpiece of Victorian
innuendo *The Dolly Dialogues* but better known for his splendid Ruritanian
pot-boiler, *The Prisoner of Zenda*. It is unsurprising that Wodehouse knew
Hope, another *Strand* stalwart, but how did he first meet Birkenhead? At
one of their early meetings Wodehouse tried to talk to Smith about
politics, to no avail, but when he asked the great lawyer why he didn't get
his rugger blue at Oxford he got a twenty minute answer '. . . giving me no
chance to tell him what I did to Haileybury in 1899'.[31]

Before the First World War young Wodehouse enjoyed going to the
boisterous dinners of the now defunct Dramatists Club of which he was a
member and also belonged to the similarly defunct Yorick club. In the
thirties he had many friends at Bucks (Guy Bolton was elected a member

in 1933) and he was there so often that Evelyn Waugh thought he was a member. In New York he was for decades a member of the Lotus Club and, from 1923 until his death, a member of the Coffee House Club. Old members still tell the new of the days when Wodehouse was discreetly told that other members disliked his habit of having a dog on his lap when lunching at the club. This so incensed him that the next time he ate there he brought a guest along – and both of them had lunch with their dogs on their laps.[32] Wodehouse also belonged to a number of golf clubs including the Stage Golfing Club; as sociable a group of golfers as the Allahakbarries had been sociable cricketers.

Clearly Wodehouse was as clubbable as was usual for men of his period and class even though he told Usborne, much later, that he hated them all.[33] He also shortened his eight years membership of the Garrick, made it a general rule and turned it into a good introduction to a friend's book. It did not reflect the facts but it helped create Wodehouse's desired image of himself.

He also belonged to other sociable organizations, including the Freemasons. On mainland Europe the Masons have a reputation for being involved in all sorts of strange and dark rituals. In England they are a mutual benefit society for the senior business and professional classes and involved in a lot of charity work, largely for each other. 'So kind to our rich and to their poor', not that there are many poor Masons. The fraternity claims it is not, as often alleged, 'A secret society' but 'A society with secrets'. So what went on in Lodge meetings, including the names of members, used to be wrapped in impenetrable mystery – and Wodehouse always abided by the rules even if most of his heroes and heroines made up their own. In fact Lodge meetings are mostly taken up with significant rituals stretching back into the mists of history (or, some say, juvenile charades), good dinners and business deals. Masons noting the occasional use of Masonic phrases in Wodehouse's writing tend not to mention the fact while non-Masons are unlikely to notice them. I have found only two, but there will be more. Gally Threepwood, conspiring with Beach, says 'The meeting is tiled',[34] a Masonic expression meaning confidential. And in a letter to Bolton, expressing fury at post-war restrictions on moving money from one country to another, Wodehouse uses another Masonic phrase 'Oh, Architect of the Universe' and longs for the days when he could win a couple of hundred thousand francs at Monte Carlo, ship it straight over to his London bank account and then take it over to New York if he wanted to.[35] For long Wodehouse's Masonry has been subject to much ill-informed speculation. In fact he was a member of an old and distinguished Lodge, the Jerusalem Lodge Number 197 in London, of which the reformer John Wilkes and the actor Sir Henry Irving were

among other notable members. Wodehouse was 'initiated' on 22 March
1929, 'passed' on 26 April and 'raised' on 22 November that year. His
friends Ian Hay Beith and Rafael Sabatini were members, as was his
friend Roland Pertwee, the author ('raised' the next year) and his cousin
Henry James Deane. Wodehouse resigned from the Masons on 10
November 1934.[36] It is unlikely that Wodehouse took Masonic ceremo-
nies with the required seriousness and, anyway, they cut into his writing
time.

In 1929 Wodehouse was elected to the management committee of the
Society Of Authors, whose chairman at the time, Lord Gorell, remembered his amiability at meetings.[37] Wodehouse's move to Hollywood cut
short that appointment. In 1939 he was elected to the Council of the
Society (which, when Thomas Hardy died, put on its writing-paper 'President: the late Thomas Hardy, OM').[38]

Sometimes the sociable Wodehouse would dine young writers at one of
his clubs. He and Ethel had a habit of sending invitations to lunch or
dinner to those whose books impressed him. Two of the many were Alec
Waugh and Denis Mackail the authorized biographer of his friend J.M.
Barrie. Neither of these neophytes had met Wodehouse before. Mackail
had just written *What Next?* and received a letter of praise from Wodehouse and, a little later, an invitation to dine. They met at one of Wodehouse's clubs and then went on to the Savoy Grill and:

> There he provided a considerable banquet and immediately started
> talking about writing without a moment's delay. For this – apart from
> Pekes, and cricket and football matches at his old school with which he
> also seemed obsessed – was his own great unending topic; and at all the
> evenings that we have spent together I can't remember him ever linger-
> ing, for more than a few seconds, on anything else.[39]

It was the start of a lifelong friendship. The uxorious Mackail usually
dedicated his books to his wife Diana or to his dogs but made an exception dedicating *How Amusing* 'To Plum, but for whom'. Wodehouse had
also admired Alec Waugh's *The Loom Of Youth*. So Ethel invited Waugh to
lunch.[40] Waugh and Wodehouse had one distinction in common, they had
both enjoyed their time at public school; more usually they were both keen
cricketers. A friendship sprang up that cheerfully survived twenty-five
years without a single meeting.

Established writers such as John Galsworthy, Arnold Bennett, Hugh
Walpole and Hilaire Belloc enjoyed the Wodehouses' hospitality. The
Australian writer John Farrow, later to marry Maureen O'Sullivan,

lunched at Norfolk Street which he and Hilaire Belloc left at the same time.

> He [Belloc] looked at my hat (bowler), umbrella (correctly furled), gloves and carnation (of the correct hue). 'So you wish to write?' he said in something resembling a growl. 'Yes, Sir,' I replied. 'Get rid of those things,' he said, pointing to the uniform just mentioned, 'and get back to the sea.' 'But I wish to write, Sir,' I replied. 'What better place to write than on a ship?' was his answer. And then as an afterthought. 'Conrad left too soon.'[41]

In old age Belloc became increasingly reclusive.

> His reading now consisted entirely of *The Diary Of A Nobody*, his own works and the novels of P.G. Wodehouse, which he would read with the satisfied intentness of an old priest poring over his breviary. . . . Sometimes he would mutter 'Admirable, admirable' at its perfection of phrasing. As he did so mice scampered on the coverlet of his bed and nibbled excitedly at the pockets of his scruffy camel-hair dressing gown, spread out over the bedclothes, thick with appetisingly stale crumbs.[42]

There were other authors who received such invitations and that is hardly the behaviour of a recluse; although Wodehouse did prefer meeting people one at a time, which is why he didn't care for parties. But he was not socially inept, except to those expecting a free vaudeville act from him. Beverley Nichols, a 'Bright Young Thing', wrote of Wodehouse in *Are They The Same At Home?*, a collection of pen-portraits commissioned by a newspaper, the London *Sketch*. Nichols thought it must be dreadful to have a reputation as a great humorist and was sure Wodehouse shared that view. The two first met at a House of Commons lunch where Nichols noted that whenever Plum opened his mouth the faces of the politicians seated round him prepared to twitch up into set smiles, as if saying to themselves '*Now* he's going to begin'. But Plum did not begin, behaving like an ordinary human being instead, and the politicians looked as if they felt cheated.[43] Nichols found that even though Wodehouse did not make jokes he was excellent company, radiating charm, and that, best of all, he did not talk about himself.

Other people did talk about him. Augustus Muir, writing that same year in *The Strand* caught more of the dichotomy of the man than most. 'A kindly, easy, matey, shy sort of chap. . . . A man with an eager gusto for friendship.'[44] 'Shy'? Yes. 'Matey, . . . with an eager gusto for friendship'? Certainly. Muir was as responsible and respected a journalist as Gerald Cumberland quoted earlier.

Nichols and Wodehouse were once in a party that went to the London Zoo where, Nichols tells us, Plum had a passionate desire to see the snakes, which was frustrated by the rest of the group. Whenever Plum asked after the snakes his friends drew his attention to the charms of other fauna, such as the antelopes. Wodehouse would dutifully look at the antelopes and admire them but Nichols felt that Wodehouse, in his heart of hearts, cherished a fierce resentment against those antelopes, just because they were not snakes.[45]

Wodehouse loved all animals, not excluding snakes who have frequent walk-on parts in the opus and are always sympathetically cast. Polly Lady Wetherby has a pet snake, Clarence, in *Uneasy Money* (back in 1916) and Leila York's husband owned a menagerie of snakes, inherited from his mother Herpina The Snake Queen, nearly half a century later in *Ice In The Bedroom*. Other serpentine characters occur regularly in between. The Revd Mr Deane might not have approved of a serpentophile grandson!

Wodehouse had a similar interest in parrots, which goes back even further. In 1903 in the *Daily Express*, three years after it was founded by C. Arthur Pearson 'The Champion Hustler of the Tariff Reform League', Wodehouse wrote a series of poems on their front page which concerned a parrot who capped all discussion about the matter of tariff reform with the satirical cry 'Your food will cost you more'. The verses were topical, witty and followed the paper's editorial line. These verses are another example of Wodehouse the political observer although to him they were almost certainly a job of paid work rather than an expression of his own views. But there's no doubt he liked parrots. For many years he and Ethel owned one. Writing to Townend in early 1920 he told him that the family were sailing on the *Adriatic* on 24 April with Ethel carrying the black kitten, followed by himself with parrot in a cage and Loretta, their maid, with any other animals they might have acquired in the meantime.[46] Given the longevity of parrots it could have been the same bird, Coco, that Ethel had to leave with friends in 1940 – but it is more likely this was the boarder belonging to their Le Touquet neighbour, the Countess of Dudley (the actress Gertie Millar). When their house was occupied by German officers the bird was a great hit with them for its rendering of *God Save The King*.[47] Parrots in the Wodehouse canon have similar friendly supporting roles to snakes, from Polly in 'The Man Who Disliked Cats' (in *The Man Upstairs*) to *Plum Pie*, but the most famous is anonymous – the innocent bird at Mitching Hill who narrowly escapes being vetted by Pongo Twistleton-Twistleton and Frederick Altamont Cornwallis Twistleton, fifth earl of Ickenham – who makes his debut as a Wodehouse classic, a sort of elderly Psmith, in 'Uncle Fred Flits By' from *Young Men In Spats*.

Even in Wodehouse's parrot days, with so much of his best work still to come, he was called 'Our national humorist' and he enjoyed the role. Nobody ever called Wodehouse vain but recognition of his writing was as sweet to him as to any other author. He did as was expected of him, even giving that interview to Nichols, a man so insouciantly homosexual that Wodehouse took a mild dislike to him. Once he wrote to Townend: 'Can you imagine giving lunch to celebrate the publication of a book? With the other authors, mostly fairies, twittering all over the place, screaming "Oh Lionel!" '[48] In the theatre-world he met many gay men and it never bothered him – so long as it wasn't flaunted.

Little did bother him, least of all that he was gaining a reputation for mild eccentricity. When visiting Leonora at school in Bromley on the Kent edge of London he often cycled there and would hide himself and his bike in the bushes to await his daughter. This, combined with a white handkerchief tied with four knots at the corners to protect his bald pate from the sun, caused great mirth amongst Leonora's fellow pupils even after she explained that Plum was frightened of the headmistress, Miss Starbuck.[49] Readers brought up under the beneficent protection of Dr Spock may find that funny. Anyone who was educated in a pre-war English school with a headmistress out of the Gilkes mould will feel an echo of understanding for Plum's tactics. Miss Starbuck was the inspiration for all those fearsome headmistresses, the Misses Maitland, Mapleton, Tomlinson and Dame Daphne Winkworth, in the Wodehouse opus.

Similarly if Wodehouse saw someone coming during his long afternoon walks, where often he would be laughing loudly for no apparent reason, he would pop behind a tree until they had gone by. Given his shortsightedness, other walkers got Wodehouse in clear view well before he saw them. There is a simple explanation. That perfect prose, that seamless plotting and those unique characters did not come straight from his mind onto the typewriter. They were thought out on his long walks and interruption would have broken the threads of composition.

Frances Donaldson recalls arriving with her father at Norfolk Street for one of Ethel's parties. The door was answered by Wodehouse who, seeing two friends, said, 'Don't come in. You'll hate it.' To me that shows only a dislike of big parties. Frances Donaldson also wrote, 'He thinks of himself as very shy, but that quality takes on a far more determined and complex character than it does in most other people.'[50] Exactly. Another example, told by Leonora, is of the time Wodehouse, in order to evade an invitation, told a lady reporter that he had to go to Georgia. So he went to Georgia.[57] Wodehouse, who would twist the truth as if plasticine when it came to his writing, was, in private, so truthful he even hated telling those white lies which are essential for a harmonious social life.

As an ex-journalist himself he was tolerant of the tribe, writing:

If an interviewer says to you 'What do you think of our high buildings?' and you reply 'I think your high buildings are wonderful' and it comes out as 'I think your high buildings are wonderful. I'd like to see some of those income tax guys jump off the top of them' no harm is done. The sentiment pleases the general public, and even the officials in the Internal Revenue Department probably smile indulgently, as men who know they are going to have the last laugh.[52]

So knowing the game his rule with interviewing reporters (which he was to forget on one memorable occasion) was to treat them as if they were writing fiction – a view which will make many other celebrities wince in sympathy – and invented stories for them. It was a shrewd approach by an old hand as, by making up stories about yourself, you avoid the nasty surprises when the interviewer goes away and does it for you.

On one of the many trips the family made across the Atlantic they arrived at Southampton from America and Wodehouse decided to visit friends at Emsworth, told Ethel so and simply did the Wodehouse Glide. Ethel ran his life just to the extent that he liked her to, and no more. Throughout his correspondence there is no example of Ethel ever preventing her husband from doing what he was determined to do nor of her ever forcing him to do anything he was determined not to do. The nearest he ever gets to it is wishing Ethel would agree to settle down in England when he is in France, or America when he is in London, but in fact both of them chose their homes for reasons of tax efficiency and quarantine laws. He enjoyed portraying himself as henpecked long before he started on his post-war image building. What made his marriage to so strong-willed a woman such a success was that Ethel got her own way on all everyday matters because Wodehouse didn't feel strongly about them one way or another, yet she enjoyed the comfort of knowing she was married to a strong man. Leaving Ethel in charge left Plum free for writing.

On another arrival at Southampton he decided to cycle to London, and did so.[53] That was considered eccentric but it was only the case of an unselfconscious and active man, cooped up on a liner for a week where his only alternatives in walking round the promenade deck were to go widdershins or turnwise. By cycling to London he could stretch himself thoroughly with hundreds of alluring routes open to him. Wodehouse had real self-confidence, the sort where you aren't bothered by what other people may think of you but judge yourself by your own standards.

As Wodehouse rode those eighty-four miles to London he would have been planning further stories. During the twenties, of books not yet mentioned, he wrote *Money For Nothing* sitting in a punt in the moat at Hunstanton Hall in Norfolk with his typewriter propped upon his knees. The plot centred round a fake burglary – the Wodehouses having suffered a real burglary at Norfolk Street a few months previously. *Fish Preferred* (UK *Summer Lightning*) was a new Blandings novel beginning the great saga of sequential stories and containing his classic preface:

> A certain critic – for such men, I regret to say, do exist – made a nasty remark about my last novel that it contained 'all the old Wodehouse characters under different names'. . . . With my superior intelligence I have outgeneralled the man this time by putting in all the old Wodehouse characters under the same names. Pretty silly it will make him feel, I rather fancy.

Fish Preferred also introduces us to Wodehouse's first middle-aged hero, the Hon. Galahad Threepwood, brother of Clarence ninth earl of Emsworth, a *Beau Sabreur* of the old Pelican Club, a man bookmakers call by his pet name and under whose chaff barmaids simper. A frequenter of Romano's and a reader of the Pink 'Un (*The Sporting Times*, like *The Globe* printed on pink paper); a brother-in-arms of 'The Coroner', 'The Pitcher', 'Ducks', 'The Mate' and a host of other ingenious sportsmen. The Pelican Club was started in London in the 1880s by 'Shifter' Goldberg and 'Swears' Wells for the more raffish element of Victorian society and the extraordinary stories told about them were true. Captain Fred Russell, a Pelican known as 'Brer Rabbit', was asked by the Duke of Cambridge, Commander-in-Chief of the British Army, 'What is the role of cavalry in modern warfare?' His reply swept England in a week: 'I suppose it's to give tone to what would otherwise be a mere vulgar brawl.'[54]

Wodehouse was a good friend of at least one Pelican, Owen Hall, whose nick-name was 'Owing All', and so would have known other members as well. He also owned all Arthur Binstead's books, the main surviving record of the club, after Norman Murphy made him a present of one missing volume. He used them as an ore-body which he mined for ideas. Binstead tells of three hard-up Pelicans, 'The Punching Machine', 'The Man Behind The Face' and Joe Scott, who organized a Great Hat Stakes for whatever hat first came through the door of the American Bar of the Criterion in Piccadilly Circus after seven o'clock one evening. As the clock struck seven a hush fell over the Bar – and the first man through the door (almost certainly bribed by the organizers) was a waiter from the adjoining Indian restaurant – wearing a turban. A skinner for the book with not a single bet laid on a turban.[55] That became the Great Clothes

Stake organized by 'Mustard' Pott in *Uncle Fred In The Springtime*, the
Wodehouse reworking even better than the original story.

We also *Meet Mr Mulliner*, the Munchausen of 'The Angler's Rest'. E.
Phillips Oppenheim did so at the Sporting Club at Monte Carlo when
Wodehouse, using, possibly for the first time, 'The Angler's Rest'
nomenclature, asked him 'Who's that long, sandy, Gin-and-tonic over
there?'[56] Wodehouse hated the dust-jacket of *Meet Mr Mulliner* and said
that 'God may have forgiven Herbert Jenkins for it but I never shall'.[57]
The illustration on the jacket shows nothing but a genial, portly, pipe-
smoking man who is the spitting image of another Wodehouse fan, the
Prime Minister of the day, Stanley Baldwin. (But for a really awful dust-
wrapper look at the UK first edition of *Ice In The Bedroom*.) *Meet Mr
Mulliner* is dedicated to the Earl of Oxford and Asquith (former Prime
Minister Asquith) who, after his defeat at Paisley in the October 1924
Parliamentary elections, which spelled the end of his political career, sat
in the train back to London and, according to his daughter, 'Produced
from his bag the latest P.G. Wodehouse and lived again'. Wodehouse
knew Asquith and got on well with him but not with Baldwin who, he
complained after breakfasting with him, talked to his fellows as if they
were a public meeting.[58] *Mulliner Nights* and *Mr Mulliner Speaking* complete the trilogy. J. B. Priestley reviewed the latter book in the London
Evening News writing 'If anybody wants a test of real high-and-dry-
browism here is one to hand: an inability to enjoy Mr Wodehouse.'[59]
Later Priestley much annoyed Wodehouse who complained to Mackail
that not only had Priestley analysed his book but had drawn attention to
things Plum wanted hushed up '. . . viz that I have only got one plot and
produce it once a year with variations' and he wished that novelists
wouldn't review novels.[60] If any carping critic accused Wodehouse of
using the same old plot time and time again he would innocently agree
with them.

Meanwhile Jeeves and Bertie carried on in *Carry On Jeeves* and *Very
Good Jeeves*. There were finally fifteen Bertie and/or Jeeves books with
twenty-one titles – as only seven books have the same title on both sides of
the Atlantic and *My Man Jeeves* has not been published in America. Jeeves
gets his name on fourteen of them, Bertie on only two and five carry
neither name. It sounds like favouritism. Jeeves also got his name in the
title of both the first two films made about him and Bertie by Hollywood,
whose seductive purse was now calling, irresistibly, to Ethel and Plum.

12

DOTTYVILLE-ON-THE-PACIFIC

A stout man with a face rather like that of a vulture which
has been doing itself too well on the corpses.[1]

'The Castaways'

THAT is the boss of Metro-Goldwyn-Mayer, Louis B. Mayer –
both looks and character summed up in twenty-two deft words
– masquerading as Jacob Z. Schnellenhamer, President of the
Perfecto-Zizzbaum Motion Picture Corp. Entire biographies by other
pens give us less idea of the man. Wodehouse had a lot of fun with
Hollywood but didn't care much for the place W.C. Fields christened
Dottyville-On-The-Pacific; he preferred Droitwich which, he said, also
gave him more of a kick than the Grand Canyon (which he found disap-
pointing).[2] Ethel loved Hollywood and Plum liked the big money it paid
him. Hollywood made much greater use of Wodehouse than is generally
realized. He had been premiered on the silver screen back in 1915 with *A
Gentleman of Leisure* produced by The Jesse I. Lasky Feature Play Co. Inc.
with John Stapleton (who had helped dramatize the book for the stage)
Cecil B. deMille and Wodehouse as scriptwriters. There are at least forty-
one English language films (outside India) either based on Wodehouse
stories, with his lyrics or where he worked upon the screenplay (with or
without screen credits), plus a silent film – in German. In India, which has
a vast domestic film industry, foreign copyright-holders are not always
told of domestic projects and there are many unreported Indian films
based on Wodehouse stories.

In the autumn (in Tudor England they called it 'the fall') of 1929
Wodehouse was working on a new musical for Florenz Ziegfeld, *East Is
West* where not much was happening (and nothing ever did) while rehear-
sals for *Candle-Light*, starring Gertrude Lawrence, were ending ahead of
the pre-Broadway, out-of-town, run. So Wodehouse glided off to inspect
Hollywood having had, like every major author at the time, approaches to

work there on film scenarios. He stayed for three days and liked what little he saw of the place and expected to return there in the summer, having had three offers of a year's work, but he held out for only five months.[3]

The trouble with Wodehouse's trip is that he hadn't told anyone he was going. The rumour went round Broadway that Wodehouse had succumbed to the lures of Hollywood, never to return. With no forwarding address for Plum (Ethel was in London) the irate Ziegfeld could not even send one of his furious and famously lengthy telegrams. Gertrude Lawrence was displeased.

Nine days after he left, Wodehouse turned up again and, as *Candle-Light* was a great success, was forgiven. (When Wodehouse was asked what the title of the play had to do with a romantic comedy about a Hapsburg heir and a chambermaid he replied that it came from an old Austrian proverb 'Choose neither women nor linen by candle-light'.[4] This ancient proverb was probably born the moment Wodehouse had to answer the question.)

As always Plum got material out of his trip and Hollywood found it would be feeding the hand that bit it as Wodehouse published 'Slaves Of Hollywood' in the *Saturday Evening Post* of 7 December and in the London *Daily Mail*.

In every studio in Hollywood there are rows and rows of hutches, each containing an author on a long contract at a weekly salary. You see their anxious little faces peering through the bars. You hear them whining piteously to be taken for a walk. And does the heart bleed? You bet it bleeds. A visitor has to be very callous not to be touched by a spectacle such as this.[5]

Visiting Hollywood was not essential for satirizing the place. An aspiring young playwright, Moss Hart, wrote *Once In a Lifetime* which George S. Kaufman polished up and produced at the Music Box Theatre on Broadway the following year. One of the characters, Lawrence Vail, is part of a shipment of sixteen authors and he has been waiting in his office for nearly a year and a half without a word of instruction and suffers a breakdown from underwork.

It was during Wodehouse's first Hollywood trip that Marion Davies, from the old Princess days, worked Wodehouse into an important MGM studio lunch given for Winston Churchill, the founder of The Other Club. Wodehouse came to the conclusion that he had one of those meaningless faces which make no impression whatsoever on the beholder. He had met Churchill about seven times before and could see that he came upon the politician as a complete surprise once more. Not a trade of that 'Why, of course I remember you, Mr Addison Simms of Seattle'* stuff.[6] Which was unfair to Churchill, even though they were both members of The Other Club, for by then our hero had long perfected the Wodehouse Glide. In passing we might note that in those days the 'reclusive' author often lunched at the House of Commons and had met Churchill there on several occasions.

Back in London a cable came from Hollywood asking Wodehouse to do a picture for Evelyn Laye and arranging for him to see Samuel Goldwyn on his forthcoming visit to discuss the details.[7] Goldwyn was one of the few Hollywood moguls who recognized the value of good writers and treated them with respect. But he had an even greater respect for money. Wodehouse had some sessions with Goldwyn who wanted the author to write for him but wouldn't pay realistic money for the job, offering about half the rate Wodehouse could get for a serial involving much less work. Wodehouse respected money too. Ethel, however, liked the idea of Hollywood and in late 1929 Plum sent her there to agree a contract for him. While Ethel Wodehouse was in Hollywood, P.G. Wodehouse in London quietly resigned his command of *HMS Pegasus*, one of Britain's early aircraft carriers.†

Hollywood was then the centre of a dynamic industry which had been given a major adrenalin injection with 'the talkies' replacing mere 'movies'. Like all such industries, striving to keep up with rapidly increasing demand and developing technologies, there were extraordinary characters, intrigue, scandals, nepotism, corruption, exuberance, waste and extravagance. The great Hollywood studios assiduously cultivated that image. It was good for business. Yet, while true, it was only part of the truth. The Dream Machines, the great studios, were manufacturing companies like any others supplying a consumer need, competing fiercely with each other for market share and with the primary purpose of making money – which they did in abundance.

An important raw material was plots for the movies and, additionally, dialogue for the talkies. Irving Thalberg, the young head of production at Metro-Goldwyn-Mayer, felt good stories were the most important ingredient for a profitable picture and the most difficult to find. So did Goldwyn. The price of so scarce a commodity as writing talent rose steadily under the free-market laws of supply and demand.

Thus Ethel was able to agree a contract for Wodehouse to work for

---

* At that time a well known advertising slogan for an American memory-training course.
† That is, Captain Philip George Wodehouse, RN, DSO, a first cousin of Pelham Grenville.[8]

MGM at $2,000 per week with the studio having an option (which they took up) to keep him on for a further six months. In the spring of 1930 Wodehouse and Leonora arrived in Dottyville-On-The-Pacific. Wodehouse's old friends, George Grossmith and playwright Freddy Lonsdale were already there in the MGM writers' block. In July Ethel joined them and the family took over Norma Shearer's old house (she had married Thalberg two years earlier) from another old friend from the theatre, Elsie Janis who had acted in *Miss 1917* and *Oh Kay!*.

MGM was then under the leadership of Mayer, who was widely loathed, and Thalberg who was widely loved. It was an effective combination which created the foremost of the great Hollywood studios. Wodehouse worked under Sam Marx, MGM's powerful story editor, and sometimes with Thalberg, part of whose genius lay in reshaping other people's ideas into better ones producing finer films and fatter profits.

The culture gap immediately began to show between the workaholic author and the Hollywood system. Sam Marx recalled Wodehouse's first assignment:

Thalberg had hoped to make *Those Three French Girls* distinguished by Wodehouse's unique flavour and told Beaumont to have the British humorist rewrite it. Wodehouse usually worked in the sunlit garden of his Beverly Hills mansion. I advised him that the director wanted him to do the revision at the studio for immediate shooting. A studio limousine was sent to fetch him but when it got there, Wodehouse wasn't home.

Two hours later he showed up and announced he had walked the five mile distance in record time. He assured the director he could easily fix up the scene but wanted to do it outdoors. I found a sunny spot for him on a saloon porch in the Western street and provided him with desk, chair and writing paraphernalia.

Beaumont waited until late afternoon, with no word or words from Wodehouse. An assistant director was then dispatched to the back lot, but returned to say the saloon set was uninhabited. The equipment had also disappeared.

It was subsequently learned that Wodehouse developed a ravenous appetite from his long walk, so he went to lunch. While he was gone a watchman saw the deserted desk and typewriter and thought it was mislaid by the prop department and so returned it. When Wodehouse saw that it had been removed he took it as a hint his work wasn't needed after all. He went home the same way he came to the studio. He walked.[9]

There was nothing contrary to Hollywood studio contracts in walking around Los Angeles County (probably because it had never occurred to the studio attorneys) or working at home but to the denizens of the Hollywood zoo they simply confirmed that all Englishmen are mad. Ruth Howard, Leslie Howard's daughter, remembers, in an autobiography irritatingly written in the third person:

> P.G. Wodehouse was in Hollywood when the Howards were there and they were hugely entertained by his determination to walk to work every day. They would pass him striding along, quite oblivious to the stares of gardeners, maids and delivery boys, all driving to their work. No one else was ever seen to walk in Beverly Hills and Ruth was even warned against it in case the police picked her up on suspicion. 'What of?' asked Ruth in high dudgeon. 'Surely I will not be mistaken for a prostitute?' She was quickly assured that even these ladies did not walk in Beverly Hills.[10]

Similarly Wodehouse was given work that he could complete in an afternoon and discovered that it was expected to take him six weeks. Had he delivered the required words the following day the whole system would have been upset. Not only would the director have assumed the work was slapdash and no good, but his fellow script-scribes would have been highly offended at such a breach of the restrictive practices of the craft. So the unworldly Wodehouse wisely took six weeks over the task, which is to say he spent six weeks (less an afternoon) working on his own projects. This kept him happily occupied in his garden and during this first stint in Hollywood he wrote 'The Story of Webster' and at least two other unnamed short stories, two acts of the play *Leave It To Psmith* co-written by post with Ian Hay and most of *If I Were You*. That novel has a most unsatisfactory ending with the reader uncertain whether Antony Claude Wilbraham Bryce Chalk-Marshall or Sid Pryce is rightfully the Earl of Droitwich – but Wodehouse thought otherwise, telling Reynolds Jr. that he had gone to pains and exercised consummate artistic genius to keep the question doubtful.[11]

Meanwhile Ethel was enjoying herself giving and attending parties, usually graced with appearances by Plum before he went back to his beloved Monarch. He disliked the California climate and told Townend that by sticking to his garden all the time and shutting his eyes when going out it was possible to get by, but he still had time for his friends. The actress Heather Thatcher came for a long stay; the San Francisco stock-broker, Raven Barnikow, was a good friend and frequent guest and they met many greater and lesser Hollywood luminaries from Clark Gable and

Fred Astaire to Douglas Fairbanks and his wife Mary Pickford to minor actors such as Werner Plack.

The playwright Roland Pertwee, a Mason in the same Lodge as Wodehouse, wrote of his time in Hollywood. 'Another cause of irritation was the total lack of ordinary people. I thanked God for such men as P.G. Wodehouse, flapping around in a damned awful pair of slippers'.[12] Marion Davies invited the Wodehouses to stay with her and Hearst at Castle San Simeon – the incredible amalgam of numerous ancient European buildings reconstructed in the California sunshine.

Meals are in an enormous room, and are served at a long table with Hearst sitting in the middle on one side and Marion Davies in the middle on the other. The longer you are there, the further you get from the middle. I sat on Marion's right the first night, then found myself being edged further and further away till I got to the extreme end, when I thought it time to leave. Another day, and I should have been feeding on the floor.[13]

The story Wodehouse didn't tell was of his host's decree that the party that weekend was a Hawaiian *luau* and that all his guests were to appear in grass skirts and leis imported specially for the occasion. Hearst, a man to whom presidents deferred and congressmen grovelled, was always obeyed – except by Wodehouse, who attended the party in a dinner jacket. As Ethel couldn't bully Plum, Hearst had no hope of doing so.[14]

Wodehouse also helped C. Aubrey Smith, later Sir Aubrey and a Sussex and England cricketer when Plum was at Dulwich, to found the Hollywood Cricket Club. At the inaugural meeting he took the minutes and offered to help with the cost of the equipment and later paid $100 for life membership.[15] Smith was elected president and the vice-presidents were Wodehouse along with Ronald Colman, George Arliss and Leon Errol. Another founder member was Plum's friend Boris Karloff; both were public school, cricket enthusiasts, and Greek scholars. Karloff's real name was William Henry Pratt, but you can't play film fiends with a name like that. Other keen members in those days included Nigel Bruce, Errol Flynn, Herbert Marshall, Alan Mowbray, Philip Merivale, David Niven, Reginald Owen, Basil Rathbone, Pat Somerset and H.B. Warner. Laurence Olivier played for the club only once.[16] Gubby Allen, England's cricket captain visiting Hollywood on his way home from the notorious bodyline tour in Australia, was conscripted by Smith and played twice for the Club in the spring of 1937.[17] Wodehouse records spending a lot of time with him.[18] The club became the social centre for the British colony in Los Angeles.

One of the Wodehouses' many house guests – although he was a close friend of Ethel's rather than Plum's – was Gerard Fairlie, who succeeded Col H.C. McNeile as 'Sapper', writer of the Bulldog Drummond books. (The Germanophobic, anti-Semitic, McNeile's first name was, pleasingly, Herman.) Fairlie wrote:

> During the morning following the despatch of my letter to him, Plummy Wodehouse called on me at the hotel. He was entirely unlike what I had expected him to be. He was very kind and pleasant, and asked me to come out that evening and dine with him at his house in Beverly Hills. I gladly accepted.
>
> When it came for the moment for me to thank them for a lovely evening and to leave, Plummy stated that I must obviously stay with them at Linden Drive until my plans were a little more definite, which would give him and his family an opportunity to introduce me to some of the personalities of Hollywood, and also to show me round the place. I was, of course, delighted and asked him when it would be convenient to start my visit. I shall never forget Plummy's reply.
>
> 'You have already arrived,' he said. 'I had all your things brought to the house some time ago.'[19]

Conrad Nagel, the long-forgotten child star, remembers the times.

> Hollywood was always a strange place. Whether you worked or not depended mostly on chance. For example, once they were going to do a picture with British (*sic*) dialogue. 'Nobody can write this except P.G. Wodehouse – or a man of his calibre. That's it. Get P.G. Wodehouse.' So they started calling, looking all over for him. They couldn't find him. It turned out he was right there in the studio. He had an office there for six months and was drawing a salary right along.[20]

That is typical of the nonsense recorded about Hollywood – and widely believed. Wodehouse's arrival had been reported in all the trade and local papers and his habit of walking everywhere was a matter for incredulous filmworld gossip. He met Mayer and worked with Thalberg and Marx – while nobody earning $2,000 a week would be forgotten.

Those Three French Girls, released in October 1930, was produced by Harry Rapf, directed by Harry Beaumont and starred Fifi D'Orsay and Plum's old friend George Grossmith. Wodehouse enjoyed a modest screen credit as part of the regiment of writers who had worked on the script. The film was shot in thirty days, cost $284,000 to produce and made a profit of $99,000.[21] His next known assignment was *Rosalie*, the musical comedy for which he and Ira Gershwin had written the lyrics. MGM had bought the film rights intending to make a picture for Marion Davies. He also worked on *The Man In Possession*, which MGM released in July 1931, winning another minor screen credit.

In March 1931 he was put to work on *By Candlelight*, the retitled *Candle-Light* which MGM had bought. They never produced the film, apparently selling the rights to Universal who released it in 1933. This has echoes of Wodehouse's Hollywood story *The Castaways* where writers are contracted to remain working for the studio, Perfecto-Zizzbaum, until the film *Scented Sinners* is completed – which shows no sign of ever happening. The writers are released when it is discovered that all along the film rights to *Scented Sinners* were owned by another studio!

Plum was gratified when Thalberg told him that *Leave It To Psmith* was his favourite novel but when he suggested that Thalberg should come across with money for the movie rights the producer merely smiled sheepishly and the matter dropped. A couple of years later *Leave It To Me*, based on the Wodehouse-Hay play rather than the original Psmith novel, was filmed in Britain with Monty Banks directing.

Plum's contract with MGM had expired in May 1931 but in June they asked him to give an interview to Alma Whitaker of the *Los Angeles Times*. He agreed and it took place at his home in Benedict Canyon Drive. While making polite conversation before getting down to the formal interview Wodehouse made some commonplace remarks about the way the studio had paid him a lot of money and then made hardly any use of him. Commonplace because everyone in Hollywood knew that the Hollywood studios, like all creative businesses, were often inefficient – but the rule was not to do anything to shock the servants or frighten the horses. Miss Whitaker's article, mostly those innocent pre-interview remarks, appeared in the paper on 7 June 1931. The abridged *New York Times* story of 9 June, based on the Associated Press wire-service copy, has always been cited in the past but the original *Los Angeles Times* piece is worth reprinting in full, for the first time.

WODEHOUSE OUT AND STILL DAZED

England's Famous Humorist Ends Film Contract

After A Year He Still Wonders Why He Was Engaged

Studios Nice But P.G. Feels They Were Cheated

By Alma Whitaker

P.G. Wodehouse, England's most famous humorist, has just concluded his year's contract with MGM.

'They paid me $2,000 a week, – $104,000 – and I cannot see what they engaged me for,' he said wonderingly as we sat beneath the coconut palms beside his glistening swimming pool in Benedict Canyon. 'The motion picture business dazes me. They were extremely nice to me – oh, extremely – but I feel as if I have cheated them. It's all so unreasonable.

'You see, I understood I was engaged to write stories for the screen. After all, I have twenty novels, a score of successful plays, and countless magazine stories to my credit.

'Yet apparently they had the greatest difficulty in finding anything for me to do. Twice during the year they brought completed senarios of other people's stories to me and asked me to do some dialogue. Fifteen or sixteen people had tinkered with those stories. The dialogue was really quite adequate. All I did was to touch it up here and there – very slight improvements.

NO HURRY INVOLVED

'Then they set me to work on a story called *Rosalie* which was to have some musical numbers. No, it wasn't my story. But it was a pleasant little thing, and I put in three months work on it. No one wanted me to hurry. When it was finished they thanked me politely and remarked that as musicals didn't seem to be going so well they guessed they would not use it. That about sums up what I was called upon to do for my $104,000. Isn't it amazing? If it is only names they want, it seems such an expensive way to get them, doesn't it?

'Naturally my reputation is for light humor, jolly nonsense. I was led to believe they felt there was a field for my work in pictures. But I was told my sort of stuff was "too light". They seem to have such a passion for sex stuff. I wonder if they really know the tastes of their audiences. It seems to me that the most successful pictures of the year have been almost devoid of "sex",' he said, naming, among others *Cimarron*.

'Personally, of course, I received the most courteous treatment. But see what happened to my friend Roland Pertwee at Warner Brothers. He did a story for Marilyn Miller, and they slapped him on the back and said it was great. I think the expression is that "everything was hunky-dory".

'He returns to the studio as usual the next morning, and is informed by the policeman at the gate that he cannot be let in as he is fired. Such very poor manners. If such were the case, why not a courteous intimation the day before?

'After all, Roland has a fine reputation in his profession, was invited to come here, apparently did good work – yet it remained for the policeman at the gate to give him his first intimation that his services were no longer needed, and actually to bar him from the studio.

'It's so unbelievable, isn't it? Of course I know they have their problems, but really now, good manners are so inexpensive, yet so important in pleasant business relations.'

At this point I could not resist mentioning *Once In A Lifetime*.

'I can see that the play was only the slightest possible burlesque,' he admitted. 'But really; I don't want to be critical. I am merely trying to understand their point of view. For instance, I cannot see why just two people should not be sufficient to collaborate on a scenario – the author and a good continuity writer. Why must it be sixteen or more? How can an author's idea possibly materialise as he envisioned it when so many people take a hand in its preparation for the screen?'

CONDITIONS BAFFLE

Now, all this was said conversationally, not as a diatribe against Hollywood. P.G. Wodehouse, whose light airy wit has entranced his readers for more than twenty years, has much too keen a sense of humor to wax oracular. He merely admits the condition baffles him. He came out to work and has been paid $104,000 for loafing. Which seems to him poor business even when he's richer for it.

He says he loves California and loves the home at Beverly Hills which he is renting. 'This sunny garden with the palms – it is what every Englishman dreams about on a muggy day at home.' So as there are five months to run of his lease he will remain and finish his *American* magazine contract stories here. He is accompanied by his wife and daughter.

While the *New York Times* indicated its view of the unimportance of the story by burying it on page thirty-three, the *New York Herald Tribune* of 10 June carried an editorial on the subject titled 'All So Unbelievable' and considered Plum had performed a considerable public service.

Mr Wodehouse must be among the first to bring it all out into the open, to mention names and firms, and thus assure us of the truth of the astounding legends. He confirms the picture that has been steadily growing – the picture of Hollywood the golden, where 'names' are bought to be scrapped, talents are retained to be left unused, hiring of distinguished authors is without rhyme and firing without reason.

What Plum said about himself wasn't really news. Some time before the film journal *Variety* had carried a catty little paragraph:

Following *Variety*'s report of the ludicrous writer talent situation, eastern executives interrogated the studios as to instances such as concerned one English playwright and author who has been collecting $2,500 [*sic*] a week at one of the major studios for eleven months, without contributing anything really worthwhile to the screen.[22]

Hollywood and Wodehouse knew it referred to him.

Then the soft-boiled-eggs hit the fan – if Plum and Townend are to be believed. They called it the interview that was to rock Hollywood to its foundations and, quite unintentionally, bring about what amounted to a major revolution. The yes-men of Plum's Hollywood stories, they claimed, had become portents of the storm that was to break with such devastating fury over the studios. Townend added 'Before nightfall Plum was the most talked-of man in the United States of America and the bankers went into action' and Plum claimed he expected to be blacklisted by the studios for ever.[23] Plum and Townend are not to be believed. None of the subsequent histories of Hollywood mention the interview at all while the industry bible, *Variety*, (then weekly) ignored the story on 9 June. The *Motion Picture Herald* treated the interview as a minor joke while *Film Daily* and *Motion Picture* ignored it entirely.

The whole story was nonsense for three main reasons. It was wrong, firstly, because Wodehouse, unusually for him, got his facts wrong. Warner Brothers had merged with First National Films and there were the inevitable redundancies. Jack Warner called Pertwee to his room, said how sorry he was about the turn of events, gave him a cheque for the unexpired portion of his contract and told him to take his own time in leaving the studio office. By the time the *Los Angeles Times* interview was published Pertwee was on an Atlantic liner and unable to give the facts. Arriving at Cherbourg he was not pleased to discover headlines in the film papers such as 'Roland Pertwee Gets The Ozone'.[24] He set the record straight with a letter to Jack Warner, copied to the *New York Times* which ran the story.

DEFENDS HOLLYWOOD
Roland Pertwee Denies Wodehouse
Referred to Him.

A defense of Hollywood's methods of doing business with authors is offered in a letter received by J.L. Warner, vice-president in charge of Warner Brothers productions, from Roland Pertwee, English playwright. Mr Pertwee until recently was under contract to write seven plays at the Warner studios. P.G. Wodehouse in his widely published interview told a story of a [*sic*] playwright who went out to lunch and returned to find himself out of a job. This was generally thought to refer to Mr Pertwee.

'I very much regret that Mr Wodehouse should have laboured under the delusion that I was slung out of Burbank by the "cop",' Mr Pertwee said in his letter. 'I knew nothing about the article until I read it all at Cherbourg. On arriving in London I instructed the reporters who met me to deny the incident as having happened to myself.

'Also I asked them to say that I had received at your hands nothing but the greatest courtesy and consideration. These words were quoted by several London newspapers and if I can find the clippings I will forward them to you. Naturally the news value of enthusiasm is small compared with the value of criticism. What I said, therefore, did not inspire very much publicity.

'Subsequent to the upheaval in the administrative affairs of First National many lively stories were current. At least twenty people told me that one of the writing staff first heard the news of his decline from the policeman at the gate and I daresay Mr Wodehouse got it from as many different quarters.

'Let me categorically deny that I was the writer in question. I would like to say again that I enjoyed every hour of my employment with you and have carried away from Hollywood nothing but feelings of friendship for you all. I would add further that, unlike my friend Wodehouse, I am in no sense appalled at the amount of salary I drew, nor am I troubled by any pangs of conscience about the amount of work I did. I only hope that work will not have turned out too badly.'[25]

For the second time Wodehouse lost a friend and his embarrassment at inadvertently slandering Pertwee triggered his resignation from their mutual Masonic Lodge and from the Masons.

Secondly Wodehouse's story was nonsense because the bankers who funded film production had no say in the running of the studios. Bankers only get involved in running companies if the security for their loans is at risk. There was then no risk in their Hollywood loans. The great studios suffered from the Depression but far less than did most sections of the American economy. While the American working man and his family had little spare cash and the army of the unemployed even less, they persistently used some of it to escape from the nasty realities of the actual world into the agreeable fantasy worlds produced by the Dream Machines of Hollywood.

The people who did have the right and the muscle to interfere were the studios' shareholders. MGM was then owned by Loew's Inc, the New York-based cinema and theatre chain, whose President, Nicholas M.

Schenck, telephoned Thalberg to ask about the Wodehouse furore. 'You are silly boys out there. You throw away our money.' The economical Thalberg, who when running Universal had scattered notices around the studio telling people to switch off lights to save on the electricity bills, was exasperated, replying 'Nick, if you know how to make pictures without writers, tell me how', and that was an end to the matter. It's easy to see why. MGM's record and profits during the period were:[26]

Season	Pictures Made	Cost $ million	Profit $ million
1929/30	44	15.7	5.9
1930/31	49	20.8	6.3
1931/32	43	17.7	5.2

When a business is making that sort of money – around $50 million a year at today's values – the executives running it have a pretty free hand. Loew's remembered the watchmaker's maxim: 'If it works don't mend it'. Later RKO and Paramount nearly went bankrupt – not because of extravagance in film production but because of paying excessive prices to build up their tied cinema chains.

Lastly the studio bosses were ambitious business people in a highly competitive industry. While often uneducated, they were able and if a tenth of the stories about their spendthrift incompetence had been true the studios would never have got started in the first place and, if they had, they would have been bankrupt within six months.

Wodehouse also declined the chance to become a Broadway star. Having read the *Los Angeles Times* interview, impresario Sam H. Harris offered Wodehouse the role of Lawrence Vail in his Broadway hit, *Once In A Lifetime*. Wodehouse sent a telegram declining the opportunity as 'Sudden work after all this might prove fatal'.[27]

With the end of his Hollywood contract in sight Ethel wanted to take a round-the-world cruise on the *Empress Of Britain*. Plum toyed with the idea, writing to friends that 'we are thinking about it'. But then he made up his mind and wrote to Reynolds in the first person singular 'I have decided against it'[28] – so they did not go. Ultimately Plum was the undisputed boss in his own household.

Instead he and Leonora returned to London, arriving back in November 1931. 'Do you realise that all that year I was away from London, when everybody supposed that I was doing a short stretch at Dartmoor, I was actually in Hollywood?'[29] Despite the humour he felt bitter about Miss Whitaker, he was kind but not saintly. It merely took a lot more to arouse his dislike than it would an ordinary man. In the original text of *Performing Flea* he called *La Whitaker* charming on the outside but beneath the surface as hard-boiled as a gila monster and as poisonous[30] but the libel lawyers insisted the comment be cut out.*

After Hollywood Ethel stayed behind for a five-week holiday before joining Plum at Cannes, and tried to put right the damage, such as it was, telling the press that what her husband really meant was that he regretted that he had not done better work: 'A smash hit of some sort'.[31] Both of them, she explained diplomatically, were crazy about Hollywood – but she won few column inches.

Wodehouse expected never to return to Hollywood and if his stories about the effect of his *Los Angeles Times* interview had been true he wouldn't have done. In 1934 Paramount offered him a contract at $1,500 per week and the only reason he didn't accept was because of a dispute at that time with the US tax authorities which made it unwise for him to visit America. He also had other offers.[32] In any event, shortly after that tax dispute was settled he accepted an offer from MGM for another six-month stint (and another six at the studio's option) at a salary increased to $2,500 per week. He returned to Hollywood in September 1936 and rented a spectacular house on Angelo Drive, high up in the Hollywood Hills overlooking the entire city of Los Angeles in those pre-smog days.

His first assignment was, to his astonishment, *Rosalie* upon which he had been working five years earlier! However he soon got the impression that he was being 'edged out' and was finally told that the studio wanted Bill McGuire to do the script on his own.[33] MGM released *Rosalie*, starring Nelson Eddy and Eleanor Powell, in 1937 with no mention of Wodehouse in the screenwriter credits.

Hollywood and the great studios were little changed, for all the alleged activity by those East Coast bankers. Wodehouse busied himself as before doing what was asked of him – which as before, was not much – and with his writing. He also socialized with old friends such as Nesbitt Kemp, now a California millionaire, and his colleague from the early days of *The Captain*, C.B. Fry, who recalled:

I sat in a cool salon and listened to Herbert Marshall, David Niven, Nigel Bruce [the actors], P.G. Wodehouse, three scenario writers (all engaged in writing the scenarios which P.G. had been imported at a high price to write), G.O. Allen [the England cricket captain] and half a dozen others. All were talking at once, all on different subjects, and nobody was listening to anybody else. In fact I was the only one who

* A gila monster is a large, venomous lizard found in the south-western United States. Note for libel lawyer: Miss Whitaker died in 1956.

was not talking. I was trying to listen to P.G. Wodehouse telling the air how he thought his own stories ought to be portrayed.[34]

At the time Twentieth Century Fox were filming *Thank You Jeeves*, released in October 1936, starring David Niven as Bertie Wooster and Arthur Treacher as Jeeves. This was a great success. Frank Nugent wrote in *The New York Times*:

> Mr Wodehouse must have been one of the fates in attendance at [Niven and Treacher's] births marking them to play the characters he has been writing about these many years.[35]

To cash in on that success Fox released a quickie sequel in 1937, *Step Lively Jeeves*, with Arthur Treacher – Wodehouse had nothing at all to do with the story or the script but the credits acknowledged his role saying the story was 'After Wodehouse': as one critic said 'A long way after Wodehouse'.[36]

Meanwhile Wodehouse was writing *Summer Moonshine* which has perhaps the most remarkable character in all the canon: Heloise, Princess von und zu Dwornitzchek. Wodehouse himself pointed out that a real character in one of his stories stood out like a sore thumb. The Princess's stepson, Joe Vanringham, gave his reasons for parting company with her.

> I left because I have a constitutional dislike for watching murder done – especially slow, cold-blooded murder. . . . My father. He was alive then – just. She didn't actually succeed in killing him till about a year later. . . . Oh I don't mean little-known Asiatic poisons. A resourceful woman with a sensitive subject to work on can make out quite well without the help of strychnine in the soup. Her method was just to make life hell for him.

The Princess is totally alien to every other character ever allowed into Wodehouse's Edwardian Elysium. Wodehouse got the Princess's name from a character in Molnar's *The Play's The Thing*, Johann Dwornitschek, but not even the redoubtable Norman Murphy has suggested on whom she must have been based. Wodehouse tells us she was a large, sinuous woman, with a beautiful figure and a supple way of moving herself from spot to spot. Miss Whitaker was not the model, her photograph showing a determined lady with all the sinuousness of an overstuffed armchair.

Wodehouse again became involved in the real world, getting caught in the cross-fire of the Hollywood Writers' Wars between the Screen Playwrights and the Screen Writers' Guild. Philip Dunne, the improbable,

Ivy-League, chairman of the membership committee of the Guild, wrote
to Wodehouse – whom he had met previously at a drinks party at Southampton, Long Island – and recalls:

> We in the Guild considered it [the Screen Playwrights] to be a company
> union and I said as much in a letter to the English humorist P.G.
> Wodehouse, who had been publicised as one of its members.
>
> I had been brought up on Wodehouse's Jeeves and Bertie Wooster
> and, before I came to the Coast, had enjoyed his company over drinks
> in Southampton. My letter was intemperate to say the least. In effect I
> asked Wodehouse if he realised that he was consorting with scabs and
> scallywags in an organisation whose sole malign purpose was to break
> our virtuous Guild. Wodehouse, whose right-wing leanings I didn't
> suspect, showed my letter to the officers of the Playwrights.[37]
>
> The letter I wrote Wodehouse was never intended for publication. It
> was quite obviously ill-considered, but I thought that I was writing to a
> friend.[38]

The Playwrights promptly sued the officers of the Guild (including
Wodehouse's old stablemate at *Vanity Fair*, Dorothy Parker) for libel and
$250,000 damages.[39] Fortunately for the Guild and for Wodehouse a
cheerfully biased Democratic judge, Robert W. Kenney (later attorney to
the Guild [died 1944]), threw out the case before it ever came to trial.[40]
Thus the world missed the spectacle of P.G. Wodehouse giving evidence
from the witness box – much to his relief.

When his contract expired he had offers from other studios for single-
picture work. One was a joy: working with Guy Bolton adapting their own
musical *Anything Goes* for the screen. They took up the offer from Paramount who released the picture in January 1936 starring Bing Crosby and
Ethel Merman. Remarkably Bing Crosby also starred in Paramount's
1956 remake of the film, in which the screenplay was reworked by Sidney
Sheldon. *Show Boat* was also released in 1936, not a Wodehouse film but
with his lyric for 'Bill'. He also accepted an offer from RKO to work on
the screen version of his own book *A Damsel In Distress* which the studio
had bought as a Fred Astaire vehicle commissioning George Gershwin to
write the score. As a charming tribute to Wodehouse Astaire sang the title
song on the lawns of Totleigh Castle (*sic*) located at Upper Pelham
Grenville, Wodehouse, England.[41] The film was released in November
1937.

That picture should have established not only how filmable Wodehouse
stories are with intelligent direction but also that he was a highly competent scriptwriter – it's hard to imagine such a good playwright being

anything else. He was also used to rewriting scenes under impossibly short deadlines for egocentric directors. That is what he had done for so many plays as they were polished on their pre-Broadway tours. Similar techniques were required for the film industry. Bolton pointed out that Wodehouse never learned to make use of the camera's ability to follow events off-stage but that minor deficiency is the sort of shortcoming a director should cheerfully put right for the benefit of sparkling dialogue and plot construction. Unfortunately, in a piece of casting so absurd as to make any story about Hollywood inanities believable, Joan Fontaine was given the starring role opposite Astaire. She was a fine actress but neither a singer nor a dancer. Predictably this damned the film to faint, almost inaudible, praise – and on the Hollywood rule, you're only as good as your last picture, nobody wanted Wodehouse as scriptwriter.

After working on *A Damsel In Distress*, but before it was released, he worked on a film with Eddie Goulding telling Townend that the money was fine, $10,000 for six weeks work and $2,000 a week after that but that it wasn't his sort of story and he wasn't enjoying the work.[42] That film was almost certainly *That Certain Woman*, a Bette Davis weepie – no wonder Plum didn't like it. With that Wodehouse's work in Tinseltown was ended but a few links occurred from time to time. In 1946 MGM released *Till The Clouds Roll By* based on an original script by Guy Bolton. It was a highly glamorized life of Jerome Kern, the sort of extravagant (in both senses of the word) tribute to its own great and good that Hollywood loves. Although Wodehouse does not appear in the film it contains three of his lyrics and was a success. James Agee reviewed it thus.

A little like sitting down to a soda fountain de luxe atomic special of maple walnut on vanilla on burnt almond on strawberry on butter pecan on coffee on raspberry sherbert on tutti frutti with hot fudge, butter-scotch, marshmallow, filberts, pistachios, shredded pineapple and rain-bow sprills on top: to go double on the whipped cream.[43]

There was to be one more Wodehouse film, apart from *The Helen Morgan Story* which featured Kern and Wodehouse's song 'Bill'. In 1962 Knights-bridge, a UK company, produced *The Girl On The Boat* released with United Artists starring Millicent Martin. Then Wodehouse was disco-vered by television. His Hollywood times were finally over but they gave us two full length novels, *Laughing Gas* and *The Old Reliable*; six short stories, 'Monkey Business', 'The Nodder', 'The Juice Of An Orange', 'The Rise of Minna Nordstrom', 'The Castaways' and 'George and Alfred' and major characters for *Bachelors Anonymous*, *The Luck Of The Bodkins* and its sequel, *Pearls, Girls And Monty Bodkin* (US *The Plot That*

Thickened), Wodehouse's most unsatisfactory novel. Not even such Wodehouse scholars as John Fletcher can reconcile the abrupt changes between the two books of such things as a pearl necklace to a diamond necklace and Monty Bodkin's sudden demotion from the noble line and wealth of Crusader the Sieur de Bodkin to a money newly made in trade by a working class uncle-by-marriage. Wodehouse made those changes to accommodate a new plot line in the later title.

The Wodehouses left Hollywood in October 1937. Plum was glad to turn his back on Tinseltown which largely forgot him. The money it yielded had been much appreciated but it was Wodehouse's writing for magazines and book publishers that was making him seriously rich.

— 13 —

BIG MONEY

An air of deep innocence which holds up even when he drops a bit of information culled from the *Wall Street Journal*.[1]

Newsweek interview

WODEHOUSE was intensely interested in money and he was not unworldly about it, although he pretended to be so once he married. It was another of those private jokes where nobody else realized they were having their legs pulled. All those scenes of authors with level business heads fighting for higher advances and royalties were based on himself. And there's a lovely bit of wishful thinking in 'Sleepy Time' from *Plum Pie* where publisher Cyril Grooly is talking to an author, Professor Pepperidge Farmer ('Pepperidge Farm' is the brand name for a large American cookie or biscuit maker) to whom he has given a $5,000 advance. He should have paid no more than the agreed $200 limit, but doesn't remember paying more even when his partner tells him he has done so. Grooly confronts the Professor and accuses him of hypnotizing him. 'Of course I did, my dear fellow. It was one of the ordinary business precautions an author has to take. The only way to get a decent advance from a publisher is to hypnotise him.'

The dreamy publishers wanting to be artists were partly counterpoint to those hard-headed authors – of whom none was more hard-headed than Wodehouse – and partly based on Herbert Jenkins, publisher and author of the *Bindle* stories, highly popular in their day. He died of overwork in 1923 and the realistic Wodehouse had earlier insisted on a clause in his contract enabling him to revoke it if Jenkins died or left the firm.[2]

Wodehouse loved nothing more than writing and hated not writing – but while he wrote firstly because his nature impelled him to, he wrote secondly and lastly for money.[3] This was a legacy of those urgent times at the bank when he was racing against that two-year deadline to earn enough from his pen to avert the horror (to his mind) of being sent out to the East. There was no time to be arty or self-indulgent. Wodehouse's approval of the commercial author shows in his admiring pen-portraits of such writers of superfatted fiction as Rosie M. Banks and Leila York who know they write sentimental tripe and Rockmetteller Todd who writes meaningless modern poetry – all with the cynical and worthy aim of exploiting their talents to pile up the doubloons in the old oak chest. Wodehouse's contempt for pretentious, arty writers in general and poets in particular appears throughout his work. He was a considerable poet himself but his work went under the disguise of lyrics or light verse, not poetry. Percy Gorringe in *Jeeves And The Feudal Spirit* is considered an ass for writing *avant garde* poetry – 'Caliban At Sunset' for the trendy poetry periodical *Parnassus* for which he got 15 shillings – but then admired when it turns out that he also writes blood-and-corpse detective stories under the pen-name of Rex West, from which he makes £800 a year – likely to double with his agent establishing him in the American market. The Wodehouse view of unworldly poets comes over equally clearly with Lancelot Mulliner who reluctantly agrees to debase his Muse by writing an advertising jingle in praise of the Briggs's Breakfast Pickles produced by his wealthy uncle, Jeremiah. The result, 'Darkling (A Threnody)', must, he tells his uncle, be printed in hand-set type on deep cream paper with bevelled edges, bound in limp violet leather and produced in a limited edition of 105 copies signed by the author.[4] Wodehouse had to adapt both his talent and the style and matter he wrote about so that his writing would sell. Not only was he concerned that his work be bought but he kept a sharp eye on how much he was paid for it – and he retained that attitude to the end of his life.

George Lorrimer, Editor of the *Saturday Evening Post* once sent Wodehouse $2,000 for *The Crime Wave At Blandings* asking if that was all right. Wodehouse was quick to point out that while he was so intensely spiritual that money meant nothing to him he found that $2,000 was a bit of a sock on the jaw, as he had always thought that a short story was supposed to fetch a tenth of the price of a serial and that he had been looking forward to getting $4,000.[5] He got his extra $2,000 but that story strips away any pretence that he was naive about money. So does Wodehouse's extensive correspondence with his US agent, Paul Reynolds and his son, Paul Jr. known as Revere. It contains scores of similar examples of Wodehouse taking a detailed, intense and obsessive interest in the commercial side of his writing. He knew just how the magazines worked – he had been contributing editor on *Vanity Fair* – and no item of his contracts was too small to attract his interest. He was concerned with getting the best prices; the speed with which he would be paid; the co-ordination of publication

dates of short stories and serials in different magazines and the publication of his books; the internal politics within magazines; the state of the
market for his work and how editors treated his contributions compared
with other authors. He was concerned not only with getting the maximum
sums for his work but also with the benefits of building up relationships
with magazines, which might pay slightly less but would ensure a regular
market for his work. He discusses the trade-off between the intangible
benefits, such as prestige, from appearing in top quality papers like the
Saturday Evening Post and the bigger bucks that could sometimes be
obtained from lesser magazines. He told Reynolds, paraphrasing Ambrose
Beirce, that in the business of making concessions to editors, if one did it
at all, it should be from a lively sense of benefits to come.[6]

Yet Wodehouse, while so interested in money, never made an icon of it.
Reynolds says that Wodehouse was angry with him for threatening to go
elsewhere if Wesley Stout, Lorrimer's successor at the *Saturday Evening
Post*, did not pay $50,000 for a new serial instead of the previous
$45,000.[7] That was exactly the sort of commercial suasion at which
Wodehouse himself was adept and the story rings as true as a cracked bell
– unless the guileful but truthful Plum said it so he could repeat his
remark to Stout. Wodehouse had a keen sense of loyalty as well as a sharp
sense of business but when the two clashed, as they often did, while
loyalty usually got the better of the compromise, compromise there always
was.

All of which flatly contradicts Reynolds Jr.'s assertion in his memoirs
that 'Wodehouse . . . never understood the business side of his writing or
the function of an agent'. From an agent's point of view, however, he was
right. Professional people like their clients to accept their professional
advice without argument. The rationale for Reynolds' view is, perhaps,
given a few lines later. 'Wodehouse adored my father and always did what
my father wanted. I was a new personality whom he did not like'.[8]

This intense interest in money is at odds with the picture Leonora gave
in an article she wrote for *The Strand* in which she said that Wodehouse
had no real sense of money and that a cheque for a thousand pounds
meant nothing to him except as a sort of good conduct mark. She also
claimed that he would sell a cheque for fifty pounds to anyone at any time
for seven shillings and sixpence cash – and that was how she kept her
financial head above water.[9] Ex-banker Wodehouse was not that dumb,
but what a delightful way to hand over money to a much-loved daughter.
Leonora was not that dumb either and knew just what he was doing but,
like Plum, she knew how to tinker with and polish the truth to make a
good yarn.

The Wodehouse letters are plentifully sprinkled with observant, detailed and shrewd comment on financial matters. He writes of box office takings for *Her Cardboard Lover* not dropping below $2,200 a week; of *Candlelight* taking $18,060 (accurate to the dollar) in its first week. He notes that in 1932 the *Saturday Evening Post* had to pass its dividend when it had paid $8 a share. He knew what the dividend had been – which is not the sort of thing you look up in order to impress Old Bill Townend. Richard Usborne, inspecting the Wodehouse family archive, wrote:

> Within reach of the armchair in the sanctum are books from Plum's Remsenburg shelves in which he had marked passages or scribbled remarks in pencil. Occasionally these markings suggest that Plum had found an idea for a plot, or a plot twist, or a shape for a new hyperbole or 'nifty'. But his scribble on the fly-leaf of his copy of H.G. Wells's *Select Conversations With An Uncle* is what looks like American stock-market quotations [they are]: Radio 100, B. [Bethlehem] Steel 109½, Pullman 82¾, West [Westinghouse] 148, G.M. [General Motors] 85½, E.C.L. & Powers 13¼, F.P. 64½, C.P. [Canadian Pacific] 234¼, Pub Serv of Jersey 79½.[10]

All of those are sound, blue-chip, stocks; the sort an interested and sensible private investor buys who follows the stock market but knows he is not a professional fund manager.

Wodehouse also comments upon *Cosmopolitan* paying him in instalments for *Thank You Jeeves* instead of a lump sum, and draws the correct inference from that about the state of the market for both magazines and their authors. He is pleased at being paid $10,000 for six weeks' work on a picture for Eddie Goulding and $2,000 a week thereafter. He remarks on the small prices Conan Doyle got for stories that are now world famous. He is gratified by the saving made when dining at home on ham instead of paying restaurant prices in Paris. He is cheerfully impressed by S.H. Behrman investing $2,000 for ten per cent of *Oklahoma* when it looked like sinking on the out-of-town tour before its New York premier and calculates that Behrman must have earned half a million dollars from his investment. He writes with knowledgeable detail about the rising costs of mounting a new musical show in America. In 1920 a conman tried to sell Wodehouse shares in a dud gold mine but got a shrewd *nolle prosequi* (from him, not Ethel)[11] and, as a consolation prize perhaps, was immortalized as that smooth-talking salesman of dud oil stock Soapy Molloy and his doppleganger Oily Carlisle. When the US tax authorities held on to some of Wodehouse's money pending a court decision he noted that they had to pay him six per cent interest – as much as he could get on an unfrozen investment.[12] When Wodehouse was ninety he told Graham

Lord of the *Sunday Express* that he didn't even think about money – a blatant fib but Lord noted 'He spatters his conversation with questions, most of them about money'[13] and that is obvious, though unstated, in other interviews. Money is as omnipresent in Wodehouse's books as death in Ivy Compton-Burnett's. Note how, even through the mists of love, Wodehouse intrudes money into his stories. Pongo Twistleton, when hoping to marry Angelica Briscoe a clergyman's daughter, wonders if he will get the marriage service at cut rates or even absolutely on the nod.[14] There is hardly a book or short story where money does not play a role, usually a pivotal one.

It is obvious that Wodehouse was not only extremely interested in money and that he talked about it constantly and shrewdly but also that he ran his financial affairs himself. Throughout his letters to the Reynolds, the Grimsdicks at Herbert Jenkins, Peter Schwed at Simon & Schuster, to Scott Meredith and to A.P. Watt & Co in London, he gives instructions on the payment of his royalties and other sums and he instructs his bankers on payments from one account to another and raises with them such matters as foreign exchange controls and changing currency rates between the French franc, sterling and the dollar. He writes always in the first person singular about his financial affairs and there is rarely any mention of Ethel. Indeed Ethel wrote to Reynolds Jr. on one occasion that her husband's secretary, Margaret Matusch, knew far more about Wodehouse's affairs than she did.[15] However Wodehouse sometimes used Ethel for his hatchet work. It was Ethel, not Plum, who wrote to Reynolds Jr. in 1931 saying that, devoted as her husband was to Reynolds Sr., he could not continue with the firm, under any circumstances, at ten per cent commission. So thereafter Wodehouse paid Reynolds only five.[16] In 1933 Ethel felt they should accede to demands by the US Internal Revenue Service (the IRS) but her husband was far shrewder on financial matters and disagreed.[17] So they fought on and eventually won a less onerous settlement. Furthermore the Wodehouse financial affairs could not be suspended during Ethel's many absences, sometimes for up to two months at a time. Yet this paradoxical man was less interested in spending and managing money than in earning it, or winning it at the casino or race-track.

While Wodehouse was careful with his money he was also generous, but in his own way. To those he loved his purse was always open. Ethel could spend what she liked (and she did) and Plum was happy that she was happy. He enjoyed giving Leonora money and presents. He was also kind and wise enough to help his friends tactfully.

In helping Townend, ex-banker Wodehouse sometimes used 'back-to-back loans' where money in a bank deposit account in his name was used

as security for an overdraft, at the same bank, for his friend. He also wrote
to influential friends, such as Kipling and Conan Doyle, praising Townend's work and urged publishers to take his friend's books[18] and on the
occasions when he urged Herbert Jenkins to do so they did so. Wodehouse was the best selling author on their list and without him the firm
might not have survived. Throughout his adult life Townend was a pen-
sioner of Wodehouse's, whose generosity is undoubted, if not his judgement. He was always praising Townend's writing (which a host of
publishers found as wooden as his illustrations for *The White Feather*) but
this could have been simple encouragement in the hope that an inspired
Townend would cease to be the responsibility of the Wodehouse coffers.
He later admitted to novelist Tom Sharpe (*Riotous Assembly*, *Porterhouse
Blue* et cetera) that, in fact, he found Townend's books dull. The Code of
The Wodehouses seems to have been as potty as The Code of The
Widgeons. In 'Freddie, Oofy And The Beef Trust'[19] the Widgeon Code
decrees that when you have saved a chap's life you have a responsibility to
him for ever thereafter. The Wodehouse Code meant that having once
subsidized Old Bill Townend you had to go on doing so, but Plum never
gave any sign of being unhappy with the duty.

Townend and his wife Rene lived a comfortable middle-class existence
in Folkstone in a charming Georgian house with a maid. Taking Plum's
money reflects badly on his character and must have had a debilitating
effect on his endeavours although, whatever his faults, he was not lazy. He
wrote forty-three published books. In spite of them he remains a slightly
shadowy character. Little is known about him and when the publishers of
Yours Plum looked for a photograph of him not even the redoubtable
Margaret Slythe at Dulwich was able to find one. I was excited to discover
an unknown half-page profile of Wodehouse by Townend in the *Daily
Mail* to herald their serialization of *The Code Of The Woosters* in 1938 – yet
it has not one insight nor quotable phrase.[20] Ethel surely looked upon
Townend as a sponger and, if so, it is hard to disagree with her. That is
why Wodehouse took trouble to keep Ethel in ignorance of his permanent
subsidies to Townend, repeatedly telling his friend in letters not to mention his financial help when replying in case Ethel saw the letter. Wodehouse did so only to avoid Ethel's reasonable recriminations and, perhaps,
because he enjoyed the intellectual exercise of helping Townend without
Ethel knowing. It was not because Ethel ran his finances, because she
didn't. The shrewd and worldly Ethel probably knew full well what was
happening, but she also knew that on the few things that mattered to her
husband he was immovable and she was more than wise enough not to let
on that she knew all. But Ethel was not a simple character either. From
New York, during the food rationing Britain suffered after World War

Two under its socialist government, she sent the Townends frequent and generous food parcels.

While Townend was Wodehouse's private charity with a signeurial gulf between them, Bolton was looked upon as an equal and acts of charity towards him were, while generous, more commercial. Wodehouse frequently halved royalties with Bolton where he, not Guy, had often done most of the work. Such joint deals included not only *Bring On The Girls* but other books such as *French Leave*, based on a Bolton idea, and *Ring For Jeeves*, based on a Bolton–Wodehouse play *Come On Jeeves*, which in turn was based on Wodehouse's ideas, while the pair shared the royalties on the lyric for 'Bill'. Wodehouse would send Bolton cheques but did not tell Ethel. The Wodehouse Glide applied not only to parties but to such things as the Ethel–Guy antipathy – both were jealous of Plum's affection for the other – but Plum never let this bother him.

Twice these joint Bolton–Wodehouse royalty arrangements almost caused breaches between the friends. At one stage Wodehouse made over to Bolton certain rights in *Leave It To Psmith* on the excuse that Guy had provided him with the idea for one good scene[21] and then in 1933 the two settled a dispute agreeing that Bolton would waive his claimed rights on the play, *Leave It To Psmith* in exchange for Wodehouse's rights to the play of *Piccadilly Jim*.[22] This actually required a formal, legally drafted, letter from Plum to Guy. A year later they almost went to court to settle their differences. Wodehouse wrote to Reynolds that in an argument over royalties on *If I Were You* (he may have meant *Who's Who*, the play from his book) 'I settled with him out of court'.[23] The friendship was soon resumed, as before, although it also got interrupted by Bolton's habit of trading the old Mrs Bolton in for a different model every few years. Plum found adjusting to a new Mrs Guy, just when he had got used to the old one, rather unsettling.

Wodehouse was also generous to Dulwich. As they were published, he provided copies of all his books for the college library where they were read by the boys until they fell to pieces. Nobody then realized the future values of those books, including an inscribed first edition of *The Pothunters*, for which any rich collector would now willingly pay £10,000, that is $20,000 or more. The college received nothing under Wodehouse's will but after his death Ethel carried out his wishes by funding two scholarships for upper school boys and assisted with the refurbishment of the college library in 1981. During his life Wodehouse was good to the college, sending biggish cheques to every fund-raising appeal and helping in other ways. Old Alleynian Trevor Bailey, later a great English cricketer, recalls that in the 1938 season, when the college's First XI won all their matches, Wodehouse generously stood the team dinner in London's West

End and a show at the London Palladium.[24] He was not present – and one should read no more into that than a sensible fifty-seven year old realizing that he would no longer feel at ease with a team of noisy, celebrating adolescents and that his presence would cramp their enjoyment of his bounty.

For those not so close to him, such as Armine, he was not a soft touch – intelligent, money-wise people never are – but there is no evidence he was mean. In *A Maypole In The Strand* the then editor of the magazine, Reginald Pound, wrote of his old contributor: 'I remember the kindly letter that passed through my hands when I was on the *Daily Express*: he was anxious that we should help a once-famous cricketer who had fallen on evil days. It is firmly held in this office that Wodehouse was the author of many private good deeds as well as a lot of public good fun'.[25] But those good deeds were always executed very quietly. Frances Donaldson relates that when she and her husband Jack asked Wodehouse to become godfather to their daughter Rose he agreed on the strict understanding that after the obligatory christening gift there would be no expectation of annual presents – the basis on which Oofy Prosser became godfather to Algernon Aubrey Little in *Leave It To Algy*. This seems inconsistent with Plum leaving each of his three godchildren who survived him – Mrs Rose Worlidge, Miss Julie Howard and Mike Grenville Griffith – $1,000 each in his will,[26] a worthwhile bequest in those days. A man of ninety who took no interest in his godchildren would be unlikely even to remember who they were. In money, as in most things, Wodehouse was a complex man. He did not love money, but he loved the things it could buy, especially the privacy to get on with writing. Most of all he looked on money as a benchmark, a public recognition of his status as an author, and by that test he couldn't be faulted. In the 1930s he was one of the highest paid authors in the world. *The Strand* was paying him £500 for a short story and *The Saturday Evening Post*, with the larger American market, $3,000 or $4,000 while he was paid $40,000 for the US magazine rights of *Summer Moonshine* and similar amounts for other novels. There were also the advances and royalties on new books as well as the royalties on old ones and on all his plays and lyrics plus film, foreign language and republication rights. It totted up to a large amount of money and with it, under Ethel's guiding hand, the Wodehouses, if not Wodehouse, lived in some style.

For several summers they rented a fine country house, usually Hunstanton Hall in Norfolk owned by Wodehouse's kinsmen the Le Stranges, and one year Rogate Lodge in Hampshire. Then in 1928 Ethel bought a lease on an imposing London mansion, 17 Norfolk Street (now Dunraven Street) in fashionable Mayfair just off Park Lane costing in rent the large sum of £450 per month before running expenses. Wodehouse went on to the butler standard. (He never emulated his friend Edgar Wallace whom he admired for having both a day-butler and a night-butler, so that at whatever time one arrived *chez* Wallace there was always buttling going on.) There were seven other servants – cook, footman, two housemaids, a parlourmaid, a scullerymaid and a gardener – and they also bought a Rolls Royce which meant a chauffeur as well. Ethel loved it all and it must have been ideal for launching Leonora into London society, but it didn't seem to make any difference to Wodehouse at all, apart from having a new cable address 'Blandings, Audley, London'.[27] Audley was the postal sub-district. George Grossmith remembers Wodehouse from those days.

> In a charming house in Norfolk Street his wife personally supervised the decorating and furnishing of a perfect study and library for her husband to work in. Beautiful old books and prints filled the shelves and relieved the panelling. Rich but subdued hangings, costly but comfortable furniture, completed a workroom any man might envy. 'PG' gave one look at it, complimented Mrs Wodehouse on her perfect taste and asked for permission to descend to the kitchen. Here he borrowed a small deal table and chair.
>
> These he carried up himself to an empty attic at the top of the house, and installing his beloved typewriter on the one and himself on the other, began to rattle off one of the immortal adventures of 'Jeeves' or 'P'Smith' (sic).[28]

Wodehouse worked back-to-window, face-to-wall, to avoid distraction. While his simple tastes cost the family very little he was happy that Ethel lived more fashionably and expensively. When a casino bystander had the impertinence to criticize her gambling to Wodehouse, his acerbic rebuke was simple: 'It's my money'.[29] Both Ethel and Plum liked gambling but while she was an ill-disciplined punter he was not. In gambling and money he was, as in so much else, a complicated and contradictory man. Oppenheim described the Wodehouse gambling system.

> A few years ago he and his wife rented a delightful villa near Grasse and during the season were almost nightly visitors at the Cannes Casino. P.G. liked his own peculiar form of gambling which consisted chiefly in walking from table to table, taking a Banco of any size at *chemin de fer*, or, if roulette was more in evidence, backing in *mille* notes a special little combination of his own of red or black associated with the columns. He had a method, too, of covering the board so that only five numbers remained on which he had not staked. I imagine that one

or other of those five numbers turned up a little too often, for it is a
system which he afterwards abandoned. Tall, broad-shouldered and
with a kind of hidden smile, looking more like an Oxford professor than
a writer of humorous stories, he walked about at Le Touquet with a
handful of *mille* notes and a studious, I fancy acquired, habit of seeing
no one until he had either won or lost as much as he intended to during
the evening. (I was never able to risk all the money I could afford for
the evening's entertainment in three or four coups and then treat the
game as though it had no existence.) Sometimes it was all over in an
hour, then quite a different man strolled over to where his wife was
playing baccarat at the big table. If he found her occupied, he was
immediately ready for a drink with any of his friends.[30]

Wodehouse's letters often mention his gambling and Ethel's. On one
occasion he won £1,000 at the Cannes casino – a huge sum then, equal to
£30,000 today.[31] On another he went to a casino, had a shot at roulette,
won three *mille* in two minutes and came home. At seven in the morning
one of the Pekes, Miss Winks, was restless so he took her out and met
Ethel arriving home having been at the casino all night, losing three *mille*.
So they took the dogs for a walk and went into the casino for breakfast.[32]
Wodehouse was an extraordinarily self-disciplined gambler. He would
enter the casino having decided how much he was prepared to play with
and if he lost it he quit, making him not only a psychological rarity but
proving his strength of character.

One very ordinary characteristic Wodehouse, and Ethel, held in
common with most people was a dislike of paying taxes in general and
income tax in particular. Indeed Evelyn Waugh complained that at his
only and eagerly anticipated meeting with Wodehouse at a *Vogue* editorial
lunch in New York after the war all The Master would talk about was
income tax.[33] (Wodehouse later denied this story to Tom Sharpe and on
such matters Plum was always right, yet the story is absolutely in character
but for the fact that Wodehouse was too well mannered to be a lunch-
party bore.)

Some people get paid a lot of money and some people earn it. Wodehouse and his peers felt they earned their money. One reason for the
Wodehouses' peregrinations between the wars was to reduce their heavy
tax burden. As early as 1921 the Wodehouses left England for Paris
because Plum was appalled to discover that if he stayed in Britain for
more than six months of the financial year (which runs to 6 April in the
UK) he would have to pay British income tax not only on everything he
earned in the UK but also, in full, on everything left from his American
income after the US authorities had taxed it. 'This is no good to our

Pelham so I am skipping,' he told Townend.[34]

Thus Wodehouse limited his tax liabilities by living in countries with less punitive tax rates or by not living long enough in one country to become resident there for tax purposes. Not being a permanent resident of any country could save a lot of money. Wodehouse sometimes talked wistfully of settling down in England, perhaps in the Chippenham area of Wiltshire, surrounded by enough acres for lots of pets and animals.[35] At times he said he hated living abroad, but not as much as he hated paying taxes, yet he would also say 'I pine for America' if he was away from God's Own Country for too long.[36] During his peak earning period in the thirties he had to ration his visits to England, writing to Leonora of having to eke out his visits to England in case the taxman claimed him as a resident. In fact many letters show he slipped over to England from Le Touquet on the Channel ferry to spend the weekend at Fairlawne on numerous occasions in the thirties, apparently without telling the taxman.

From the early twenties, when Wodehouse began to earn huge sums of money, he and his advisers worked hard to minimize his tax bills but with varying success. At one stage most of his US earnings were channelled into companies which paid lower taxes than individuals. There was Jeeves Dramatics Inc. and Jeeves Inc. in the US and Jeeves Ltd. in the UK and Siva Aktiengesellschaft SA in Switzerland.[37] On 26 April 1934 Siva bought the North and South American rights to all Wodehouse's work for a period of four years for the sum of $400,000. These financial convolutions were not always entirely successful for the multinational business Wodehouse conducted and Siva was put into liquidation in the autumn of 1937. Plum considered trying to treat his work sold in America as 'Articles manufactured out of the country' which would have meant payments for them were not liable to US tax. However that would have meant admitting to the UK authorities that his US earnings did not belong to Jeeves Dramatics Inc. – and thus they would become liable to UK income tax. Wodehouse's letter to Reynolds on this problem[38] showed his clear understandings of the complications and ramifications of international tax planning. This was the time when tax rates had only recently become punitive and the tax avoidance industry was still in its infancy, as was the drafting of international tax legislation. As an author resident in France, most of whose income came from the US and UK, Wodehouse did not fit into any statutory pigeon-hole – always a sure recipe for oven-hot problems. So I do not think it a severe reflection on Wodehouse and his advisers that some of his tax disputes actually reached court and a credit to them that, on each occasion, his lawyers put up a strong case on his behalf – and in every instance they either won outright or won a favourable compromise. These cases indicate how hard he was prepared to fight to minimize his tax payments. He was in the company of many other highly paid people but few were as tenacious as he was.

The first of his tax disputes came to court on 19 January 1934 in London[39] winning for Raymond Needham KC, who acted for Wodehouse, the dedication to *Right Ho Jeeves* which simply says 'With affection and admiration'. Usborne tells us that Needham had to talk Wodehouse out of using the original, highly provocative, dedication which was to have been: 'To Raymond Needham KC, who put the tax-gatherers to flight when they had their feet on my neck and their hands in my wallet' or words to that effect.[40]

The Inland Revenue in the UK had summoned Wodehouse for the payment of £25,000 in back taxes. The tax inspector, long in charge of the Wodehouse case, thought he had at last got his quarry trapped. Wodehouse's solicitors thought so too but they retained Needham, then the top tax silk, who exploited a minor error in the taxman's presentation of his case and got the whole thing dismissed. The furious inspector told Needham he intended to appeal against the judgement to which the lawyer responded, 'Well anyway, come and have some lunch with us now.' 'Us? Who else?' said the inspector. 'My client, P.G. Wodehouse,' replied Needham 'Savoy Grill at one.' The inspector and Wodehouse came out of the Grill after lunch arm-in-arm like Abercrombie & Fitch or Marks & Spencer. The Inspector had been at Bedford when Wodehouse was at Dulwich and they had played rugger against each other. The appeal against the court's judgement in favour of Wodehouse was never lodged[41] – which proves not that tax inspectors can be diverted from stern duty's call but that they, too, are human.

That same year, on 8 August 1934, the IRS claimed no less than $250,703.59 from Wodehouse in alleged back taxes and penalties and froze his US income and assets. In June 1936 an out-of-court settlement was reached with Wodehouse paying the IRS some $80,000 – but that case was just a beginning.[42] The IRS in America was enthusiastically attempting to dig more deeply into the coffers of foreign authors with American earnings, making a series of large tax demands of them on behalf of Uncle Sam. Rafael Sabatini, the swashbuckling author of pirate tales, took up the cudgels on behalf of all overseas authors and fought the IRS through the courts, as did Sax Rohmer, creator of the fiendish Dr Fu Manchu. It took two decades to resolve the principles of such taxation. The whole matter was much complicated by a new US Revenue Act in 1936 which aimed to settle the matter in favour of the tax authorities but was badly drafted. Meanwhile some of the world's highest paid authors were, literally, on the brink of penury. Plum's pen-friend Agatha Christie, for example, was taxed in the UK on her post-tax US earnings, so she needed her US earnings to pay her British taxes upon them. Yet her American funds were frozen pending agreement with the IRS. 'I can't understand how one is supposed to live if you get £7,000-odd income and pay £5,000 surtax out of it,' she remarked.[43] After the war UK tax rates went up to 97.5 per cent for top incomes and Wodehouse tartly observed that if a man making £100,000 a year could only get as much for himself as a man making £10,000 a year there was no inducement to sweat oneself to the bone. (Not that this stopped him working as hard as ever.) He added that it was the £100,000 a year men who really made a country's prosperity.[44]

In April 1947 Wodehouse wrote to Townend of his problems with the US tax authorities suddenly deciding he had not paid his taxes for 1921 to 1924 and impounding all his US funds. This was an obvious nonsense as, in those days, no one could leave the US without a chit saying that his taxes had been paid and Wodehouse had been in and out of the country many times since then.[45] Finding tax records twenty-three years old is difficult enough in normal times and impossible when your house has been commandeered by Germans during a war. Eventually the US courts decided Wodehouse had in fact paid up but the IRS still stuck to $20,000 and Wodehouse got back $19,000 – which made him feel $19,000 to the good instead of $20,000 to the bad.[46]

Some while earlier Sabatini and Rohmer, at substantial cost to themselves in time and legal fees, had both lost their cases in lower courts and retired from the lists having tried to do their best for their fellow authors. Their place was taken by a benign, short-sighted, elderly figure who had never buckled a swash in his life: P.G. Wodehouse.

The case of *Commissioner Of Internal Revenue* v. *Wodehouse* was argued on 10 and 13 December 1948 before the Justices of the US Supreme Court. Watson Washburn, on behalf of Wodehouse, was appealing against IRS assessments of additional tax claimed on Wodehouse's US income of $11,806.71 for 1938, $8,080.83 for 1940 and $1,854.85 for 1941. In effect he was appealing against the Sabatini judgement and also arguing some arcane points on the difference between income and capital. Wodehouse had sold some of his work for capital sums rather than income as there was then no tax on capital gains.

The judgement takes up fifty-six pages of *Cases Adjudged In The Supreme Court*[47] and contains much of incidental interest. *The Code Of The Woosters* was originally to be called *The Silver Cow* and the North American serial rights were sold for $40,000. Out of that Reynolds took his five per cent agent's fee and ten per cent of the balance was paid in withholding tax to the IRS. That left $34,200, half of which was paid directly to Ethel and the other half to Plum. (That split was purely for reasons of tax minimization – and failed in that. It tells us nothing more than that about how the Wodehouse finances were run.) *My War With Germany* was originally *My Years Behind Barbed Wire* and the same magazine rights fetched $2,000. It also shows the considerable effort the Wodehouses and their advisers had put into minimizing his US tax liabilities.

In a split decision Wodehouse lost the case by five to three. Justice Harold H. Burton gave the 25,000 word majority judgement. The opinion of the three dissenting justices was delivered by Mr Justice Frankfurter who was also considered one of the finest exponents of the English language ever to sit on the Supreme Court. He observed that the majority judgement 'Appears to be guided, in however low a key that consideration is pitched, by the urgent need for revenue'. But 'twas ever thus. It's a pity Wodehouse didn't attend the hearings. He would surely have created as memorable a character as A.P. Herbert's litigious Albert Haddock of the *Uncommon Law* stories and made something of such cases cited as *Photo Drama Motion Picture Co.* v. *Social Uplift Film Corp.* At least eight of Wodehouse's tax disputes went to court – one of which was before the aptly named Judge Learned Hand[48] – while many others reached the court house steps before a settlement was agreed. Not until 6 December 1950 was a settlement reached on the last of Wodehouse's numerous tax cases.

It is just as well that the IRS never knew of the Wodehouse dodge with the US serialization rights of *Laughing Gas*. The *New York Herald Magazine* paid him $10,000 for the rights but did so with a cheque from their Paris office 'Thus utterly baffling the USA tax people and making them look pretty silly'.[49] Like the great majority of rich men Wodehouse took a freebooting attitude to his tax obligations and filing his returns, whether in America, Great Britain or France. Not only did he slip into England to see Leonora without telling the taxman but he regularly sent cheques from ASCAP (for American royalties on his theatre work) to Townend. This was not to deceive Ethel but for two better reasons, both of which delighted the money obsessed, tax-hating, Wodehouse. Firstly sending Townend ASCAP cheques, rather than personal cheques drawn on his own account, meant Plum could cheerfully forget to declare that income on his tax return as the money never passed through his bank. Secondly as gifts such sums were tax free in Townend's hands.[50] To get the better of both the US and UK tax authorities in one deft move must have been especially satisfying. Sometimes it didn't work and Wodehouse was most annoyed when his instruction to W.P. Watt in London to pay £1,250 of royalties directly to Townend arrived too late as the money had already gone into his account at Barclays Bank in London.[51]

The idea that Wodehouse didn't understand money and let Ethel handle his financial affairs comes from the usual unreliable informer, Wodehouse himself, sometimes aided and abetted by Ethel, although late in life she gave the game away. Talking to *The New Yorker* she said 'Plummie loves America. He loves A.T.&T. He loves the dividend.'[52]

What was this man, who was supposed to have nothing to do with handling the family finances, doing noting down stock prices? What was this financial innocent doing, casually dropping information culled from the *Wall Street Journal?* Why should a man whose every interview, letter and story has some sensible mention of money take no interest in his own? Who is this fiscally naive man whose interest in tax rivals that of Bertie Wooster's Uncle Tom Portarlington Travers? The facts in his letters show that the idea of Wodehouse remaining uninvolved in his own finances is as false as the other facets of the myth he created about himself, not just fiction but farce. Ethel was only the joint treasurer in the Wodehouse household. Wodehouse and Ethel had separate bank accounts as well as joint ones. For example, in a letter to Mackail he complained about foreign exchange controls preventing him getting at his UK assets while his US funds were frozen pending settlement of a tax dispute, and he adds cheerfully that Ethel is in the money and he will borrow from her.[53] Even in the thirties Wodehouse seldom had need for cash and the small change from his earnings was more than enough for his requirements, of which his quasi-pensioner Townend, and in a different class altogether, his adored Leonora, were the most significant, costing him much more than he spent on his own simple needs. One of the reasons he liked his next house, Low Wood at Le Touquet, was that it was simple and comfortable rather than grand.

— 14 —

HE RATHER ENJOYED IT

That Lord of Language, Dr P.G. Wodehouse, no quotation could represent nor synopsis clarify.[1]

L.A.G. Strong

I T was partly due to the casino at Le Touquet on the north French coast that, in August 1934, the Wodehouses leased a villa there, Low Wood, which they bought a year later. Another advantage was the more relaxed French quarantine laws (important to a pair of dog-lovers). Wodehouse once wrote of taking their Peke, Miss Winks, to England disguised in a cat skin;[2] cats were not then quarantined. Had he done so the scene in the customs hall would surely have rivalled anything he ever wrote. The situation of Le Touquet also enabled residents and their visitors to travel between the resort and Paris or London fairly quickly – either by rail and ferry or, for the adventurous, Imperial Airways flew from Le Touquet to Croydon Aerodrome in South London in under an hour. Wodehouse made the trip once, the first and last time he ever flew. 'I was scared stiff although it only lasted half an hour.'[3] Ethel never flew. They were both adult when – at almost exactly the time when the Wright brothers made the first powered flight at Kitty Hawk, North Carolina, in 1903 – distinguished scientists such as the American astronomer Simon Newcomb proved conclusively that practical air travel was impossible.[4] Le Touquet was also convenient for the transatlantic liners sailing to New York as Cherbourg was within easy motoring distance, while Townend and his wife were then living just across the Channel at Dover and later Folkstone. Most of all the Wodehouses liked the easier tax system for foreign authors. But the principal cause of their move to Le Touquet was the failure of producer Vinton Freedley's show *Pardon My English*.

After sunning himself in the Pearl Islands to allow his creditors to cool down Freedley returned to the US with plans for a guaranteed hit. Thus he chose Bolton and Wodehouse to write the book and Cole Porter for the score and lyrics. Freedley suggested setting the story on a pleasure cruise with the ship later wrecked at sea. At the time the Wodehouses were living in Paris and Bolton in London, so the two authors agreed to meet and work on the script at a town halfway between the two. They chose Le Touquet which Plum and Ethel liked better and better the more they saw of it.

Guy and Plum sent their script to New York in mid-August 1934 and Freedley wasn't satisfied with it – no impresario ever is satisfied with a first script. Wodehouse believed that Howard Lindsay, the producer and 'the man on the spot' poisoned Freedley's mind against it.[5] (Wodehouse knew how bitchy the theatre world could be and he was neither naive nor weak. Nineteen years later he noted that a Lindsay and Crouse play had come off in London after only seven performances and told Bolton, with evident pleasure, that he thought it showed the right spirit.[6]) Then on 8 September the *SS Moro Castle* was wrecked off the New Jersey coast with a loss of over 100 lives. The original authors were not free for the total rewrite now essential as Bolton was in a Brighton hospital with a burst appendix. So Howard Lindsay got the job and asked Russel Crouse to assist him. (Thus was born another of the great partnerships of the American musical stage.) *Anything Goes* was a smash hit running for 415 performances although, per Lindsay and Crouse, there remained only a couple of lines of the original authors' book. Because of Plum and Guy's contract with Freedley they made far more money from the show than did Lindsay and Crouse who, understandably, felt sore. Wodehouse wrote in detail about the matter noting with satisfaction that he still got one and a half per cent of the gross takings;[7] poor Crouse got only a half of one per cent. The show was also a great success when produced in London the following year. It continued to be so. In later life Bolton said: 'Amateurs are still doing it all over the place. Ginnie [his fourth wife] and I practically live off it. I don't know where they find all the amateurs.'[8]

In fact it was the amateurs who found the play and Wodehouse was proud of its success although whether the original Bolton–Wodehouse script was ever produced or still exists is unknown. While modest about himself Plum had enough vanity to make him human. He was delighted when the Marquess of Crewe on behalf of the Council of The Royal Society of Literature invited him to become a Fellow in 1926.[9] He was gratified when a letter addressed to 'P.G. Wodehouse, London'[10] reached him with no trouble and when a critic in *Playhouse* described an actor as 'Good as a P.G. Wodehouse sort of character' and a book reviewer in *The Times* wrote 'The author at times reverts to the P.G. Wodehouse manner'. As Plum wrote to Leonora 'This is jolly old Fame'.[11] He also asked Leonora to send him a copy of *The Georgian Literary Scene* as 'It's all about how good I am'.[12] While he showed no interest in photography he was not camera shy but always obliging to press photographers and happily co-operative whenever publicity photographs were required. He was bucked when press photographers buzzed around him and Ethel when they arrived in New York once and disappointed not to find any of the pictures in the next day's papers.[13] In Hollywood he and Ethel enjoyed being interviewed on radio by Hedda Hopper.[14] Shrewdly he wrote a script for the interview which gave Miss Hopper all the best gags. He also took an acquiescent part in his publishers' promotional activities for his books, writing cheerfully to Townend about an entire week being taken up by 'duty-lunches',[15] although unlike Hugh Walpole he didn't actually initiate lunches with the literary critics. In 1933 Wodehouse dutifully posed for the famous cartoon by Low, who remembered:

> As I had expected the humorists were personally not funny, but looked rather as if they were studying for the undertaking business. Even P.G. Wodehouse, a cheerful big chap easy to get on with, was not funny in the sense of jokey, apart from his peculiar wish to pose after he had just had drops in his eyes for treatment so that he would have impressively large and luminous pupils like Edgar Allen Poe.[16]

Wodehouse happily spent half a day autographing his books at Harrods, signed twelve copies of each of his titles at the Jenkins offices[17] and at the age of eighty signed 1,000 copies of his books for a US book club. Similarly he treated his fans with as much respect and courtesy as any author ever did, always replying to their letters personally, although some-times finding it a bore. Nor was he like so many authors, including Mark Twain and Thomas Hardy, who refused to inscribe copies of their books. He invented a piece of doggerel for the purpose. 'You like my little story do ya? Oh, glory, glory, Halleluya'.[18] Herbert Mayes, the great editor of *McCall's*, recalls another. 'My favourite inscription is used by writer P.G. Wodehouse, "Tell your friends to buy this book" would appear on the flyleaf of anything he wrote "because I need the money".'[19]

His modesty did not extend to his work. On the one hand he accepted editorial comments and when, for example Erd Brandt, an editor at the *Saturday Evening Post*, criticized the original draft of *The Code Of The Woosters* as having too many stage waits, Wodehouse at once realized he was right, said so, and cut them out.[20] To the end of his life he valued constructive criticism from editors, writing to Bolton that the comments of his editor at *Colliers* on *Pigs Have Wings* left him with a large respect for outside opinion.[21] He also valued, highly, the comments of Leonora and Ethel. All of which shows real self-confidence. But he was his own sternest critic. He knew when his writing failed to achieve the right effect in the right way, judged by his own stratospheric standards, and then worked hard to correct his faults and bring about the required result.[22]

On the other hand, when he'd achieved what he sought he didn't mind congratulating himself. He wrote the last chapter of *Bring On The Girls* at speed and when he read it over he was 'Stunned how good it is'.[23] Rereading *Blandings Castle* he told Sheran, Leonora's daughter, that he was 'Lost in admiration for the brilliance of the author'.[24] Jokily phrased but not a joke. He took the same robust view of *America I Like You* in commenting to Peter Schwed in 1956.[25] In writing to Bolton he expresses a low opinion of Larry Hart as a lyric writer: 'Ira [Gershwin] is worth ten of him'. He also had a low opinion of many of Cole Porter's lyrics, especially in *Anything Goes*, which he discusses in great technical detail with Bolton, telling him that he always felt that Porter sang his lyrics to Elsa Maxwell and Noel Coward in a studio stinking of gin with his audience saying 'Oh Cole *darling*, it's just too marvellous'.[26] In private Wodehouse was often as anodyne as a razor blade. He considered Porter's trouble was that he had no power of self-criticism. Yet Plum had a high opinion of Noel Coward's lyrics (and novels)[27] although he and Coward were about as antipathetic as two men can be. Wodehouse also told Bolton that he was lost in admiration of the lyrics for *Inside USA* and had no idea that Howard Dietz was such a wizard.[28] Those are not the comments of a modest man but of an unselfconscious master of his art, pleased by fine craftsmanship and irritated at inferior work. However in public he was modest, as required by the public school code. 'I haven't a very high opinion of my work. I think it's all right for what it intends to be, but I wouldn't say it is very important.'[29] That is modesty vanquishing truth.

Similarly, his criticisms were never made publicly for, unlike Hugh Walpole, Wodehouse was sensitive to other people's feelings, as well as his own – although agents and publishers were occasionally exceptions to the rule. Derek Grimsdick told Margaret Slythe that, sometimes, when Wodehouse entered the Herbert Jenkins offices the staff hid. They could tell by his attitude that he had taken a decision, which they wouldn't like, upon which he would insist. In those days before the war no one at York Street, St James's, had any misconceptions about Wodehouse's strength of character and interest in his business affairs. Lord Tenby, who worked for Herbert Jenkins in the nineteen-fifties, said that in his day Wodehouse still took a shrewd and detailed interest in every aspect of the UK publication of his books, especially everything to do with money, and that the firm still did just as Wodehouse bid them.[30] It had to as it depended on Wodehouse throughout most of its independent existence. In 1963

Derek Grimsdick worked out that, while Jenkins published over 400 authors, Wodehouse accounted for eleven per cent of their sales and seventy-three per cent of sums received for paperback royalties.[31] Wodehouse treated his publishers courteously, but as his employees – which in practical terms they were.

Like any other author he was not fond of unrequested criticism and had a thoroughly normal dislike for the critics, wondering whether he hated them more when they praised him or roasted him. He gave up taking a UK press clippings service for his book reviews in 1934[32] having given up the same service in America some years previously – but he continued to get copies from his publishers and agents (thus saving the cost of a service) and his correspondence remained full of comments about the reviews of his work. In 1952 he renewed his subscription to a press cuttings agency and complained that the first thing he got was thirty-five obituaries of Ian Hay where he, Wodehouse, received a passing mention.[33] At all times he took to heart criticism that he recognised as valid.

> I get a lot of reviews sent to me. They are invariably favourable and somehow I always read them carefully. You do get tips from them. Now that last Jeeves book of mine, *Jeeves And The Tie That Binds* [UK *Much Obliged Jeeves*], I forget which critic it was, but he said that the book was dangerously close to self-parody. I know what he meant. I had exaggerated Jeeves and Bertie. Jeeves was always reciting some poetry or something. I'll correct that in the next one. I do think one can learn from criticism. In fact I'm a pretty good critic of my own work. I know when it isn't as good as it ought to be.[34]

An unusual and perceptive literary critic was the cow that lived in a tiny village in India. Writer Verrier Elwin found that, faced with his library shelves including the works of Armine's mentor theosophist Mrs Annie Besant and Jerome K. Jerome, the bovine critic preferred to eat a copy of *Carry On Jeeves*.[35] Wodehouse, whatever his expressed feelings about the critics, continued to take a normal pleasure in favourable reviews and read them avidly as they arrived from his publishers or agents.

In 1935 A.P. Watt & Co became his UK literary agent (and the firm is still agent to the Trustees of the Wodehouse Estate). W.P. Watt was an imposing figure and young Derek Grimsdick, now mostly looking after Wodehouse at Herbert Jenkins in place of his father John, confessed that he always felt like calling the agent 'Sir' and was staggered to learn that, among his intimates, Watt was known by Plum's favourite name, 'Bill'. Grimsdick would have felt dumbfounded had he known that Townend referred to Watt as 'Willie'.[36] Wodehouse struck up a strong rapport with

Watt and Grimsdick both of whom he met only a few times in his life. He took a particular interest in young Mike Grimsdick's cricketing prowess at grandfather Deane's old school, the Merchant Taylors'.

Plum usually got on well with publishers, one of whom, for just one book, was his friend George Blake; a Peke-fancying Scot who wrote numerous novels set in Scottish shipyards. He was also the assistant editor at *The Strand* who looked after Wodehouse. Blake had just been tempted to join the board of publishers Faber and Faber. Wodehouse, to help his chum in his new job, dug into his files and put together a book made up mostly of his old journalism, mainly articles from *Vanity Fair*. The result, *Louder And Funnier* (not published in the US), is one of Wodehouse's weakest books but has probably the finest dust-wrapper of any of them: a Rex Whistler design based on a bust of Plum looking like a genial Roman Emperor. The dedication reads 'To George Blake, a splendid fellow and very sound on Pekes' with a footnote 'But he should guard against the tendency to claim that his Peke fights Alsatians. Mine is the only one that does this.' Like so many journalists, Blake found publishing didn't suit him and went back to writing shortly after *Louder And Funnier* was published.

However the major event in 1932 was Leonora's engagement to Peter Cazalet, the son and heir of the Wodehouses' friends, William and Molly Cazalet who owned the 1,000 acre Fairlawne estate at Shipbourne near Tonbridge in Kent. The Cazalets were a racing family and Peter was eventually to train the horses of Her Majesty, Queen Elizabeth The Queen Mother, coincidentally, a devotee of Wodehouse's writing. The wedding took place quietly at 9.30 a.m. on 14 December at the parish church of St Giles due to the recent death of the father of the groom. At the ceremony the father of the bride was uncharacteristically immaculate in full morning coat, wing collar and silk top-hat. Leonora's first child, Sheran, was born sixteen months later and Plum – whose previous view was that all babies look like a cross between a homicidal poached egg and Winston Churchill or Boris Karloff – was in raptures, writing to Leonora that he had never seen such a beautiful baby[37] (although he later polished and used Leonora's description of her daughter as 'Looking like an old Chinese gangster'). A son, Edward, was born to the couple in 1936.

Wodehouse was extremely close to his son-in-law Peter while Leonora was alive. He called him 'The Puss', followed his racing career both as a rider and trainer and took his advice on backing horses. Sometimes Wodehouse gave his son-in-law money to bet on horses, using his own judgement, on his father-in-law's behalf. Plum was also close to Peter's sister, the Member of Parliament, Thelma Cazalet, later Thelma Cazalet-Keir. It was the Cazalet family who reintroduced him to Hugh Walpole at

Shipbourne one weekend. The two authors went to Twickenham together to watch a rugby match and Wodehouse dragged Walpole off to a lunch at the House of Commons to meet Winston Churchill (again) – but a real friendship never developed. Wodehouse, noting that Walpole kept a list of his friends, was worried that he might have been bunged on at number fourteen and relieved when, after declining to join a trip to Majorca, he felt he must have been relegated to number thirty or, better, struck off altogether.[38]

However Wodehouse allowed Beverley Nichols to maintain a slight friendship, which yields us another demonstration that Wodehouse was, when he turned his mind to it, still a shrewd observer of the world and in particular of other people's follies. In 1938 Nichols, considerably bothered by the threat of Russian Communism, planned a warning book on it and wondered how on earth to get his message over without a mass of boring statistics no one would ever read. The answer was provided, unexpectedly, by Wodehouse. During a lunch with Nichols he pulled a copy of *The Daily Worker*, the communist newspaper, out of his pocket and underlined passages in an essay, *For Purity of Marxist–Leninist Theory In Surgery*. He then read some aloud and told Nichols, 'If I were having my piles out and saw that article sticking out of the surgeon's pocket I should leap off the operating table like a startled antelope.'[39] After that Nichols used laughter to achieve his ends. (That such a money-obsessed conservative with 'the blood of an hundred earls running in his veins' read a Communist newspaper should no longer surprise us.)

A minor tragedy took place in the Wodehouse household in December 1935. Plum's beloved Monarch was given the last rites and laid to rest. It was replaced with a Royal, which he learned to love, but never as deeply as he had the Monarch and there was no period of official mourning when the Royal was replaced by an electric model in 1956.

Plum's achievements as a writer were now recognized by almost everyone except Hugh Walpole, the Irish litterateur Sean O'Casey and the Cambridge don, F.R. Leavis (and his wife 'Queenie') who dismissed Wodehouse's writing as 'stereotyped humour' but whose own pretentious and sterile ideas are now largely derided. He wrote of Wodehouse: 'There has never been a question of an art or any influence to be taken in any way seriously. I should never have insulted an undergraduate audience (my habit being to address them as intelligent adults) by suggesting otherwise.'[40] Queenie wrote: 'His humour is a cross of prep-school and *Punch*, his invention puerile, the brightness of his style the inane, mechanical and monotonous brightness of the worst schoolboy slang.'[41] Leavis lived long enough to hear Wodehouse described as 'The highbrow's lowbrow',[42] and for the remark about himself, 'A man from whom dispraise were no faint praise',[43] to sweep deliciously through academia – which must have caused him well-deserved fury.

On 26 June 1936 Wodehouse was awarded the medallion of the International Mark Twain Society 'In recognition of your outstanding and lasting contribution to the happiness of the world'.[44] It was particularly pleasing to Wodehouse that an earlier recipient of the society's medallion was one of his heroes, Rudyard Kipling, while it amused him that the fascist dictator, Benito Mussolini, quondam journalist and novelist, had also been awarded the medal.

Possibly the society was influenced by a broadcast Hilaire Belloc had made in America at that time (and repeated in his introduction to *Week-end Wodehouse*) calling Plum 'the best writer of English now alive. The head of my profession . . . the ancient, the burdensome, the out-at-elbows trade of writing. The trade of Homer, of Swift, of Theocritus'.[45] Belloc was in crowded company. Sir Ian Moncreiffe recalled:

> When I was at Stowe our English tutor was that remarkable falconer-pacifist-huntsman, T.H. White, who wrote *The Sword In The Stone* and *The Ill-Made Knight*. One morning [in 1936] Tim White came into our beautiful Georgian classroom and announced 'G.K. Chesterton died yesterday. P.G. Wodehouse is now the greatest living master of the English language.' He then read out a number of passages to show us the skill with which Wodehouse could, as he put it, 'turn a phrase better than any other writer'.[46]

To match the American award came one from England; an honorary Doctorate of Letters from Oxford University. When Wodehouse first received the news he thought it must be a hoax and worried about this until the ceremony itself. Leavis was the only academic to criticize the award, claiming that the whole point of Wodehouse's humour was the refusal of maturity – which was looked upon as a virtue by many, including Evelyn Waugh who considered what others called immaturity to be that rare quality of innocence. By this I believe Waugh meant not the innocence of the unworldly but that precious quality of remaining unsullied by a corrupt world.

The Oxford honour must have been especially sweet remembering those anguished letters to 'Jeames' and dashed hopes of an Oxford degree forty years before. Wodehouse was also pleased that Mark Twain appeared to be the only man previously to have received the honour outside the dull stodgy birds, quite unknown to the public but who seem to get honours showered on them.[47] David Cartwright, Head of Classics at Dulwich, had the inside story from John Griffith, his tutor at Jesus

College. Griffith's father, the late I.O. Griffith, was a Fellow of Brasenose College and on the Hebdomadal Council, Oxford University's ruling body for such awards.

At a meeting in the Spring of 1939 my father, as a distinguished physicist, was asked to name an eminent scientist for an Honorary Degree. As, at that time, there was no obvious person to put forward my father (never lacking in a sense of the unconventional) said: 'Mr Vice-Chancellor (who was the President of Magdalen, George Gordon), I should like to propose Mr P.G. Wodehouse.' An incredulous silence fell and my father wished he had not spoken, but this was broken by the ever genial Gordon with 'Griff, I've always wanted to propose that name but I've never had the courage to do so. There can't be any opposition, can there?' and the proposal went through with acclamation, as was right.

When informed of the task ahead of him, the humane and in his way splendidly whimsical Public Orator of the time, Cyril Bailey (the Classics Tutor at Balliol) wrote to say that he had never read a line of P.G. Wodehouse in his life and could he have some help please, from the proposer?

So my Dad 'phoned me and asked me to come round from Jesus to Brasenose to prepare a selected reading list for the further education of the Public Orator and to throw in a few 'leading thoughts'. Luckily I remembered Julius Caesar's verdict on the Greek poet Menander (*puri sermonis amator*) and, for his part, my Dad insisted on a reference to Augustus Fink-Nottle and Clarence's prize sow of Blandings and we lent Cyril B. our own copies for his use.

What neither of us had expected was what Cyril produced – not a speech in prose listing some of these deathless books but twenty, sensitive Latin hexameters in the manner of Horace's literary Epistles admirably suited to the subject, to the occasion, to the honorand and a masterpiece of the Latin versifier's craft.[48]

It seems likely that Bailey only had to read one Wodehouse story to realize that he would be addressing a man with a proper appreciation of the Latin citation he had to declaim in the Sheldonian theatre, which probably explains the extra trouble he took composing his fine oration.

The night before the ceremony, the Encaenia, Wodehouse stayed with Gordon at Magdalen – Bertie's old college* as he, Bertie, mentions in *The*

---

* See 'Bertram Wooster: Dark Blue' (and '*Wodehouse Fairy-Land*') in *Motley* by Verrier Elwin, one of the best and scarcest books of literary criticism.[49]

Code Of The Woosters when told that the Revd Harold Pinker had been there (as had G. D'Arcy 'Stilton' Cheesewright). Hugh Walpole was also a guest of Magdalen having given a lecture at the Bodleian Library earlier in the day. He was much puzzled by the esteem surrounding Wodehouse, epitomized by Belloc's remarks. Plum told Townend:

> It was just a gag of course, but it worried Hugh terribly. He said to me, 'Did you see what Belloc said about you?' I said I had. 'I wonder why he said that.' 'I wonder,' I said. 'I can't imagine why he said that,' said Hugh. I said I couldn't either. Another long silence. 'It seems such an extraordinary thing to say!' 'Most extraordinary.' Long silence again. 'Ah well,' said Hugh having apparently found the solution, 'the old man's getting very old.'[50]

Unless one believes Wodehouse was lacking in all humour he must have had a hard job keeping a grave face to match Walpole's earnest enquiries. Today you can go into any branch of W.H. Smith or Barnes & Noble and have trouble in finding a single book by Hugh Walpole. You will find at least ten by Wodehouse and probably nearer twenty.

The Encaenia took place on 21 June in the Sheldonian with Wodehouse resplendent in a scarlet gown with facings and sleeves of grey silk. The Public Orator, in his last appearance in the office, took each honorand and presented him to the university's Vice-Chancellor. Bailey's original Latin hexameters appear in the appendices and while no English translation does them full justice, the following makes a valiant attempt to do so.

> And now a famous author, best of those
> Who use the magic medium of prose.
> To make new characters and with a word
> Bring each to life, incomparably absurd.
> Who does not know that youth of wealth and virtues
> Who may not act without his staunch Achates,
> Arbiter of his dress and devious plotter?
> Who has not heard tales of the rubicund talker
> Whose family, cousins and nephews, in their ways
> Lead wondrous lives, at least by what he says.
> Far famed is Clarence with his family lands,
> His prized pig and Psmith – Leave It In His Hands.
> Augustus too, observer of newts amours
> And all the others born to stranger stars.
> Our author yet does not condemn man's folly

But notes it with affection, finds it jolly
And while he fills his books with simple prose
His words run rhythmically, where'er he goes,
The elegance and wit and neatness shows.

Why say more? This man of whom we all know does not need my testimony. I present to you that great humorist, – should I say our Petronius or our Terence? – Pelham Grenville Wodehouse, Fellow of the Royal Society of Literature, to be admitted, for honour, to the degree of Doctor of Letters.

The Vice Chancellor then presented the degree and said (in Latin):

Most delightful, witty, charming, amusing and humorous Sir, with my authority and that of the whole University I admit you together with your entourage of pleasantries, witticisms, jokes and humours to the degree of Doctor of Letters *honoris causa*.[51]

Among the other honorands were Sir Hubert Grierson the English scholar, Sir Edmund Chambers the great lexicographer, Lord Lothian the British Ambassador to Washington, Charles Massey the Canadian High Commissioner, and Felix Frankfurter, of The United States Supreme Court. Wodehouse made the ten minute walk from All Souls to the Sheldonian with Bailey, who attempted to make conversation but without success – Plum did not utter a word. Put that down, if you like, to the shy and unworldly recluse terrified at the public ordeal to come. Or, if you prefer, note that it was one of the mere handful of days in the last seventy-five years of his life when Wodehouse would be unable to spend an hour at the typewriter or writing with pad and pen. He was getting his fix as best he could by working out plot or text in his mind as he always did when walking. That afternoon, at the garden party at Magdalen, John Griffith (who himself became Public Orator in 1973) recalls Wodehouse looking bemused but enjoying himself. Perhaps only then did it sink in that there was no hoax.

The evening of the Encaenia saw Wodehouse on the top table for the Gaudy Dinner at Christ Church. In response to a clamour from the body of the hall, 'We want Wodehouse. We want Wodehouse', he got to his feet, said, 'Thank you very much' and sat down.[52] At fifty-eight he was coming to prefer worlds he could control like Blandings or Valley Fields, not those he couldn't, like Oxford.

Wodehouse's honorary doctorate from Oxford had a disturbing effect on O'Casey. He wrote to his friend, Gabriel Fallon in March 1941, 'The civilization that could let Joyce die in poverty and crown with an Litt. D. a thing like Wodehouse, deserves fire and brimstone from heaven: and is getting it.'[53] He wrote in similar vein at every opportunity (and none) to everyone from the editor of the *Totnes Times* to the *Daily Telegraph*. These two ideas drove O'Casey paranoid. Why he linked them together he probably didn't know in his own mind, but he appeared to think that, by accepting the honour, Wodehouse was personally to blame for Joyce's destitution. Poor O'Casey was not an intimate of Joyce, who died in Zurich two years after that Encaenia, and he may not have known that his hero spent his last years living most comfortably, on the largesse of his American *patronne*, Harriet Weaver. The Irish writer Ulick O'Connor calculates that Mrs Weaver gave Joyce the equivalent of £438,000 in 1991 pounds in the decade 1923 to 1933.[54]

Unaware of his responsibility to Joyce, Wodehouse was able to use the Oxford visit to meet Townend at Dulwich in early July, watch the college first cricket XI play St Paul's, and to write up the match for *The Alleynian*. His report of 'This frightful game, probably the dreariest ever seen on the school grounds'[55] still grips today when read in the Dulwich library by someone whose interest in cricket is long dead (except when I'm talking to baseball fanatics when it springs to life). Wodehouse then returned to Le Touquet and never saw Townend or England again.

As the decade came to an end Wodehouse could look back on ten years which produced much of his finest work. Books not yet mentioned include *Quick Service*, in my view as good as anything he ever wrote. I was gratified to learn that Wodehouse also regarded it as one of his best books. *Big Money* is called by Usborne 'A *locus classicus* for Valley Fields'. There are also two of Wodehouse's best books of short stories; *Eggs, Beans And Crumpets* and *Lord Emsworth And Others* (US *The Crime Wave At Blandings*).

He was now fixed in his ways, had settled down for good at Le Touquet and could look forward to an uneventful old age with increasing veneration and honours: the Order of Merit or perhaps being made a Companion of Honour. He might well, like his friends J.M. Barrie and Owen Seaman, have been made a baronet as older men without male heirs always had a better chance of scooping this honour than more fecund authors.

A regular reader of the London *Times*, Wodehouse remained well informed about world affairs and, when he bothered to apply his mind to them, a shrewd commentator. Two examples will do. In *The Code Of The Woosters*, he perceptively satirized Hitler's Black Shirts. Bertie discusses Spode, a would-be British dictator (recognizably Sir Oswald Mosley, the British fascist leader), whose followers are The Black Shorts.

'When you say "shorts" you mean "shirts", of course.'
'No. By the time Spode formed his association, there were no shirts left. He and his adherents wear black shorts.'
'Footer bags, you mean? Bare knees?'
'Yes.'
'How perfectly foul.'

Wodehouse was, as usual, spot on. At the time there were the black shirts of the British Union of Fascists, the blue shirts of Commander O. Locker-Lampson's anti-Communist vigilantes, the green shirts of Major T.C. Douglas's Social Credit protagonists, the red shirts of the Independent Labour Party's Guild of Youth and the brown shirts of the British Fascists Association.

Bertie, with his typical good sense, addresses Spode thus.

The trouble with you, Spode, is that just because you have succeeded in inducing a handful of half-wits to disfigure the London scene by going about in black shorts, you think you're someone. You hear them shouting 'Heil, Spode!' and you imagine it is the Voice of the People. That is where you make your bloomer. What the Voice of the People is saying is: 'Look at that frightful ass Spode swanking about in footer bags!'

That paragraph showed a worldly awareness that such 'movements' were dangerous gangs of bullies, while many people of his class and generation were looking on the fascists as a bulwark against the communist menace. Secondly the allegedly naive Wodehouse wrote to Townend in 1932 criticizing the American Hawley-Smoot Act. He pointed out then that the big tariffs barriers it erected (and the American insistence on debt repayments) were only making the Depression far worse.[56] It took thirty years before the consensus of economic historians came round to Wodehouse's viewpoint.

Those judgements are inconsistent with a remark Wodehouse is said to have made early in 1939 when staying at the Cazalets' home in Kent when Jack and Frances Donaldson were also guests. In a discussion about the possibility of war, Frances Donaldson – prefacing her remarks with 'I cannot remember the full details of this' – quotes Wodehouse as saying 'What I can't see is what difference it makes. If the Germans want to govern the world, why don't we just let them?' (There actually were extreme pacifists in that era of appeasement who took that view.) That sensationally stupid remark from the highly intelligent Wodehouse admits to only two explanations. Either he believed it or he was teasing his friends, especially Old Etonian Jack Donaldson whose socialist convictions always puzzled him. Given his shrewd comments on other political matters I believe that, as his fatuous remark was taken seriously, even he must have had a hard task keeping a solemn expression with the success of his private joke.

The only other remark frequently quoted as evidence of his innocence in political matters was his comment to Townend in April 1939 that he thought the world had never been further from war than it was then.[57] The wish was surely the father to the thought and his wiser friends such as Jack Donaldson could see that war was inevitable. But Wodehouse's remark was neither as unworldly nor as naive as it appears in the nineteen-nineties to those with 20/20 hindsight. The British Prime Minister Neville Chamberlain had come back from Munich proclaiming 'Peace in our time' and many sensible, worldly people in the press, Parliament and the country at large believed him.

Wodehouse's political judgements were invariably sensible but not always right. This was to cost him dear as, unseen, in the background Fate was quietly slipping the lead into the boxing-glove. On September 3 1939 Britain declared war on a Germany led by a man with no sense of humour.

15

HEAVY WEATHER

Wodehouse was a distinguished and highly original writer and, as such, entitled to be kept clear of the atrocious buffooneries of power maniacs and their wars.[1]

Malcolm Muggeridge

WODEHOUSE was one of the unlikelier spoils of war acquired by the Germans in their conquest of northern France, which swept into Le Touquet on 22 May 1940. Hitler, and more importantly his propaganda minister, Josef Goebbels, were unaware of the treasure they had acquired. It would have been different under the old regime. The historian Sir John Wheeler Bennett was visiting ex-Kaiser Wilhelm at Doorn, his retreat in Holland, the previous year and there was some confusion over the appointment. 'He [the Kaiser] said frankly that his gentlemen had been at fault. "Sometimes they are very naughty," he told us confidentially, "and do you know how I punish them? I read P.G. Wodehouse to them – in English." '[2] Wilhelm had probably chuckled over a learned debate on Hitler.

> The situation in Germany had come up for discussion in the bar parlour of the Angler's Rest, and it was generally agreed that Hitler was standing at a crossroads and would soon be compelled to do something definite. His present policy, said a Whisky and Splash, was mere shilly-shallying.
>
> He'll have to let it grow or shave it off. . . . He can't go on sitting on the fence like this. Either a man has a moustache or he has not. There can be no middle course.[3]

Fortunately for Wodehouse the Führer was not a fan and had Hitler known of that passage the author would probably have been sent to a concentration camp, a thought that probably occurred to Ethel. She and

Plum had both been reassured by the large number of Royal Air Force officers in the neighbourhood, most of whom were frequent guests at Low Wood, and he was not only busy writing but doing his best to thrust the war entirely from his mind. So the ageing couple left it rather late to flee the advancing German armies. Sadly, in a farce worthy of a Wodehouse novel, both times they tried to do so their car broke down. Typically they intended to drive the 1,300 miles to Portugal, then catch a liner to America a further 3,000 miles away. Going to England, fifty miles from Le Touquet, would have meant months of quarantine for their pets.

At first Wodehouse had only to report to the Kommandatur each day and put up with the German soldiery looking upon the Wodehouse larder, home and bathroom as legitimate perks of war. Then, on 21 July, with the channel coast of France now the German front-line, all the male foreigners in Le Touquet were deported to the prison at Loos, a suburb of Lille. Wodehouse had time to pack only a small suitcase, forgetting his passport but taking a mutton chop, a pair of pyjamas and the complete works of William Shakespeare. At Loos, Plum's name was entered in the ledger as 'Widhorse' and his crime as 'Anglais'.[4] It would prove to have been better for him had he kept that anonymity. Soon it was learnt that all men over sixty were to be released and Plum was then only fifteen months from his sixtieth birthday.

Over the next eleven months Wodehouse and his fellow prisoners endured severe privations. At Loos he had to sleep on a granite floor with only his clothes and macintosh for bedding. Then there was a twenty-hour journey, standing in a cattle truck with forty other men, to a Belgian army barracks near Liege which was cold, unprepared and disgustingly filthy. Here the internees had to root around an old rubbish dump for items to use as plates and cups and then clean the latrines and the rest of the barracks. After that Plum was moved to the Citadel at Huy and finally to a lunatic asylum at Tost in Upper Silesia (then in south-west Germany but now part of Poland). This involved a three-day journey during which each internee had one bowl of thin soup, half a sausage and two half-loaves of bread. Throughout this period they were separated from their families and the food was both nasty and little above starvation level. The internees had to do all the heavy work needed to run their camps, sleep was often interrupted by roll-calls and the very fact of imprisonment undermines the strongest morale. It was, perhaps, worse for Wodehouse than the others as for the previous quarter of a century he had earned and enjoyed a cosseted lifestyle devoted to writing. Photographs of him after his release show a haggard and harrowed stranger. He lost forty-two pounds in weight during his internment and prompted his only known serious mention of religion. He attended the services held every Sunday at Tost by a Salvation Army Colonel. 'There's something about the atmosphere of a camp which does something to you in that way.'[5]

One commentator thought Wodehouse was never happier than when interned as the structure and discipline would have been so like his schooldays at Dulwich. He did write that he didn't find internment terrible after the first few months[6] but to expect Wodehouse to go around saying how terrible internment was is to misread the man. True to form he not only clothed the unpleasantness of internment with humour but by pretending he was happy he made life bearable for himself. He also played cricket for the first time in twenty-seven years and found that his bowling arm still retained all its cunning.

While at Tost Wodehouse did what little he could as a patriotic Anglo-American. His New York literary agent, Reynolds Jr., then running his father's firm, tells how.

Occasionally during the next few months we would hear from Wodehouse. He would write to us on postal cards in blocked letters. One card asked us to send five dollars to a person in Canada. We did so, saying that our check was at the request of P.G. Wodehouse. Back came the check with a letter of appreciation from the father of a boy in the Canadian Air Force. The boy had been reported missing in action. Now the father knew that the boy was a prisoner of war in Germany in the same concentration camp that held Wodehouse. Wodehouse had circumvented the German censor. Other similar five-dollar request cards were received; in each case with the same purpose and the same result.[7]

Had the Germans learned the real message of those cards Wodehouse would have been shot – as he must have realized.

The first news Wodehouse's family and friends had of him since the fall of France came after Angus Thuermer, an Associated Press reporter visiting Tost on Boxing Day 1940, met Wodehouse and wrote about him. (As an agency report this was never printed in full but used by newspapers taking the AP service as source material for their own news stories.) His friends and admirers immediately began lobbying the German authorities for Plum's release. In Euope Demaree Bess, the European representative of the *Saturday Evening Post*, and his wife wrote to the German Foreign Office and also arranged for Plum to have the use of a typewriter. In neutral America, Guy and Virginia Bolton organized a petition signed by many influential people of the day, asking for their friend to be sent to America. It was presented to the German Ambassador by Senator

W. Warren Barbour that June. That petition alerted the Germans, and the Nazi Ministry of Propaganda in particular, to 'Mr Widhorse'.

To Wodehouse the war was simply something that hampered his writing (and dealing with his agents and publishers). Internment and separation from his family were of secondary importance. So, as ever, he continued working. In June 1941 he wrote an article 'My War With Germany' which was published in America in the July issue of the *Saturday Evening Post* and, slightly abridged, in the London *Daily Mail* of 17 July under the headline 'This was written by P.G. Wodehouse The Prisoner'. It was a lighthearted piece, including such things as the probable bad effect of internment on the Wodehouse table manners. In peacetime it would have been lauded as vintage Wodehouse. With the benefit of hindsight it was totally insensitive in wartime but Wodehouse had been almost completely out of touch with the real world for eleven months. In spite of his having shut war out of his mind ever since the First World War it seems likely that, but for that eleven months' isolation, his intelligence would have stopped him behaving so unwisely. His fans, friends and family were happy to know that Wodehouse was safe and they admired the way he made light of his travails.

Soon after 'My War With Germany' was dispatched the Lager Führer at Tost, Oberleutenant Buchelt, called Wodehouse to his office to discuss the typewriter he had hired for Plum and said how much he had enjoyed the text of 'My War With Germany' before casually suggesting 'Why don't you do some broadcasts on similar lines for your American readers?' At the time it never occurred to Wodehouse to wonder what so relatively junior a German official was doing suggesting that an internee make broadcasts and that he would not do so without instructions from a higher, very much higher, authority. So Wodehouse replied he thought that was a good idea. It had strong appeal to him for three reasons. Firstly as a way of replying to all the letters of good wishes he had received from America. All his life he replied, himself, to every fan letter he ever received and his apparent bad manners in not doing so now irked him greatly. Secondly it would be essentially a writing project, the broadcasts were given from his written scripts, and a real job (as distinct from writing novels for stock) had great appeal. Thirdly, he had agreed to broadcast to America, then a neutral country. This struck him as being as unexceptionable as writing for the *Saturday Evening Post*. His author's professionalism and concentration on his writing to the exclusion of almost everything else were to cost him dear.

On 21 June 1941 Wodehouse was released – he assumed because he was almost sixty – but he was instructed to live in the Hotel Adlon in Berlin with two 'minders'. The day after his release Wodehouse was told by one of them to come with him to the lobby of the hotel. There the minder bought a newspaper and sat down to read it leaving Wodehouse to wander around the hotel courtyard where he met his old friend from San Francisco, Eric Barnikow. Wodehouse had never thought of him as German since, in Hollywood, 'He was so entirely American'[8] but now he was Major the Baron Eric Raven von Barnikow, but as friendly as ever. He had come to meet Wodehouse having learned of his release from Werner Plack, their mutual Hollywood acquaintance, now a German Foreign Office official. As the two wandered back into the lobby of the Adlon, there was Plack. Within a few days all the arrangements had been made for Wodehouse to make five broadcasts to America and also to take part in a short radio interview with Harry Flannery, Columbia Broadcasting System's correspondent in Berlin, which went out on 26 June. The five talks were recorded between 25 June and 26 July and transmitted to America on 28 June, 9, 23 and 30 July, and 6 August. The German Foreign Office had cleverly trapped Wodehouse into giving them a modest propaganda coup.

It never occurred to Wodehouse (nor, to be fair, to von Barnikow or Plack) that the Nazis would rebroadcast the talks to England. Goebbels' Ministry of Propaganda demanded the tapes and did so on 9, 10, 11, 12 and 14 August.

Plum was interned during the so-called 'phoney war' when the full ghastliness of the horrors to come was unforeseen and, since then, he had been locked away from the world and any outside advice – but that might not have made much difference. The strange yet unsurprising thing is that in his correspondence at the time, mostly through Reynolds in New York, he had shown little interest in anything but his writing, the sale and publication of his work and how this would be affected by the war. He seemed oblivious to the worries of Leonora and his friends about his welfare and made only perfunctory enquiries about theirs.

His two cables to Reynolds in August and November are indicative. With all the troubles of the war and internment the first asks only about Wesley Stout accepting *Money In The Bank* for serialization in the *Saturday Evening Post*. The second says 'Tell Leonora Ethel well. Give her my love' and then deals with the important matter of American reaction to the *Post's* serialization of his book.[9] Of the small number of letters he sent to Reynolds, one of November 1941 – probably his last before America joined the war and that channel closed – is typical. In one and a half single-spaced pages he writes only about the publication of his work and his standing with the American reading public apart from a short note on why Berlin is a good city for walkers and a postscript about his food parcels and magazine subscriptions. Ethel is only mentioned as having brought the manuscript of *Joy In The Morning* to him from France and there is no message for Leonora at all.[10] Such an ability to focus on one's work to the exclusion of all else is a hallmark of genius but to ordinary people it can be quite frightening. To Leonora it must have been hurtful as well. (Ethel, in occupied France, received postcards directly.)

The morning after Wodehouse recorded the fifth and last talk Ethel arrived in Berlin, together with their Peke, Wonder. In such a crisis all the qualities that enabled her to fight her way up to social success in London, New York and Hollywood as the wife of a great writer came to the fore. Her home was requisitioned by the Germans shortly after her husband was taken to Loos and she went to stay with friends. She then raised all the money she could, even selling her jewellery. Most wives would have done that only after some agonizing, for a wife's jewellery represents more than value; it is a series of demonstrations of love by the man you love. Ethel, who adored jewellery, sold hers for what she could get, a fraction of its real value, and did so without hesitation. She wrote cheerful letters to Plum when she could not have been anything other than frightened and worried, despite her courage. Then she learned Wodehouse had been freed and she rushed to him in Berlin as fast as the German authorities and wartime conditions allowed. The worldly Ethel would surely have stopped her husband from foolishly making those broadcasts had she arrived only a month earlier. The Germans made sure that she did not.

British reaction to the broadcasts, judged on those who made themselves heard, was hysterical fury. By the time of the broadcasts, events of the war had moved to Britain's disadvantage. Alone in Europe she was matched against the German war machine which had conquered almost the entire Continent. Facing nightly bombing raids, imminent starvation, invasion and defeat there was no time for careful consideration of peripheral matters. Few, if any, of his detractors had heard his broadcasts, let alone read the texts as the British Broadcasting Corporation's monitoring service at Caversham Park had, apparently, recorded all the broadcasts but only transcribed the first of them and summarized the others. The very fact that Wodehouse had broadcast at all was, for many people, enough to damn him unheard. A.P. Ryan observed of the broadcasts 'As an essay in detachment they were magnificent. But they were not war.'[11] Exactly. Wodehouse was detached to a degree an ordinary person can barely imagine.

Anthony Eden, then British Foreign Secretary, deplored the broadcast in the House of Commons on 9 July and the Minister of Information, Plum's one-time lunch companion, Alfred Duff Cooper, urged the *Daily Mirror* columnist, William Connor (pen name Cassandra) to broadcast what was probably the most vituperative attack on an individual ever heard on British radio. It began 'I have come to tell you tonight of the story of a rich man trying to make his last and greatest sale – that of his own country'. Then it becomes nasty. Frances Donaldson bravely published almost the entire text. I am made of weaker stuff. Even half a century later reading the full text of Connor's flood of bile is sickening. About the mildest barb in it was ridiculing the names Pelham Grenville. Connor may not even have heard the broadcasts nor read texts of them and his libels against Wodehouse were based on an almost total ignorance of the truth. Cooper later claimed to have shown Connor's draft text to another of Plum's old dining companions, Prime Minister Winston Churchill.[12] (This claim may have been, to quote Churchill 'A terminological inexactitude'.) The Prime Minister's only comment, Cooper told Connor, was that the language seemed rather mild. That language showed the application of superb journalistic gifts to an unworthy end. To their credit the BBC refused to transmit Cassandra's polemic but then did so following a direct wartime order from Duff Cooper (only later discovering that he probably did not have the powers so to instruct them). It went out on 15 July.

From the public there came a mixture of support and disgust and none were more disgusted than the BBC, but under wartime regulations the governors were not allowed to say that they were forced to transmit it by Cooper, although their pressure did force the minister to write to *The Times*[13] accepting responsibility for Connor's broadcast. Many local authorities responded more emotionally. Several of them withdrew Wodehouse's books from their public libraries' shelves and to their shame the councillors of Colne and of Southport voted to pulp (but not, as sometimes reported, burn) their Wodehouse books.[14] Reverence for books, which freed the advance of human knowledge from the limits of the human mind, is part of every civilized person's inheritance. The destruction of books, of any book, is a crime against humanity – and it typified the Nazis. Fortunately, on legal advice, Colne and Southport did not actually destroy their Wodehouse volumes and instead withdrew them from circulation. Wodehouse was also banned in Hungary at one time, which he thought as strange as the Hungarians reading him in the first place.[15] He was in noble company: Mark Twain's *Huckleberry Finn* was banned in Massachusetts; Conan Doyle's Sherlock Holmes stories in Russia; Anon's Robin Hood in Indiana (because Robin was a Communist); Lewis Carroll's *Alice In Wonderland* in China and Walt Disney's Mickey Mouse in Nazi Germany, Communist East Germany, Fascist Italy, Russia and Yugoslavia.[16] Those few examples are from a distressingly interminable list.

One group showed that civilized judgements can be maintained in wartime. The Society of Authors, led by their president the Poet Laureate John Masefield, protested to the BBC at the Connor broadcast. Masefield also wrote a statement which was to have been issued on behalf of the council, almost all of them fully agreeing with their president, but Dame Ethel Smythe (who made up in strength of character what she lacked in talent) was adamantly anti-Wodehouse. So the statement appears never to have been issued and has been lying, unread, in a file for the last half century. Today it still sums up the matter perfectly.

> The Council of the Incorporated Society of Authors, Playwrights and Composers wish to draw the attention of the Minister of Information to an attack on Dr P.G. Wodehouse, made by the British Broadcasting Corporation in the evening of Tuesday July 15th.
>
> This attack was (supposedly) meant as a reply or rebuke to Dr Wodehouse for a talk lately broadcast by him to the United States from Germany.
>
> Perhaps few members of this Council, and very few of the people of this island, know the nature of the talk broadcast by Dr Wodehouse. It was addressed to America by one who knows that country; it was, no doubt, the sincere, honest utterance of a man no longer young, used to speaking his mind and famous all over the world: it was certainly entitled to a fair hearing and reasoned judgement.
>
> Such judgement was to be expected from the B.B.C. if, indeed, judgement of any kind were necessary.
>
> The commentator on Tuesday night quoted only one sentence, or part of a sentence, from Dr Wodehouse's talk; the rest of his comment was mainly malignant suggestion, designed, seemingly, to poison public opinion against a famous man now in adversity. In this design some success has been obtained; some measure of bitterness has been roused against Dr Wodehouse. But very little measure compared with that roused against the B.B.C.
>
> The Members of the Council feel that such a comment was a disgrace to a country which has a great name for just dealing. To most of them, it seemed of a special quality of infamy and a pollution to the air. They hope that by this expression of their feelings they may hope to make any other such abuse of the B.B.C. impossible.[17]

Few others were so sensible and nobody stopped to wonder how anyone could be thought a Nazi who had so hilariously satirized Hitler's moustache and his Black Shirts.

Letters to the newspapers about the Wodehouse broadcasts mostly condemned him in harsh terms, unfettered by knowledge of the facts.

Fifteen years later when researching *Wodehouse At Work* Usborne could only find three people who ever heard any of them, and two of those were the Mackails. A small number of temperate letters were published. In *The Times* and *The Daily Telegraph* these came from, among others, old friends Bill Townend, Arthur Thompson of Teignmouth and Lord Newborough and authors Sax Rohmer, Dorothy L. Sayers, Gilbert Frankau, and Ethel Mannin who wrote, 'May I suggest that judgement be withheld until we know the facts?' Ian Hay wrote a gently condemnatory but not unkind letter.

Against those views, E.C. Bentley of Clerihew fame, in a spiteful little letter, suggested Plum's D. Litt. should be removed on the odd grounds that Wodehouse 'Had never written a serious line'. But it was A.A. Milne who, consumed by *schadenfreude*, libelled his friend most viciously. Ann Thwaite, in her distinguished biography of Milne (who by 1941 was famous as the author of the 'Pooh' books for children featuring his son, Christopher Robin) writes, 'How much he would have preferred to have had, before 1941, Wodehouse's reputation rather than his own. How much he would have liked to have been thought of as a successful humorist, not as a writer of children's books and books so peculiarly vulnerable to attack and parody.'[18] In his letter to *The Daily Telegraph* Milne said:

> I remember he told me once he wished he had a son; and he added characteristically (and quite sincerely): 'But he would have to be born at the age of 15, when he was just getting into his House eleven.' You see the advantage of that. Bringing up a son throws a considerable responsibility on a man; but by the time the boy is 15 one has shifted the responsibility on to the housemaster.[19]

He then added a few remarks about Plum spending the First World War in America and on his US tax problems. Coming from a man who had sanctimoniously exploited his son for commercial gain, that was breathtakingly hypocritical. It was also untrue. Wodehouse never made any such comment to Milne who had taken it from a remark made by Mike Jackson in *Psmith In The City* when, over high tea in Clapham, he was being interrogated by his host's obnoxious young son, Edward. 'Small boys, however, filled him with a sort of frozen horror. It was his view that a boy should not be exhibited publicly until he reached an age when he might be in the running for some sort of colours at a public school.'

Sir Compton Mackenzie wrote to *The Daily Telegraph* professing 'An old-fashioned prejudice against condemning a man unheard' adding 'I feel more disgusted by Mr Milne's morality than by Mr Wodehouse's irresponsibility'[20] but that letter was not published 'for lack of space'. Thwaite adds, 'As it was, Milne was appalled [at the broadcasts] and joined in the correspondence with a vehemence and inaccuracy which sometimes seem, absurdly, to have made him come out of the whole business with rather less credit then Wodehouse himself.'[21] Quite.

From Teignmouth, Arthur Thompson wrote letters to local papers, wherever councils had banned Wodehouse's books, defending his friend, to whom he later sent copies of the correspondence.

Wodehouse wrote to the British Foreign Office through the Swiss Embassy on 21 November 1942 explaining his actions and attempted several times to return to England via neutral countries in order to clear his name. The Germans refused to let him go, while friends at home were in no position to clear him without the facts only he could provide. Sir Seymour Hicks complained that he couldn't find out what Wodehouse was supposed to have done wrong and noted, 'Looking at photographs of him taken in Berlin [actually by Angus Theurmer in Tost], huddled in an armchair and wrapped in a rug, they appeared to be pictures of a broken man, if not worse than that, and small wonder when one considers that a person of his type – at the age of sixty – had spent months in a concentration camp.'[22] For the rest of the war, and long thereafter, any slander about what Wodehouse did or said during the period was widely believed. As Evelyn Waugh said, 'There is a hideous vitality about calumny.'[23] Two examples (of too many) suffice. It was reported that when the Germans arrived in Le Touquet the Wodehouses were giving a cocktail party to which German officers were invited. In fact 'I gave no cocktail party. At the time of the German occupation of Le Touquet I was fully occupied trying to get away – first in my own car, which broke down after going two miles, and then in a truck belonging to a neighbour, which broke down in the first hundred yards. The only German officer I ever saw at Le Touquet was the Kommandant with the glass eye.'[24] Other Britons resident in Le Touquet at the time verified that statement. An American newspaper in Boston said the Wodehouses used to lie in bed in wartime Berlin feeding their dogs pork chops. How Plum and Ethel were supposed to have an abundance of pork chops in wartime Berlin was not explained. In fact they gave Wonder their minute meat ration and ate vegetables themselves.

So what were the terrible things Wodehouse actually said in his broadcasts? The only full and accurate publication of all five texts is in Ian Sproat's *Wodehouse at War*, the definitive work on this period of Plum's life. I have made much use of that essential book in writing this chapter.

In the October and November 1954 issues of *Encounter* Wodehouse published the texts of the first three broadcasts but his *daemon* was too strong and even on so sensitive a matter he couldn't help tinkering and polishing. There's a lovely line about an internee's intention, after the war, of buying himself a German soldier to keep in the garden and count six times a day, as internees had been counted in their camps – but it was not in the original broadcasts. The verbatim texts show, on the worst interpretation, a man joking about serious matters. A fair view is of an unbelligerent and tolerant man bravely making light of severe hardship by doing as he had always done with unpleasantness; clothing it in humour. At best his broadcasts can be seen for masterly anti-Nazi propaganda. Montgomery Ford, a theatrical friend of Plum's, wrote to Wodehouse after the war:

> When I last talked to Watty Washburn a few days ago, he said that he hadn't yet informed you of the sensational discovery I made recently through a friend of mine, who during the war was a Major in Intelligence and who graduated from the US Army Intelligence School at Camp Ritchie, Maryland. [Now Fort Ritchie.] During his training at Camp Ritchie (in early 1944) your broadcasts (3 of them) were played to the student officers in his section as examples of *anti*-Nazi propaganda. Any of the students who said your broadcasts contained any pro-Nazi sentiments was flunked on this test and asked where his sense of humour was. . . . My brother-in-law, Colonel Shipley Thomas, was Director of Training at Camp Ritchie throughout the entire war. I phoned him immediately on learning the above to get corroboration from him. All he would say was that it is possible your broadcasts were used; but you must understand, as I do through much first-hand experience, that trying to get anyone in Intelligence to give you the right time of day is a complete impossibility.[25]

The following extracts from the broadcasts show why the Camp Ritchie experts took the view they did. That twenty-hour journey crammed standing in a cattle truck, for example.

> One drawback of being an internee is that, when you move from spot to spot, you have to do it in company with eight hundred other men. This precludes anything in the nature of travel *de luxe*. We made the twenty-four hour trip in a train consisting of one of those *Quarante Hommes, Huit Chevaux* things – in other words, cattle trucks. I had sometimes seen them on sidings in French railroads in times of peace, and had wondered what it would be like to be one of the Quarante Hommes. I now found out, and the answer is that it is pretty darned awful. Eight horses might manage to make themselves fairly comfortable in one of those cross-country loose boxes, but forty men are cramped.

. . . and of sleeping on a stone floor without blankets at the age of fifty-nine he said:

> An internee does not demand much in the way of bedding – give him a wisp or two of straw and he is satisfied – but at Huy it looked for a while as if there would not even be straw. . . . Of blankets there were enough for twenty men. I was not one of the twenty. I don't know why it is but I never am one of the twenty men who get anything.

. . . and of his work fatigue: 'Without wishing to be indelicate, I may say that, until you have helped to clean out a Belgian soldiers' latrine, "you aint seen nuttin".'

Apart from the courage there was much vintage Wodehouse.

> The cell smell is a great feature of all French prisons. Ours in Number Forty-Four at Loos was one of those fine, broad-shouldered, up-and-coming young smells which stand on both feet and look the world in the eye. We became very fond and proud of it, championing it hotly against other prisoners who claimed that theirs had more authority and bouquet. . . .
>
> Nevertheless, in spite of the interest of hobnobbing with our smell, we found that time hung a little heavy on our hands. I was all right. I had my Complete Works of William Shakespeare. But Algy had no drinks to mix, and Cartmell no pianos to tune. And a piano-tuner suddenly deprived of pianos is like a tiger whose medical adviser has put it on a vegetarian diet. Cartmell used to talk to us of pianos he had tuned in the past, and sometimes he would speak easily and well of pianos he hoped to tune in the future, but it was not the same. You could see that what the man wanted was a piano to tune *now*.

Scarcely the stuff of treasons, stratagems and spoils, but then there was music within Wodehouse.

Air Vice-Marshal Owen Boyd, who either heard the broadcasts or read the transcripts, told his assistant, the author John F. Leeming, when both were later prisoners of war in Italy, 'Why the Germans ever let him say all that I cannot think. They have either got more sense of humour than I credited them with or it has just slipped past the censor. There is some stuff about being packed in cattle trucks and a thing about Loos jail that you would think would send a Hun crazy. Wodehouse has probably been shot by now.'[26]

There were many things Wodehouse said in his broadcasts that were utterly insensitive given the psychology of wartime but the only thing he said that could reasonably have incensed his compatriots was in his broadcast with Flannery. 'I'm wondering whether the kind of England and the kind of people I write about will live after the war – whether England wins or not I mean'. What nobody spotted until years later was that the entire script for the interview, Wodehouse's words and his own, was written by Flannery. That is not a Wodehouse excuse. In his book, *Assignment To Berlin*, published in 1942,[27] a weak imitation of his predecessor William L. Shirer's famous *Berlin Diary*, Flannery admits he wrote Wodehouse's words – but this subtle point was ignored by Wodehouse's critics and missed by his defenders. Flannery had clearly taken Wodehouse in dislike at earlier meetings and assumed him to be a fool and a collaborator without evidence for either assumption. Flannery is probably the only man who ever caused Wodehouse bitterness. Plum accepted that Cassandra was simply doing a wartime job but Flannery, who met Wodehouse only three times, invented damaging libels and, worst of all, 'Gave me such rotten dialogue'.[28]

Meanwhile, as the controversy and the war raged on, the Wodehouses stayed in Germany either at the Adlon, or as guests of von Barnikow's fiancee, Baroness Anga von Bodenhausen, or as paying-guests of Graf von Wolkenstein in Upper Silesia. They paid their hotel bills themselves surviving on the money Ethel had realized and on borrowing from friends. Wodehouse was also paid 40,000 marks for dramatizing *Heavy Weather* for the Berliner Film Co. but insisted on a clause in the contract guaranteeing that the film would not be made until after the war. He also sold to Tauchnitz rights to *Money In The Bank*. Then in September 1943, having stoically survived the horrors of Allied air raids on Berlin, the Wodehouses were allowed to move to Paris, lodging at the Hotel Bristol.

Paris was freed by the Allies on 25 August 1944 and the following day Wodehouse reported to the American military authorities. Soon he was interviewed by Malcolm Muggeridge, then a British Intelligence Corps Major liaising with the French *Services Speciaux*. During their conversation Muggeridge told Plum that his beloved Leonora had died. 'After a longish pause he said: "I thought she was immortal." '[29] Leonora had entered the London Clinic for a minor gynaecological operation. She died unexpectedly on 16 May 1944, aged forty. Peter Cazalet, then serving with the Welsh Guards, called in the most eminent forensic scientist of the day, Sir Bernard Spilsbury, who conducted a post-mortem and said that Leonora died of 'Myocardial degeneration and early atheroma of the arteries', which the coroner put on the death certificate. The distress caused by her Plummie's internment and broadcasts cannot have helped. Wodehouse had been unmoved when his mother died in 1941 but Leonora's death shattered him. This was something that could never be clothed in humour and the pain never eased. He simply masked his abiding grief with silence.

Muggeridge knew little of Wodehouse's books – 'With my strict socialist childhood, Bertie Wooster and Jeeves had about them a flavour of forbidden fruit' – but he took the view that 'Wodehouse was a distinguished and highly original writer and, as such, entitled to be kept clear of the atrocious buffooneries of power maniacs and their wars'.[30] Upon arriving at the Bristol he was immediately impressed with Plum's courage. Wodehouse, knowing full well that he might be meeting the man delegated to take him back to Britain to face prison and a treason trial (in the wake of Cooper's hate campaign), was courteous and calm. Muggeridge rapidly came to like Wodehouse, gave him good advice and helped him and Ethel as much as he could, even after their case was taken out of his hands by Major E.J.P. Cussen (later His Honour Judge Cussen) on behalf of MI5. Cussen investigated the whole matter of Wodehouse's activities from the German occupation of Le Touquet to the liberation of Paris.

The Cussen report is dated 28 September 1944. His investigation was as thorough as possible at the time but took place before he could interview everybody concerned and examine German archives. Cussen was so convinced of Wodehouse's innocence that he never bothered to do much more work on the case and so his report is not conclusive but, combined with the further evidence gathered by Iain Sproat and given in *Wodehouse At War*, Plum was innocent of everything apart from stupidity. In writing this book I looked for evidence that Wodehouse had fooled everyone – he certainly had the brains to do so and later successfully gave the world a wildly partial image of himself – but I could find none. Ethel, never a conventional moralist, would have done anything, without scruple, to get the funds required to look after her husband (and Wonder) but there is no evidence that she did anything worse than behave as her normal flamboyant self, ignore the war as far as she could and enjoy herself as far as possible. The Wodehouses were technically guilty of minor breaches of Section 2A of the wartime Defence Regulations because of the means by which they raised the money on which to live. But unless the British government expected them to starve in the Berlin streets or get shipped off to perish in work-camps there was nothing else they could do.

On 23 November 1944 the Director of Public Prosecutions, Theobald Matthew, decided there was no evidence on which to prosecute Wodehouse. In the House of Commons on 6 December Anthony Eden stated 'There are no grounds upon which we could take action' and on 23 December the Attorney General, Sir Donald Somervell, repeated that decision.

Low Wood near Le Touquet, the Wodehouse home in France

Rex Whistler was one of the few illustrators who did Wodehouse justice

PGW and Leonora arrive in Los Angeles in 1930

Proud Papa

The Empress of Blandings. 'Are you under the impression', Lord Emsworth said, for when deeply moved he could be terribly sarcastic 'that I want to enter my pig for the Derby?'

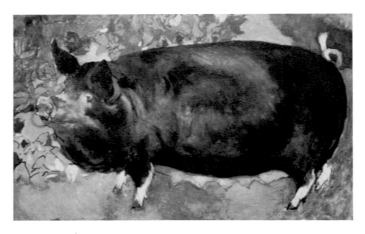

Dr Wodehouse. At first
Plum thought the offer of
an honorary doctorate
from Oxford University
was a joke

Wodehouse, emaciated after internment, is
hardly recognisable as he stands in front of
the Brandenburg Gate in Berlin with Werner
Plack, circa June 1941

Wodehouse with mutt, Bill, 1953

Bill and me
P.uun
March 11-1953

A woman is only a woman
but a good cigar can be
shredded for pipe tobacco

At Remsenburg it rained dogs but only showered cats

Wodehouse and Peke both find somewhere comfy to relax

Wodehouse, Ethel and mutt at the P.G. Wodehouse Shelter for stray animals at Westhampton on Long Island. This was the only one of his many charitable acts that was not private

The daily walk down Basket Neck Lane, Remsenburg
to collect the papers and post

A small sample from a huge output

The Master's study replicated in a corner of the
P.G. Wodehouse Library at Dulwich College with
items from Remsenburg, the gift of Ethel Wodehouse

Indeed Wodehouse's courage and good-humour in the face of adversity should inspire admiration. The following extracts about his internment are from the full text of his statement to Major Cussen.[31]

Conditions were hard as we had no correspondence or parcels and the potato ration was very small. Then quite suddenly everything began to improve. Instead of three potatoes we received eight or nine . . . apart from the anxiety about the welfare of my wife – largely dispelled by the cheerful tone of her letters – I was definitely happy at Tost.

Not an atom of self-pity. Wodehouse, as always, acted as an intelligent Pangloss, looking only on the bright side of things. While he was suffering, the British public (suffering too) gave their verdict on his broadcasts: some 450,000 copies of his books were bought in Britain between 1941 and 1945.[32]

Yet successive British governments refused to publish the Cussen report and associated papers. It took thirty-five years plus the persistence of Iain Sproat, the Member of Parliament and later a government minister, who refused to accept the farcical reasons given for them remaining classified information, before they were released.

There was no great crime in Wodehouse's condemnation: in war there is no time for nice judicial judgements of peripheral matters. Wodehouse having inadvertently placed himself in the crossfire of Allied and Axis ministries of propaganda had to suffer, and he did, for his detachment. After the war Cassandra did what the British government should have done. He reviewed the matter, came to the conclusion that he had wronged Wodehouse and apologized to him privately and in a later *Daily Mirror* article.[33] No such apology ever came from Cooper. The great crime against Wodehouse was withholding, for those thirty-five years, the evidence that cleared his name and letting him go to his grave with it unpublished. Auberon Waugh argues that Wodehouse's 'crime' was to ignore politicians, who do not take kindly to anyone with an imperfect appreciation of their importance.[34] That view accords worryingly well with the facts: politicians would rather be excoriated than ignored. But Wodehouse was even more on target. He shrewdly thought that the reason might be any government's general dislike of admitting it had been wrong.[35] Cooper's hate campaign, which was contrary to all the principles for which the Allies were fighting the Nazis, could easily have been excused as one of those mistakes, sometimes unavoidable due to the stresses of war, corrected and forgotten. Three able lawyers, Cussen, Matthew and Somervell had decided there was no case for Wodehouse to answer but the politicians were not going to admit to any mistakes.

Eventually Sproat forced the government to tell him why they were refusing to publish the Cussen report. Wodehouse was taken from Tost to Berlin with another internee who might, or might not, have been a German spy or possibly a double agent or possibly not, and his name is mentioned several times by Cussen. Sproat suggested the report be shown to him with the other man's name blanked out. This simple idea had proved beyond the intelligence of successive ministers and civil servants over thirty-five years. The report was finally released to Sproat on 25 June 1980, repaying him for his years of persistence. *Wodehouse At War* appeared in 1981 and the following year came the authorized biography which ungenerously says of the report, 'Then in June 1980 it was unexpectedly released.' In fact everyone who has ever enjoyed reading Wodehouse owes Iain Sproat their thanks for his persistent efforts which finally forced the release of the report.

After the liberation of Paris the Wodehouses were forced to move from the Hotel Bristol. This was because the Wodehouses' presence there was embarrassing to another guest, the new British Ambassador to France, who sent an urgent note to London in the diplomatic bag.

> I think you should know that Mr and Mrs P.G. Wodehouse are staying in Paris at the Hotel Bristol which is supposed to be reserved for the Corps Diplomatique and where I myself together with the majority of the Foreign Representatives are living. . . . In view of the difficulties that might arise if the Press were to get hold of the story, I am trying to arrange for Wodehouse to be moved to another hotel.[3]

No one could accuse the new Ambassador, Alfred Duff Cooper, of lacking self-importance and petty vindictiveness. Plum and Ethel were forced to move to the Hotel Lincoln when the French authorities suddenly wondered if Plum was a threat to the safety of the republic. So they arrested him and Ethel. For those French policemen, forbidden to gag prisoners, being in charge of an angry and verbose Ethel must have been a foretaste of purgatory. They soon released her, but not her husband. To save Wodehouse staying in prison under preventive detention the guileful Muggeridge had him deposited in hospital where he enjoyed comfortable working conditions and with characteristic *sang froid* simply worked. Eight weeks later the French Republic satisfied itself that it faced no threat from Wodehouse – it was, he said, one of the nicest republics he had ever met – and he was released on 17 January 1945. He and Ethel, shepherded by Muggeridge, then moved to Barbizon, back to the Lincoln, then to apartments at 78 Avenue Paul Doumer and 36 Boulevard Souchet and finally

to St Germain-en-Laye. They also visited Low Wood, which was in great
disrepair, and eventually decided to sell it.

Muggeridge perceptively said of Wodehouse, 'It wasn't that he was
other-worldly or un-worldly, as much as that he was a-worldly. Wodehouse's true offence was to have disinterested himself in the war.'[37] In
those two simple sentences Muggeridge set down the core of the matter.

Not only the Conservative politicians felt offended at Wodehouse's
disinterest. In the new post-war socialist government the new Attorney
General, Old Alleynian Sir Hartley Shawcross, made a menacing statement in the House of Commons in answer to a member's question. 'The
question of instituting proceedings against this man will be reconsidered if
and when he comes within jurisdiction of our courts.' After being cleared
by Cussen, Matthew and Somervell that was a blow. With the next change
in government in 1951 the incoming Attorney General, Sir David Maxwell Fyfe, privately gave a similar reply. One can easily imagine how petty
and mean the politicians would have looked had kindly Wodehouse
arrived in England to be surrounded by questioning British reporters.

For a long time Wodehouse was unable to believe that his harmless
broadcasts had caused so much anger and done him so much harm.
Similarly his love for Leonora was overwhelming but it never seems to
have occurred to him how much anguish and distress his broadcasts must
have caused her and others who loved him. Once he did realize the
sickening truth he applied himself to his problem and knew he could not
win. There was too much of that vital calumny about. He knew that
almost anything he said, however true, would be treated as a feeble and
maladroit excuse. He could have hammered away at the fact he agreed to
broadcast only to neutral America. He could have mentioned his postcards to Reynolds. He could have pointed out that the British Government's hysterical hate campaign was far more fatheaded than anything he
had done. Instead he said the one thing that would be accepted: that he
had been unbelievably foolish and that he was very sorry. He never
complained about the injustice which it is now recognized was done to
him. Instead he did the only realistic thing and set about convincing the
world how naive and unworldly he was. Those are not the actions of a
naive and unworldly man. They are the actions of a courageous and
formidably intelligent man.

During those harrowing war years Wodehouse continued to write producing some of his best work. *Joy In The Morning* was completed in Berlin
and such respected critics as Usborne consider it as fine as any of his
books.

Money In The Bank was written entirely at Tost and joins such distinguished works as *Fanny Hill*, *Le Morte d'Arthur* and the beginning of

Don Quixote, all written while their authors were incarcerated.[38] Wodehouse got the idea for the lateral thinking George, sixth Viscount Uffenham (perhaps his last great comic creation) from a fellow internee at Tost, Max Enke. His Lordship also appears in *Something Fishy* (US *The Butler Did It*) which I think is as fine a book as any Wodehouse wrote. Sadly Enke's daughter, Mrs Ruth Chambers, thought Lord Uffenham a cruel caricature of her father[39] which it was not. The Viscount is honest, courageous and shrewd – pointing out, for example, that a safe simply affords an indication to a burglar of where to start looking and gives the fellow a sort of official assurance that if he is prepared to take a little trouble he will find something to his advantage. (Mrs Chambers was as wrong as those who think that *The Merchant of Venice* is anti-Semitic when Shylock is actually the only man of honour and integrity in the story. The Nazis knew this full well and never allowed the play to be staged in the Third Reich.) *Money In The Bank* was published in New York in 1942, and by Tauchnitz in Stuttgart in 1949 with a dedication unique to their edition: 'To Bert Haskins with deep affection'. Look in *Performing Flea* and you will find 'When I was in camp I had the most tremendous liking and admiration for the War Graves Commission men. With one of them, Bert Haskins, I formed a friendship that will last all our lives. He was pure gold.' On Wodehouse's instructions, Herbert Jenkins sent Haskins, who retired to Birmingham, free copies of all his old cell-mate's new books to the end of his life. Wodehouse also paid for him to have a holiday every year while Haskins used to send his friend British papers and magazines.

   Spring Fever was written, and *Joy In The Morning* completed, in Germany while *Uncle Dynamite* was written in France as was *Full Moon*. Wodehouse also wrote ten short stories during the war, all of them *crème de la crème*, and he kept a diary, the *Camp Diary*. Separately from that he wrote a book of his experiences entitled *Wodehouse In Wonderland* (also called *The Camp Book*) which he intended to publish but he later accepted advice not to do so, although extracts were included in *Performing Flea*. It has since disappeared, possibly destroyed by Ethel.

   There was much debate on when to publish *Money In The Bank* in England. Herbert Jenkins were milky-hearted about the idea while, with Plum's best interests at heart, Thelma Cazalet-Keir and A.P. Watt gave Grimsdick instructions, without consulting the author, to postpone production of the book.[40] It is strange that one close business associate and one close friend should have so little understanding of Wodehouse. Because he was gentle and unassuming it did not follow he lacked strength of character; far from it. The instruction so annoyed Wodehouse that he told Grimsdick to publish immediately and, happily, with the best of results. The book, out in May 1946, was a best seller. Most critics were kind and the few who weren't got ticked off by their peers. G.W. Stonier, writing in *The Observer*, said, 'The old fascination has gone; if he hasn't changed, we have.' Hugh Kingsmill shot back.

> The humour of Wodehouse is as rich and inexhaustible as ever; the delicate perceptions and sensitive intelligence of Mr Stonier [are] still hampered by a temperament that, in his less amiable moments, makes him condescend from a height which to others looks like a depression.[41]

As Lord David Cecil wrote, 'Comic masterpieces are composed to make us laugh so that the critic who writes of them with an unsmiling face reveals himself as comically unable to appreciate the primary intention of these writers.'[42] The *New York Times Book Review* wrote, in a comment that pleased Wodehouse:

> Maybe Wodehouse uses the same plot over and over again. Whatever he does, it's moderately wonderful, a ray of pale English sunshine in a gray world. . . . There is, of course, the question of Mr Wodehouse's 'war guilt'. Upon mature post-war reflection, it turned out to be about equal to the war guilt of the dachshunds which were stoned by super-heated patriots during World War I.[43]

That, I think, is the most sensible comment ever made about those wretched broadcasts. It is much better than the story Muggeridge tells of the Germans, in their literal way, taking Wodehouse's works as a guide to English manners and actually parachuting an agent into Lincolnshire wearing spats, which led to his speedy capture. I would like to think this charming tale was true but there was a German Embassy in London until the outbreak of war, full of intelligence staff who knew just how Englishmen dressed.

In the spring of 1945, at Muggeridge's instigation, George Orwell (the socialist with a private income) bought Plum and Ethel 'a very good lunch' in a Paris restaurant near *Les Halles*. Orwell, who had been a fan of Plum's public-school stories from his prep-school days, then wrote an article, 'In Defence Of P.G. Wodehouse', which appeared in *The Windmill* that November. He concluded: 'In the case of Wodehouse, if we drive him to retire to the United States and renounce his British citizenship, we shall end up by being horribly ashamed of ourselves.'[44] We did, he did and we certainly should be.

16

SUNSET AT REMSENBURG

The plain man was drawn to him for the endless sunshine of his humour, the critic for the purity of his style and the ingenuity of his plots, the scholar for his lightly worn erudition.[1]

Anthony Curtis

THEL and Plum set sail from Cherbourg for New York on the aptly named *S S America* on 18 April 1947. He was never to see England again. The delay was caused mainly by the British Government's tardiness in sending the US authorities the findings of the Cussen report showing that Wodehouse was innocent of any wartime offence.[2] In a Jeevesian move he suggested to his lawyers that they enlist the IRS to help him get a US visa as, living in America, the tax boys would the better be able to mulct his income.[3] Before they sailed Ethel went to London to see Sheran and Edward and visit her friends. She also insisted on getting a new wardrobe in Paris and, somewhat unfairly, this was given as the major reason for the delay.[4] Plum and Ethel arrived in New York on 26 April 1947. Fortunately they were not short of money for together they had some £105,000 in British Government securities plus bank deposits in the US of around $100,000,[5] totalling a respectable fortune and now equal to approximately $5,000,000 or £2,500,000 at 1991 prices.

The priority ought to have been to clear Wodehouse's name beyond all doubt, but that would demand publicity. He had already done three things. Firstly, and to him most important of all, he set out to reassure his friends at Dulwich by writing a full letter to C.T. Rees, Chairman of the Old Alleynians, who had long extracts of it published in *The Alleynian* of July 1945.

Then against the strong advice of his US publishers, Doubleday, who had wanted to bring out his next book, *Joy In The Morning*, without any publicity about the broadcasts, he wrote a letter to the editor of *Variety*, published on 8 May 1946. As Wodehouse knew full well the clipping of the *Variety* piece went into all the newspapers' library files and the first thing any journalist does upon writing a piece is to call for the clippings. Thus all the reviewers of his new book had read his explanation for the broadcasts and as a result he won favourable reviews – which he certainly would not have done had he adopted Doubleday's approach.

He also gave an interview to Hubert Cole of *Illustrated*, a UK magazine, which appeared on 7 December 1946. All three articles set the record straight – but briefly – and did not garner the publicity that a full book would have done. In the UK the insistent advice of Herbert Jenkins and W.P. Watt was to say as little as possible and certainly not to publish *Wodehouse In Wonderland* but to issue, 'at the right time' the accumulation of books written during the war.[6] With hindsight that policy of the low-profile was probably wrong and also more influenced by the desire to sell as many books as possible than other factors. Plum, with forgiveness failing to materialize, bitterly hurt and missing Leonora eventually became glad to go along with that advice.

One man who had argued strongly in favour of publishing *Wodehouse In Wonderland* was Scott Meredith who, when still a corporal in the American Air Force in Ohio, had written to Plum, expressing good wishes. Later Meredith became angry at the lack of effort to clear Wodehouse's name and wrote to Plum's New York lawyer, Watson Washburn, urging 'tell all'. While his advice was ignored it developed his growing relationship, all by post, with Wodehouse. Upon demobilization Meredith bought a small, inert, literary agency and began making a success of it.

Wodehouse's US agent, Paul Reynolds Sr., had died in 1944 and Plum had never felt in tune with his son, Reynolds Jr., who was loyal and competent but lacked the flair of his father. For many years the son had looked after the day-to-day handling of Wodehouse's affairs at the agency and his client had tried to become friendly with him, at one stage writing to him as 'Dear Revere'. He didn't feel comfortable with this and soon reverted to 'Dear Reynolds' but he still expected a total service from the firm above and beyond that due from a literary agent. Paul R. Reynolds & Son had to act as Wodehouse's bankers when required, sometimes by advancing him money before royalties had come in; to pay numerous small American bills for him from his account; to send him money in likely breach of IRS regulations and risk facing proceedings themselves;[7] to send flowers to people on his and Ethel's behalf; to act as an accommodation address and message bureau; to obtain copies of US press clippings, papers, magazines and books for him and to send copies of his books to various people; to send him tobacco and chocolate at Tost and Berlin as well as acting as his US literary agents getting the best possible prices from the top magazines with prompt payment and publication.[8] All of that was expected for their cut-rate, five per cent commission. They had to act as Sebastian Beach to his Galahad Threepwood and had Wodehouse desired that pigs be stolen, incarcerated in the old game-keeper's cottage in the West Wood and illicitly fed there at the dead of night there is no doubt that he would have required Paul R. Reynolds & Son to get on with the job with no dallying.

In spite of all those services Wodehouse wrote Reynolds a brief unfeel-ing letter of 14 September 1945 dismissing him as his US agent.[9] When it came to business Wodehouse could be as unsentimental and ruthless as Jeeves, Senator Opal or any of his tainted millionaires. Soon thereafter Meredith, still in his early twenties and with the same sort of flair Rey-nolds Sr. had enjoyed, was appointed in Reynolds Jr.'s place and with echoes of Seth Moyle forty-five years before sold two stories to *Cosmopoli-tan* just before Ethel and Plum arrived back in New York. Meredith became a good friend of the Wodehouses and played an important role in re-establishing Plum in the American market; two years later Wodehouse was telling Townend that his new man was making things hum and was the agent of his dreams.[10] Meanwhile there were more prosaic matters to hand.

Wodehouse was met off the ship by a swarm of reporters and soon whisked off to a press conference with newspaper, magazine, radio and television interviews to follow as Doubleday were publishing *Full Moon* the next month. Ever the professional author, he obliged. The couple put up at the Weylin Hotel and Wodehouse settled down to work. Then, in September, he and Ethel were able to pick up the threads of life in New York with the return of Guy and Virginia Bolton from a trip to Europe. They took Plum off to their home at Remsenburg in Suffolk County, Long Island, while Ethel house-hunted, finally taking a set of rooms at the Hotel Adams on East 86th Street. Eventually they ended up for many years with an apartment at 1,000 Park Avenue.

Encouragement came in 1948 with the successful New York revival of Plum's *The Play's The Thing* and a London success with a new Wodehouse and Bolton play, *Don't Listen Ladies*, although Plum, perhaps worried about how he was thought of in England used the pen-name Stephen Powys. It wasn't much camouflage as when Samuel French published the play the copyright holders were listed as Guy and Plum. Ethel visited London that August, arriving back in England aboad the *S S America* to see the show and visit Edward and Sheran. She also went to Paris to buy a few more clothes before going home. Plum had thought about coming but didn't. For the rest of his life he always intended to visit England again but always, at the last moment, found a good reason not to do so.

Muggeridge again put it better than anyone else. 'His attitude is like that of a man who has parted in painful circumstances from someone he loves, and whom he both longs and dreads to see again.'[11] In 1950 the BBC, which had behaved so well in 1941, began the thaw in England's 'official' relations with Plum with a request to broadcast *A Damsel In Distress*. In the spring of 1953, Muggeridge, now editor of *Punch*, provided Wodehouse with further encouragement by begging Plum to renew his contributions to the magazine. His first post-war article, 'This Is New York', appeared that July.

Another offer must have given Wodehouse a pleasing sense of old times. 'The plastic surgeon of the theatre' was commissioned to rewrite a flop called *The House On The Cliff*. This had to be done in a hurry and it required Wodehouse to travel with the company to Skowhagen, Maine, for rehearsals, and then on tour, and eventually to Watkins Glen, New York State. Suddenly Ethel was there. Having decided to join Plum she typically visited a car showroom, bought a Nash and drove straight off to Watkins Glen.

Shortly thereafter Wodehouse had a giddy attack which was diagnosed as a tumour on the brain. He faced this quietly and with courage telling Townend that if this was correct it was presumably the finish, as he didn't suppose he could survive a brain operation at his time of life.[12] Later, medical opinion changed its diagnosis to 'don't know'. Plum's well-maintained constitution kept him going but at seventy he was slowing down. Sales of his books were not, with his readers' loyalty as strong as as ever. His publishers calculated that by 1951 he had lifetime sales of at least five million books in the UK plus four million in the US and a million elsewhere in the world (excluding pirate editions).[13] The current total is unknowable but certainly over fifty million, including translations into over thirty languages.

American sales did not add as much to the sum as Wodehouse felt they should. He concluded that his US publishers, Doubleday, were no longer doing all they could to boost the grand total of his sales. Arriving in New York after the war he soon concluded they had become a soulless assembly-line book producer with no interest in their authors or their books but only in their profits.[14] Wodehouse was interested in profits too, although he had more than enough money, and he didn't take kindly to getting only a $2,500 advance on his books plus a fifteen per cent royalty, even though most other authors only got ten per cent. So he moved to Didier for a couple of books, then back to Doubleday for four more books before, in 1953, beginning his long and happy association with Simon & Schuster with, as his editor, Peter Schwed, to whom he wrote, 'What a joy working for an editor like you who makes constructive

suggestions.'[15] The feeling was mutual. Schwed wrote, 'That's what I like
to see – an author who is also an editor – it leaves me time for visiting the
nightclubs and playing tennis.'[16] Scott Meredith asked Simon & Schuster
for an advance of only $2,000 per Wodehouse book but insisted on a
straight fifteen per cent royalty on all sales as Wodehouse knew that was
what Ernest Hemingway received and so he wasn't going to settle for any
less.[17]

Schwed, now retired, was a great editor with only one fault, his titles.
There had always been some variation in the US and UK titles of
Wodehouse's books. 'Fresh' has in America a meaning synonymous with
impertinent in England so *Something Fresh* in the UK was, sensibly,
Something New in America. In post-war years the habit got out of hand,
most notably in two extraordinary titles. *Galahad At Blandings* in the UK
became *The Brinkmanship of Galahad Threepwood* in America and Wode-
house told Grimsdick he thought it the worst title he had ever heard.[18] *A
Pelican At Blandings* in England became the improbable *No Nudes Is Good
Nudes* in America. Only one book, *The Catnappers* (US) and *Aunts Aren't
Gentlemen* (UK) had equally suitable titles both sides of the Atlantic.
Wodehouse imagined an 'Order of Installation' for publishers where each
initiate had solemnly to swear that however suitable the title of any novel
submitted to him by the author he would immediately alter it to one of his
own choosing, thus upholding the ancient privileges of his profession.[19]
However Wodehouse was far too fond of Peter Schwed (who is the
dedicatee of four Wodehouse books, more than anyone else except Leonora) to argue very much about titles.

Now was the time for a little mild revenge. In *The Mating Season* Gussie
Fink-Nottle is given fourteen days without the option at Bosher Street
Magistrates Court for newt-hunting in Trafalgar Square fountains at five
in the morning and 'Showing unexpected intelligence, gave his name as
Alfred Duff Cooper'. (Evelyn Waugh wrote waspishly of '. . . the Master's
great ignorance of Cooper's habits. Nothing is more likely than that he
would be found wallowing in evening dress at five in the morning' adding
'Cooper as a writer *manqué* [he wrote biographies of Tallyrand, the first
Earl Haig and himself] had a peculiar hatred of good writers.')[20] Then in
Cocktail Time came 'Literary composition is not entirely barred to those
whose ambition it is to carve for themselves a political career, but it has to
be the right sort of literary composition – a scholarly life of Tallyrand, for
instance'. Later in *Author! Author!*, mincing his words carefully, Wodehouse called Cooper a book thief. As a mere politician, not worthy of
much notice, Cooper got off lightly.

Milne got more attention. With the prisoner Alfred Duff Cooper in
gaol Bertie has to masquerade as Gussie and recite Christopher Robin

poems at the King's Deverill village concert. Bertie notes that it is unnerving to know that in a couple of days one will be up on a platform in a village hall telling an audience, probably well provided with vegetables, that Christopher Robin went hoppity, hoppity, hop. Indeed Bertie is a spent force as far as Christopher Robin is concerned although he does vaguely remember that the little chap had ten toes. Luckily Wodehouse takes pity on Bertie and gives the job to Esmond Haddock – he of the five resident aunts. There was another published dig at Milne in 1950 with 'Rodney Has A Relapse' in *Nothing Serious*. It is one of Wodehouse's finest short stories and he clearly enjoyed writing it. Rodney Spelvin's young son Timothy has caused a revival of the dormant poetry virus within his father, previously cured by golf. Timothy's Uncle William confides to The Oldest Member that Rodney Spelvin now refers to his son as Timothy Bobbin and gives an example of the proud father's verse

Timothy Bobbin has ten little toes.
He takes them out walking wherever he goes.
And if Timothy gets a cold in the head
His ten little toes stay with him in bed.

Timothy Bobbin also went hoppity, hoppity, hop but Rodney was not sure of that verse having written after it 'Reminiscent?'. Timothy's uncle is rightly worried that Rodney is laying up a lifetime of misery for his son, as Milne did for his. Eventually when Timothy, hamming it up for the audience, asks his father at the climax of an important golf match 'Daddee, are the daisies little bits of stars that have been chipped off by the Angels?', golf (the usual fifty-six holes a day) and sanity prevail.

There was one more jibe at Milne which Wodehouse wrote, but never published, telling of the time he founded the Try To Like Milne Club. After much canvassing he could sign up only one member and he, a week later, wrote saying he would have to resign from the Try To Like Milne Club as 'I've just met him'.[21]

Milne had broken the public school code in the worst possible way and he joined that small band, along with E.C. Bentley, Winston Churchill, Flannery, Dorothy Parker and Alma Whitaker, whom Wodehouse actually disliked although he was too wise to waste much effort on the task or to let his feelings cloud his judgement. He admitted to Denis Mackail that, while nobody could be more anxious than him that Alan Alexander Milne should trip over a loose boot-lace and break his bloody neck, he still read Milne's early work with all the old enjoyment.[22] However he wrote also to Mackail in May 1946 expressing great satisfaction when Milne's *Clary*

Marr was described in the *Daily Mail* as the silliest book of the year.[23]

In March 1952 *The Strand* ceased publication. It was the end of an era for Wodehouse as most of his work published in the UK had first appeared in that magazine and in letters to Reynolds and Grimsdick he admitted it was the only magazine about which he felt sentimental; all the others were judged purely on the terms they offered for his work. He commented to Townend[24] that he was not surprised at *The Strand*'s demise for he thought he had never seen anything sicker-looking than the little midget it had shrunk to and, in its last year or two, he never found anything worth reading in it either.

That same month the Wodehouses were again staying with the Boltons and, while Guy and Plum were busy working on a play, *Come On Jeeves*, Ethel bought a house on the Atlantic shore of the island at Basket Neck Lane, an area Wodehouse had always liked. The new house had the great advantage of being little more than a mile away from Guy and Virginia Bolton. Initially the Wodehouses only used the house during the summer but in 1955 they sold their Park Avenue apartment and lived in Remsenburg the year round. With five acres of grounds there was room for Wodehouse to walk and for the menagerie that accumulated as soon as word got round the animal kingdom that a couple of soft-touches had bought the house. To maintain their privacy the couple bought all the surrounding land they could, ending up with twelve acres, seven of them woodland which ran down to a little creek running off the Atlantic ocean. In isolated Remsenburg a car was essential – the only means of transport – so, typically Ethel drove around Long Island without a licence until she passed her test a couple of months later.[25]

Remsenburg was their last home. The party-giving, party-going Ethel once more showed her mettle and her love for her husband; Remsenburg was Plum's ideal, not hers, but she not only accepted their departure from New York for his sake but was actually responsible for it.

Meanwhile Plum worked on the first of his image building books, *Performing Flea*, using as a vehicle an idea which Townend had first suggested to him back in 1936.[26] The title was chosen from one of Sean O'Casey's vituperative comments in a wartime letter to the *Daily Telegraph* – where he revealed his own level of judgement.

> The harm done . . . is the acceptance of him by a childish part of the people and the academic government of Oxford, dead from the chin up, as a person of any importance whatsoever in English humorous litera-ture. If England has any dignity left in the way of literature she will forget for ever the pitiful antics of English Literature's performing flea.[27]

The Irishman was no match for Wodehouse who blandly took the remark as a compliment noting that all the performing fleas he had ever met had impressed him with their sterling artistry and that indefinable 'something' that made a good trouper.[28]

In *Performing Flea* Wodehouse knew exactly what he intended to achieve – a pen-portrait of himself as that amiable and unworldly recluse – and exactly how to do so. In a shoal of letters[29] he told Grimsdick it was to show him as calm and detached; just getting on with his writing, with no worries about how he might be treated by the British authorities, while there was to be nothing that might be misconstrued as whining or complaining and no hint of his reasonable fears was to be seen. (That meant that the reader did not see the full extent of his courage either.) Thus all mention of a day trip to Switzerland, to consult his old friend Raymond Needham about his legal position in England due to the broadcasts, was omitted.[30] This was not because Wodehouse had been frightened – his contemporary letters make it clear he was not – but because the trip might be misconstrued that way. Townend's contributions were to be ruthlessly rewritten to assist in this aim, and they were,[31] but Townend was given half the royalties. For the book Wodehouse wrote an introduction which is one of the finest and funniest gems he ever penned but it was thought too light for the importance of the book and so Wodehouse, always a ruthless cutter, took it out. Out too went references to Charles Graves, Howard Spring, Ian Hay and every mention of 'The Cazalet crowd . . . so they won't have much to complain of'.[32] The Cazalets, led by Thelma Cazalet-Keir, felt it would not serve Plum's best interests to publish the book.[33] The book was vetted by London's best libel lawyers who strongly advised deleting the phrase 'lawyers really are the damndest fools'.[34] Grimsdick was delighted with the book, writing:

> I am living for the day when I can press this book into the hands of some of the authors I meet from time to time who proudly confess they write two thousand words an hour straight onto the machine and 'never revise a line afterwards'. These are the people who go about believing they have some sort of 'gift' and that they need therefore make no greater effort to ensure success than the physical one of pounding the typewriter. I have long wanted a means of showing them that success, even in the highest places, comes in great measure from hard graft. This book is the perfect answer.

The same year that *Performing Flea* was published Wodehouse received another boost. Penguin issued five of his titles simultaneously – *The Inimitable Jeeves, Right Ho Jeeves, The Code Of The Woosters, Leave It To*

Psmith and *Big Money* – with a combined print run of a million books. This helped introduce a whole new generation of younger or impecunious readers to The Master.[35]

In *Performing Flea* Wodehouse, remembering Cassandra accusing him of having the Christian names Pelham Grenville, idly hoped that Connor's initials W.D. stood for Walpurgis Diarmid and that some day the man would have to own up to them in public. Connor was in New York at the time and wrote a characteristically robust reply in the *Daily Mirror*.[36] He said that he would not today use such words and phrases as he had done in his 1941 broadcast but pointed out, fairly, that war is not a time of reasonableness. He then turned to his victim's notion of his own given names and reproduced a letter he had just sent to Wodehouse.

Dear Mr Wodehouse

Walpurgis Diarmid Connor presents his compliments. But I feel disgruntled, or at any rate far from gruntled, you may recall the phrase, at your choice of the name Diarmid. It carries not one tittle of red-facedness about it. It is devoid of embarrassment.

Now Walpurgis is a corker. It has the smell of the charnel house, the mood of the wake held in the lair of the white worm.

But Diarmid – NO. It has a certain Celtic charm and that, I am sure, is not your purpose. Then another thing. It is true that my first initial is W but my second name does not begin with a D. The initial is N. So cannot we both start again? W for Walpurgis – but N for what?

You must help me. N for Nebuchadnezzar? Not very good. N for Neanderthal? An improvement I think – Walpurgis Neanderthal Connor. We are getting somewhere – can you hear the sound of something plunging about the graveyard. The mixture of the gruesome and the sub-human takes shape.

But you can do better. You suggest what the N stands for. You tell me and I will come to a fair compact with you. Within a few days I am going to Detroit, Chicago, Seattle, San Francisco, Albuquerque, Houston and Chattanooga. To the hotel clerks I will announce myself as Walpurgis Connor.

That ought to shake 'em and will also fulfil your wish that someday I will have to admit to such a string of formidable names in public. I shall enjoy it immensely.

Come now Mr Wodehouse. N stands for what?

Yours sincerely

Walpurgis Connor.

Cassandra wrote some venomous articles but didn't whinge when he was on the receiving end – he hit back. A lunch was arranged by the *Daily Mirror*'s chief US correspondent, Ralph Champion, and took place at the Warwick Hotel, New York.

When Wodehouse turned his mind to a problem his acute intelligence perceived both the problem and the solution to it in ways not apparent to lesser brains. I believe that Wodehouse approached that lunch with Connor having decided to become friends with him as a matter of calculated policy. Supporting that view is Wodehouse telling Connor that 'Even before I met you, I never had any ill feelings about that BBC talk of yours'[37] which is flatly contradicted by what Wodehouse wrote to Bolton and Townend about Connor just after the War. That Connor turned out to be as worthwhile in private as he was base in public just made the task easier.

Connor, in a later *Mirror* article (mainly concerned with attacking Evelyn Waugh for daring to criticize Connor), told of that lunch with Wodehouse.

> He replied, addressing me as 'Dear Walp'.
>
> He invited me to meet him for lunch. We did. He turned up in grey flannel bags at a fashionable New York restaurant and god-dammit or god-blessit, we got on famously. I found him, slightly to my consternation, to be a man of genuine charm and immense likeability. I was, I admit, criminally influenced in the defendant's favour by the sinister fact that Mr Wodehouse, like myself, is reprehensibly fond of cats.
>
> For me, growing old, it is easy to bury the whole story and to forgive and, where necessary to hope to be forgiven.[38]

It is easy to see why the two became genuine friends, lunching together whenever Connor was in New York and maintaining a warm correspondence. To Wodehouse, his friend Connor always remained 'Walp'. That friendship yielded the benefits that Wodehouse expected from his calculated policy. It made many people realize that, as Cassandra had become friendly with Plum, the accusations against him must have proved wrong, while it also made Wodehouse's other wartime critics like Milne, Cooper and Bentley look petty, mean and vindictive.

Connor told Wodehouse of Churchill's alleged comment on the script of the infamous broadcast. This strengthened Plum's dislike of the founder of The Other Club and when Rolf Hochhuth's virulently anti-Churchill play *Soldiers* was staged at London's National Theatre in 1969 it gave Wodehouse much quiet pleasure.[39] There were limits to the kindliness of this kindly man who told Townend that Churchill was one of the few unpleasant personalities he had come across.[40] This was unfair as the only evidence we have that Churchill approved of Cassandra's broadcasts is Cooper's word – a most dubious currency. On the other hand Wodehouse did not allow such personal feelings to influence his political judgement. He felt the country had been wrong to reject Churchill in the 1945 General Election and was pleased when the great man regained power in 1951.[41] Wodehouse's interest in politics was still sufficiently detailed that he was writing to Townend about chances of the Conservatives winning the 1947 by-election in Liverpool and was pained when they lost.[42] Two years later he was making pertinent observations about the anti-Israel policy of the British Foreign Secretary, Ernest Bevin, wondering if the man had the' faintest idea what he was doing since, when US support for British economic recovery was so vital, it was foolish to antagonize the powerful and influential Jewish community in the US over a less important matter.[43] This was the man who, at the same time, was busy portraying himself as a naive and non-political author with just enough brains to open his mouth when he was hungry.

Meanwhile there were more pleasant people in the world, including Arthur Thompson of Teignmouth. Wodehouse made him a gift of his play, *Joy In The Morning* (originally *Phipps*, based on *The Old Reliable*) as a gesture of thanks for his loyalty and friendship and also to help the struggling amateur group, the Buckfast Players. Thus the world premier of a new Wodehouse play took place in a converted barn at Ashburton in Devon in August 1954. On the first night the box-office took £12.[44] It was a far cry from a first night at the magnificent New Amsterdam Theatre on Broadway taking $16,000 in pre-World War I dollars but the play was as well received by an enthusiastic audience of almost a hundred as by 2,000 at a Princess show in New York.

Wodehouse hardly ever went to the theatre any more but instead he finally bought a television set. In an objective, unbiased and balanced assessment of the medium he wrote that, apart from thinking it the foulest, ghastliest, loathsomest nightmare ever inflicted on the human race, he did not positively object to it.[45] He thought it worthwhile just for the boxing, of which he was still an avid fan. However he no longer attended fights since, in 1948, Ethel had paid a huge price for a couple of seats to watch the second Joe Louis v Jersey Joe Walcott fight at Yankee Stadium.[46] They were so far from the ring that Wodehouse's sturdy dislike of wasting money overcame his love of the craft and they never again went to a fight. As he got older that veteran reader of trash got a lot of pleasure from television, becoming a devoted fan of soap operas, particularly *Edge of Night* and *Love Of Life*.

By 1955 there had been no word of official forgiveness from England so

Wodehouse did as Orwell feared he would. On 16 December 1955 in front of Justice D. Ormonde Ritchie in the Riverhead, Long Island Court Buildings he took the oath of allegiance and became an American citizen. Typically he noted that he had to pay another fifty cents for taking the oath after already having paid a ten dollar fee when filing his application papers.[47] Wodehouse had often referred to his own Englishness and at one time said vehemently that he was an Englishman and always would be an Englishman, although he hardly ever referred to himself as British, which is not surprising for someone coming from such an ancient English family. Publicly Wodehouse offered England the most tactful reason he could; it seemed sensible and good manners to be a citizen of the country in which one lived.[48] The real reason was simpler. While the authorities in England had not forgiven him, and the hurt was still alive deep within him, America had succoured him. So more in pain than joy he showed America his gratitude and wrote to Townend, 'Thank God for being an American (I don't mean God is, I mean I am).'[49] For many years Wodehouse had thought of himself as both English and American and found no more difficulty in doing so than other men did in thinking of themselves as both English and British. It is fitting that so great an Anglo-American writer should have had citizenship of both countries during his life. The humorist Frank Sullivan was one of the many Americans who were gratified, writing to Wodehouse, 'Your becoming an American citizen makes up for our loss of T.S. Eliot and Henry James combined.'[50]

One effect of Wodehouse becoming a US citizen was that he had to remit his capital to America, apart from immovables such as UK copyrights. In England wills are public documents (unlike America) and when he died his UK estate was valued at only £31,733.[51] The value of his American estate, the bulk of which went to Ethel, is private but some years before Peter Schwed said that he was a millionaire many times over. Ethel, who never became a US citizen, left an estate in England valued at £504,327 and probably an American estate worth several times that figure. The bulk of her estate went to the Wodehouse English Settlements One Two and Three, whose purpose and beneficiaries are not a matter of public record.[52]

The real sign of Wodehouse's adoption of America was not his accent, it remained purely English, but his apostasy on the holy matter of cricket. In his introduction to a rare book – the 1968 US edition of *Mike At Wrykyn*[53] where he is explaining cricket for the American reader – he writes, 'Take a line through baseball, which incidentally I consider a far superior game.' (Wodehouse was a fan of the New York 'Mets' team.) No English gentleman can make a greater commitment to America than that.

Unless, of course, the statement was merely good manners towards his American readers. As late as 1964 he was still an avid reader of *The Cricketer*. One of his close friends was Old Alleynian S.C. 'Billy' Griffith, who captained the Dulwich rugger XV without defeat through the 1932/3 season, was also a fine cricketer who later kept wicket for England and then became secretary to the ruling body for cricket, The Marylebone Cricket Club, from 1964 to 1972. Wodehouse took a great interest in Griffith's son, his godson, Mike Grenville Griffith, and his cricketing prowess at Grandfather Deane's old school, the Merchant Taylors'. Mike became Captain of the Sussex county cricket XI. Wodehouse also chided Derek Grimsdick for not including in his letters full details of the 1961 test matches against Australia[54] and also followed the cricket career of Grimsdick's son – another Mike. When this Mike did especially well at cricket Wodehouse would send him a ten pound tip and Grimsdick's two daughters thought it frightfully unfair that Wodehouse took no interest in netball.[55] When young Grimsdick went up to Cambridge Plum gave him the original author's manuscript of *Plum Pie*, a valuable item even then, for him to sell. To his credit Mike never did so.

Once Wodehouse became an American the English began to realize how badly they had treated their greatest humorous author. There was still a clutch of carping critics, like John Wain of the *Observer* who, in reviewing *French Leave*, called it a poor book, but Wodehouse's defenders were legion. Evelyn Waugh in an understated yet masterly rebuke proved Wain could not have read the book properly. 'Years and years ago, before it reached its present magisterium, I was one of the regular reviewers on the *Observer*. We were far from dedicated but we had certain old fashioned ideas of fair play. One of them was that you did not abuse a book unless you had read it.'[56]

Wodehouse wrote to friends that Ethel had come to loathe seeing anyone but him and the dogs and that she really loved solitude.[57] That was what she told Plum and to his discredit he allowed himself to believe her – but he had always sacrificed Ethel (and anyone and everything else) to his writing. Ethel had not suddenly changed from the vivacious party-goer she had been all her life – and had still been in post-war Paris where she and Plum met over a hundred Allied servicemen,[58] and in one week went out to three evening functions, having given a party at their home the week before.[59] But she gave her beloved Plum that impression, to keep him happy. At eighty-six the irrepressible Ethel gave a big party at the Henry Perkins hotel in nearby Riverhead[60] and when any visitor hove into view at Remsenburg she immediately recovered all her old vivacity and hospitable instincts. Until their very last years such visitors were numerous, many of them journalists. Ethel did not rigorously protect her Plum from the outside world, nor did he wish to be protected from it, to the degree legend claims. I have noted some eighty interviews Wodehouse gave at Remsenburg, twenty-six of them just for his ninetieth birthday,[61] and have probably missed at least as many more. Those visitors were about the only personal contact with the everyday world left to The Master.

As he withdrew almost totally into the isolation of Remsenburg he found it suited him well – and he even became more relaxed about money – but that perceptive intelligence was as alert as ever. To Townend he wrote of how pressure groups had made it impossible to put a negro on the stage unless he was made very dignified, thus making comic negro characters absolutely taboo and noting that the result was that all the negro actors were out of work, because the playwrights wouldn't write any parts for them.[62] Before the broadcasts that would have made a tellingly gentle piece of satire in a book. Not now, although he did take a mild swipe at post-war socialist Britain with Jeeves explaining, 'We are living now in what is known as the Welfare State, which means – broadly – that everybody is completely destitute.'[63]

In 1959 New York saw the revival of the Bolton, Wodehouse and Kern musical, *Leave It to Jane*. Guy, Plum and the three surviving members of the 1917 cast went to see the show. It was Wodehouse's first visit to the theatre for four years and he enjoyed it, although he let slip one of his rare, public criticisms, admitting that he had hated *My Fair Lady*,[64] the musical based on Bernard Shaw's *Pygmalion*, to which he went with his granddaughter Sheran. Needless to say he told his hosts, Guy and Virginia Bolton, how much he had enjoyed it, but told Mackail 'a manager' had taken him and that he found it the dullest, lousiest show he had ever seen.[65] The revival of *Leave It To Jane* was also enjoyed by the public, for whom the original magic was still there. It achieved 928 performances making it for many years one of the five longest-running Broadway musicals in the history of the theatre.

During the fifties Wodehouse's output remained at the same high level and of the same high quality. Of books not mentioned there were two more in the Bertie-Jeeves cycle: *Jeeves And The Feudal Spirit* (US *Bertie Wooster Sees It Through*) and *How Right You Are Jeeves* (UK *Jeeves In The Offing*). The Blandings saga developed with as fine a book as any in the line, *Pigs Have Wings*. Uncle Fred was in sparkling form in *Cocktail Time* and many of our old favourites appeared in another volume of short stories, *A Few Quick Ones*. In 1960 Wodehouse was honoured by election to the *Punch* table, although unable to go to London to execute the tradition of carving his initials thereon. That 14 October, Simon & Schuster took a big advertisement in the *New York Times*, an authors'

salute to The Master, to celebrate his eightieth birthday – and had to alter
it to salute him entering his eightieth year. It was headed:

Happy Birthday, Mr Wodehouse

WHEREAS P.G. Wodehouse is tomorrow entering his eightieth year, and
WHEREAS none of us had come of age without having read anywhere
from one to eighty of his books with profit and delight, and WHEREAS
P.G. Wodehouse is an international institution and a master humorist:
    We the undersigned salute him with thanks and affection.

Then followed the facsimile signatures of eighty authors. They included
Kingsley Amis, W.H. Auden, S.N. Berhman, John Betjeman, Agatha
Christie, Ivy Compton-Burnett, Ira Gershwin, Graham Greene, Moss
Hart, A.P. Herbert, Aldous Huxley, Christopher Isherwood, Nancy Mit-
ford, Ogden Nash, Cole Porter, V.S. Pritchett, Richard Rodgers, Stephen
Spender, Frank Sullivan, Lionel Trilling, James Thurber, John Updike,
Evelyn Waugh and Rebecca West.

   The next year, when the British got round to The Master's eightieth
birthday, there was much celebration too. Back in 1955 he had agreed
that Herbert Jenkins could commission a book about his writing for the
occasion and having read *Clubland Heroes*, Richard Usborne's fine study of
Dornford Yates, Sapper and John Buchan, The Master suggested him for
the task. Usborne was flattered and agreed to the request, in spite of the
miserly terms offered, modestly assuming that several bigger names in the
literary firmament must have turned the job down, perhaps because of the
money, or rather lack of it. Jenkins had not the wit to tell Usborne that he
was The Master's choice, which would have cost nothing and given a
valuable boost to Usborne's self-confidence.[66] As Jenkins would not pay
the cost of a trip from London to Remsenburg, and their advance would
not bear it, the book was written on the correspondence course principle.
It was ten years before Usborne was in New York (not, of course, at
Jenkins' expense) and met Wodehouse for the first and last time. *Wodehouse At Work* was published in 1961 to well-earned critical praise and it
confirmed, beyond debate, Wodehouse's place in English literature.
Initially Wodehouse was angry at the draft book which included a chapter
on the Berlin broadcasts but he was impressed when it finally came out
(without the broadcasts chapter): 'It is now really all of a piece, a study of
my work. I think Usborne has done a wonderful job.'[67] Usborne did do a
wonderful job, in spite of the fact that Wodehouse virtually acted as
publisher's editor for the book. He was determined that this book, too,
should play its part in his image building. It was not a case of him making

suggestions of how he thought the book should fulfil its function but of him telling Grimsdick how it would do so.[68] It is a tribute to Usborne that his book remains an objective, yet affectionate, classic of its kind. Much as Wodehouse liked the book he remained disconcerted at Usborne's depth of analysis and intuitive perceptions referring to him as 'One learned Usborne'. (After Wodehouse died the book was updated, becoming *Wodehouse At Work To The End*.) Then Evelyn Waugh gave a radio talk on BBC Home Service, *An Act Of Homage And Reparation To P.G. Wodehouse* on 15 July (the same date as Cassandra's broadcasts). Typically Wodehouse asked Waugh not to berate Cassandra who is therefore never mentioned by name in the talk.[69] In a magnificent peroration, Waugh, at his unique best, talks of the pristine, paradisaical innocence of the Wodehouse world.

> For Mr Wodehouse there has been no Fall of Man, no aboriginal calamity. His characters have never tasted the forbidden fruit. They are still in Eden. The Gardens of Blandings Castle are that original garden from which we are all exiled. The *chef* Anatole prepares the ambrosia for the immortals of high Olympus. Mr Wodehouse's world can never stale. He will continue to release future generations from captivity that may be more irksome than our own. He has made a world for us to live in and delight in.[70]

In 1965 the BBC began their television series *The World Of Wooster* with Dennis Price playing Jeeves in what for many was the definitive piece of casting. Wodehouse thought him the best Jeeves ever and that Ian Carmichael played a fine Bertie, although a *Sunday Times* journalist thought him too old for the part and so attributed that view to Plum, much to his annoyance.[71] The series won the Guild of Television Producers and Directors' best comedy award for 1965 with OA Richard Waring and Michael Mills winning the best script award for their skilled adaptations.

In September 1964 Wodehouse invited Armine's widow, Nella, to come to live with him and Ethel at Remsenburg[72] – which she did until his death. Naturally he did not let the inevitable quarrels between Ethel and Nella bother him in the slightest bit. He treated them in the same way he did dog-fights, something in nature of the species and which a wise man ignores. In his will he made a number of bequests which lapsed if he died before Ethel (as he did), but he left Nella $100,000 absolutely.[73]

Wodehouse had always been charitable in both senses of the word, although his only *public* donation to charity was the $20,000 he and Ethel gave to the Bide-A-Wee Association in 1966 to build the 'P.G. Wodehouse Shelter' for stray animals at nearby Westhampton – and the public nature of the gift was only to encourage others to give too.[74] Six Wodehouse pets are buried at Westhampton beneath a common gravestone. Under the name 'Wodehouse' this simply lists the pets' names and says underneath 'We loved them'. More characteristic is the encomium to a nearby poodle: 'Darling Binky-boo. Mommie will join you in Heaven one day'.

Ethel visited the shelter frequently, feeding and petting the animals – until a new manager imposed revised rules forbidding anyone but the staff to feed the animals or stay in the shelter after 5 p.m. (This is what Christopher Fildes calls the 'Restaurant closed for staff lunch' principle of running a business.) Virginia Bolton relates that Ethel asked 'Does that apply to everyone?' and was told that it did. And ' "Bang went the $300,000 the association would have got when Plum died," Virginia remarked.'[75]

In January 1965 grandson Edward became engaged to the Hon. Camilla Gage and was married that April. Plum wanted to come over for the wedding but, predictably, didn't. Ethel wanted to come and, unpredictably, did not. The same thing happened when Sheran married Simon Hornby three years later. It is pleasing that Mr (now Sir Simon) Hornby became chairman of the family firm, W.H. Smith, which sells more Wodehouse titles than any other company in the world.

As the years passed Wodehouse, both his writing and the man, became the object of affectionate veneration. In 1973 under the inspiration of Thelma Cazalet-Keir, *Homage To P.G. Wodehouse* was published containing twelve essays from friends and admirers ranging from Lord David Cecil to Auberon Waugh. Wodehouse probably told each author his essay was his favourite but wrote to Thelma that he thought the one by Richard Ingrams, then editor of *Private Eye*, the magazine everyone denies reading, the best of the lot.[76] Ingrams' theme was the immortality of Wodehouse's writing. 'People . . . should consider for a start just how many literary reputations have blossomed and died during his long lifetime while his has remained unfaded. Mr Wodehouse is not a thing of the past because he has never been a thing of the present.'

Remsenburg was becoming a place of literary pilgrimage. Wodehouse liked the proof that his readers, who had never deserted him, held him in continuing affection and it's doubtful if he disliked the way that they drove gaps through his defences, or he would have had Ethel turn them away. In 1968 after seeing one boorish and incompetent interviewer Wodehouse swore he would never see any of the pests again[77] – but he did, often. Most guests were good company such as Frank Muir and Richard Usborne. David Jasen continued the series of visits that culminated in his bibliography and biography. Madame Tussaud's sent John Blakely over to record Plum's features in wax – not for posterity but for rubbernecking *hoi polloi* trooping through their London museum. David Emms, then Master of Dulwich, had his bottom pinched by Ethel, saucy as ever at ninety. Tom Sharpe visited Remsenburg but modestly went there as a photographer (which he had been) rather than a novelist. Later Wodehouse was to speak highly of *Porterhouse Blue*. That The Master should commend such bawdy black humour is superficially surprising, given his dislike of anything raunchy, but he must have appreciated that he had met another comic master who could also make the language dance to his bidding.

He told William Davis, then the new editor of *Punch*, that he had shortened his books at the request of his publishers in England so that they could sell them at under £2. Dutifully he did so for his next book – which they published at £2.25p.[78]

Scott Meredith and Peter Schwed were regular visitors. In *Biffen's Millions* (UK *Frozen Assets*) Lord Tilbury, having been debagged, asks his lawyer if he can sue the man who did it and is told he can not.

The case would be on all fours with Schwed versus Meredith LR3 HL 330, though in that case the *casus belli* was an overcoat. Schwed sued before the magistrates of South Hammersmith [Albert Haddock's favourite court] sitting in petty court and was awarded damages.

Another of the private jokes found throughout the canon.

Meredith and Wodehouse gave each other a unique bibliographical distinction in the *The Best Of Modern Humor* which they edited jointly and which is dedicated by each of them to the other.

From England, Sheran and Edward Cazalet came to see their grandparents. The democratic Wodehouse was delighted (and perhaps surprised) that his step-grandson was no snob calling him a charming chap and very democratic.[79] Christopher Maclehose of Barrie and Jenkins, who had brought a needful dose of enthusiastic professionalism to the handling of Plum's UK editions, was another welcome visitor. So was Malcolm Muggeridge whenever he visited America; and there was a steady stream of other famous and less well known fans.

Scores of journalists from papers, periodicals, radio and television came from America and around the globe. Plum, with more brains than any of them and, as an old journalist himself, well aware of the tricks of the craft, was always in full control of these interviews. He directed them gently where he wished and nearly all his guests wrote exactly what he wanted them to write. (He never repeated the mistake he made with Miss Whitaker.) Whenever plausible, each writer got the impression that his or her publication was Wodehouse's favourite reading.

Many of these visitors, such as Gerald Clarke who wrote profiles of

The Master in *Esquire* and *The Paris Review*, were the unconscious butts of those private jokes Wodehouse loved. Clarke telephoned in advance to find out how to get to Basket Neck Lane from the nearest railway station at Speonk, and Wodehouse, playing Lord Emsworth, said he had absolutely no idea. Having baited the trap Wodehouse met Clarke on arrival at the house and plaintively asked for assistance as he couldn't get through to New York on the telephone. It turned out that this charming but confused old man didn't know that you had to include the 212 area code when dialling the city from Remsenburg. This left Clarke with a warm feeling of useful competence and friendly superiority.[80] If you believe Wodehouse, even at ninety, when he could still write a Wodehouse novel each year, didn't know or had forgotten how to telephone New York, you will believe that *Aunts Aren't Gentlemen* was ghost-written by Enid Blyton and *The Catnappers* by Dr Seuss. In fact six months later Wodehouse gave another journalist, Ruth Inglis of *Nova*, such clear instructions on how to drive from Manhattan to Basket Neck Lane that she arrived ten minutes early.[81] Other journalists got the same treatment as Clarke. Wilfred De'Ath was asked by the well-informed reader of the *Wall Street Journal* 'What is the Common Market?' and to explain Britain's new decimal currency. The doddery old man was suitably grateful when De'Ath translated the price of his latest English book from £2.20p into two pounds and four shillings.[82] Sometimes Ethel joined in the game, firmly correcting her husband with a bravura show of expertise when he became 'confused' talking to a journalist about tax law. It all helped create the image of an amiable and unworldly recluse. So did his claim made to Tom Sharpe and Edward Cazalet among others that, of all his characters, he felt most like the unworldly and woolly-minded Lord Emsworth. Upon reading that 'I inspected my imagination. Jeeves was quite right. It boggled'.

Occasionally Plum and Ethel tripped each other up. Usborne, when shown Plum's study by The Master, had pointed out to him a big pile of letters ready for posting and was told, plaintively, 'Ethel insists on my answering all the letters I get.' But Ethel had already shown Usborne the study and pile of letters, remarking with wifely disapproval, 'Plummie insists on answering every letter. I wish he wouldn't.'[83]

Welcome and unwelcome, all Wodehouse's visitors were received with the same inbred courtesy. Visitors apart, the days at Remsenburg followed a gentle pattern. The daily exercises first thing in the morning before making his own breakfast, work till twelve, then watching television until lunch. After that taking the dogs for a walk to collect the mail, a little more work or thinking about it, a bath at five o'clock then cocktails, dinner and reading. His favourite writers covered so vast a range that it would be unwise to single any of them out. They ranged from the highbrow to the lowbrow, from the classical to the contemporary, but to visiting journalists he usually mentioned the popular lowbrows – in keeping with the image of Wodehouse the dumdum. Unsurprisingly he often cited writers such as Rex Stout and Agatha Christie whose style is unmemorable but whose mastery of plot is unbettered and whose use of language to achieve their aims is total. After reading, Wodehouse might take another walk with the dogs and write a few more letters before bed.

Sometimes he played two-handed bridge with Ethel after dinner. In earlier years, being what he called 'a wise owl' he never played bridge with his wife.[84] He enjoyed the game but never took it too seriously. When an angry partner once asked him why he hadn't played his ace earlier he answered in injured tones, 'I played it as soon as I found it.' He also wondered why South always got the best cards! Then he hit upon the answer; South deals. He pictured South as a Mississippi gambler of the old school with a thin face, thin lips, a small moustache and eyes that could be grafted onto a crocodile. South and his old friend North had been freshmen at Sing-Sing together while East and West were just a couple of raw boys up from the country with whom North had scraped an acquaintance at the bar.[85] In the early years at Basket Neck Lane there were dinners of the New York Old Alleynians, later changed to Sunday lunches so their most famous member could get there and back in a day from Remsenburg.

On most days Wodehouse visited Bolton. 'For that, among many reasons, Guy garnered Ethel's almost ceaseless animosity.'[86] It was Guy who claimed that Ethel ruled Plum ruthlessly and in later years kept him short of money, allowing him only five dollars (or, when Bolton felt benign, twenty) a week. Bolton is a highly untrustworthy source of information about Ethel. In old age Wodehouse never carried money in Remsenburg and like the Queen or the President never needed to. Anything he wanted he either ordered on account from New York by post or telephone, or he bought from the local shops where it was also charged to the Wodehouses' accounts. Ethel never ruled her husband, except to the extent that he wished her to, and the Guy-Plum friendship ended only with death.

As Wodehouse observed, somehow that repetitive daily routine never got boring. Not for him, anyway. In 1946 he said he couldn't ever remember being bored during the previous twenty years;[87] an unconscious tribute to the quality of his mind and character which enabled him to think about his work and plan it out, even on a twenty-hour journey standing up in a horse carriage.

For Ethel it was not such fun. She was as vivacious and tastefully dressed as ever, 'She is still an excellent hostess. She stands behind the bar and for four people takes enough Martini to fill a fish tank, building it strongly enough to send the unsuspecting guest into outer space, with just enough Vermouth to fill an eye-dropper. Plummy sips his warily, she is more adventurous.'[88]

After nearly sixty years of marriage Plum and Ethel were as close as ever, leaving around the house for each other little love-notes of a sentimentality more suitable for adolescents. To her husband, Ethel was Bunny, The Boss and, adopting Edward's name for his grandmother, The Colonel. Three nicknames are always a sign of strong affection. The couple still spent most hours apart with Wodehouse in his study still producing a book a year. In the sixties other titles were *Service With A Smile*, an Uncle Fred-Blandings novel and one of his best books, *Stiff Upper Lip Jeeves*, and *The Purloined Paperweight* (UK *Company for Henry*). That last book and his 1970 offering *The Girl In Blue* are the first to show any sign that Wodehouse was getting older and writing below the almost faultless level he had maintained for fifty-seven years. The plotting is less complex, the seams occasionally show and there are far fewer new images than we have come to expect. But in 1973 with *Bachelors Anonymous* The Master was back in mid-season form.

In February 1970 Guy Bolton contributed 'Unforgettable P.G. Wodehouse' to the *Reader's Digest*, written in the rose-tinted marshmallow style favoured by the magazine. It portrays a rose-tinted marshmallow personality with as much strength of character as a soggy flannel – which was the way Plum wanted it. P.G. Wodehouse had created his finest fictional character – himself.

17

PEERLESS P.G. WODEHOUSE

To criticise him is like taking a spade to a souffle.

Sir Compton Mackenzie *Punch*

AT the age of ninety Wodehouse's place in English letters was assured. He was then and is still today almost certainly the best-selling humorous writer in the world – though no one has undertaken the task of proving him so. Sales alone are proof of appeal to readers (if not to critics) but, unlike most contemporary commercial authors who sell in their millions, Wodehouse enjoys enormous breadth and depth of sales. He appeals as much to the most lordly professors in ancient universities, such as the philosopher Anthony Quinton, as to the ever so 'umble daily commuter on the municipal bus, such as myself; to subtle theologians such as Monsigneur Ronald Knox; to the inbred aristocrat and mongrel citizen of the world. Peter Schwed uncovered a cabal of at least three ambassadors to the United Nations in New York who read Wodehouse to while away the tedium of UN Council meetings.[1] Wodehouse also noted his appeal to 'A rather specialised public. Invalids like me. So do convicts. And I am all right with dog stealers.' (He then admitted he was swanking, only one dog stealer, and a not very good one at that – he was caught at his first attempt at dognapping.)[2]

Unlike Henry James, the other great Anglo-American author, Wodehouse did not have to wait until after his death to become a best seller. He has been one since 1915 with the publication of *Something New* in the *Saturday Evening Post* (then the pinnacle of achievement for every fiction writer in America). As a book it has remained in print ever since. So he was a best seller for the next fifty-eight years until his death and still passes the test of time. Arthur Waugh, chairman of publishers Chapman and Hall, wrote a fan-letter to Wodehouse in 1936.[3] Both his sons, Alec and Evelyn, were fans as is his grandson Auberon who, seeing his daughter chuckling over a Wodehouse novel, realized that she was the fourth generation of his family to do so.[4] Wodehouse continues to sell as well and as widely since his death as he did when alive.

He is also one of that elite band of authors who sell strongly in translation, having been published in dozens of languages – the total is unknown – from Arabic to Esperanto, from Burmese to Bulgarian. In Holland and Sweden there are usually over twenty Wodehouse titles in print and in Italy over forty. This is odd since, in translation, many of the finer points of any writer's felicity with his own language are lost. Using the translate-retranslate technique, the sentence ' "Jeeves" I said, wiping the brow and gasping like a stranded goldfish, "it's beastly hot" ' becomes in Arabic 'O Jeeves! This atmosphere is hot in a savage fashion' which doesn't quite have the subtle bounce of the original. What gives Wodehouse enormous appeal in all languages is the taut, original and seamless plotting plus the joy and jollity which surge through in even the weakest translations.

George Orwell records, 'Some foreign readers regard Wodehouse as "a penetrating satirist of English society" and "a social satirist of the first order".'[5] And still from the English speaking world, the critic John Selby, in the Augusta, Georgia, *Chronicle* wrote, 'He is a social satirist of the first order. Ask the old order in England.'[6]

Humourless Marxists occasionally attack Wodehouse for being an apologist for an outworn aristocracy. Alastair Cooke, another great Anglo-American wordsmith, vividly imagines 'The preconceptions of the foreigner, especially of the Communists, who must at this moment be learning the dreadful truth about the West by commuting between *Leave It To Psmith* and *Little Dorrit* in order to strike a proper balance between the life of the oppressors in their castles and the oppressed in their factories.'[7] Wodehouse agreed this was very likely. Even a sensible socialist like Orwell wrote, 'Wodehouse's real sin has been to present the English upper classes as much nicer than they really are'[8] – which is like berating Kenneth Grahame for presenting toads as better at driving motor cars than they are in *The Wind in the Willows*.

One enthusiast, John Hatton, kept a straight face to make a conversion; difficult, as he had his tongue in his cheek at the time.

Only the other day Mr Peter Johnson, of the Socialist Workers Party in Scunthorpe, was telling me that he could not share my enthusiasm for Blandings Castle and Mr Bertram Wooster. I told him there is a great deal of social comment in the Jeeves books. Jeeves, the educated, perceptive member of the proletariat, is sought out by bumbling members of the aristocracy to help them out with their difficulties. In these books the dignity of the working man, as portrayed by Jeeves, compared with the fecklessness of the upper orders, as portrayed by Wooster, his aunts, Gussie Fink-Nottle and Bingo Little, is made clear for all to see.

'Do you know, I'd never looked at it that way before' replied Mr Johnson, who, I hope, is even now ploughing through all ninety-six of Plum's novels looking for any other social or reforming message I may have missed.[9]

Auberon Waugh tells us that at a left-wing conference in Vienna his friend Claud Cockburn, the radical journalist, 'Exerted himself to persuade his deeply serious audience that the Jeeves-Wooster relationship offered a microcosm of the class struggle: despite the apparently effortless intellectual superiority of the proletarian Jeeves and despite the apparent inanity of his employer, Wooster, Jeeves allows his enormous fish-fed intelligence to be exploited. This demonstrates the power and cunning of the ruling class, which progressive thinkers underestimate at their peril.'[10] It also demonstrates that Bertie – like Wodehouse – is not the simpleton he pretends to be.

At that same conference a Swedish lady asked Cockburn if Wodehouse was really sound on the vital question of Woman's Struggle For Freedom and on Animality-Aggressiveness in The Male. Such humourless feminists have sometimes attacked Wodehouse for the male chauvinism of his characters – which shows extraordinary obtuseness. Most of the Wodehouse men, with a few exceptions led by Jeeves, are bossed about by their womenfolk, and even the Hon. Galahad Threepwood has to use all his guile to thwart Lady Constance and his other nine sisters.

Wodehouse is not only well read but, as any antiquarian bookdealer will aver, one of the most collected of all authors and has been for decades. The true bibliomaniac finds him particularly satisfying to collect for three reasons: unknown articles can still be discovered, a valuable collection can be built up cheaply, and the task is never complete. Between 1901 and 1914 Wodehouse produced hundreds of articles for London and New York newspapers and periodicals: many are known but many still await the diligent fanatic to rediscover them for posterity. To collect Wodehouse through the salerooms is now an expensive business – with rare titles in fine condition fetching thousands (dollars or pounds) – but it is still possible to find affordable Wodehouse first editions in thrift or charity shops, at car boot sales and the more casually managed second-hand book shops. Lastly the task is never done. Having set out to collect a set of US or UK first editions the novice discovers he or she needs both because of variations either side of the Atlantic. The initiate is impelled to seek out Wodehouse's lyrics, plays, theatre programmes, records, tapes, and video cassettes; but that is far from the end. The enthusiast must have books about Wodehouse and his work, memoirs with mention of him, foreign language editions and newspaper clippings of his journalism. Now the bibliomaniac enthusiast has to assuage his craving for Wodehouse memorabilia – especially such things as letters from the Master (not uncommon) and signed copies of his books (rare). There could scarcely be a more innocent mania, even though it does include collecting twenty issues of *Playboy*.

Yet distinct from the rest of *Playboy*, Wodehouse's own stories are inoffensive to the most rigid Puritan – unlike, say, the Rabelaisian black comedy of Tom Sharpe. He, like so many authors, has been strongly influenced by The Master to whom he happily acknowledges his debt, as did Evelyn Waugh who said: 'One has to regard a man as a Master who can produce on average three uniquely brilliant and entirely original similes to every page.'[11]

Waugh was just one of many of Wodehouse's peers to hold his prose in awed admiration. Some people treated Belloc's famous remark 'The best writer of English now alive' as hyperbole but most of Wodehouse's peers didn't think so, nor did the Oxford dons when they made him an honorary Doctor of Letters. Today the remark does not seem much overstated, if at all. It would be hard to argue that any other writer alive in the thirties was a greater master of the language than Wodehouse. *The Times*, in a leader on Wodehouse's ninetieth birthday, gave its measured judgement on Belloc's comment: 'He exaggerated only just, if at all.'[12] Who else had not only twenty-four ways of calling someone mildly drunk – ranging from awash to woozled via oiled, ossified, pie-eyed, plastered and polluted[13] – but gives one character, Lord Tidmouth, five different ways of saying goodbye (excluding goodbye) in one book? 'Bung-ho', 'Teuf-teuf', 'Tin-kerty-tonk', 'Poo-boop-a-doop', and 'Honk-honk',[14] while Bertie adds a couple more, 'Toodle-oo' and 'pip-pip'.

Wodehouse invented many phrases, such as 'Down to earth', which are now so much part of the English language that we assume they are of ancient provenance instead of being only a few decades old. Other examples are 'To have a dash at something', 'Dirty work at the crossroads', 'Foggy between the ears', 'Loony-bin' and that splendid back formation, 'Gruntled'.[15] 'He spoke with a certain what-is-it in his voice, and I could see that, if not actually disgruntled, he was far from being gruntled.' He also fathered three other words now sanctioned by the Oxford English Dictionary (OED): Wodehousian (traced back to the *Times Literary Supplement* in 1931), Jeeves (first used by Evelyn Waugh in *Labels* in 1930) and Wooster (first used by W.H. Auden and Christopher Isherwood in *Journey To War* in 1939). A measure of the effect Wodehouse has had on the English language is that the OED refers to his work 1,255 times! Of those 143 apply to the invention of a word by Wodehouse or to the first use by him of a word with a specific subsense.[16]

Such language has become a code between enthusiasts. The great jazz musician, Bix Beiderbecke, could quote great junks of Wodehouse verbatim, as could his peers Frank Norris and Squirrel Ashcraft. All three could spot the exact character who said any chosen line and the right book – at a time when Wodehouse had already written some forty-eight.[17] Sir Robert Birley was once talking to M.R. James, 'the most learned scholar I have ever known', who referred to a house where Queen Elizabeth I had once stayed. Birley said to himself, 'One of those houses, no doubt, at which Queen Elizabeth had spent a night in her snipe-like migrations about the country.' James caught the *sotto voce* comment; 'My dear Birley, do you read him too?'[18] Such experiences are common among The Master's fans.

Notwithstanding enthusiasts such as Dr James, there is a long tradition – stretching back to at least Samuel Johnson with his definition of a humorist as 'A mere humorous person' – of reluctance by many critics and academics to treat humour as real literature. They appear to feel that by lauding humour they might be accused of lacking gravitas, the charge the second-rate most dread. So much safer to go to the other extreme. For example, it is as difficult to find an educated person's library without a copy of James Joyce's *Finnegans Wake* as it is to find an educated person who has actually read the whole book. Most of them accept Joyce as great literature at the same time as they find him unintelligible.

If your criteria for great literature require *Sturm und drang* with penetrating insights into the human predicament then Wodehouse is not great literature. If those criteria include total mastery of written English, the ability to make it dance to your bidding with a poetic beauty and to any job desired and to give joy to readers across the entire spectrum, then Wodehouse is great literature. 'His narrative and dialogue could not be improved, and he passes the supreme test of being re-readable. I don't know how many times I have read the stories, but plenty. I know exactly what is coming and how it is all going to end, but it doesn't matter. That's *writing.*'[19] Not me on Wodehouse but Wodehouse on Rex Stout – but it applies just as much to Plum. Each re-reading of Wodehouse gives us the pleasure and the joy of appreciating further twists and layers of humour and felicitous use of English missed on earlier readings. Today it is hard to suggest any contemporary humorous author who might approach Wodehouse's stature.

What enthralled his fellow writers was that use of language. The effortless way he made it do almost impossible tasks with grace and economy;

the combination of verbal felicity, faultless dialogue, the beauty of his English, the deft characterization with so few words and his seamless convoluted plots – they knew how difficult that was.

It is not a faculty that can be imitated. The McIlvaine bibliography lists twenty-nine Wodehouse pastiches, of which I have read over half. They attempt to catch the flavour of the original and fail, although J. McLaren Ross comes closer than most.

Wodehouse told us more about how he wrote than almost any other author and Townend received a torrent of wise technical and tactical advice (although it never made him a noticeably better author). Wodehouse started explaining his methods in 1927 with an article titled 'How I Write My Books' in a little *Strand* volume called *What I Think* and tackled the matter in depth in *Performing Flea* and *Author! Author!*. He noted that for short stories the plot grew out of the characters but that for novels the characters grew out of the plot. He talks of working and reworking both plot and characters for his novels. 'I stand no nonsense from my characters. The pickle-manufacturer has to become a duchess – and like it – in order to fit the scene where the dog fancier (now a blackmailer once more) goes to the Hunt Ball so as to keep in with the girl's aunt, whose rabbits have been taken away from her and replaced by a racing stable.'[20] He wrote short stories at great speed and then corrected them, while with novels he just plugged steadily away. As he grew older he spent more and more time on working out the plots of his novels, sometimes compiling 400 pages of notes before writing a word of the text. As always, it was the plot famine that bothered him most and growing older he wrote far fewer short stories as these used up plots that might more profitably be developed into a novel.

He talked of introducing major characters early on and getting to the dialogue as soon as possible; of the value of giving minor characters ordinary names; of never giving major characters minor scenes; of splitting stories into scenes as if they were stage plays; of never humanizing villains. (He did not pin sheets of continuous typing paper on the wall, with those where the story sagged a bit put lower down, and those that had not quite the right feel at an angle. That was one more story Bolton wished on Wodehouse.) What is not so obvious from his letters is any painstaking research. In *Performing Flea* there is one letter where Wodehouse asks Townend eight portmanteau questions about life on a tramp steamer – for just half an intended chapter about Sam Shotter of *Sam In The Suburbs*. In fact that letter was made up just for the book. Strangely Wodehouse never talked or wrote about the actual writing itself. The penning of that peerless prose came to him as unconsciously as sleeping and breathing. It was only plots, and to a small extent his characters, which ever caused him any trouble. The actual writing of a story, he said, always gave him a guilty feeling, as if he was wasting his time. The only thing that bothered him was thinking the stuff out.[21] In the late forties he wrote to Bolton, bemoaning the fact that it now took him six months to write a novel instead of three.[22] Most writers would be proud to write one novel of Wodehousian calibre in six years.

Wodehouse was our greatest master of the quote and the cliche, resurrecting them from limbo to do extraordinary tasks with youthful vigour. 'When the Woosters put their hands to the plough, they do not readily sheathe the sword'. While he used a few old favourites time and time again the full range of his repertoire is unknown. A Richard Usborne will spot the classical allusions. A Tony Quinton will spot allusions from great English literature. A Benny Green will spot the allusions from the theatre. But which Wodehouse scholar will spot references to the classics, great English literature and poetry, the musical theatre, whodunnits, English public-school stories, nearly all the humorous writers of the nineteenth and twentieth century including many forgotten for decades, trash magazine writers spanning eight decades, popular novelists no longer popular, Gilbert and Sullivan and much more including the *Wall Street Journal*? None.

In any extended essay on Wodehouse a comparison between the Bard of Avon and the Bard of Blandings appears obligatory. Wodehouse's writing shows he was a Shakespeare buff long before internment gave him the habit of reading the entire works every year or two. Both had a musical sense of language and Shakespeare scholars take a particular delight in Wodehouse. One can see why.

> The fact I am not a haggis addict is probably due to Shakespeare. . . . Macbeth happens upon the three Witches while they are preparing the evening meal. They are dropping things into the cauldron and chanting 'Eye of newt and toe of frog, wool of bat and tongue of dog' and so on, and he immediately recognises the recipe. 'How now, you secret, black and midnight haggis' he cries shuddering. This has caused misunderstandings and has done injustice to the haggis.[23]

Shakespeare himself never wrote anything quite like that!

Wodehouse wrote two articles in *Punch* on the hotly debated question of the relative merits of himself and Shakespeare and concluded, generously, 'Who am I to say which is superior? Bill's stuff is good. I'm good. Both good lads is the way I look at it, and I deprecate the pitting of author against author.'[24] He also dealt firmly with those who argued that the plays had actually been written by Francis Bacon, Lord Verulam. While

Bertie is permitted this popular misconception the aunt of Archibald Mulliner's amorata Aurealia Cammarleigh is elegantly exposed.

'What needs my Shakespeare for his honour'd bones? The labour of an Age in piled stones? Or that his hallowed Reliques should be hid under a star-y pointing Pyramid. . . . As in the Plays and Sonnets we substitute the name equivalents of the figure totals.' . . . The aunt inflated her lungs.
'These figure totals are always taken out in the Plain Cipher, A equalling one to Z equals twenty-four. A capital letter with the figures indicates an occasional variation in the name count. For instance, A equals twenty-seven, B twenty-eight, until K equals ten is reached, when K, instead of ten becomes one and R or Reverse and so on, until A equals twenty-four is reached. The short or single digit is not used here. Reading the Epitaph in the light of this Cipher, it becomes "What need Verulam for Shakespeare? Francis Bacon England's King be hid under W, Shakespeare? William Shakespeare. Fame, what needest Francis Tudor,. King of England? Francis. Francis W. Shakespeare. For Francis thy William Shakespeare hath England's King took W. Shakespeare. Then thou our W. Shakespeare Francis Tudor bereaving Francis Bacon Francis Tudor such a tomb William Shakespeare".'
The speech was unusually lucid and simple for a Baconian.[25]

Using the same system Plum's fan, Monsigneur Ronald Knox, proved that Queen Victoria wrote the works of her Poet Laureate, Alfred Lord Tennyson.[26] The only concession Plum was prepared to make on the question of the Bard's ghost writer was that his works might have been written *by someone else with the same name.*
Sir Iain Moncreiffe also had something to suggest about Plum and his ancestral fifth cousin.

Talking of Shakespeare, did Wodehouse write Bacon? For, through the marriage of PGW's forefather Sir Armine Wodehouse (fifth Baronet, died 1777), to Letitia Bacon, daughter and co-heiress of Sir Edmund Bacon, sixth Baronet, the great Sir Francis Bacon was his ancestral uncle. Perhaps, however, the question should really be did the ghost of uncle Bacon have a hand in typing Wodehouse?[27]

Bernard Levin gives the best comparison between Shakespeare and The Master.

I would not normally compare Wodehouse to Shakespeare, but that line ['in my heliotrope pyjamas with the old gold stripe'] puts me in mind of Macbeth after the murder:

. . . this my hand will rather
the multitudinous seas incarnadine,
Making the green one red.

Shakespeare did not, of course, consciously strive to balance the rolling thunder of the polysyllabic second line with the hammer blows of the mono-syllables in the third, and Wodehouse was likewise not consciously choosing his words to make the line I have quoted into perfect music. But it is perfect music; and his instinctive feel for the rhythm in it is, in its way, the same as Shakespeare's in the mighty lines he gives to Macbeth.[28]

Apart from finally resolving the 'Who wrote the works of Shakespeare?' conundrum, Wodehouse pops up in all sorts of unexpected ways. One fan, writer Truman Capote, was introduced to his works by another fan, the film star Elizabeth Taylor who is also a close friend of Wodehouse's granddaughter Sheran. Miss Taylor took her husband, actor Richard Burton, to meet Sheran and she corrected him on the pronunciation of Wodehouse. When asked what made her an authority on this matter she replied firmly, 'Because he's my grandfather.' Burton, another of Wodehouse's unexpected friends, wrote to him saying, 'I loved your granddaughter on the spot and pencilled her in for my third wife, should the occasion rise. The occasion hasn't arisen and isn't likely to as Sheran went off and married a Hornby (very nice too, though a trifle tall for my 5″11″).'[29]

There are several Drones Clubs around the world and there is a valeting service in London called 'Jeeves of Belgravia' while American golfers repeated the feat of Ralph Bingham and Arthur Jukes who, in *The Long Hole*, golfed their way sixteen miles from the clubhouse to the Majestic Hotel. An expensive provision merchants called Duff & Trotter after the emporium from *Quick Service* was established in London. In 1930 some Cambridge undergraduates founded 'The Wooster Society' and repeated *The Great Sermon Handicap* with a field that included the bishops of Ely and Singapore, Monsigneur Ronald Knox and a missionary, the Rev H.C. Read, who won 'riding' the parish church of St Andrew-the-Great.[30]

Sir Robert Birley, who had been Headmaster of Eton, wrote a scholarly pamphlet, *One Hundred Books In Eton College Library*.[31] Mentioning their prized copy of the Gutenberg Bible, one of only forty-eight known, he continued, 'To the recorded copies of the Gutenberg Bible should be added one in the library of Blandings Castle in Shropshire'. H.P. Kraus, the great New York bookdealer, was considerably worried about the Blandings Gutenberg until he found out it was fictional.

The achievements of Wodehouse and comparable authors will never be equalled because the nature of our culture and communications has changed too much, quite apart from the absence of a grounding in the classics. We are witnessing the busy replacement of physical communication (talking face to face, print on paper) and electromechanical communication (cinema, records, telegrams) with electronic communication (radio, video, television, electronic mail-boxes, EDP, et cetera). Those of us who enjoy writing, reading and collecting books should not blind ourselves to the fact that we are an endangered species with a survival expectancy of perhaps 100 years. Marshall McLuhan, the prophet of the electronic age, argued that our affection for books and periodicals will not preserve them from the onslaught of newer technologies.[32] McLuhan is being proved right. Electronics is now the dominant medium of communication.

Wodehouse understood this. In spite of adopting the facade of an *ingénue* he looked at the world with objective innocence asking, 'Where have all the humorists gone?' and answering, 'Television I suspect.' The young wordsmith who might one day compete for Plum's laurels is now lucratively ensnared by the electronic media.

An author of a book still has individuality, one of a film-script has not, the directors having appropriated for themselves the role of *auteur* for each film. This was shown clearly enough during Wodehouse's two stints as a scriptwriter in Hollywood. In television the writer is often supreme – talent has always been a scarce commodity – but his individuality takes a different direction from that of an author writing to be read. His script has to be designed to give the show instant appeal to millions of viewers, inevitably tending towards a lowish common denominator while there is little time for subtlety. The present generation of top television writers were nourished by print, but their younger peers grew up nurtured by television, resulting perhaps in better television but an ever-widening gap between scripts and literature written to be read.

The scripts of *Soap* and *Cheers* in the US and of *Yes Minister* and *Porridge* in the UK produced some of the best television humour ever, with dialogue Wodehouse would have been proud to write. Yet the nearest we have to latter-day Wodehouse is the scripts of such shows adapted to a book format. The talent is there but the result is not the same as a book written to be a book, but any books, whatever their provenance, must be welcomed.

Apart from that McLuhanite analysis there is more old-fashioned support for my view. Murphy reports the opinion of the headmaster of a major public-school.

> His view was unequivocal – that Wodehouse was the end of a line. Never again would any writer have the solid grounding in the classics that Wodehouse had, unmarred by radio and television. He felt that the combination of the classics background, the printed word as the only medium of communication and Wodehouse's own temperament and omnivorous reading produced an almost Shakespearean range of language that we shall never see again.[38] [Why 'almost'?]

Thus there seems no chance that television scriptwriters will be in any position to compete with the great humorous writers of the past and little chance that any prospective writer of humorous prose will find much of a market for his or her work elsewhere. Now there are hardly any such markets for the tyro humorist. *The New Yorker* still exists while newspapers take occasional humorous articles, but that is all. Some newspaper columnists are writing great humour but theirs is a different craft to that of the humorous novelist and short story writer.

Most commentators say firmly that Wodehouse had no message. David Jasen argues that he did, that it imbues all he wrote from his first article to his last book, and that message is a call for tolerance and kindliness. The argument is one of semantics but it is impossible to imagine anyone reading a Wodehouse novel and then doing something malevolent.

If Wodehouse had been born a generation earlier he would have lived in a more formal and restricting age while his prose would not have been enriched by words from around the globe, nor would there have been so large a market for the embryonic writer. Had he been born a generation later he would have been too young to experience properly that magical Edwardian era from which the Wodehouse world evolved – which would also have been the case had he been brought up anywhere else in the world.

As Wodehouse approached ever closer to the inevitability of death it did not bother him. In 1965 he told *Sunday Express* reporter Clive Hirschborn who asked him if he feared death, 'Heavens no. I am far too well balanced. The only thing I ever fear is that the last chapters of any book I write won't work out.' He added, 'I'm a Spiritualist, like my friend Conan Doyle.'[34] After Wodehouse's death sixty-two books on spiritualism and related subjects were found on his shelves. Between 1923 and 1925 he attended at least three seances, two of them with Leonora, at the home of H. Dennis Bradley. At one of these the 'voice' of one Ernest Wodehouse, a cousin, claimed to have been with Plum at Harrogate the year before.

When Wodehouse said he had been at Harrogate but not with any Wodehouse relation the voice explained he had been there with Plum *in spirit*.[35] Not a convincing proof of spiritualism. Even so in 1925 Plum told Townend that he thought spiritualism was the goods.[36] Clearly the subject fascinated him but how much he believed in it we cannot tell. No one has been able to prove or disprove the tenets of spiritualism and so intelligent a man as Wodehouse is likely to have suspended judgement. He told Wilfrid De'Ath, in the same vein, 'I'm an agnostic.' (Compulsory church-going for the young can be counter-productive.) 'My attitude has always been, we'll have to wait and see.'[37] There is only one important ghost in his works, that of Leila J. Pickney, writer of sentimental slosh, who haunts 'Honeysuckle Cottage' (which Wodehouse chose for an anthology, *My Funniest Story*) turning her cousin, James Rodman, from an author of wholesome murder mysteries into one who writes her kind of saccharin romance. The one significant spiritualist is the wealthy widow, Mrs Spottsworth, in *Ring For Jeeves*. Alas we shall never know if the ghosts of Rowcester Abbey travelled with her when she rebuilt that ancient pile, *a la Hearst*, in the California sunshine.

As The Master waited to learn what was on the other side his fans were pressing for his contribution to English literature and human happiness to be recognized by the award of a suitable honour before it was too late. In 1971 Prime Minister Edward Heath had curtly turned down the sugges-tion of a ninetieth birthday honour. This earned him the emnity of Auberon Waugh who thus anticipated the national consensus by several years. Many of Wodehouse's fans, such as Mr H.S. Edwards of Padd-ington, had earlier gone through the proper procedure of making the suggestion to the Prime Minister's Patronage Secretary at 10 Downing Street, but to no avail. In the end Wodehouse was given his knighthood through the endeavours of a most unlikely fan; a man with only an elementary education, an electrician, a red-in-tooth-and-claw socialist, a trade union leader, a knight, then a peer – Walter Citrine.

For two decades until 1946 Citrine had been the undisputed and dominant General Secretary of the Trades Union Congress and one of the most powerful men in Britain. He and Wodehouse started corres-ponding some time before 1960 due to Citrine's compensatory enthu-siasm for English public-school stories. They became good pen-friends. His lordship gave Plum *The Head Of Kay's* and *The Gold Bat* to fill gaps in his collection and also a great deal of technical advice on the geography and procedure of the House of Lords for *Service With A Smile*. Plum was planning a meeting of the earls of Ickenham and Emsworth in London and adopted Citrine's idea of them doing so at the Brothers Moss when handing back their hired Parliamentary robes. (Sir Iain Moncrieffe pointed out in a letter to *The Times* that Lord Emsworth, as usual, ordered the wrong kit as he hired a coronet and ermine trimmed robes, worn at a coronation. For an ordinary Opening of Parliament an earl would have worn robes trimmed only with miniver.)

It was in 1967 that Citrine had a letter from H.S. Edwards asking for help in persuading the Prime Minister to honour Wodehouse. So Citrine, wondering why he hadn't thought of the idea himself, wrote to Harold Wilson urging him to recommend that the Queen grant Wodehouse an honour and then went to see him at 10 Downing Street on 13 April that year. He received a sympathetic hearing and so continued to press Wilson, suggesting that making Wodehouse a Companion of Honour would be most appropriate. Seven years later his determination to win recognition for his friend paid off.[38]

In November 1974 when Wodehouse was ninety-three there came a discreet, non-committal, telephone call from the British Consul General in Washington. The Queen had it in mind to confer upon him the honour of knighthood: if she decided so to do would Mr Wodehouse be minded to accept? He was so minded and it is pleasing that he had a couple of months in which to savour the pending recognition by England of the wrong it had done him and of his greatness as a writer.

In that same 1975 New Year's Honours list Charlie Chaplin was also made a knight, aged eighty-five (and Florence Nightingale was eighty-seven before she got her only honour, the Order of Merit). By this one action Harold Wilson gave lustre to what was otherwise a lustreless premiership. 'When technological white heat and Lady Falkender's pastel paper are at one with Nineveh and Tyre, it may well be that Sir Harold Wilson will be remembered for one good and gracious act. A knighthood conferred on P.G. – Sir Pelham – Wodehouse.'[39] So Plum became Sir Pelham, a Knight of The British Empire or KBE, and Ethel became Lady Wodehouse. He was far too old to travel to London to be dubbed by the Queen; Her Majesty Queen Elizabeth The Queen Mother, then aged seventy-four herself, wanted to go to America for the ceremony but, alas, could not do so. It would have been fitting for, as she later telegraphed at the time of Plum's centenary celebrations in New York:

> Throughout my life I have been a devoted admirer of his work; in fact I think I have read and enjoyed almost all the ninety-eight books that he wrote and found delight in so many of the fifty plays and musical comedies with which he was involved.[40]

A month after his knighthood Sir Pelham was taken to the Southampton Hospital, Long Island, suffering simply from old age. With him he took the latest, half completed, Blandings novel on which he was working and which was later sympathetically edited by Richard Usborne and published as *Sunset At Blandings*. Forty-four days after his knighthood Sir Pelham died quietly on St Valentine's Day 1975 aged ninety-three, having spent his life giving pleasure to millions of readers and theatre lovers all around the world.

Sir Pelham Grenville Wodehouse, KBE, D.Litt. (Oxon), the greatest humorous English writer of all time, was cremated on 18 February 1975 after a service at the Remsenburg Presbyterian church conducted by the Revd Gordon G. Dickson.

> Throughout the ceremony Lady Wodehouse did not weep although her face appeared contorted with grief. Occasionally her grandchildren would gently touch her arm as if to reassure her.
>
> Sir Pelham's body, in a deep brown cherrywood coffin, was taken to a crematorium. Tonight the ashes were brought to the Remsenburg cemetery. It was only then that Lady Wodehouse wept openly.[41]

The world wept too. Other authors have written as well, or as much, or been as funny but none have written so much humour, of such sustained and unsurpassed quality, over so long a period. For this reason, if for no other, P.G. Wodehouse is without peer and we shall never, alas, read his like again. A rare genius, a narrow moment in history and the luck of geography combined to make him uniquely P.G. Wodehouse.

— 18 —

ENVOI

When he died, I asked a Carmelite friend of mine* to remember him at Mass. He looked at me from two deep, dark, blue Kerry eyes.

'Well I will, since you ask me. But in the case of someone who brought such joy to so many people in the course of his life, do you think it's necessary?'

Owen Dudley Edwards.[1]

---

* Father Noel Dermot O'Donoghue, author of *Patrick Of Ireland* and other books.

—Appendix 1—

REFERENCES

Books by P.G. Wodehouse. For details see Appendices 7 and 8.
Books about P.G. Wodehouse, his life and work. For details see Appendix 9.

WODEHOUSE AND ME: INTRODUCTION

1. Geoffrey Jaggard, *Wooster's World*.
2. *The Economist* Research Department, London.

1 THE MYTH

1. David A. Jasen, *P.G. Wodehouse: A Portrait of A Master*.
2. P.G. Wodehouse and Guy Bolton, *Bring On The Girls*.
3. P.G. Wodehouse. From the author's introduction to the new UK 1972 edition of *The Little Nugget*.
4. P.G. Wodehouse, *Over Seventy*.
5. P.G. Wodehouse to Peter Schwed 25 Jan. 1961. 'The Burbling Pixie' description of Wodehouse has also been attributed to *The New Yorker*.
6. Derek Grimsdick to P.G. Wodehouse 6 July 1962.
7. David A. Jasen, *A Bibliography And Readers' Guide To The First Editions of P.G. Wodehouse*.
8. P.G. Wodehouse to Denis Mackail 7 Feb. 1952.
9. P.G. Wodehouse to Guy Bolton 4 Nov. 1952.
10. P.G. Wodehouse to Richard Usborne 30 Dec. 1955.
11. P.G. Wodehouse to William Townend 4 Aug. 1936 and 6 Oct. 1951.
12. Jasen, *P.G. Wodehouse*.
13. N.T.P. Murphy, *In Search Of Blandings*; Frances Donaldson, *P.G. Wodehouse*; *ibid*; Ernest Newman quoted in the *Observer* (26 Sep. 1982); Anthony Burgess, the *Observer* (26 Sep. 1982); *Daily Telegraph* (17 Feb. 1975); *Northern Echo*, Darlington (16 Oct. 1981); *Sunday Express* (16 Feb. 1975); *Glasgow Herald* (17 Feb. 1975); *Winston-Salem Journal* (27 Oct. 1981); Charles Trainor, Professor of English at Illinois College, from an article in the author's collection; Wilfred De'Ath, *London Illustrated News* (Feb. 1973); David Scrivens, *Toronto Globe & Mail* (22 Jan. 1983).

2 THE MAN

1. Frank Crowninshield, 'Crowninshield in the Cubs' den', *Vogue* (US, 15 Sep. 1944).
2. In conversation with the author.
3. Charles E. Gould Jr., 'The toad at Harrow: P.G. Wodehouse in perspective', *Kent*, (Fall edition 1981). Gould has slightly condensed Wodehouse's text.

3 GENEALOGY, GENES AND GENIUS (SEE ALSO APPENDIX 3)

General sources in this chapter include Burke and Debrett's peerages, Blomefield (see note 5 below), the *Dictionary of National Biography* UK, *Who Was Who* UK, the British *Army Lists*, *Crockford's Clerical Directory* UK and N.T.P. Murphy, *In Search of Blandings*.

1. 'Noblesse Oblige', *Our Old Nobility* (London, The Political Tract Society, 1879).
2. P.G. Wodehouse, *Right Ho, Jeeves*.
3. Sir Harris Nicholas, *History Of The Battle Of Agincourt* (London, Johnson & Co. 1832).
4. P.G. Wodehouse, *The Code Of The Woosters*.
5. Revd Francis Blomefield, *An Essay Towards A Topographical History Of Norfolk* ('Blomefield's Norfolk') (printed at Fersfield, 1734).
6. Quoted by Blomefield, see note 5 above, from a family pedigree then (1734) in the possession of Sir John Wodehouse Bart, MP.
7. P.G. Wodehouse, *Thank You Jeeves*.
8. *The Victoria History Of The Counties Of England*, Norfolk, vol. II (London, Archibald Cox & Co, 1906).
9. Charles Dalton, *Waterloo Roll Call* (London, Eyre & Spottiswoode, 1904).
10. P.G. Wodehouse, 'Uncle Fred Flits By', in *Young Men In Spats*.
11. See note 1 above.
12. Lord Kilbracken, *Reminiscences* (London, Macmillan, 1931).
13. Walter Rye, *Norfolk Families* privately published for subscribers and printed by Agas H. Goose & Son, Rampant Horse Street, Norwich, 1913 and *Norfolk Antiquarian Miscellany*, 2nd series, vol. 1 (Norwich, 1877).
14. Sir Iain Moncreiffe of that Ilk, Bt., article in *Books And Bookmen* (UK, April 1975).
15. G.E. Cockayne, *The Complete Peerage by G.E.C.*, eds. H.A. Doubleday and Lord Howard de Walden, vol. VII (London, St Catherine Press, 1929).
16. See note 1 above.
17. P.G. Wodehouse, *Stiff Upper Lip, Jeeves*.
18. John, First Earl of Kimberley, *A Journal Of Events During The Gladstone Ministry 1868–1874*, Camden misc., vol. XXI, (London, Royal Historical Society, 1958).

19. P.G. Wodehouse, *Service With A Smile*.
20. P.G. Wodehouse, *Laughing Gas*.
21. Mary Deane, *The Book Of Dene, Deane, Adeane* (London, Elliot Stock, 1899).
22. Murphy, *In Search Of Blandings*.
23. Jasen, *P.G. Wodehouse*.
24. Mrs E.P. Hart (ed.), *Merchant Taylors' School Register 1561–1934* (London, Merchant Taylors' School, 1936).
25. F.M.W. Draper, *Four Centuries Of The Merchant Taylors' School* (Oxford, OUP, 1962).
26. *The Taylorian*, (September 1888). Magazine of the Merchant Taylors' School.
27. St Helen's Bishopsgate. Vestry Minutes at the Guildhall Library, London.
28. Revd John Bathurst Deane, *The Worship Of The Serpent* (London, J. Hatchard & Son, 1830).
29. P.G. Wodehouse, 'Sleepy Time' in *Plum Pie*.
30. Revd John Bathurst Deane, *A Life Of Richard Deane, Major General and General At Sea In The Service Of The Commonwealth* (London, Longmans Green, 1870).
31. Deane, *The Book of Deane*.
32. P.G. Wodehouse to Leonora Wodehouse 28 Nov. 1920.
33. Frances Donaldson, *P.G. Wodehouse*.
34. P.G. Wodehouse, *Jeeves And The Feudal Spirit*.
35. P.G. Wodehouse, *Over Seventy*.
36. Lt. Col. E.W.C. Sandes, *The Royal Engineers in Egypt and The Sudan* (Chatham, Institute Of Royal Engineers, 1937).

4 A SURGING SEA OF AUNTS

1. Song title.
2. P.G. Wodehouse, *The Mating Season*.
3. Saki (H.H. Munro), 'Sredni Vashtar' in *The Chronicles Of Clovis* (London, John Lane The Bodley Head, 1911).
4. Rosemary Sutcliffe, *Rudyard Kipling* (London, The Bodley Head, 1960).
5. P.G. Wodehouse to William Townend 16 Apr. 1935.
6. Richard Usborne, *Dr Sir Pelham Wodehouse, Old Boy*.
7. *The Captain* (London, April 1907).
8. P.G. Wodehouse, *Over Seventy*.
9. Quoted by Jasen in *P.G. Wodehouse*.
10. Bernard Levin, 'As Jeeves would have said: perfect music, Sir' in *The Times*, (London, 18 Feb. 1975).
11. P.G. Wodehouse, *Heavy Weather*.
12. P.G. Wodehouse, 'The Aunt And The Sluggard' in *My Man Jeeves*.
13. Mary Bathurst Deane, *A Book Of Verse* (London, Elkin Matthews, 1921).

14. Mary Bathurst Deane, *Seen In An Old Mirror* (London, Charing Cross Publishing, 1878).
15. Geoffrey Jaggard *Wooster's World*.
16. A.P. Ryan, 'Wooster's progress' in *The New Statesman And Nation* (London, 13 Jun. 1953).
17. Ian Hay Beith to P.G. Wodehouse c. 1939 quoted by Jasen in *P.G. Wodehouse*.

5 ALMA MATER – WODEHOUSE AT DULWICH

1. Wilfrid Sheed, *The Good Word – And Other Words* (London, Sidgwick and Jackson, 1978).
2. Augustus Muir, *The Popularity Of P.G. Wodehouse* in *The Strand* (London, Feb. 1927).
3. J.R. Piggott, *Dulwich College* (London, Valley Fields, Dulwich College, 1990).
4. From the Report No. 5 of the Executive and Finance Committee of the Governors of the College, 8 June 1900.
5. James Morris (now Jan Morris), *Pax Britannica: The Climax Of An Empire* (London, Faber & Faber, 1968).
6. P.G. Wodehouse, *Over Seventy*.
7. P.G. Wodehouse to William Townend 2 Dec. 1935.
8. From information given to the author by Margaret Slythe, Head Of Library, Dulwich College, 1981–1991.
9. P.G. Wodehouse, *The Pothunters*.
10. P.G. Wodehouse, 'Junior Cup Matches' in *The Alleynian* (Oct. 1894).
11. Peter Southern (formerly a master at Dulwich College), 'Dulwich Schooldays' in *P.G. Wodehouse: A Centenary Celebration*, and Murphy.
12. P.G. Wodehouse, 'Episode Of The Dog McIntosh' in *Very Good Jeeves*.
13. P.G. Wodehouse to William Townend 6 Mar. 1932.
14. P.G. Wodehouse to William Townend 11 June 1934.
15. Sir Compton Mackenzie, 'As A Contemporary' in *Homage To P.G. Wodehouse*.
16. P.G. Wodehouse to William Townend Mar. 1932.
17. Isabel Quigly, *The Heirs Of Tom Brown* (London Chatto and Windus, 1983).
18. *The Alleynian* (May 1900).
19. *The Alleynian* (Sep. 1899, Mar. 1900 and July 1900).
20. 'Mr Treadgold's House' bound record book.
21. *The Alleynian* (Sep. 1899).
22. *The Alleynian*, vol. XXVIII, (Feb./Dec. 1900).
23. Roger Lancelyn Green, *A.E.W. Mason: The Adventures Of A Storyteller* (London, Parrish, 1952).
24. C.S. Forester, *Life Before Forty.* (London, Michael Joseph, 1967). (Published posthumously.) Reprinted with the permission of Peters Fraser & Dunlop Group Ltd.

25. Frank McShane, *The Life Of Raymond Chandler* (London, Jonathan Cape, 1976).

26. Dennis Wheatley, *The Time Has Come The Young Man Said 1897–1914: The Memoirs Of Dennis Wheatley* (London, Hutchinson, 1977).

27. *Daily Mail*, (London, 12 July 1939), said to have been provided by Ethel Wodehouse.

28. Richard Usborne, *Wodehouse At Work To The End*.

29. Copy in the author's collection.

30. P.G. Wodehouse, *Over Seventy*.

31. See note 8 above.

32. J.A. Smith, *John Buchan And His World* (London, Thames and Hudson, 1979).

33. See note 8 above.

34. Cosmo Hamilton, *People Worth Talking About* (London, Hutchinson, 1934).

35. P.G. Wodehouse, *Something Fishy*.

6 Money in the Bank

1. W.S. Gilbert, *Iolanthe*.

2. Professor H.H. King, *The History Of The Hong Kong & Shanghai Banking Corporation*. vol. 1 *The Hong Kong Bank In Late Imperial China 1864–1902: On An Even Keel* (Cambridge, Cambridge University Press, 1987).

3. P.G. Wodehouse, *Performing Flea*, *Over Seventy* and Jasen *P.G. Wodehouse*.

4. Murphy, *In Search Of Blandings*.

5. Copy in the author's collection.

6. Zoe Farmer, interview with Wodehouse in the *Daily Express*, (London 15 Oct. 1936).

7. P.G. Wodehouse and Guy Bolton, *Bring On The Girls*.

8. Ibid.

9. P.G. Wodehouse, author's introduction to the new UK edition of *The Man With Two Left Feet* (1971).

10. John Adlard, *Owen Seaman: His Life And Times*. (London, The Eighteen-nineties Society, 1977).

11. Denis Mackail, *The Story of J.M.B.* (London, Peter Davies, 1941).

12. P.G. Wodehouse, 'Grit: A Talk With Sir Arthur Conan Doyle' *V.C. A Journal Of The Brighter Side Of Life*, (London, 2 July 1903).

13. P.G. Wodehouse, introduction to Sir Arthur Conan Doyle, *The Sign Of Four* (New York, Ballantine Books 1975).

14. P.G. Wodehouse, 'From A Detective's Notebook' in *The World Of Mr Mulliner*.

15. 'Dudley Jones – Borehunter', *Punch* (London, 29 Apr. 1903 and 6 May 1903).

16. 'Back To His Native Strand', *Punch* (London, 27 Mar. 1903).

17. 'The Prodigal', *Punch* (London, 23 Sep. 1903).

18. Notably W.S. Bristowe's 'The Influence Of Holmes On Wodehouse' *The Sherlock Holmes Journal* (Summer 1976); Linda Jeffery 'The Rummy Affair Of

P.G. Wodehouse And Sherlock Holmes' *The Baker Street Journal* (December 1974), and Andrew Malec 'Early Wodehouse Doyleana And Sherlockiana' *Baker Street Miscellanea*, no. 27 (London, Autumn 1981)

19. J. Randolph Cox, 'Elementary My Dear Wooster' *Baker Street Journal*, 17, no. 2, (June 1967).

20. P.G. Wodehouse, *Right Ho, Jeeves.*

21. Hesketh Pearson, *Conan Doyle: His Life And Art* (London, Methuen, 1943).

22. Alec Waugh, 'Lunching With Plum' in *P.G. Wodehouse: A Centenary Celebration.*

23. C.B. Fry, *Life Worth Living* (London, Eyre & Spottiswoode, 1939).

24. Sir William Beach Thomas, *A Traveller In Time* (London, Chapman and Hall, 1925).

25. P.G. Wodehouse's cashbook which he later gave to Derek Grimsdick.

26. P.G. Wodehouse's cashbook, author's research and James H. Heineman, *P.G. Wodehouse: A Comprehensive Bibliography and Checklist.*

27. Denis Mackail, *Life With Topsy* (London, William Heineman, 1941).

28. Jasen, *P.G. Wodehouse.*

29. Stephen King-Hall (later Lord King-Hall), *My Naval Life.* (London, Faber and Faber, 1952).

30. P.G. Wodehouse, *Thank You, Jeeves.*

31. Beach Thomas, *A Traveller in Time.*

32. P.G. Wodehouse to James B. Pinker 17 Jan. 1906 and Jan. 1907.

33. Herbert W. Westbrook, *The Cause Of Catesby* (London, Catesby & Sons, 1905).

34. P.G. Wodehouse to William Townend 28 Mar. 1935.

35. William Townend writing in *Performing Flea.*

36. Notably in P.G. Wodehouse's introduction to William Townend's *The Ship In The Swamp* (London, Herbert Jenkins, 1928).

37. Hon. Theodora Benson, *The First Time I . . .* (London, Chapman & Hall, 1935).

38. P.G. Wodehouse to William Townend 3 Mar. 1905.

39. Herbert W. Westbrook, *The Booby Prize* (London, Simpkin Marshall, 1924).

40. P.G. Wodehouse to William Townend 19 Aug. 1954.

41. P.G. Wodehouse's cash book.

42. See note 5 above.

7 TALES OF ST AUSTIN'S AND ELSEWHERE

1. Arthur Calder-Marshall reviewing *The Heirs Of Tom Brown* by Isabel Quigly (London, Chatto and Windus, 1982) *Evening Standard* (London, 21 July 1982).

2. Brian Doyle, *The Who's Who Of Children's Literature* (London, Hugh Evelyn, 1968).

3. Jacynth Hope-Simpson, *Tales In School* (London, Hamish Hamilton, 1971).

4. C.S. Forester, *Life Before Forty* (London, Michael Joseph, 1967). (Published

posthumously.) Reprinted with the permission of Peters Fraser & Dunlop Group Ltd.

5. *Ibid.*
6. *Ibid.*
7. *Ibid.*
8. P.G. Wodehouse, *Mike.*
9. *Ibid.*
10. Frances Donaldson, *P.G. Wodehouse: The Authorised Biography.*
11. W.O.G. Lofts and D.J. Adley, *The Men Behind Boys' Fiction.* (London, Howard Baker, 1970).
12. Benny Green, *P.G. Wodehouse: A Literary Biography.*
13. John W. Houghton, lyrics for *Queen Of Hearts* by C. Burnette and H.C.W. Newte (London, 1902).
14. Barry Phelps, 'To the critics these pearls: P.G. Wodehouse dedications' *Antiquarian Book Monthly Review* (Oxford, April 1983).
15. Evelyn Waugh 'An act of homage and reparation to P.G. Wodehouse' *Sunday Times Magazine* (London, 16 July 1961).
16. A.J.A. Morris, *The Scaremongers* (London, Routledge & Kegan Paul, 1984).
17. Samuel Hynes, *The Edwardian Turn Of Mind* (New Jersey, Princeton University Press, 1968).
18. Morris, *The Scaremongers.*
19. Tim Jeal, *Baden-Powell* (London, Hutchinson, 1989).
20. Auberon Waugh, introduction to *The Parrot And Other Poems* by P.G. Wodehouse (London, Hutchinson, 1988).
21. P.G. Wodehouse, *Over Seventy.*
22. P.G. Wodehouse, *Mike.*
23. P.G. Wodehouse to L.H. Bradshaw 16 Nov. 1909.

8 America I Like You

1. P.G. Wodehouse, *Over Seventy.*
2. Rudyard Kipling, 'Mandalay'.
3. Jasen, *P.G. Wodehouse.*
4. *New York Times* (29 May 1909).
5. P.G. Wodehouse, 'The First Time I Went To New York' in *The First Time I . . .*, ed. Hon. Theodora Benson (London, Chapman & Hall, 1935).
6. P.G. Wodehouse, author's introduction to the new UK edition of *The Man Upstairs* (1971).
7. Leonora Wodehouse, 'P.G. Wodehouse At Home' in *The Strand*, (London, January 1929).
8. Leslie H. Bradshaw, 'Impressions Of P.G. Wodehouse' in *The Captain* (London, Mar. 1910).
9. P.G. Wodehouse to L.H. Bradshaw, undated c. 1910.
10. P.G. Wodehouse's cashbook, *P.G. Wodehouse: A Comprehensive Bibliography And Checklist*, and author's research.

11. John Ebbel, *George Horace Lorrimer And The Saturday Evening Post* (New York, Doubleday, 1948). See also the list of Wodehouse contributions to US periodicals in *P.G. Wodehouse: A Comprehensive Bibliography And Checklist.*
12. P.G. Wodehouse to William Townend 28 Feb. 1920.
13. P.G. Wodehouse to L.H. Bradshaw 20 Jan. 1915.
14. Ira Gershwin, *Lyrics On Several Occasions* (New York, Viking Press, 1973).
15. Robert Strunsky reviewing *Young Men In Spats*, *The Saturday Review* (USA, 25 July 1936).
16. J.B. Priestley reviewing *Mr Mulliner Speaking*, *Evening Standard* (London, 31 May 1929).
17. *Playboy Illustrated History Of Organised Crime* (Chicago, Playboy Press, 1975).
18. Max Eastman, *Enjoyment Of Laughter* (London, Hamish Hamilton, 1937).
19. *The New York Times Review* (c. mid-May 1952), quoted by Jasen.
20. P.G. Wodehouse, *Author! Author!.*
21. P.G. Wodehouse to William Townend 20 Feb. 1920.
22. Joyce Kilmer, interview with P.G. Wodehouse in the magazine section of the *New York Times* (7 Nov. 1915).
23. P.G. Wodehouse, *Ring For Jeeves.*
24. Gerard Fairlie, *With Prejudice* (London, Hodder & Stoughton, 1922).
25. P.G. Wodehouse, introduction to *The Bindle Omnibus* by Herbert Jenkins. (London, Herbert Jenkins Ltd, 1932).
26. Paul R. Reynolds Jr., *The Middle Man: Adventures Of A Literary Agent* (New York, William Morrow, 1971).

9 THE MATING SEASON

1. Malcolm Muggeridge, *Chronicles Of Wasted Time* (London, Collins, 1973).
2. Maureen O'Sullivan, 'The Wodehouses In Hollywood', in *P.G. Wodehouse: A Centenary Celebration.*
3. Iain Sproat, *Wodehouse At War.*
4. Records of the Registrar General for England And Wales (births, marriages and deaths) St Catherine's House, London and the Probate Registry, Somerset House, London.
5. Frances Donaldson, *P.G. Wodehouse*
6. See note 4 above.
7. *The London Gazette* John Wayman: Bankruptcy Petition 3 July 1912, Receiving Order No. 797 of 25 July 1912, Adjudication Order 22 Aug. 1912, Release of Trustees 22 May 1913.
8. P.G. Wodehouse lyrics, 'The Church Round The Corner', copyright T.B. Harms and Co, New York.
9. Muggeridge, *Chronicles of Wasted Time.*
10. P.G. Wodehouse to L.H. Bradshaw 10 Oct. 1914.
11. P.G. Wodehouse, introduction to *Son Of Bitch* by Elliott Erwin (London, Thames and Hudson, 1974).
12. P.G. Wodehouse to L.H. Bradshaw 24 Oct. 1914.

13. P.G. Wodehouse to Paul R. Reynolds Jr. 28 Dec. 1930.

14. P.G. Wodehouse to Leonora Wodehouse 24 Nov. 1920.

15. P.G. Wodehouse to William Townend 1 Dec. 1932.

16. P.G. Wodehouse to Paul R. Reynolds Jr. 28 Dec. 1930.

17. P.G. Wodehouse to Guy Bolton 14 Aug 1963 and 26 Jan. 1964.

18. Graham Lord, *Sunday Express* (London, 3 Jan. 1971).

19. P.G. Wodehouse, 'Being 80 And What I Make Of It' in the *Sunday Telegraph* (London, 15 Dec. 1961).

20. P.G. Wodehouse to Leonora Wodehouse 20 Sep. 1922.

21. P.G. Wodehouse to R.T.B. Denby, telegram of 22 Jan. 1927.

22. Charles E. Gould Jr. 'On Collecting P.G. Wodehouse' in *P.G. Wodehouse: A Centenary Celebration.*

23. O'Sullivan, in *A Centenary Celebration.*

24. Donaldson, *P.G. Wodehouse.*

25. Sir Compton Mackenzie, 'As A Contemporary' in *Homage To P.G. Wodehouse.*

26. Godfrey Winn, *The Infirm Glory* (London, Michael Joseph, 1967).

27. P.G. Wodehouse, *Yours Plum.*

28. P.G. Wodehouse to William Townend 27 June 1922.

29. P.G. Wodehouse to Leonora Wodehouse 10 Feb. 1929.

30. J.F. Whitt, *The Strand Magazine 1891–1950: A Selective Checklist.* Published by the author, London, 1979.

31. P.G. Wodehouse to Denis Mackail 12 Apr. 1931.

32. P.G. Wodehouse to Leonora Wodehouse 10 Feb. 1929 and similarly 23 Nov. 1923.

33. In correspondence with the author, 1983.

34. P.G. Wodehouse to L.H. Bradshaw 10 Oct. 1914.

35. P.G. Wodehouse to L.H. Bradshaw 19 Oct. 1914.

36. P.G. Wodehouse to William Townend 28 Feb. 1920.

37. Cleveland Amory, ed., *Vanity Fair: A Cavalcade Of The 'Twenties And 'Thirties* (New York, Viking, 1960).

38. Babette Rosmond, *Robert Benchley: His Life And Good Times.* (New York, Doubleday, 1970).

39. Robert B. Shuman, *Robert Emmet Sherwood* (Boston, Twayne, 1964).

40. Not General Karl von Clausewitz! Correct attribution found for the author by Lt. Col. Norman Murphy in the Ministry of Defence Library, London.

41. Back numbers of *Vanity Fair c.*1914/1920 in the New York City Library, 43rd Street Annexe.

42. *Vanity Fair* (Aug. 1915).

43. P.G. Wodehouse to William Townend 16 Dec. 1949.

44. Frank Crowninshield, 'Crowninshield In the Cubs' Den' *Vogue* (15 Sep. 1944).

45. P.G. Wodehouse, *Vanity Fair* (May 1914).

46. Heywood Broun and Margaret Leech, *Anthony Comstock: Roundsman Of The Lord.* (London, Wishart, 1928). Also Alec Craig, *The Banned Books Of England And Other Countries* (London, George Allen and Unwin, 1962).

47. P.G. Wodehouse, *Vanity Fair* (Mar. 1915).

48. Crowninshield, 'Crowninshield in the Cubs' Den'.
49. P.G. Wodehouse. 'Jeeves Takes Charge' in *Carry On, Jeeves*.
50. Richard Usborne, *Manchester Guardian* (11 Aug. 1971).
51. Marion Meade, *Dorothy Parker: What Fresh Hell Is This?* (London, Wm Heinemann, 1988).
52. See note 50 above.
53. Arthur F. Kinney, *Dorothy Parker: Her Life*. (Boston, Twayne, 1978).
54. Rosmond, *Robert Benchley*.
55. Amory, *Vanity Fair*.
56. Information from Messrs Wetherbys.

10 THE TRIO OF MUSICAL FAME

See also the bibliography for Appendices 4 and 5.

1. Gerald Boardman, ed., *The Concise Oxford Companion To The American Theatre* (New York and Oxford, OUP, 1984).
2. Quoted in P.G. Wodehouse, *The Parrot And Other Poems*.
3. Gerald Boardman, *Jerome Kern: His Life And Music* (New York and Oxford, OUP, 1980).
4. Kurt Ganzl, *The British Musical Theatre 1865–1914*, vol. I, (London, Macmillan, 1986).
5. Ellaline Terriss (later Lady Hicks), *By Herself* (London, Cassell, 1928).
6. Ellaline Terriss, *A Little Bit of String* (London, Hutchinson, 1955).
7. P.G. Wodehouse to William Townend 28 Feb. 1920.
8. P.G. Wodehouse to William Townend 27 June 1922.
9. Review of *Nuts And Wine* in *The Times* (London, 5 Jan. 1914).
10. P.G. Wodehouse and Guy Bolton, *Bring On The Girls*.
11. *Ibid*.
12. Michael Freeland, *Jerome Kern: A Biography* (London, Robson Books, 1978).
13. P.G. Wodehouse, *Vanity Fair* (Mar. 1915).
14. Benny Green, *P.G. Wodehouse: A Literary Biography*.
15. P.G. Wodehouse, *Vanity Fair* (Sep. 1915).
16. Boardman, *Jerome Kern*.
17. Elizabeth Marbury, *My Crystal Ball* (London, Hurst and Blackett, 1924).
18. P.G. Wodehouse, *Vanity Fair* (Dec. 1915).
19. P.G. Wodehouse, *Vanity Fair* (Apr. 1916).
20. Sheridan Morley, *Spread A Little Happiness* (London, Thames and Hudson, 1987).
21. Gilbert Seldes.
22. Frances Donaldson, *P.G. Wodehouse*.
23. Hugh Fordin, *Jerome Kern: The Man And His Music*. (Santa Monica, T.B. Harms and Co., 1975).
24. P.G. Wodehouse, *Vanity Fair* (Apr. 1918).

25. Dorothy Parker, *Vanity Fair* (Apr. 1918).

26. P.G. Wodehouse introduction to Guy Bolton, *Gracious Living Limited* (London, Herbert Jenkins, 1966).

27. Guy Bolton, 'Working With Wodehouse' in *Homage To P.G. Wodehouse.*

28. Wodehouse introduction to Bolton, *Gracious Living.*

29. Wodehouse and Bolton, *Bring On The Girls.*

30. David Ewan, *The Story Of Jerome Kern* (New York, Henry Holt & Co, 1953).

31. Freeland, *Jerome Kern.*

32. *Ibid.*

33. See note 12 above.

34. Jerome Kern to John Rumsey 29 Sep. 1943: copy with Guy Bolton annotation.

35. Frederick Nolan, *The Sound Of Their Music: The Story Of Rodgers & Hammerstein* (London, J.M. Dent, 1971).

36. Alec Wilder, *American Popular Song* (New York, OUP, 1972).

37. Miles Kreuger, *Show Boat* (New York, OUP, 1977).

38. In correspondence with the author 30 Sep. 1991.

39. Green, *P.G. Wodehouse.*

40. Dorothy Parker, *Vanity Fair* (Apr. 1918).

41. Howard Dietz, *Dancing In The Dark* (New York, Quadrangle, 1953).

42. Alan Jay Lerner, *The Street Where I Live* (London, Hodder and Stoughton, 1978).

43. Ira Gershwin, BBC Radio interview, 1960 quoted by Benny Green in *P.G. Wodehouse: A Literary Biography.*

44. P.G. Wodehouse to Leonora Wodehouse 20 Sep. 1922.

45. P.G. Wodehouse to William Townend 24 Aug. 1923.

46. George Grossmith *"GG"* (London, Hutchinson, 1935).

47. P.G. Wodehouse to Leonora Wodehouse 2 Apr. 1921.

48. (Leslie) Ruth Howard, *A Quite Remarkable Father* (New York, Harcourt Brace, 1959).

49. P.G. Wodehouse to Paul R. Reynolds Jr. 24 Aug. 1928.

11 Spring Fever

1. Quoted by Frank Swinnerton in *The Georgian Literary Scene.* (London, Hutchinson, 1935.)

2. P.G. Wodehouse, 'Extricating Young Gussie', *Saturday Evening Post* (New York, 15 Sep. 1915).

3. Lady Cynthia Asquith, *Portrait Of Barrie* (London, James Barrie, 1954).

4. Denis Mackail, *The Story Of JMB* (London, Peter Davies, 1941).

5. Reginald Jeeves, 'Bertie Changes His Mind' in *Carry On Jeeves.*

6. P.G. Wodehouse, 'Jeeves And The Old School Chum' in *Very Good Jeeves.*

7. Quoted by Richard Usborne in *Wodehouse At Work To The End.*

8. Gerald Cumberland, *People Worth Talking About* (London, Grant Richards, 1922).

9. Story given to the author by Margaret Slythe, Head of Library, Dulwich College, 1981–1991.

10. E. Phillips Oppenheim, *The Pool Of Memory* (London, Hodder and Stoughton, 1941).

11. The *Daily Mail* (London, 15 Aug. 1938).

12. P.G. Wodehouse, 'The Purification Of Rodney Spelvin' in *The Heart Of A Goof.*

13. P.G. Wodehouse, introduction to *The Heart Of A Goof.*

14. George Grossmith, *"GG"* (London, Hutchinson, 1935).

15. Stanley Naylor and George Grossmith, *Gaity And George Grossmith* (London, Stanley Paul, 1913).

16. Grossmith, *"GG"*.

17. From the Archive of the Society Of Authors.

18. Letter to the author from Lord Kimberley 10 June 1991.

19. Grossmith, *"GG"*.

20. P.G. Wodehouse in *Performing Flea.*

21. Daphne Fielding, *The Duchess Of Jermyn Street* (London, Eyre & Spottiswoode, 1964). This story may be apocryphal.

22. Mary Bathurst Deane, *A Book Of Verse* (London, Elkin Matthews, 1921).

23. P.G. Wodehouse to William Townend 12 Nov. 1928.

24. Denis Mackail, *Life With Topsy.* (London, Wm Heineman, 1947) by permission of A.P. Watt Ltd. on behalf of Mary Ryde.

25. P.G. Wodehouse, introduction to Charles Graves' *Leather Armchairs.* (London, Cassell, 1963).

26. Details provided by the Garrick Club to the author.

27. Artemis Cooper, ed., *A Durable Fire: The Letters Of Duff And Diana Cooper 1913–1950* (New York, Franklin Wall, 1984).

28. Details provided by the Savage Club to the author.

29. Rupert Hart Davis, *Hugh Walpole* (London, Macmillan, 1952).

30. Sir Colin Coote, *The Other Club* (London, Sidgwick and Jackson, 1971).

31. P.G. Wodehouse to William Townend 18 Apr. 1953 in *Performing Flea.*

32. Gerald Gold speaking to the P.G. Wodehouse Convention, New York, 12 Oct. 1991. This story may be apocryphal.

33. Usborne, *Wodehouse at work.*

34. P.G. Wodehouse, *Heavy Weather.*

35. P.G. Wodehouse to Guy Bolton 17 June 1948.

36. From the records of the United Grand Lodge Of England, Freemasons' Hall, London.

37. Lord Gorell, *One Man . . . Many Parts* (London, Odhams Press, 1956).

38. Archive of the Society of Authors.

39. Mackail, *Life with Topsy.*

40. Alec Waugh, 'Lunching With Plum', in *P.G. Wodehouse: A Centenary Celebration.*

41. Robert Speaight, *Hilaire Belloc* (London, Hollis and Carter, 1957).

42. A.N. Wilson, *Hilaire Belloc* (London, Hamish Hamilton, 1984).

43. Beverley Nichols, *Are They The Same At Home?* (London, Jonathan Cape, 1927).

44. Augustus Muir, 'The Popularity Of P.G. Wodehouse' in *The Strand* (London, Feb. 1927).

45. Nichols, *Are They The Same At Home?*.

46. P.G. Wodehouse to William Townend 28 Feb. 1920.

47. P.G. Wodehouse to Denis Mackail 7 Aug. 1945.

48. P.G. Wodehouse to William Townend 10 Mar. 1934.

49. Frances Donaldson, *Freddy Lonsdale* (London, Wm Heineman, 1957).

50. *Ibid.*

51. Leonora Wodehouse, *P.G. Wodehouse At Home* in *The Strand*, (Jan. 1929).

52. P.G. Wodehouse, *Peforming Flea*.

53. Nichols, *Are They The Same At Home?*.

54. Murphy, *In Search Of Blandings*.

55. *Ibid.*

56. Oppenheim, *The Pool of Memory*.

57. P.G. Wodehouse to William Townend 30 June 1945.

58. Michael Davie, interview with Wodehouse in the *Observer* (London, 10 Oct. 1971).

59. J.B. Priestley, review of *Mr Mulliner Speaking*, *Evening News* (31 May 1929).

60. P.G. Wodehouse to Denis Mackail Oct. 1932.

12 DOTTYVILLE-ON-THE PACIFIC

See also Appendix 6.

1. P.G. Wodehouse, 'The Castaways' in *Blandings Castle And Elsewhere*.

2. P.G. Wodehouse to William Townend 29 Jun. 1931, 19 May 1931.

3. P.G. Wodehouse to William Townend 8 Jan. 1930.

4. Sheridan Morley, *Gertryde Lawrence* (New York, McGraw Hill, 1991).

5. P.G. Wodehouse, 'Slaves Of Hollywood', *Saturday Evening Post* (7 Dec. 1929) and the London *Daily Mail*, Dec. 1929.

6. P.G. Wodehouse to William Townend 2 Oct. 1929.

7. P.G. Wodehouse to William Townend 8 Jan. 1930.

8. *The Times* (London, 29 Nov. 1929), Naval Appointments.

9. Sam Marx, *Mayer and Thalberg – The Make Believe Saints* (New York, Random House, 1975).

10. (Leslie) Ruth Howard, *A Quite Remarkable Father* (London, Longmans Green, 1970).

11. P.G. Wodehouse to Paul R. Reynolds Jr. 11 Mar. 1931.

12. Roland Pertwee, *Master Of None* (London, Peter Davies, 1940).

13. P.G. Wodehouse to William Townend 5 Feb. 1931.

14. Samuel Marx, *A Gaudy Spree: The Literary Life in Hollywood in The 1930's When The West Was Fun* (New York, Franklin Wallace, 1987).

15. P.G. Wodehouse to Paul R. Reynolds Jr. 18 Sep. 1931.

16. David Rayvern Allen, *Sir Aubrey* (London, Elm Tree, 1982).

17. E.W. Swanton, *Gubby Allen: Man Of Cricket* (London, Hutchinson, 1985).

18. P.G. Wodehouse to William Townend 7 May 1937.

19. Gerard Fairlie, *With Prejudice* (London, Hodder and Stoughton, 1952).
20. Conrad Nagel, 'The Player' in *The Real Tinsel* (New York, Macmillan, 1970).
21. Marx, *Mayer and Thalberg.*
22. Quoted by Jasen in *P.G. Wodehouse.*
23. P.G. Wodehouse and William Townend in *Performing Flea.*
24. Pertwee, *Master of None.*
25. *New York Times* (30 July 1931).
26. Marx, *Mayer and Thalberg.*
27. *New York Times* (16 June 1931).
28. P.G. Wodehouse to Paul R. Reynolds Jr. 7 Dec. 1931.
29. P.G. Wodehouse, *Louder & Funnier.*
30. Oswald Hickson Collier and Co's libel report to Herbert Jenkins Ltd., 28 July 1952.
31. Ethel Wodehouse quoted in *The Republican* (Connecticut, Waterbury, 27 Dec. 1931).
32. P.G. Wodehouse to William Townend 11 June 1934.
33. P.G. Wodehouse to William Townend 8 Mar. 1937.
34. C.B. Fry, *Life Worth Living* (London, Eyre and Spottiswoode, 1939).
35. Quoted by Charles Francisco in *David Niven – Endearing Rascal* (London, Virgin, 1987).
36. Sheridan Morley, *The Other Side Of The Moon: The Life Of David Niven* (New York, Harper & Row, 1985).
37. Philip Dunne, *Take Two: A Life In The Movies And Politics* (New York, McGraw Hill, 1980).
38. Philip Dunne in correspondence with the author 23 Nov. 1991.
39. Nancy Lynn Scharz *The Hollywood Writers' Wars.* (New York, Knopf, 1982).
40. See note 38 above.
41. Ira Gershwin, *Lyrics On Several Occasions* (New York, Viking Press, 1973).
42. P.G. Wodehouse to William Townend 4 Sep. 1937.
43. Leslie Halliwell, *Halliwell's Film Guide*, 7th ed., (New York, Harper and Row, 1989).

13 BIG MONEY

1. Interview with Wodehouse *Newsweek* (New York, 6 Feb. 1961).
2. P.G. Wodehouse to William Townend 23 July 1923.
3. P.G. Wodehouse, *Over Seventy.*
4. P.G. Wodehouse, 'Came The Dawn' in *Meet Mr Mulliner.*
5. P.G. Wodehouse to William Townend 7 Nov. 1936.
6. The Wodehouse-Reynolds correspondence in the Butler Library, Columbia University, New York, Bierce paraphrase 7 Dec. 1931.
7. Paul R. Reynolds Jr., *The Middle Man: The Adventures Of A Literary Agent.* (New York, William Morrow, 1972).
8. *Ibid.*

9. Leonora Wodehouse, 'P.G. Wodehouse At Home' in *The Strand* (London, Jan. 1929).

10. Richard Usborne, *After Hours With P.G. Wodehouse* (London, Hutchinson, 1991).

11. P.G. Wodehouse to Leonora Wodehouse 27 Sep. 1920.

12. P.G. Wodehouse to William Townend 11 May 1947 and 22 Apr. 1951.

13. Graham Lord, *Sunday Express* (London, 3 Jan. 1971).

14. P.G. Wodehouse, 'Tried In The Furnace', in *Young Men In Spats*.

15. Ethel Wodehouse to Paul R. Reynolds Jr. 13 Nov. 1929.

16. Ethel Wodehouse to Paul R. Reynolds Jr. 15 Jan. 1931.

17. P.G. Wodehouse to William Townend 5 June 1933.

18. P.G. Wodehouse to William Townend 18 Oct. 1928 and 23 Jan. 1935. Two of many examples.

19. P.G. Wodehouse, 'Freddie, Oofy And The Beef Trust' in *A Few Quick Ones*.

20. William Townend, 'P.G.: Close Up of The Father Of Jeeves' in the *Daily Mail* (London, 8 Sep. 1938).

21. P.G. Wodehouse to Guy Bolton 13 July 1946.

22. P.G. Wodehouse to Guy Bolton 8 June 1933.

23. P.G. Wodehouse to Paul R. Reynolds Jr. 27 Aug. 1934.

24. Trevor Bailey, *Wickets, Catches And The Odd Run* (London, Willow Books, Collins, 1971).

25. Reginald Pound, *A Maypole In The Strand* (London, Ernest Benn, 1948).

26. Last Will And Testament of P.G. Wodehouse made 29 June 1973.

27. P.G. Wodehouse to Paul R. Reynolds Jr. 3 Jan. 1933.

28. George Grossmith, *"GG"* (London, Hutchinson, 1935).

29. Frances Donaldson, *P.G. Wodehouse*.

30. E. Philips Oppenheim, *The Pool Of Memory* (London, Hodder and Stoughton, 1941).

31. P.G. Wodehouse to William Townend 1 Dec. 1932.

32. P.G. Wodehouse to Leonora Cazalet 24 Aug. 1934.

33. Frances Donaldson, *Evelyn Waugh: Portrait Of A Country Neighbour* (London, Weidenfeld & Nicholson, 1967).

34. P.G. Wodehouse to William Townend 2 Feb. 1921.

35. P.G. Wodehouse to Leonora Wodehouse 30 May 1925 also to William Townend 23 Apr. 1932.

36. P.G. Wodehouse to Guy Bolton 23 Dec. 1939.

37. P.G. Wodehouse to Paul R. Reynolds Jr. 2 May 1934 (Siva), and 15 June 1933 (Jeeves).

38. P.G. Wodehouse to Paul R. Reynolds Jr. 15 Jun. 1933.

39. Donaldson, *P.G. Wodehouse*.

40. Richard Usborne, *Vintage Wodehouse*.

41. *Ibid*.

42. P.G. Wodehouse to William Townend 7 Jan. 1934.

43. Janet Morgan, *Agatha Christie* (London, Collins, 1984).

44. P.G. Wodehouse to William Townend 14 Oct. 1949.

45. P.G. Wodehouse to William Townend 12 Apr. 1947.

46. P.G. Wodehouse to William Townend 12 Apr. 1947.
47. *Cases Adjudged In The Supreme Court*, vol. 337, October Term 1948, US Government Printing Office (Washington DC, 1949).
48. *US Tax Cases* (Commerce Clearing House Inc, 1949).
49. P.G. Wodehouse to Leonora Cazalet 18 Oct. 1934.
50. P.G. Wodehouse to William Townend 15 Apr. 1952.
51. P.G. Wodehouse to William Townend 5 Jan. 1956.
52. *The New Yorker* (15 Oct. 1960).
53. P.G. Wodehouse to Denis Mackail Jan. 1946.

14 He Rather Enjoyed It

1. L.A.G. Strong, *The Spectator* (London, 1950).
2. P.G. Wodehouse to Denis Mackail Oct. 1932.
3. Ruth Inglis, *Nova* (Oct. 1974).
4. Arthur C. Clarke, *Profiles Of The Future* (London, Gollancz, 1962).
5. P.G. Wodehouse to Guy Bolton 8 Mar. 1937.
6. P.G. Wodehouse to Guy Bolton 8 Jan. 1953.
7. P.G. Wodehouse to William Townend 4 Dec. 1934.
8. E.J. Kahn Fr., a profile of Guy Bolton in *Far Flung And Footloose* (New York, Putnam, 1979).
9. Details supplied to the author by The Royal Society Of Literature.
10. P.G. Wodehouse to Leonora Wodehouse 12 Sep. 1924.
11. P.G. Wodehouse to Leonora Wodehouse 7 Aug. 1920.
12. P.G. Wodehouse to Leonora Wodehouse 3 Apr. 1935.
13. P.G. Wodehouse to Leonora Wodehouse 13 July 1937.
14. P.G. Wodehouse to Leonora Wodehouse 2 Apr. 1921.
15. P.G. Wodehouse to William Townend 17 Aug. 1929.
16. David Low, *Low's Autobiography* (London, Michael Joseph, 1959).
17. P.G. Wodehouse to Leonora Wodehouse 20 Nov. 1920.
18. P.G. Wodehouse, *Over Seventy*.
19. Herbert Mayes, *The Magazine Maze* (New York, Doubleday, 1980).
20. P.G. Wodehouse to William Townend 9 Nov. 1937.
21. P.G. Wodehouse to Guy Bolton 27 Mar. 1952.
22. P.G. Wodehouse, *Over Seventy*.
23. P.G. Wodehouse to Guy Bolton 16 Mar. 1953.
24. P.G. Wodehouse to Sheran Cazalet 28 Mar. 1948.
25. P.G. Wodehouse to Peter Schwed 30 Jan. 1956.
26. P.G. Wodehouse to Guy Bolton 2 Nov. 1961, 28 Oct. 1961, and to Ira Gershwin 10 Nov. 1961.
27. Richard Usborne, *Observer* (London, 11 Aug. 1971).
28. P.G. Wodehouse to Guy Bolton 15 Apr. 1948.
29. Graham Lord, *Sunday Express* (London, 3 Jan. 1971).
30. In conversation with the author.
31. Undated holograph memorandum from Derek Grimsdick to other directors of Herbert Jenkins Ltd.

32. P.G. Wodehouse to William Townend 4 Nov. 1952.
33. *Ibid.*
34. Gerald Clarke, interview with Wodehouse in *Paris Review*, vol. 16, no. 64 (Winter 1975).
35. Verrier Elwin, letter to *The Times Literary Supplement*, (London, 1953).
36. P.G. Wodehouse to William Townend 29 Apr. 1952.
37. P.G. Wodehouse to Leonora Cazalet 24 Aug. 1934.
38. P.G. Wodehouse to William Townend 1 Aug. 1945.
39. Beverley Nichols, *The Unforgiving Minute* (London, W.H. Allen, 1978).
40. Quoted by Alan Massie in 'Lashing Of Plum Pudding' in the *Observer* (London, 18 Oct. 1981).
41. Q.D. Leavis, *Fiction And The Reading Public* (London, Chatto and Windus, 1932).
42. Colin Welch, *The Spectator* (London, 20 Aug. 1983).
43. Quoted by Colin Welch in *The Spectator* (London, 20 Aug. 1983).
44. Copy of citation in the author's collection.
45. Hilaire Belloc writing in *John O'London's* c. 1940.
46. Sir Iain Moncreiffe of That Ilk, Bt., in *Books And Bookmen* (UK, Apr. 1985).
47. P.G. Wodehouse to Paul R. Reynolds Jr. 3 June 1939.
48. Quoted by permission of the late John Griffith.
49. Verrier Elwin, *Motley* (Calcutta, Longmans Orient, 1955).
50. P.G. Wodehouse to William Townend 1 Aug. 1945 in *Performing Flea*.
51. The full Latin text appears as Appendix 10.
52. Richard Usborne, 'A Very Private Man' in *P.G. Wodehouse 1881–1981*.
53. Sean O'Casey, *The Letters Of Sean O'Casey 1910–1941*, ed. David Krause (New York, Macmillan, 1975).
54. Ulick O'Connor, *Biographers* (Dublin, Wolfhound Press, 1991).
55. P.G. Wodehouse, *The Alleynian* (July 1939).
56. P.G. Wodehouse to William Townend 1 Dec. 1932.
57. P.G. Wodehouse to William Townend 23 Apr. 1939.

15 HEAVY WEATHER

Much of this chapter has relied upon the definitive book on Wodehouse between 1940 and 1945, *Wodehouse At War* by Iain Sproat. (New York, Ticknor and Fields, and London, Milner, 1981). '*Passim*' as indexers say, so I have not cited it on the many occasions I have used it by kind permission of Mr Sproat.

1. Malcolm Muggeridge, 'The Wodehouse Affair', *New Statesman And Nation* (London, 4 Aug. 1961).
2. Sir John Wheeler Bennet, *Knaves, Fools And Heroes* (London, Macmillan, 1974).
3. P.G. Wodehouse, 'Buried Treasure' in *Lord Emsworth And Others*.
4. Jasen, *P.G. Wodehouse*.
5. P.G. Wodehouse to William Townend 11 May 1942.

6. P.G. Wodehouse to William Townend 11 May 1942.

7. Paul R. Reynolds Jr., *The Middle Man: Adventures Of A Literary Agent* (New York, Morrow, 1971).

8. P.G. Wodehouse to Guy Bolton 1 Sep. 1945.

9. Telegrams, P.G. Wodehouse to Paul R. Reynolds Jr. 6 Aug. 1941 and 18 Nov. 1941.

10. P.G. Wodehouse to Paul R. Reynolds Jr. 27 Nov. 1941.

11. A.P. Ryan, 'Wooster's Progress', *New Statesman And Nation* (London, 20 June 1953).

12. W.N. Connor (Cassandra), *Daily Mirror* (London, 17 July 1961).

13. Quoted in full in Iain Sproat's *Wodehouse At War*.

14. Anthony Hugh Thompson, *Censorship In Public Libraries In The Twentieth Century* (London, Bowker, 1975).

15. Alastair Cooke, *Chronicle* (San Francisco, 19 Oct. 1961).

16. Robert Hendrickson, *The Literary Life & Other Curiosities* (New York, Viking Press, 1981).

17. John Masefield, statement drafted c. end-July 1941 from the archive of the Society of Authors.

18. Ann Thwaite, *A.A. Milne: His Life* (London, Faber and Faber, 1990).

19. A.A. Milne, *Daily Telegraph* (London, 3 July 1941). Quoted by permission of Curtis Brown Ltd, London, on behalf of the Estate of A.A. Milne.

20. Sir Compton Mackenzie, 'As A Contemporary' in *Homage To P.G. Wodehouse*.

21. Thwaite, *A.A. Milne*.

22. Sir Seymour Hicks, *Hail Fellow Well Met* (London, Staples Press, 1949).

23. Evelyn Waugh, 'An Act Of Homage And Reparation To P.G. Wodehouse' *Sunday Times* (London, 16 Oct. 1961).

24. Quoted by Jasen in *P.G. Wodehouse*.

25. Montgomery Ford to P.G. Wodehouse 30 Mar. 1947.

26. John Leeming in a letter to P.G. Wodehouse of 23 Apr. 1946.

27. Harry W. Flannery *Assignment to Berlin* (London, Michael Joseph, 1942).

28. P.G. Wodehouse to William Townend 30 Dec. 1944.

29. See note 1 above.

30. See note 1 above.

31. The only full publication of the Cussen report (now in the UK Public Records Office) is in Iain Sproat's *Wodehouse At War*.

32. P.G. Wodehouse to William Townend 22 Apr. 1945.

33. W.N. Connor (Cassandra), *Daily Mirror* (London, 17 July 1961).

34. Auberon Waugh, *The Observer Review* (London, 11 Oct. 1981).

35. P.G. Wodehouse to Guy Bolton 5 July 1946.

36. Telegram from A. Duff Cooper in Paris to the British Foreign Office of 29 Sep. 1944.

37. See note 1 above.

38. Hendrickson, *The Literary Life*.

39. Murphy, *In Search Of Blandings*.

40. P.G. Wodehouse to William Townend 11 Sep. 1946.

41. Hugh Kingsmill, *The Progress Of A Biographer* (London, Methuen, 1949).

42. Lord David Cecil, preface to *Homage To P.G. Wodehouse*.

43. *New York Times Book Review*, (25 Aug. 1946).

44. George Orwell 'In Defence Of P.G. Wodehouse', *The Windmill*, no. 2, (London, Wm Heinemann, 1945).

16 SUNSET AT REMSENBURG

1. Anthony Curtis, obituary for Wodehouse in the *Financial Times* (London, 17 Feb. 1975).

2. P.G. Wodehouse to William Townend 5 July 1946.

3. P.G. Wodehouse to William Townend 22 May 1946.

4. P.G. Wodehouse to Nelson Doubleday 2 Dec. 1946 quoted by Jasen in *P.G. Wodehouse*.

5. The Cussen report, Public Record Office, London.

6. P.G. Wodehouse to William Townend 11 Sep. 1946.

7. Paul Reynolds Sr. to P.G. Wodehouse 26 Apr. and 27 Apr. 1933.

8. See the Wodehouse-Reynolds correspondence at The Butler Library, Columbia University, New York.

9. P.G. Wodehouse to Paul R. Reynolds Jr. 14 Sep. 1945.

10. P.G. Wodehouse to William Townend 6 June 1947.

11. Malcolm Muggeridge, *Tread Softly For You Tread On My Jokes.* (London, Collins, 1966).

12. P.G. Wodehouse to William Townend 8 Mar. 1951 in *Performing Flea*.

13. P.G. Wodehouse to Guy Bolton 29 June 1951.

14. P.G. Wodehouse to William Townend 31 Jan. 1953, and 29 Apr. 1946.

15. P.G. Wodehouse to Peter Schwed 22 Aug. 1961.

16. Peter Schwed to P.G. Wodehouse 22 Apr. 1953.

17. Peter Schwed to the author at the P.G. Wodehouse Convention, New York, 1991.

18. P.G. Wodehouse to Derek Grimsdick 24 Mar. 1964.

19. P.G. Wodehouse, author's introduction to the new UK edition of *French Leave*, (1974).

20. Evelyn Waugh to Nancy Mitford 16 Nov. 1949 and to Ann Fleming 5 Oct. 1960 in *The Letters Of Evelyn Waugh*, ed. Mark Amory. (London, Weidenfeld and Nicholson, 1980).

21. Richard Usborne, *After Hours With P.G. Wodehouse*.

22. P.G. Wodehouse to Denis Mackail 27 Nov. 1945.

23. P.G. Wodehouse to Denis Mackail 20 Apr. 1946.

24. P.G. Wodehouse to William Townend 13 Dec. 1949.

25. P.G. Wodehouse to William Townend 18 June 1952 and 15 July 1952.

26. P.G. Wodehouse to William Townend 3 July 1936.

27. Sean O'Casey, letter to the editor of the *Daily Telegraph*, (London, 8 July 1941).

28. P.G. Wodehouse, *Performing Flea*.

29. P.G. Wodehouse to Derek Grimsdick 21 Mar. 1952, 2 Apr. 1952, 15 Apr. 1952, 13 Aug. 1952 and 16 May 1953.

30. P.G. Wodehouse to William Townend 11 Sep. 1952.
31. P.G. Wodehouse to William Townend 6 May 1952.
32. P.G. Wodehouse to Derek Grimsdick 13 Feb. 1953.
33. P.G. Wodehouse to William Townend 18 June 1952, see also 11 Sep. 1946 and 18 May 1962.
34. Report by libel lawyers Oswald Hickson Collier and Co to Herbert Jenkins Ltd. of 28 July 1951.
35. P.G. Wodehouse to Ira Gershwin 26 July 1953.
36. W.N. Connor (Cassandra), *Daily Mirror* (London, 9 Oct 1953).
37. W.N. Connor (Cassandra), *Daily Mirror* (London, 17 July 1961).
38. *Ibid.*
39. P.G. Wodehouse to Guy Bolton 31 July 1969 and to William Townend 25 Nov. 1953.
40. P.G. Wodehouse to William Townend 25 Nov. 1953.
41. P.G. Wodehouse to William Townend 1 Jan. 1945, 1 Aug. 1945 and 31 Oct. 1951.
42. P.G. Wodehouse to William Townend 22 Sep. 1947.
43. P.G. Wodehouse to William Townend 15 Jan. 1949.
44. *Daily Mail* (London, 20 Aug. 1954).
45. P.G. Wodehouse to William Townend 10 Sep. 1952 in *Performing Flea.*
46. P.G. Wodehouse to Peter Schwed 12 Dec. 1955.
47. P.G. Wodehouse to Peter Schwed 12 Dec. 1955.
48. Jasen, *P.G. Wodehouse.*
49. Quoted by Jasen in *P.G. Wodehouse.*
50. Frank Sullivan to P.G. Wodehouse 17 Dec. 1955.
51. Probate Registry, Somerset House, London. Probate granted 1 Sep. 1975.
52. Probate Registry, Somerset House, London. Probate granted 14 July 1988.
53. P.G. Wodehouse, *Mike At Wrykyn* (New York, Meredith Press, 1968).
54. P.G. Wodehouse to Derek Grimsdick 4 Mar. 1961.
55. Derek Grimsdick to David Emms, Master of Dulwich, 12 Oct. 1982.
56. Evelyn Waugh, 'Dr Wodehouse And Mr Wain', *The Spectator* (London, 24 Feb. 1956).
57. P.G. Wodehouse to Denis Mackail 1 May 1954 and 24 June 1956.
58. P.G. Wodehouse to Guy Bolton 30 May 1945.
59. P.G. Wodehouse to Denis Mackail 23 Dec. 1945.
60. P.G. Wodehouse to Guy Bolton quoted by Frances Donaldson in *P.G. Wodehouse.*
61. P.G. Wodehouse to Ira Gershwin 23 Dec. 1971.
62. P.G. Wodehouse to William Townend 30 Mar. 1949.
63. P.G. Wodehouse, *Ring For Jeeves.*
64. Contemporary US Press reports quoted by Jasen in *P.G. Wodehouse.*
65. P.G. Wodehouse to Denis Mackail 8 June 1947.
66. Richard Usborne, *After Hours With P.G. Wodehouse.*
67. P.G. Wodehouse to Derek Grimsdick 21 May 1961, and 28 Nov. 1960.
68. P.G. Wodehouse to Derek Grimsdick 28 Nov. 1960.
69. P.G. Wodehouse to Evelyn Waugh 10 May 1961.
70. Evelyn Waugh, 'An Act Of Homage And Reparation to P.G. Wodehouse',

radio talk published in the *Sunday Times* (London, 16 July 1961).

71. P.G. Wodehouse to Guy Bolton 31 July 1969.
72. P.G. Wodehouse to Guy Bolton 16 July 1964.
73. Last Will and Testament of P.G. Wodehouse made on 29 June 1973.
74. Undated note from P.G. Wodehouse to Peter Schwed, also Scott Meredith to Peter Schwed 19 Sep. 1966.
75. Donaldson, *P.G. Wodehouse*.
76. P.G. Wodehouse to Thelma Cazalet-Keir 25 May 1973.
77. P.G. Wodehouse to Guy Bolton 13 July 1968.
78. William Davis, *Punch* (London, 23 Oct. 1974).
79. P.G. Wodehouse to William Townend 19 Aug. 1954, and P.G. Wodehouse to Guy Bolton 16 Oct. 1959.
80. Gerald Clarke, 'Checking In With P.G. Wodehouse', *Esquire* (New York, May 1974).
81. Ruth Inglis, *Nova* (Oct. 1974).
82. Wilfred De'Ath, *Illustrated London News* (Feb. 1973).
83. Usborne, *After Hours*.
84. George Grossmith, *"GG"* (London, Hutchinson, 1935).
85. P.G. Wodehouse on bridge, *Sunday Times* (London, 12 Dec. 1958).
86. Lee Davis, 'Champagne Days', *The Hampton Chronicle-News* (Long Island, 22 Nov. 1984).
87. P.G. Wodehouse to William Townend 7 Mar. 1946.
88. Catherine Stott, interview 'Bunny And Plummy' in the *Manchester Guardian* (1 Nov. 1968).

17 PEERLESS P.G. WODEHOUSE

1. Peter Schwed to P.G. Wodehouse 14 Jan. 1972.
2. P.G. Wodehouse, *Over Seventy*.
3. Reproduced in *Performing Flea*.
4. Auberon Waugh, 'Father Of The English Idea' in *Homage To P.G. Wodehouse*.
5. George Orwell, 'In Defence Of P.G. Wodehouse', *The Windmill*, no. 2 (London, Wm Heinemann, 1945).
6. John Selby reviewing *Uncle Fred In The Springtime* in *The Chronicle* (Augusta, Georgia, 28 Aug. 1939).
7. Alastair Cooke, 'The Hermit Of Remsenburg', *Manchester Guardian* (13 Oct. 1961).
8. See note 5 above.
9. John Hatton 'Day By Day', *Scunthorpe Evening Telegraph* (16 Oct. 1981).
10. Auberon Waugh, article in the *Observer Review* (London, 11 Oct. 1981).
11. Frances Donaldson, *Evelyn Waugh: Portrait Of A Country Neighbour* (London, Weidenfeld and Nicholson, 1967).
12. *The Times* (London, 15 Oct. 1971).
13. Collected by Geoffrey Jaggard in *Wooster's World*.
14. P.G. Wodehouse, *Doctor Sally*.

15. Giles Brandreth, *The Pears Book Of Words* (London, Pelham Books (*sic*), 1979).

16. Oxford University Press, computer analysis of the *Oxford English Dictionary* prepared for the author.

17. Martin Williams, ed., *The Art Of Jazz* (London, Cassell, 1960).

18. Frances Donaldson, *P.G. Wodehouse: The Authorized Biography*.

19. P.G. Wodehouse, introduction to *Rex Stout: A Biography* by John McAleer, (Boston, Little Brown, 1977).

20. P.G. Wodehouse, 'How I Write My Books' in *What I Think*. Ed. Herbert Greenhough Smith (London, George Newnes, 1927).

21. P.G. Wodehouse to Denis Mackail 4 July 1946.

22. P.G. Wodehouse to Guy Bolton 24 Jan. 1947.

23. P.G. Wodehouse 'I Explode The Haggis', *Daily Mail* (London, 30 Nov. 1935).

24. P.G. Wodehouse, *Over Seventy* and two articles in *Punch*.

25. P.G. Wodehouse, 'The Reverent Wooing Of Archibald' in *Mr Mulliner Speaking*.

26. Monseigneur Ronald Knox, *Essays In Satire* (London, Secker and Warburg, 1928).

27. Sir Iain Moncreiffe of That Ilk, Bt., *Books And Bookmen* (UK, April 1975).

28. Bernard Levin, 'As Jeeves would have said: Perfect music, Sir', *The Times* (London, 18 Feb. 1975).

29. Lady (Sheran) Hornby (née Cazalet), introduction to Richard Usborne's *After Hours With P.G. Wodehouse*.

30. *Sunday Dispatch* (London, 1 June 1930).

31. Sir Robert Birley, *One Hundred Books In The Eton College Library*, published by the Provost and Fellows, Eton, 1970.

32. Marshall McLuhan, *The Gutenberg Galaxy* (London, Routledge and Keegan Paul, 1967).

33. Murphy, *In Search Of Blandings*.

34. Clive Hirchhorn, *Sunday Express* (London, 27 June 1965).

35. Dennis H. Bradley, *The Wisdom Of The Gods* (London, T. Werner Laurie, 1925).

36. P.G. Wodehouse to William Townend 17 Dec. 1925.

37. Wilfred De'Ath, interview with Wodehouse in *London Illustrated News* (Feb. 1973).

38. From copies of the Citrine correspondence made available to the author.

39. Geoffrey Wheatcroft, 'Plum Right' in *Observer* (London 18 Oct. 1981).

40. James H. Heineman, introduction to *P.G. Wodehouse 1881–1981*.

41. *New York Times* 19 Feb. 1975.

18 ENVOI

1. Owen Dudley Edwards, *P.G. Wodehouse: A Critical And Historical Essay* (London, Martin Brian and O'Keefe, 1977).

—Appendix 2—

THE P.G. WODEHOUSE
CHRONOLOGY

1277–83	Sir Bertram de Wodehouse fought for Edward I in his wars against the Scots.
1402	John Wodehouse granted lands at Kimberley in Norfolk.
25 Oct. 1415	John Wodehouse, *alter ego* for the Sieur de Wooster, fought for Henry V at Agincourt.
July 1547	Thomas Wodehouse, MP, killed at the battle of Musselburgh (or Pinkie) in Scotland.
1587	Philip Wodehouse knighted on the field of battle for his valour at the capture of Cadiz.
26 June 1611	Sir Philip Wodehouse created a baronet by King James I and VI.
13 Sep. 1619	Dulwich College, founded by Edward Alleyn in 1605, formally opened.
6 Aug. 1788	Philip Wodehouse, PGW's grandfather, born.
26 Oct. 1797	Sir John Wodehouse, MP and sixth baronet created first Baron Wodehouse of Kimberley.
27 Aug. 1797	John Bathurst Deane, PGW's maternal grandfather, born at the Cape of Good Hope.
18 June 1815	Captain Philip Wodehouse, PGW's grandfather, fights under Wellington at Waterloo.
14 July 1845	(Henry) Ernest Wodehouse, PGW's father, born.
15 Dec 1846	Col. Philip Wodehouse dies.
1861	Eleanor Deane, PGW's mother, born, the fifth of fourteen children.
1 June 1866	Lord Wodehouse, the third baron, created first Earl of Kimberley.
1867	Ernest Wodehouse started work in Hong Kong Civil Service.
3 Feb. 1877	Ernest Wodehouse married Eleanor Deane in Hong Kong.
26 Sep. 1877	Philip Peveril John Wodehouse, PGW's eldest brother, born to Ernest and Eleanor.
11 May 1879	(Ernest) Armine Wodehouse, PGW's brother born.
27 July 1881	William Townend born.
15 Oct. 1881	Pelham Grenville Wodehouse born at Guildford while his mother was at home in England from Hong Kong.
1881–82	Eleanor took PGW back to Hong Kong.
1883	Eleanor took Philip, Armine and PGW home to England, left them in charge of a governess and returned to Hong Kong.

284

23 Nov. 1884   Guy Reginald Bolton born at Broxbourne, Hertfordshire of American parents.

23 May 1885   Ethel Newton born in Kings Lynn, Norfolk.

1886   Ernest in London to receive the CMG from Queen Victoria. He and Eleanor placed their three boys at dame school in Croydon.

12 July 1887   Revd John Bathurst Deane died.

1888   Aged six, PGW read the whole of Homer's *Iliad*.

1889   The three Wodehouse brothers sent to a small school on Guernsey.

1891   PGW sent to Malvern House, a preparatory school in Kent.

30 May 1892   Richard Lancelot Deane Wodehouse, PGW's younger brother, born.

2 May 1894   PGW started at Dulwich College, boarding with an assistant master, H.V. Doulton.

Sep. 1894   Became a boarder at Dulwich at Ivyholme.

1896   Ernest Wodehouse retired and took a house in Dulwich. PGW became a day-boy at the college.

1896   PGW's parents moved to Stableford in Shropshire and he became a Dulwich boarder again, this time at Elm Lawn, Housemaster E.C. Treadgold.

Sep. 1897   PGW won school colours as a member of the first XV Rugby team, a position he held for two years.

1898   *The Public School Magazine* founded.

Sep. 1898   William Townend became a pupil at Dulwich and PGW's closest school friend.

Feb. 1899   Won Dulwich first XI colours.

Apr. 1899   *The Captain* founded.

31 July 1899   PGW sang *Hybrias The Cretan* at the college concert.

Sep. 1899   Looked forward to going to Oxford University.

Oct. 1899?   Learnt Ernest could not afford to let him go to Oxford.

11 Nov. 1899   Won Dulwich first XV colours.

1900   Finally got his school colours as a member of the first XI cricket team.

1900   Appointed one of the editors of *The Alleynian*.

Feb. 1900   Won writing competition run by *The Public School Magazine* with 'Some Aspects Of Games Captaincy'.

July 1900   Left Dulwich College.

Sep. 1900   Started work at the Hongkong & Shanghai Bank in Lombard Street. Took a room in Markham Square, Chelsea.

Dec. 1900   Began writing Under-The-Flail column for *The Public School Magazine*.

3 Nov. 1900   As a member of the Bank's rugby team played against the London & Westminster Bank.

Nov 1900   First humorous article 'Men Who Missed Their Own Weddings' appeared in *Tit-Bits*.

June 1901   Caught mumps and convalesced at Stableford.

16 Aug. 1901	First played truant from the bank to work on *The Globe* newspaper for the day.
Oct. 1901	First piece appeared in *The Captain*. A St Austin's school story.
1902	Parents moved to 3, Wolseley Terrace, Cheltenham.
Mar. 1902	*The Public School Magazine* closed.
2 Apr. 1902	Spent a week working on *The Globe*.
9 Sep. 1902	Resigned his position at the Hongkong & Shanghai Bank.
17 Sep. 1902	First article appeared in *Punch* called 'An Unfinished Collection'.
18 Sep. 1902	A. and C. Black published his first book: *The Pothunters*.
Sep. 1902	Spent five weeks working on *The Globe*.
c. 1902/03	Played for the Authors and Punch cricket teams. Moved to better lodgings at 23 Walpole Street, also in Chelsea. Visited there by Herbert W. Westbrook. Soon thereafter visited Westbrook at Emsworth House preparatory school in Hampshire.
c. 1903	Played for J.M. Barrie's cricket team, the Allahakbarries.
Early 1903	Took lodgings above the stables at Emsworth House. Soon afterwards rented Threepwood Cottage at Emsworth.
2 July 1903	Interview with Sir Arthur Conan Doyle appeared in the *V.C.* magazine.
Aug. 1903	Became the deputy on the By-The-Way column of *The Globe*.
15 Sep. 1903	Ethel Newton married Leonard Rowley in Nottingham.
16 Apr. 1904	PGW sailed on the *SS St Louis* for his first visit to the US arriving on the 25th.
Aug. 1904	Became editor of the By-The-Way column.
10 Dec. 1904	First commercial lyric 'Put Me In My Little Cell' sung in *Sergeant Brue* at London's Strand Theatre.
1905	Leonard Rowley took his wife and daughter to India.
July 1905	PGW's first article in *The Strand* called 'The Wirepullers'.
Sep. 1905	First US magazine publication with 'Kid Brady – Lightweight' in *Pearson's Magazine* of New York.
6 Mar. 1906	Started work for Seymour Hicks as resident lyricist at London's Aldwych Theatre.
19 Mar. 1906	Met Jerome Kern at the Aldwych, both working on *The Beauty Of Bath*.
6 June 1906	PGW's first adult novel, *Love Among The Chickens*, published in the UK starring Ukridge.
17 Nov. 1906	Bought Seymour Hicks' car, a Darracq. Crashed it.
6 Dec. 1907	Joined Gaiety Theatre as lyricist.
1908	First appeared in UK *Who's Who*. The Armstrong family sold *The Globe* to Hildebrand Harmsworth.
May 1909	On second visit to the US sold two stories in two days and wired resignation to *The Globe*.
11 May 1909	*Love Among The Chickens* became PGW's first book to be published in the US.

15 Sep. 1909	*Mike* heralded the arrival of Psmith.
Feb. 1910	Returned to UK from New York.
Mar. 1910	A 1,500 word pen-portrait by H.L. Bradshaw appeared in *The Captain*.
11 May 1910	*A Gentleman Of Leisure* became PGW's first book to be published in the US before the UK.
8 June 1910	Leonard Rowley died in Mysore, India.
12 Dec 1910	Ethel Rowley granted probate in London for Leonard Rowley's estate.
1911	Ella King-Hall married Herbert Westbrook.
28 Jan. 1911	Ethel Rowley married John Wayman in London.
24 Aug. 1911	*A Gentleman Of Leisure*, PGW's first play, opened in New York.
Jan. 1912	Ella King-Hall became PGW's UK literary agent.
July 1912	John Wayman declared bankrupt in London.
Sep. 1913	PGW's last article appeard in *The Captain*.
5 Jan. 1914	*The Times* reviewed *Nuts And Wine*. A flop.
May 1914	First piece in *Vanity Fair* (US) called 'The Physical Culture Peril'.
27 July 1914	Sailed for New York with John Barrymore on board a German ship.
2 Aug. 1914	Arrived in New York.
3 Aug. 1914	Met Ethel Rowley Wayman at a party in New York.
4 Aug. 1914	First World War began.
30 Sep. 1914	PGW married Ethel Rowley Wayman.
1 Oct. 1914	Rented a bungalow at Bellport, Long Island.
24 Dec. 1914	Probable first meeting of PGW and Guy Bolton at the New York first night of *Tonight's The Night*.
25 Mar. 1915	*A Gentleman Of Leisure*, PGW's first film released.
Mar. 1915	PGW became drama critic of *Vanity Fair*.
15 Sep. 1915	Jeeves and Bertie made their first appearance in *The Saturday Evening Post* (US).
28 Feb. 1916	*Pom Pom*, a play and the first Bolton and Wodehouse collaboration, was a success.
25 Sep. 1916	*Miss Springtime*, first Bolton, Wodehouse and Kern show a great success.
11 Jan. 1917	*Have A Heart*, the first Bolton, Wodehouse and Kern Princess show opened – at the Liberty Theatre
20 Feb. 1917	*Oh Boy*, the second Princess show but the first at the Princess Theatre opened to rave reviews.
1918	*Piccadilly Jim* was the first of seventy-one of PGW's books to be published in the UK by Herbert Jenkins over half a century.
Mar. 1921	Arriving in New York during Prohibition, payed the bellhop at the Biltmore Hotel $17 for a bottle of Scotch.
Dec. 1921	A two-page profile of PGW appeared in *The Strand*.
1922	A portrait of PGW appeared in Gerald Cumberland's book, *People Worth Talking About*.

1923	PGW and Kern's last collaboration on *The Beauty Prize*.
17 May 1923	The first Jeeves and Bertie book, *The Inimitable Jeeves*, was published.
Mar. 1925	*The Captain* closed.
1926	Elected a Fellow of The Royal Society Of Literature.
1927	Beverley Nichols portrayed PGW in *Are They The Same At Home?*
1 Apr. 1927	Wodehouses leased 17 Norfolk Street (now Dunraven Street) in Mayfair, their London home for many years.
Nov. 1927	Sailed to New York with George Grossmith.
10 Mar. 1928	Michael Arlen dined at Norfolk Street.
25 Mar. 1928	John Galsworthy and actor Leslie Howard lunched with the Wodehouses at Rogate Lodge in Sussex. Ian Hay was a house guest and Mr and Mrs E.P. Oppenheim were visitors.
Aug. 1928	PGW, Ian Hay and A.A. Milne financed the PGW/Hay play *A Damsel In Distress* with £500 each.
Oct. 1928	Lunched with Sir Owen Seaman, editor of *Punch* at the Beefsteak.
Jan. 1929	Leonora Wodehouse wrote 'P.G. Wodehouse At Home' in *The Strand*.
27 May 1929	PGW's father Ernest died aged 83.
Aug. 1929	PGW made a flying visit, his first, to Hollywood.
Nov. 1929	Ethel went to Hollywood and agreed a $2,000 a week contract for PGW with MGM.
8 May 1930	PGW and Leonora arrived in Hollywood.
1 June 1930	PGW's contract with MGM commenced.
July 1930	Ethel joined PGW and Leonora in Hollywood.
31 May 1931	PGW's contract with MGM ended.
7 June 1931	*Los Angeles Times* interview with PGW appeared.
30 July 1931	*New York Times* carried Roland Pertwee's denial of PGW's *LA Times* story of him being fired from Warner Brothers.
13 Sep. 1931	Dined with Douglas Fairbanks and Mary Pickford at 'Pickfair'.
Sep. 1931	On the way back from Hollywood visited Canada again and spent the day with Stephen Leacock.
Mar. 1932	Wodehouses rented a house in the south of France at Arribeau near Cannes.
Aug. 1932	H.G. Wells dined *chez* Wodehouse at Arribeau.
12 Dec. 1932	Leonora married Peter Cazalet at Shipbourne.
1933	David Low drew his famous cartoon of PGW.
31 Mar. 1934	Sheran Cazalet born; a granddaughter for Ethel and Plum.
June 1934	Settled in Le Touquet.
24 Aug. 1934	Rented Low Wood near Le Touquet.
1932	Ella King-Hall (Mrs Herbert Westbrook), his UK agent, retired and died shortly thereafter.
3 June 1935	Bought Low Wood near Le Touquet.
Dec. 1935	PGW sadly gave his old Monarch typewriter the last rites.
26 Apr. 1936	Edward Cazalet born; a grandson for Ethel and Plum.

26 June 1936	Awarded medallion by the International Mark Twain Society.
9 Oct. 1936	His brother Armine died.
10 Oct. 1936	Back in Hollywood, again under contract to MGM.
May 1937	With Guy Bolton adapted his *A Damsel In Distress* for the screen for RKO.
28 Oct. 1937	Sailed for France.
4 Nov. 1937	Returned to France and Le Touquet.
21 June 1939	Accepted honorary D.Litt. from Oxford University.
8 July 1939	Reported Dulwich cricket match against St Paul's for *The Alleynian*. His last ever visit to the college.
3 Sep. 1939	Second World War began.
21 May 1940	Wodehouses attempted to flee German advance. Car broke down.
22 May 1940	German army occupied Le Touquet.
21 July 1940	As a civilian internee PGW sent to Loos Prison, Lille. Then transferred to Liege in Belgium.
3 Aug. 1940	Transferred to the Citadel at Huy, Belgium.
8 Sep. 1940	Transferred to Tost in Upper Silesia.
Dec. 1940	PGW's last contribution in *The Strand*.
26 Dec. 1940	Met Angus Thuermer of Associated Press in Tost.
21 Apr. 1941	Eleanor Wodehouse, PGW's mother, died aged eighty.
May 1941	Petition presented to German ambassador to US asking for PGW's release.
21 June 1941	While playing cricket at Tost told of his immediate release from internment. Taken to Berlin.
22 June 1941	Met Raven von Barnikow and Werner Plack at the Adlon Hotel in Berlin.
25 June 1941	Commenced recording five broadcasts to America, completing the task on 26 July.
26 June 1941	Gave an interview to Harry Flannery, CBS's Berlin correspondent, which was broadcast to the US.
27 June 1941	Went to stay with Baroness Anga von Bodenhausen at her house at Degenershausen near Magdeburg in the Harz mountains.
28 June 1941	First broadcast transmitted to UK.
July 1941	*Saturday Evening Post* published 'My War With Germany'.
9 July 1941	Second broadcast transmitted to UK. Foreign Secretary, Sir Anthony Eden, denounced PGW in the House of Commons.
15 July 1941	Vituperative attack on PGW by William Connor speaking on BBC radio.
17 July 1941	The London *Daily Mail* reprinted part of PGW's 'My War With Germany' from the *Saturday Evening Post*.
23 July 1941	Third broadcast transmitted to UK.
27 July 1941	Ethel arrived in Berlin.
30 July 1941	Fourth broadcast transmitted to UK.
6 Aug. 1941	Fifth broadcast transmitted to UK.

9 Aug. 1941	German Ministry of Propaganda rebroadcast PGW's talks to neutral America on 9, 10, 11, 12 and 14 August.
Nov. 1941	Wodehouses returned to Berlin.
Apr. 1942	They returned to Degenershausen.
Nov. 1942	They returned to Berlin.
Apr. 1943	They became paying guests of Count and Countess Wolkenstein at Lobnis in Upper Silesia.
9 Sep. 1943	Wodehouses allowed to move to Paris arriving at the Hotel Bristol on the 11th.
1944	Paul Reynolds Sr., PGW's US literary agent, died.
16 May 1944	Leonora Cazalet died unexpectedly, aged only forty.
25 Aug. 1944	Allied armies liberated Paris.
26 Aug. 1944	PGW reported himself to US military authorities.
28 Sep. 1944	Major E.J.P. Cussen completed his report clearing PGW of all but fatheadedness.
20 Nov. 1944	Arrested by French police 'Just in case'.
23 Nov. 1944	Director of Public Prosecutions decided there was no evidence on which to prosecute PGW.
15 Dec. 1944	Adjournment Debate on PGW in the House of Commons. Attorney General stated there was no evidence on which to prosecute PGW.
6 Dec. 1944	Sir Anthony Eden repeated there was no evidence on which to prosecute PGW.
20 Jan. 1945	Released from hospital detention by the French.
July 1945	PGW explained his war period to Dulwich in *The Alleynian*.
c. 1946	Scott Meredith became PGW's US literary agent.
8 May 1946	PGW's letter on his wartime period appeared in *Variety*.
7 Dec. 1946	PGW's interview with Hubert Cole about his war period appeared in *Illustrated* in the UK.
18 Apr. 1947	Ethel and PGW sailed from Cherbourg for New York on the *SS America* arriving on the 26th. They stayed at the Hotel Waylin on East 54th Street.
26 June 1948	Still keen boxing fans, Plum and Ethel saw Joe Louis fight Jersey Joe Walcott at Yankee Stadium.
2 Sep. 1948	*Don't Listen Ladies*, a new play was a hit and written by Guy Bolton and Stephen Powys, a.k.a. PGW.
1 Feb. 1949	Lunched with Evelyn Waugh in New York.
Mar. 1950	Last issue of *The Strand* appeared. PGW lunched (separately) with Michael Arlen, Evelyn Waugh and Ferenc Molnar.
28 Oct. 1950	Interviewed on radio by Eleanor Roosevelt.
Mar. 1952	While staying with the Boltons at Remsenburg, Ethel bought a house at Basket Neck Lane.
July 1952	Ethel and Plum moved to Remsenburg, keeping their New York apartment for the winter.
15 July 1953	First post-war article in *Punch*, Malcolm Muggeridge having become editor earlier in the year.

15 Oct. 1954	Wrote to J.R.D. Jones about his time at the Hongkong & Shanghai Bank.
1 May 1955	Gave up New York apartment and lived the year round at Remsenburg.
8 Sep. 1955	Filed application for US citizenship.
16 Dec. 1955	Became an American citizen.
27 Jan. 1960	Honoured by election to the *Punch* table.
1961	*Wodehouse At Work* by Richard Usborne published.
15 July 1961	Evelyn Waugh on the BBC broadcast 'An Act of Homage And Reparation to P.G. Wodehouse'.
16 Feb. 1962	William Townend died.
24 May 1964	*Jeeves* appeared as a long-playing record with Terry Thomas as Bertie and Roger Livsey as Jeeves.
Sep. 1964	Nella (Armine's widow) came to live at Remsenburg.
6 Apr. 1965	Herbert Jenkins taken over by another UK publisher, Barrie and Rockcliff.
27 May 1965	BBC began television series *The World Of Wooster* with Ian Carmichael as Bertie and Denis Price as Jeeves.
16 Feb. 1967	BBC began another television series *Blandings Castle*, starring Sir Ralph Richardson as Lord Emsworth and his wife Merial Forbes as Lady Constance.
Nov. 1967	P.G. Wodehouse Animal Shelter opened at Remsenburg.
19 Sep. 1969	*A Pelican At Blandings* was the last PGW book to be published under the Herbert Jenkins imprint.
29 Oct. 1970	*The Girl In Blue* was PGW's first book published in the UK by Barrie and Jenkins instead of Herbert Jenkins.
1974	*P.G. Wodehouse: A Portrait Of A Master* by David A. Jasen published.
1974	Madame Tussaud's Wax Museum of London sent John Blakely to Remsenburg to capture PGW in wax.
14 Apr. 1974	Last complete novel, *Aunts Aren't Gentlemen*, published in the UK.
Late 1974	BBC commenced a new television series, *Wodehouse Playhouse*.
1975	*Wodehouse Playhouse* became the third BBC television series based on Wodehouse stories.
1 Jan. 1975	Knighted by Queen Elizabeth II, along with Charlie Chaplin.
14 Feb. 1975	Died in Southampton hospital having spent his life giving pleasure to millions of readers.
18 Feb. 1975	Funeral service at Remsenburg Presbyterian Church, the Revd Gordon G. Dickson officiated.
15 Oct. 1977	Formal opening of the P.G. Wodehouse Memorial Corner of the Dulwich College Library.
5 Sep. 1979	Guy Bolton died at Goring-On-Thames in England.
25 June 1980	After a determined campaign, Iain Sproat, MP, finally secured the release of the Cussen report.
1981	*Wodehouse At War* by Iain Sproat published.

1981   *In Search Of Blandings* privately published by the author, N.T.P. Murphy.

15 Oct. 1981   Worldwide celebration of PGW's centenary.
Sheran Hornby unveiled a plaque on the Guildford house where PGW was born.
P.G. Wodehouse: A Centenary Celebration 1881–1981 published with essays and a major bibliography.

1982   *P.G. Wodehouse: The Authorised Biography* by Frances Donaldson published.

Oct. 1984   Lady Wodehouse died at Remsenburg.

Jan. 1988   The P.G. Wodehouse Prize for humorous writing established by Century Hutchinson and *The Observer* newspaper.

3 June 1988   HM Queen Elizabeth, The Queen Mother unveiled a plaque on PGW's London home, 17 Dunraven Street.

Jan. 1991   The definitive Wodehouse bibliography published by James H. Heineman.

N.B. Where this chronology differs from earlier ones I am confident that the later one is correct. B.P.

—Appendix 3—

THE DISTINGUISHED DESCENT OF P.G. WODEHOUSE

Sir Constantine de Wodehouse
Sir George de Wodehouse
Sir Henry de Wodehouse
Sir Richard de Wodehouse
Sir William de Wodehouse
Francis de Wodehouse
  (Fined for not accepting knighthood)
Sir Bertram de Wodehouse
Sir William de Wodehouse
Sir Richard de Wodehouse
Sir Thomas de Wodehouse
Sir Edward de Wodehouse
Sir John de Wodehouse
Sir John de Wodehouse

Sir Bertram de Wodehouse	m. Muriel, d. of Hamo, Lord of Felton and fought with distinction for Edward I against the Scots 1277–83.
Sir William Wodehouse	Brother of Robert de Wodehouse (Baron of the Exchequer 1318 and favourite of three Kings, Edwards I, II and III).
John Wodehouse	Constable of Castle Rising 1402. Steward of the Duchy of Lancaster 1414. Esquire to the Body and Groom To The Chamber of Henry V 1413–22, Chamberlain of The Exchequer 1415 and Executor of the King's Will. Died 1430–31.
John Wodehouse	m. Constance d. of Thomas Gedding. Died at Kimberley 1465.
Sir Edward Wodehouse	Attended the King to Scotland 1461. Knighted at Grafton Field, Tewksbury 1471.
Sir Thomas Wodehouse	Created Knight of the Bath at the marriage, by Archbishop Dene, of Prince Arthur, 1501. Ambassador to France. Died c. 1487.

Sir Roger Wodehouse	Knighted by Edward VI in 1548. m. Elizabeth, d. and co-heiress of Sir Robert Ratcliff. Attempted to end Ket's Rebellion by peaceful means. Died 1560.
Thomas Wodehouse, MP	Killed at the battle of Musselburgh (Pinkie) 1547 when the Standard Bearer with Lord Protector Somerset's army fighting against the Scots. MP for Yarmouth.
Sir Roger Wodehouse, MP	Knighted 1578 by Queen Elizabeth I who in the seame year visited Kimberley. MP for Aldborough. Died 1588.
Sir Philip Wodehouse, Bt., MP	Knighted for his valour at the capture of Cadiz, 1596. Created baronet 29 June 1611. m. Grizell, widow of Hamon L'Estrange of Hunstanton. MP for Castle Rising. Died 1623.
Sir Thomas Wodehouse, Bt., MP	m. 1605 Blanche, d. of John Carey, Lord Hunsdon and great granddaughter of William Carey, Esquire to the body of Henry VIII, by his wife Lady Mary Boleyn, sister of Lady Anne Boleyn. Kept a low profile during the Civil War. MP for Thetford. Died 1658.
Sir Philip Wodehouse, Bt., MP	Baptized 1608. MP for Norfolk and then Thetford. Died 1681.
Sir Thomas Wodehouse	Knighted by Charles II. m. Anne, d. and co-heiress of Sir William Armine Bt. Died 1671.
Sir John Wodehouse, Bt., MP	b. 1669, MP for Thetford then Norfolk. Died 1754.
Sir Armine Wodehouse, Bt., MP	First common forebear of the Barons Wodehouse, Earls of Kimberley and P.G. Wodehouse.

SIR PELHAM WODEHOUSE
THE BARONS WODEHOUSE AND EARLS OF KIMBERLEY

Sir Armine Wodehouse, MP, 5th Bt.,
1714–1758, m. 1738 Letitia, co-heiress of
Sir Edmund Bacon Bt.

Sir John Wodehouse, Bt., MP, 1741–1834 MP for Norfolk Recorder of Falmouth and 1st Baron Wodehouse of Kimberley 1797.	brothers	Revd Philip Wodehouse 1745–1811 Prebendary of Norwich. m 1775 Appolonia co-heiress of John Nourse.
John, 2nd Baron Wodehouse, 1771–1846.	1st cousins	Col. Philip Wodehouse 1788–1846. m. 1832 Lydia, heiress of Joseph Lee.
Hon. Henry Wodehouse, 1799–1834.	2nd cousins	Henry Ernest Wodehouse, CMG, 1845–1929. Hong Kong Civil Service. m. 1877 Eleanor, d. of Revd J.B. Deane.
John, 3rd Baron Wodehouse, 1826–1902, 1st Earl of Kimberley, 1866.	3rd cousins	Sir Pelham Grenville Wodehouse 1881–1975.

N.B. The early parts of this pedigree have been extracted from Blomefield's Norfolk, the later parts largely from Burke's Peerage. It must be acknowledged that modern day genealogists do not all accept the claims made for the Wodehouse pedigree prior to 1402 nor that John Wodehouse, courtier to Henry V, fought at Agincourt. See also the references relating to the chapter *Genealogy, Genes And Genius*.

—Appendix 4—

THE THEATRE OF
P.G. WODEHOUSE

10 Dec. 1904	*Sergeant Brue* Strand Theatre, London. 152 performances.	One lyric, 'Put Me In My Little Cell'.
9 Mar. 1906	*The Beauty Of Bath* Aldwych Theatre, London. 287 performances	Resident lyricist and two songs with Jerome Kern.
2 Mar. 1907	*My Darling* Hicks Theatre, London 71 performances.	Lyrics by Charles Taylor. Additional lyrics by Wodehouse.
15 May 1907	*The Girls from Gottenberg* Gaiety Theatre, London. 303 performances.	'Our Little Way'
June 1907	*The Hon'ary Degree* New Theatre, Cambridge, UK.	One Wodehouse lyric. 'My Grassy Corner Girl'
11 Sep. 1907	*The Gay Gordons* Aldwych Theatre, London. 229 performances.	Two lyrics.
11 Nov. 1907	*The Bandit's Daughter* Bedford Music Hall, London.	Co-author with H.W. Westbrook. Music Ella King-Hall.
1911	*After The Show*	Co-author with H.W. Westbrook.
24 Aug. 1911	*A Gentleman Of Leisure* The Playhouse, New York. 76 performances.	Co-author. Also called *A Thief In The Night* in Chicago
8 Apr. 1913	*Brother Alfred* Savoy Theatre, London. 14 performances.	Co-author with H.W. Westbrook.
4 Jan. 1914	*Nuts And Wine* Empire Theatre, London. 7 performances.	Co-author and lyricist with Charles Bovill.
25 Jan. 1915	*Ninety In The Shade* Knickerbocker, New York. 40 performances.	Lyric for 'A Packet Of Seeds', music by Jerome Kern.

28 Feb. 1916	*Pom Pom* Cohan Theatre, New York. 114 performances.	Joint author and lyricist with Anne Caldwell.
25 Sep. 1916	*Miss Springtime* New Amsterdam Theatre, New York. 227 performances.	Principal lyricist. Book Guy Bolton, music Kern and Kalman.
11 Jan. 1917	*Have A Heart* Liberty Theatre, New York. 78 performances.	Co-author with Guy Bolton. Sole lyricist. Music Jerome Kern.
20 Feb. 1917	*Oh Boy!* Princess Theatre, New York. 475 performances.	Bolton, Wodehouse and Kern. *Oh, Joy!* in London.
28 Aug. 1917	*Leave It To Jane* Longacre Theatre, New York. 167 performances.	Bolton, Wodehouse and Kern.
10 Sep. 1917	*Kitty Darlin'* Teck Theatre, Buffalo, NY.	Co-author with Guy Bolton. Lyricist.
24 Sep. 1917	*The Riviera Girl* New Amsterdam Theatre, New York. 78 performances.	Co-author with Guy Bolton. Sole lyricist. Music Kern and Kalman.
5 Nov. 1917	*Miss 1917* Century Theatre, New York. 48 performances.	Co-author with Guy Bolton. Sole lyricist. Music Kern & Herbert.
1 Feb. 1918	*Oh, Lady! Lady!* Princess Theatre, New York. 219 performances.	Bolton, Wodehouse and Kern.
15 Apr. 1918	*See You Later* Academy of Music, Baltimore.	Co-author with Guy Bolton. Sole lyricist.
16 Sep. 1918	*The Girl Behind The Gun* New Amsterdam Theatre, New York. 160 performances. *Kissing Time* in London.	Co-author with Guy Bolton. Sole lyricist.
4 Nov. 1918	*The Canary* Globe Theatre, New York. 152 performances.	Joint lyricist with Anne Caldwell.
27 Nov. 1918	*Oh, My Dear!* Princess Theatre, New York. 189 performances. Originally called *Ask Dad*.	Co-author with Guy Bolton. Sole lyricist. One Kern song.
25 Dec. 1919	*The Rose Of China* Lyric Theatre, New York. 47 performances!	Book by Guy Bolton. Lyrics by Wodehouse.
21 Dec. 1920	*Sally* New Amsterdam Theatre, New York. 570 performances.	Two lyrics by Wodehouse to Kern's music.

5 Oct. 1921	*The Golden Moth* Adelphi Theatre, London. 281 performances.	Co-author with Fred Thompson. Five lyrics. Music Novello.
19 Sep. 1922	*The Cabaret Girl* Winter Garden Theatre, London. 462 performances.	Co-author and lyricist with George Grossmith. Music Kern.
5 Sep. 1923	*The Beauty Prize* Winter Garden Theatre, London. 214 performances.	Co-author and lyricist with George Grossmith. Music Kern.
8 Apr. 1924	*Sitting Pretty* Fulton Theatre, New York. 95 performances.	Bolton, Wodehouse and Kern.
26 Oct. 1925	*The City Chap* Liberty Theatre, New York. 72 performances.	One lyric 'Journey's End'. Music Kern.
1 June 1926	*Hearts And Diamonds* Strand Theatre, London. 46 performances.	Joint English adapter with Laurie Wylie.
3 Nov. 1926	*The Play's The Thing* Henry Miller Theatre, New York. 326 performances.	Wodehouse (from Molnar).
8 Nov. 1926	*Oh, Kay!* Imperial Theatre, New York. 256 performances.	Co-author with Guy Bolton.
3 Jan. 1927	*The Nightingale* Jolson Theatre, New York. 96 performances.	Book by Guy Bolton. Lyrics Wodehouse.
21 Mar. 1927	*Her Cardboard Lover* Empire Theatre, New York. 152 performances.	Co-author with Valerie Wyngate.
28 Nov. 1927	*Good Morning, Bill!* Duke of York's Theatre, London. 136 performances.	Wodehouse from Fodor.
27 Dec. 1927	*Show Boat* Ziegfeld Theatre, New York. 572 performances.	One lyric, 'Bill', his most famous song. Music Kern.
10 Jan. 1928	*Rosalie* New Amsterdam Theatre, New York. 335 performances.	Co-lyricist with Ira Gershwin.
13 Mar. 1928	*The Three Musketeers* Lyric Theatre, New York. 318 performances.	Co-lyricist with Clifford Grey.
13 Aug. 1928	*A Damsel In Distress* New Theatre, London. 242 performances.	Co-author with Ian Hay.
22 Apr. 1929	*Baa, Baa Black Sheep* New Theatre, London. 115 performances.	Co-author with Ian Hay.

30 Sep. 1929	*Candle-Light* Empire Theatre, New York. 128 performances.	Wodehouse from Geyer.
27 Sep. 1930	*Leave It To Psmith* Shaftesbury Theatre, London. 156 performances.	Co-author with Ian Hay.
20 Sep. 1934	*Who's Who* Duke Of York's Theatre, London. 19 performances.	Co-author with Guy Bolton. In New York *Who's Who* *Baby*.
21 Nov. 1934	*Anything Goes* Alvin Theatre, New York. 415 performances.	Score and lyrics by Cole Porter. Book by Bolton, Wodehouse, Howard Lindsay and Russel Crouse.
21 Sep. 1935	*The Inside Stand* Saville Theatre, London. 50 performances.	P.G. Wodehouse from his novel *Hot Water*.
21 Sep. 1938	*You Never Know* Winter Garden, New York. 78 performances.	Cole Porter musical based on Wodehouse's *By Candlelight*.
2 Sep. 1948	*Don't Listen Ladies* St James's Theatre, London. 219 performances.	As Stephen Powys with Guy Bolton.
1950	Nothing Serious No major production but done in US in summer stock.	Wodehouse.
1950	*The House On The Cliff* Out of town tour, USA.	Rewritten by Wodehouse.
1954	*Come On Jeeves* No major production but staged in provinces in UK.	Bolton and Wodehouse.
Aug. 1954	*Joy In The Morning* world premier (a.k.a. *Phipps* and *Kilroy Was Here*) The Buckfast Players. The Studio Theatre, Ashburton, Devon.	Wodehouse.
4 Feb. 1964	*Josephine Baker & Her* *Company* Brooks Atkinson Theatre. 40 performances.	Sings two songs by Wodehouse.
21 Apr. 1964	*To Broadway With Love* Texas Pavilion, New York World's Fair. 97 performances.	One Wodehouse lyric.
29 Jan. 1968	*Who's Who Baby* Players, New York. 16 performances.	Musical based on the Wodehouse play *Who's Who*.
28 Aug. 1968	*Oh Clarence* Lyric Theatre, London.	By John Chapman using Wodehouse characters.

17 Oct. 1971	*Cleo Laine* Carnegie Hall, New York. One night show.	One Wodehouse lyric.
4 Nov. 1974	*Music! Music!* City Centre, New York. 37 performances.	One Wodehouse lyric, 'Bill'.
22 Apr. 1975	*Jeeves* Her Majesty's, London. 38 performances.	Based on Wodehouse characters. Music by Andrew Lloyd Webber.
21 Dec. 1975	*Very Good Eddie* (Revival) Boothe, New York. 304 performances.	Two Wodehouse songs interpolated.
30 Apr. 1980	*Blandings Castle* Westminster Theatre, London.	Book and lyrics Anne Deeve. Score Philip Case.
Aug. 1980	*Jeeves Takes Charge* Lyric Theatre, Hammersmith.	Edward Duke, author and star. From Wodehouse.
Dec. 1981	*Jeeves* Dulwich College.	Revised by Andrew Lloyd Webber.
14 Apr. 1982	*Words By Wodehouse* Olivier Theatre at the National Theatre, London.	A one-man show devised and starring David Ryalt.
2 Feb. 1983	*Ludwig & Bertie* National Theatre, London.	When Wittgenstein meets Wooster by Justin Greene and Steve Cooke.
10 Aug. 1987	*Right Ho/Stiff Upper Lip* Greyfriars Kirk House, Edinburgh Festival.	Robert Goodall and Jeremy Silbertson.

Unproduced Wodehouse Theatre

c. 1918	*The Little Nugget*	
1921	*The Blue Mazurka*	Bolton and Wodehouse, lyrics Wodehouse. Music Kern and Franz Lehar.
1922	*Pat (The Gibson Girl)*	Bolton and Wodehouse, lyrics Wodehouse and Billy Rose.
1947	*Game Of Hearts*	Wodehouse from Molnar.
1947	*Arthur* Produced on US television	Wodehouse from Molnar.
1949	*Uncle Fred Flits By* Published US 1949, possibly produced.	Dramatized by Perry Clarke (Christopher Sergal) from Wodehouse.
1955	*Too Much Springtime* Published US 1955, possibly produced.	Dramatized by Majorie Duhan from *The Mating Season*.
1971	*Leave It To Jeeves*	Bolton and Wodehouse, lyrics Wodehouse.

First New York or London performances only have been given, unless the play was never performed in either town. Many of these plays had provincial, pre-metropolis runs and also toured in America. Many of them appeared in both London and New York.

Summarized from:

Kurt Ganzl, *The British Musical Theatre* vols I and II (London, Macmillan, 1986).

Benny Green, *P.G. Wodehouse* (London, Pavilion Michael Joseph, 1981).

David Hummel, *The Collector's Guide To The American Musical Theatre* (New Jersey, Scarecrow, 1984).

David A. Jasen, *The Theatre of P.G. Wodehouse* (London, Batsford, 1979).

David A. Jasen, *P.G. Wodehouse: A Portrait Of A Master*, revised edition (New York, Continuum, 1981).

Eileen McIlvaine, *P.G. Wodehouse: A Comprehensive Bibliography* (New York, James H. Heineman Inc., 1991).

Walter Rigdon, Ed., *The Biographical Encyclopedia & Who's Who Of The American Theatre* (New York, James H. Heineman Inc., 1966).

Brian Rust with Rex Bennet, *London Musical Shows On Record 1897–1976* (General Gramophone Publications, 1977).

Rick Simas, *The Musicals No-one Came To See: 1943/83* (New York and London, Garland, 1987).

See also the references for *The Trio Of Musical Fame*.

THE LYRICS OF
P.G. WODEHOUSE

1904	*Sergeant Brue* (Liza Lehmann and Frederick Rosse)	Put Me In My Little Cell
1906	*The Beauty Of Bath* (Jerome Kern)	Oh Mr Chamberlain (later Mr Chamberlain) A Frolic Of A Breeze
1907	*My Darling*	
1907	*The Hon'ary Degree* (K.L. Duffield)	My Grassy Corner Girl
1907	*The Gay Gordons* (Guy Jones)	Now That My Ship's Come Home You, You, You
1908	*Girls From Gottenburg*	*Our Little Way
1914	*Nuts & Wine* (Frank E. Tours and Melvile Gideon)	
1915	*Ninety In The Shade* (Jerome Kern)	A Package Of Seeds
1916	*Pom Pom* (Hugo Felix)	Untraced
1916	*Miss Springtime* (Emmerich Kalman and Jerome Kern)	My Castle In The Air Once Upon A Time Saturday Night This Is Existence Throw Me A Rose A Very Good Girl On Sunday When You're Full Of Talk (All Full Of Talk)
1917	*Have A Heart* (Jerome Kern)	And I Am All Alone Bright Lights Daisy Have A Heart Honeymoon Inn I'm Here, Little Girl, I'm Here I'm So Busy Napoleon Polly Believed In Preparedness

The Road That Lies Before
Samakand
They All Look Alike
You Said Something

1917 *Oh, Boy!*
(Jerome Kern) (*Oh Joy!* in
   London)

Aint It A Grand And Glorious
   Feeling
Be A Little Sunbeam
Every Day
Nesting Time In Flatbush
An Old Fashioned Wife
A Package Of Seeds
A Pal Like You
Rolled Into One
Till The Clouds Roll By
We're Going To Be Pals
Words Are Not Needed
You Never Knew About Me

1917 *Leave It To Jane*
(Jerome Kern)

Cleopatterer
The Crickets Are Calling
I'm Going To Find A Girl
It's A Great Big Land
Just You Watch My Step
Leave It To Jane
A Peach Of A Life
Poor Prune
Sir Galahad
The Siren's Song
The Sun Shines Brighter
There It Is Again (a.k.a.
   When Your Favorite Girl's Not
   There)
Wait Till Tomorrow
What I'm Longing To Say
Why?

1917 *Kitty Darlin'*
(Rudolf Friml)

Am I To Blame?
The Blarney Stone
The Dawn Of Love
Dear Bath
Dear Caracloe
Dear Old Dublin
I'd Do The Same
Just We Two
Kitty Darling
The Land Where The Dreams
   Come True
The Maid And The Valet
A Health To Noah (a.k.a. Noah)

		Peggy's Legs
		Spread The News
		Swing Song
		The Sword Of Thy Father
		Tick, Tick, Tick
		When She Gives Him A Shamrock Bloom
		You'll See
1917	*The Riviera Girl*	Half A Married Man
	(Emmerich Kalman and Jerome Kern)	Just A Voice To Call Me Dear
		Let's Build A Little Bungalow In Quogue
		Life's A Tale
		The Lilt Of A Gypsy Strain
		Man, Man, Man
		There'll Never Be Another Girl Like Daisy
		Will You Forget?
1917	*Miss 1917*	Go Little Boat
	(Jerome Kern and Victor Herbert)	I'm The Old Man In The Moon
		The Land Where The Good Songs Go
		Peaches
		The Picture I Want To See
		Tell Me All Your Troubles, Cutie
		We're Crooks
1918	*Oh, Lady! Lady!*	Before I Met You
	(Jerome Kern)	Bill
		Dear Old Prison Days
		Do It Now
		Do Look At Him
		Greenwich Village
		It's A Hard, Hard, World For A Man
		Moon Song
		Not Yet
		Oh, Lady! Lady!
		Our Little Nest
		A/The Picture I Want To See
		Some Little Girl
		The Sun Starts to Shine Again
		Waiting Round The Corner
		Wheatless Days
		When The Ships Come Home
		You Found Me And I Found You
1918	*See You Later*	Anytime Is Dancing Time
	(Jean Schwarts and Joseph Szulc)	Desert Island

		Honeymoon Island
		I Never Knew
		I'm Going To Settle Down
		In Our Little Paradise
		Isn't It Wonderful
		It Doesn't Matter
		Love's A Funny Thing
		Lover's Quarrels
		Mother Paris
		Nerves
		See You Later, Girls
		See You Later Shimmy
		The Train That Leaves For Town
		You Whispered It
		Young Man
1918	*The Girl Behind The Gun* (Ivan Caryll) (*Kissing Time* in London)	Back To The Dear Old Trenches The Girl Behind The Man Behind The Gun A Happy Family I Like It, I Like It I've A System Oh, How Warm It Is Today Some Day Waiting Will End There's A Light In Your Eyes There's Life In The Old Dog Yet Women Haven't Any Mercy On A Man
1918	*The Canary* (Ivan Caryll)	The Hunting Honeymoon Juliet And Her Johnnies That's What Men Are For Thousands Of Years Ago
1918	*Oh, My Dear!* (Louis Hirsch) (Originally *Ask Dad*)	Boat Song Childhood Days City Of Dreams Come Where Nature Calls I Have A Musical Comedy Show I Shall Be Alright Now I Wonder Whether I've Loved You All My Life I'd Ask No More If They Ever Parted Me From You Isn't It Wonderful It Sorta Makes A Fellow Stop And Think The Land Where Journeys End And Dreams Come True You Never Know

1919	*The Rose Of China* (Armand Vecsey)	Bunny Dear College Spirit Down On The Banks Of The Subway In Our Bungalow Tao Loved Hi Li Yale Yesterday
1920	*Sally* (Jerome Kern)	The Church Around The Corner Look For The Silver Lining The Siren's Song You Can't Keep A Good Girl Down (a.k.a. Joan of Arc)
1921	*The Golden Moth* (Ivor Novello)	Dartmoor Days Dear Eyes That Shine Fairey Prince Give Me A Thought Now And Then If I Ever Lost You The Island Of Never-Mind-Where Lonely Soldiers My Girl Nuts In May Romance Is Calling
1922	*The Cabaret Girl* (Jerome Kern)	The Cabaret Girl First Rose Of Summer Journey's End London, Dear Old London Looking All Over For You Mr Gravvins – Mr Gripps Nerves Oriental Dreams The Pergola Patrol Shimmy With Me Those Days Are Gone Forever Whoop-De-Oodle-Do You Want The Best Seats, We Have 'Em
1923	*The Beauty Prize* (Jerome Kern)	Cottage In Kent Honeymoon Isle I'm A Prize It's A Long, Long Day Joy Bells Meet Me Down On Main Street Moon Love Non-stop Dancing

		When You Take The Road With Me

1924	*Sitting Pretty* (Jerome Kern)	You Can't Make Love By Wireless All You Need Is A Girl Bongo On The Congo The Enchanted Train Mr And Mrs Rorer On A Desert Island With You Shadow Of The Moon Shufflin Sam Sitting Pretty Tulip Time In Sing-Sing Worries A Year From Today
1925	*The City Chap* (Jerome Kern)	Journey's End
1927	*The Nightingale* (Armand Vecsey)	Breakfast In Bed Enough Is Enough May Moon Two Little Ships When I Meet You
1927	*Show Boat* (Oscar Hammerstein II and Jerome Kern)	Bill
1928	*Rosalie* (George Gershwin and Sigmund Romberg)	Hussars March (a.k.a. Soldiers Fine Of Mine) Oh Gee! Oh Joy! Say So West Point Song Why Must We Always Be Dreaming
1928	*The Three Musketeers* (Rudolf Friml)	March Of The Musketeers Your Eyes
1960	*Oh, Kay!* Revival	The Twenties Are Here To Stay The Pophams Home (originally Don't Ask) You'll Still Be There (originally Dear Little Girl)
1971	*Leave It To Jeeves* (Robert Wright & George Forrest)	Untraced

N.B. Changes to songs made on pre-Broadway out-of-town tours and between London and New York explain minor changes in song titles in different records.

*On his pre-1910 London writing paper Wodehouse listed the song 'Our Little Way' from the show *Girls From Gottenburg* under 'Some recent song successes'.

Summarized from:
Kurt Ganzl, *The British Musical Theatre* vols I and II (London, Macmillan, 1986).
Benny Green, *P.G. Wodehouse* (London, Pavilion Michael Joseph, 1981).
David Hummel, *The Collector's Guide To The American Musical Theatre* (New Jersey, Scarecrow, 1984).
Edward Jablonski, sleeve notes to the DRG Records CD of the 1960 revival of *Oh, Kay!*.
David A. Jasen, *The Theatre Of P.G. Wodehouse* (London, Batsford, 1979).
David A. Jasen, *P.G. Wodehouse: A Portrait Of A Master*, revised edition (New York, Continuum, 1981).
Eileen McIlvaine, *P.G. Wodehouse: A Comprehensive Bibliography* (New York, James H. Heineman, 1991).
Brian Rust with Rex Bennet, *London Musical Shows On Record 1897–1976* 1977. General Gramophone Publications.
Rick Simas, *The Musicals No-One Came To See: 1943/83* (Garland, New York and London, 1987).
See also the references for *The Trio Of Musical Fame*.

—Appendix 6—

THE FILMS OF
P.G. WODEHOUSE

(Taking The Big, Broad View)

1915	*Gentleman of Leisure* Silent	Screenplay by John Stapleton, Wodehouse and Cecil B. deMille.
1917	*Uneasy Money* Silent.	From the Wodehouse novel.
1919	*Oh Boy!* Silent.	From the Bolton, Wodehouse and Kern musical.
1919	*Piccadilly Jim* Silent.	From the Wodehouse novel.
1920	*The Prince And Betty* Silent.	From the Wodehouse novel.
1920	*Damsel In Distress* Silent.	From the Wodehouse novel.
1920	*Oh Lady! Lady!* Silent.	From the Bolton, Wodehouse and Kern musical.
1920	*Their Mutual Child* Silent.	From the Wodehouse novel.
1921	*Stick Around* Silent.	From a Wodehouse story.
1923	*A Gentleman Of Leisure* Silent.	From the Wodehouse novel.
1924	*The Clicking Of Cuthbert* *Chester Forgets Himself* *The Long Hole* a.k.a. *The Moving* *Hazard* *Ordeal By Golf* *Rodney Fails To Qualify* *The Magic Plus Fours*	Series from Wodehouse golf stories.
1926	*Sally*	From the show *Sally* which had Wodehouse lyrics.
1926	*Der Goldene Schmetterling* (*The Golden Butterfly*) Silent – in German!	From the Wodehouse play *The* *Golden Moth*.
1927	*The Small Bachelor* Silent.	From the Wodehouse story.
1928	*Oh Kay!* Silent.	From the Bolton, Wodehouse and Kern musical.

1929	*Her Cardboard Lover* Silent – star, Tallulah Bankhead.	Co-scriptwriter.
1929	*Show Boat* Poor early sound.	With Wodehouse's lyric for 'Bill'.
1930	*Sally*	From the show *Sally* which had Wodehouse lyrics.
1930	*Those Three French Girls* MGM – star, George Grossmith.	Co-scriptwriter.
1931	*The Man In Possession* MGM – star, Robert Montgomery.	Co-scriptwriter.
1932	*Brother Alfred*	From the Westbrook, Wodehouse play.
1933	*Summer Lightning* Star, Ralph Lynn.	From the Wodehouse novel.
1933	*Leave It To Me*	From the Wodehouse, Hay play, *Leave It To Psmith*.
1934	*Have A Heart* MGM.	From the Bolton, Wodehouse and Kern musical.
1935	*Dizzy Dames* Liberty Pictures. Director, William Nigh.	George Waggner, from Wodehouse's *The Watch Dog*.
1936	*Piccadilly Jim* MGM.	From the Wodehouse novel.
1936	*Anything Goes* Paramount. Stars, Bing Crosby and Ethel Merman.	Screenplay by Bolton and Wodehouse from their original musical.
1936	*Show Boat* Universal. Stars include Paul Robeson.	With Wodehouse's lyric for 'Bill'.
1936	*Thank You Jeeves* Twentieth Century Fox. Stars, David Niven and Arthur Treacher.	From the Wodehouse novel.
1937	*A Damsel In Distress* RKO. Stars, Fred Astaire and Joan Fontaine.	Co-screenwriter from his own novel.
1937	*Rosalie* MGM. Stars, Nelson Eddy, Eleanor Powell.	Uncredited co-scriptwriter.
1937	*That Certain Woman* Warner Brothers. See text.	Eddie Goulding took sole screen credit.
1937	*Step Lively Jeeves* Twentieth Century Fox. Star, Arthur Treacher.	Based on Wodehouse characters.
1946	*Till The Clouds Roll By* MGM. A life of Jerome Kern.	With five Wodehouse lyrics.
1951	*Show Boat* MGM.	With Wodehouse's lyric for 'Bill'.

1956 *Anything Goes*
Paramount.

From the Wodehouse Bolton musical.

1957 *The Helen Morgan Story*
Warner Brothers.

With Wodehouse's lyric for 'Bill'.

1961 *The Girl On The Boat*
Knightsbridge/United Artists.

From the Wodehouse novel.

Sources

British Film Catalogue 1895/1970, The (UK, David & Charles, 1973).

Richard Bertrand Dimmitt, *A Title Guide to The Talkies* (New York, Scarecrow Press, 1965).

Jack C. Ellis, *Film Book Bibliography*, Charles Derry and Sharon Kern (New Jersey, Scarecrow Press, 1979).

S.G.S. Enser, *Filmed Books And Plays 1928–1986* (UK Gower, 1987).

Leslie Halliwell, *Halliwell's Film Guide*, 75th edn. (London, Grafton, 1989).

Leslie Halliwell, *Halliwell's Filmgoers Companion*, 9th edn, (London, Grafton, 1988).

Eileen McIlvaine, *P.G. Wodehouse: A Comprehensive Bibliography* (New York, James H. Heineman, 1991).

Jay Roberts Nash, Stanley Ralph Ross, *The Motion Picture Guide 1927–1983* Chicago, Cinebooks Inc.

National Film Theatre, September 1981 programme covering their Wodehouse centenary season.

—Appendix 7—

ENGLISH FIRST EDITIONS
OF P.G. WODEHOUSE

* Preceded by the US edition.
+ Not published in the US.
   US titles, where different, in parenthesis. Includes books edited by
   Wodehouse, and Wodehouse-only anthologies published in his lifetime.

18 Sep. 1902	*The Pothunters*	A. and C. Black
11 Sep. 1903	*A Prefect's Uncle*	A. and C. Black
10 Nov. 1903	+*Tales Of St Austin's*	A. and C. Black
13 Sep. 1904	*The Gold Bat*	A. and C. Black
11 Nov. 1904	*William Tell Told Again*	A. and C. Black
5 Oct. 1905	*The Head Of Kay's*	A. and C. Black
June 1906	*Love Among The Chickens*	George Newnes
9 Oct. 1907	*The White Feather*	A. and C. Black
18 Oct. 1907	*Not George Washington* With Herbert Westbrook	Cassell
June 1908	*The Globe By The Way Book* With Herbert Westbrook	The Globe
16 Apr. 1909	*The Swoop! Or How Clarence Saved England*	Alston Rivers
15 Sep. 1909	*Mike*	A. and C. Black
23 Sep. 1910	*Psmith In The City*	A. and C. Black
15 Nov. 1910	**A Gentleman Of Leisure* (*The Intrusion of Jimmy*)	Alston Rivers
1 May 1912	*The Prince And Betty* Very different from the same US title.	Mills and Boon
28 Aug. 1913	*The Little Nugget*	Methuen
23 Jan. 1914	+*The Man Upstairs And Other Stories*	Methuen
16 Sep. 1915	*Something Fresh (*Something New*)	Methuen
29 Sep. 1915	*Psmith Journalist* Very different from the same US title	A. and C. Black
4 Oct. 1917	*Uneasy Money	Methuen
8 Mar. 1917	*The Man With Two Left Feet*	Methuen
May 1918	*Piccadilly Jim	Herbert Jenkins
May 1919	*My Man Jeeves*	George Newnes

15 Oct. 1919	*A Damsel In Distress	Herbert Jenkins
1 July 1920	*The Coming Of Bill	Herbert Jenkins
	(Their Mutual Child)	
14 Feb. 1921	Indiscretions Of Archie	Herbert Jenkins
June 1921	+Love Among The Chickens	Herbert Jenkins
	Entirely re-written, so first thus	
4 Jul. 1921	*Jill The Reckless	Herbert Jenkins
	(The Little Warrior)	
3 Feb. 1922	The Clicking Of Cuthbert	Herbert Jenkins
	(Golf Without Tears)	
15 June 1922	*The Girl On The Boat	Herbert Jenkins
	(Three Men And A Maid)	
17 Oct. 1922	The Adventures Of Sally	Herbert Jenkins
	(Mostly Sally)	
17 May 1923	The Inimitable Jeeves	Herbert Jenkins
	(Jeeves)	
30 Nov. 1923	Leave It To Psmith	Herbert Jenkins
3 Jun. 1924	Ukridge	Herbert Jenkins
	(He Rather Enjoyed It)	
13 Nov. 1924	Bill The Conqueror	Methuen
9 Oct. 1925	Carry On, Jeeves!	Herbert Jenkins
15 Oct. 1925	Sam The Sudden	Methuen
	(Sam In The Suburbs)	
15 Apr. 1926	The Heart Of A Goof	Herbert Jenkins
	(Divots)	
28 Apr. 1927	The Small Bachelor	Methuen
27 Sep. 1927	Meet Mr Mulliner	Herbert Jenkins
23 Mar. 1928	+Good Morning Bill (A play)	Methuen
	Listed here as published as a hard-cover book	
27 July 1928	Money For Nothing	Herbert Jenkins
30 Apr. 1929	Mr Mulliner Speaking	Herbert Jenkins
19 July 1929	*Summer Lightning	Herbert Jenkins
	(Fish Preferred)	
4 July 1930	Very Good, Jeeves	Herbert Jenkins
20 Mar. 1931	*Big Money	Herbert Jenkins
25 Sep. 1931	*If I Were You	Herbert Jenkins
30 Oct. 1931	+Jeeves Omnibus	Herbert Jenkins
	US Nothing But Wodehouse is similar	
10 Mar. 1932	+Louder And Funnier	Faber and Faber
7 Apr. 1932	+Doctor Sally	Methuen
17 Aug. 1932	Hot Water	Herbert Jenkins
	Simultaneous UK/US publication	
17 Jan. 1933	Mulliner Nights	Herbert Jenkins
Mar. 1933	The Great Sermon Handicap	Hodder and Stoughton
	Miniature book	
10 Aug. 1933	*Heavy Weather	Herbert Jenkins

Feb. 1934	⁺*P.G. Wodehouse* In the Methuen Library Of Humour series	Methuen
16 Mar. 1934	*Thank You, Jeeves*	Herbert Jenkins
Sep. 1934	⁺*A Century Of Humour* Edited by P.G. Wodehouse	Hutchinson
5 Oct. 1934	*Right Ho, Jeeves* (*Brinkley Manor*)	Herbert Jenkins
14 Feb. 1935	*Enter Psmith* The second half of *Mike*. Later republished as *Mike And Psmith*	A. and C. Black
12 Apr. 1935	*Blandings Castle And Elsewhere* (*Blandings Castle*)	Herbert Jenkins
11 Oct. 1935	*The Luck Of The Bodkins*	Herbert Jenkins
25 Oct. 1935	⁺*Mulliner Omnibus*	Herbert Jenkins
3 Apr. 1936	*Young Men In Spats*	Herbert Jenkins
25 Sep. 1936	*Laughing Gas*	Herbert Jenkins
19 Mar. 1937	*Lord Emsworth And Others* (*The Crime Wave At Blandings*)	Herbert Jenkins
11 Feb. 1938	*Summer Moonshine	Herbert Jenkins
7 Oct. 1938	*The Code Of The Woosters* Simultaneous UK/US publication	Herbert Jenkins
12 May 1939	*Week-End Wodehouse (*The Week-End Wodehouse*)	Herbert Jenkins
25 Aug. 1939	*Uncle Fred In The Springtime	Herbert Jenkins
26 Apr. 1940	*Eggs, Beans And Crumpets*	Herbert Jenkins
4 Oct. 1940	*Quick Service*	Herbert Jenkins
27 May 1946	*Money In The Bank	Herbert Jenkins
2 Jun. 1947	*Joy In The Morning	Herbert Jenkins
17 Oct. 1947	*Full Moon	Herbert Jenkins
20 May 1948	*Spring Fever Simultaneous UK/US publication	Herbert Jenkins
22 Oct. 1948	*Uncle Dynamite*	Herbert Jenkins
9 Sep. 1949	*The Mating Season*	Herbert Jenkins
21 July 1950	*Nothing Serious*	Herbert Jenkins
18 Apr. 1951	*The Old Reliable*	Herbert Jenkins
21 Apr. 1952	*Barmy In Wonderland* (*Angel Cake*)	Herbert Jenkins
31 Oct. 1952	*Pigs Have Wings	Herbert Jenkins
Feb. 1953	*Mike At Wrykyn* The first half of *Mike*	Herbert Jenkins
22 Apr. 1953	*Ring For Jeeves* (*The Return Of Jeeves*)	Herbert Jenkins
9 Oct. 1953	⁺*Performing Flea* Very different from US title *Author!* *Author!*	Herbert Jenkins
19 Feb. 1954	*The Week-End Book Of Humour (*The Week-End Book Of Humor*)	Herbert Jenkins

21 May 1954	*Bring On The Girls	Herbert Jenkins
15 Oct. 1954	Jeeves And The Feudal Spirit (Bertie Wooster Sees It Through)	Herbert Jenkins
20 Jan. 1956	French Leave	Herbert Jenkins
18 Jan. 1957	Something Fishy (The Butler Did It.)	Herbert Jenkins
11 Oct. 1957	+Over Seventy Very different from US title America I Like You.	Herbert Jenkins
20 June 1958	Cocktail Time	Herbert Jenkins
26 June 1959	*A Few Quick Ones	Herbert Jenkins
12 Aug. 1960	*Jeeves In The Offing (How Right You Are, Jeeves)	Herbert Jenkins
15 Oct. 1961	*Ice In The Bedroom (The Ice In The Bedroom)	Herbert Jenkins
17 Aug. 1962	*Service With A Smile	Herbert Jenkins
16 Aug. 1963	*Stiff Upper Lip, Jeeves	Herbert Jenkins
14 Aug. 1964	*Frozen Assets (Biffen's Millions)	Herbert Jenkins
26 Aug. 1965	*Galahad At Blandings (The Brinkmanship of Galahad Threepwood)	Herbert Jenkins
22 Sep. 1966	Plum Pie	Herbert Jenkins
24 Oct. 1967	*Company For Henry (The Purloined Paperweight)	Herbert Jenkins
Sep. 1968	*A Carnival Of Modern Humour (A Carnival Of Modern Humor)	Herbert Jenkins
19 Sep. 1968	*Do Butlers Burgle Banks?	Herbert Jenkins
25 Sep. 1969	A Pelican At Blandings (No Nudes Is Good Nudes – I'm not joking.)	Herbert Jenkins
29 Oct. 1970	The Girl In Blue	Barrie and Jenkins
15 Oct. 1971	Much Obliged, Jeeves (Jeeves And The Tie That Binds) Simultaneous UK/US publication.	Barrie and Jenkins
12 Oct. 1972	Pearls, Girls And Monty Bodkin (The Plot That Thickened)	Barrie and Jenkins
2 Apr. 1973	The Golf Omnibus Similar to the US 1940 Wodehouse On Golf	Barrie and Jenkins
15 Oct. 1973	Bachelors Anonymous	Barrie and Jenkins
Apr. 1974	The World Of Psmith	Barrie and Jenkins
Oct. 1974	Aunts Aren't Gentlemen (The Catnappers)	Barrie and Jenkins
17 Nov. 1977	Sunset At Blandings Not completed. Edited by Richard Usborne.	Chatto and Windus
1984	Sir Agravaine	Blandford Press

1988	*The Parrot And Other Poems*	Hutchinson
1990	*Yours Plum*	Hutchinson
1991	*A Man Of Means*	Porpoise Books

AMERICAN BOOKS NOT PUBLISHED IN ENGLAND

1932 *Nothing But Wodehouse*
1940 *Wodehouse On Golf*
1949 *The Best Of Wodehouse*
1951 *The Best Of Modern Humor* (Edited P.G.W.)
1956 *America I Like You*
1958 *Selected Stories by P.G. Wodehouse*
1960 *The Most Of P.G. Wodehouse*
1962 *Author! Author!*
1967 *A Carnival Of Modern Humor*
1976 *Uncollected Wodehouse*
1980 *The Eighteen Carat Kid*

See the table of American first editions for details of the above titles.

—Appendix 8—

AMERICAN FIRST EDITIONS OF P.G. WODEHOUSE

* Preceded by the UK edition.
+ Not published in the UK.
UK titles in parenthesis where different. Includes books edited by
Wodehouse, and Wodehouse-only anthologies published in his lifetime.

1902	*The Pothunters*	Macmillan
	All US titles published by Macmillan were from sheets imported from the UK.	
1903	*A Prefect's Uncle*	Macmillan
1904	*William Tell Told Again*	Macmillan
11 May 1909	*Love Among The Chickens*	Circle
Feb. 1910	*Mike*	Macmillan
11 May 1910	*The Intrusion of Jimmy* (*A Gentleman Of Leisure*)	W.J. Watt
Nov. 1910	*Psmith In The City*	Macmillan
14 Feb. 1912	*The Prince And Betty*	W.J. Watt
	Very different from the same UK title.	
10 Jan. 1914	*The Little Nugget*	W.J. Watt
1915	*Psmith Journalist*	Macmillan
	Very different from the same UK title.	
3 Sep. 1915	*Something New* (*Something Fresh*)	D. Appleton
17 Mar. 1916	*Uneasy Money*	D. Appleton
24 Feb. 1917	*Piccadilly Jim*	Dodd Mead
5 Aug. 1919	*Their Mutual Child* (*The Coming Of Bill*)	Boni and Liveright
4 Oct. 1919	*A Damsel In Distress*	George H. Doran
8 Oct. 1920	*The Little Warrior* (*Jill The Reckless*)	George H. Doran
15 July 1921	*Indiscretions Of Archie*	George H. Doran
1922	*The Head Of Kay's*	Macmillan
1922	*The White Feather*	Macmillan
15 June 1922	*Three Men And A Maid* (*The Girl On The Boat*)	George H. Doran
29 Mar. 1923	*Mostly Sally* (*The Adventures of Sally*)	George H. Doran

1923	*The Gold Bat*	Macmillan
28 Sep. 1923	*Jeeves*	George H. Doran
	(The Inimitable Jeeves)	
14 Mar. 1924	*Leave It To Psmith*	George H. Doran
28 May 1924	*Golf Without Tears*	George H. Doran
	(The Clicking Of Cuthbert)	
20 Feb. 1925	*Bill The Conqueror*	George H. Doran
30 July 1925	*He Rather Enjoyed It*	George H. Doran
	(Ukridge)	
6 Nov. 1925	*Sam In The Suburbs*	George H. Doran
	(Sam The Sudden)	
4 Mar. 1927	*Divots*	George H. Doran
	(The Heart Of A Goof)	
17 June 1927	*The Small Bachelor*	George H. Doran
7 Oct. 1927	*Carry On, Jeeves!*	George H. Doran
2 Mar. 1928	*Meet Mr Mulliner*	Doubleday Doran
28 Sep. 1928	*Money For Nothing*	Doubleday Doran
1 July 1929	*Fish Preferred*	Doubleday Doran
	(Summer Lightning)	
21 Feb. 1930	*Mr Mulliner Speaking*	Doubleday Doran
20 June 1930	*Very Good, Jeeves*	Doubleday Doran
30 Jan. 1931	*Big Money*	Doubleday Doran
3 Sep. 1931	*If I Were You*	Doubleday Doran
20 July 1932	+*Nothing But Wodehouse*	Doubleday Doran
	Similar to the UK *Jeeves Omnibus* of 1931.	
17 Aug. 1932	*Hot Water*	Doubleday Doran
	Simultaneous US/UK publication.	
10 Feb. 1933	*The Man With Two Left Feet*	A.L. Burt
15 Feb. 1933	*Mulliner Nights*	Doubleday Doran
28 July 1933	*Heavy Weather*	Little, Brown
28 Apr. 1934	*Thank You, Jeeves*	Little, Brown
15 Oct. 1934	*Brinkley Manor*	Little, Brown
	(Right Ho, Jeeves)	
17 Sep. 1935	*Enter Psmith*	Macmillan
	The second half of *Mike*. Later republished as *Mike And Psmith*.	
20 Sep. 1935	*Blandings Castle*	Doubleday Doran
	(Blandings Castle And Elsewhere)	
3 Jan. 1936	*The Luck Of The Bodkins*	Little, Brown
24 July 1936	*Young Men In Spats*	Doubleday Doran
19 Nov. 1936	*Laughing Gas*	Doubleday Doran
25 June 1937	*The Crime Wave At Blandings*	Doubleday Doran
	(Lord Emsworth And Others)	
8 Oct. 1937	*Summer Moonshine*	Doubleday Doran
7 Oct. 1938	*The Code Of The Woosters*	Doubleday Doran
	Simultaneous US/UK publication.	

20 Jan. 1939	*The Week-End Wodehouse* (*Week-End Wodehouse*)	Doubleday Doran
18 Aug. 1939	*Uncle Fred In The Springtime*	Doubleday Doran
10 May 1940	**Eggs, Beans And Crumpets*	Doubleday Doran
23 Aug. 1940	*+Wodehouse On Golf*	Doubleday Doran
	Similar to UK *The Golf Omnibus* 1973.	
27 Dec. 1940	**Quick Service*	Doubleday Doran
9 Jan. 1942	*Money In The Bank*	Doubleday Doran
22 Aug. 1946	*Joy In The Morning*	Doubleday Doran
22 May 1947	*Full Moon*	Doubleday Doran
20 May 1948	*Spring Fever*	Doubleday Doran
	Simultaneously US/UK publication.	
29 Nov. 1948	**Uncle Dynamite*	Didier
12 Sep. 1949	*+The Best Of Wodehouse*	Pocket Books
28 Nov. 1949	**The Mating Season*	Didier
1951	*+The Best Of Modern Humor*	Medill McBride
	Edited by P.G. Wodehouse and Scott Meredith.	
24 May 1951	**Nothing Serious*	Doubleday
11 Oct. 1951	*The Old Reliable*	Doubleday
8 May 1952	**Angel Cake* (*Barmy In Wonderland*)	Doubleday
16 Oct. 1952	*Pigs Have Wings*	Doubleday
8 Nov. 1952	**The Week-End Book Of Humor* (*The Week-End Book Of Humour*)	Ives Washburn
1953	*Mike At Wrykyn* The first half of *Mike*	Meredith Press
22 Apr. 1953	**The Return Of Jeeves* (*Ring For Jeeves*)	Simon and Schuster
5 Oct. 1953	*Bring On The Girls!*	Simon and Schuster
15 Oct. 1954	**Bertie Wooster Sees It Through* (*Jeeves And The Feudal Spirit*)	Simon and Schuster
3 May 1956	*+America I Like You* Very different from UK title *Over* *Seventy.*	Simon and Schuster
23 Jan. 1957	**The Butler Did It* (*Something Fishy.*)	Simon and Schuster
24 July 1958	**Cocktail Time*	Simon and Schuster
25 Aug. 1958	*+Selected Stories By P.G. Wodehouse*	Modern Library
13 Apr. 1959	*A Few Quick Ones*	Simon and Schuster
28 Sep. 1959	**French Leave*	Simon and Schuster
12 Aug. 1960	*How Right You Are, Jeeves* (*Jeeves In The Offing*)	Simon and Schuster
15 Oct. 1960	*+The Most Of P.G. Wodehouse*	Simon and Schuster
2 Feb. 1961	*The Ice In The Bedroom* (*Ice In The Bedroom*)	Simon and Schuster
15 Oct. 1961	*Service With A Smile*	Simon and Schuster

20 June 1962	+*Author! Author!*	Simon and Schuster
	Very different from UK title *Performing Flea.*	
22 Mar. 1963	*Stiff Upper Lip, Jeeves*	Simon and Schuster
14 July 1964	*Biffen's Millions*	Simon and Schuster
	(Frozen Assets)	
31 Dec. 1964	*The Brinkmanship Of Galahad Threepwood*	Simon and Schuster
	(Galahad At Blandings)	
12 May 1967	*The Purloined Paperweight*	Simon and Schuster
	(Company For Henry)	
12 June 1967	*A Carnival Of Modern Humor*	Simon and Schuster
	(A Carnival Of Modern Humour)	
	Edited by P.G. Wodehouse and Scott Meredith.	
1 Dec. 1967	*Plum Pie	Simon and Schuster
5 Aug. 1968	*Do Butlers Burgle Banks?*	Simon and Schuster
11 Feb. 1970	*No Nudes Is Good Nudes	Simon and Schuster
	(A Pelican At Blandings)	
22 Feb. 1971	*The Girl In Blue	Simon and Schuster
15 Oct. 1971	*Jeeves And The Tie That Binds*	Simon and Schuster
	(Much Obliged Jeeves)	
	Simultaneous US/UK publication.	
12 Apr. 1973	*The Golf Omnibus*	Simon and Schuster
	Simultaneous US/UK publication. Similar to the US 1940 *Wodehouse On Golf.*	
6 Aug. 1973	*The Plot That Thickened*	Simon and Schuster
	(Pearls, Girls And Monty Bodkin)	
28 Aug. 1974	*Bachelors Anonymous	Simon and Schuster
14 Apr. 1975	*The Catnappers	Simon and Schuster
	(Aunts Aren't Gentlemen)	
19 Sep. 1978	*Sunset At Blandings	Simon and Schuster
	Not completed. Edited by Richard Usborne.	
14 May 1979	*The Swoop And Other Stories	Seabury Press
	(The Swoop: Or How Clarence Saved England)	
1980	+*The Eighteen Carat Kid*	Continuum
1980	*Not George Washington	Continuum
	With Herbert Westbrook	
1983	*The Great Sermon Handicap*	James H. Heineman
1983	*Uncollected Wodehouse*	Continuum
1985	*The Globe By The Way Book*	James H. Heineman and Sceptre Press
	Published US and UK.	
1990	*Yours Plum*	James H. Heineman

ENGLISH BOOKS NOT PUBLISHED IN AMERICA

1903 *Tales Of St Austin's*
1914 *The Man Upstairs*
1921 *Love Among The Chickens*
Rewritten edition
1928 *Good Morning Bill*
1931 *Jeeves Omnibus*
1932 *Louder And Funnier*
1932 *Doctor Sally*
1934 *P.G. Wodehouse*
Methuen Library Of Humour
1934 *A Century Of Humour* (Edited by P.G.
Wodehouse)
1935 *Mulliner Omnibus*
1953 *Performing Flea*
1957 *Over Seventy*
1984 *Sir Agravaine*
1990 *The Parrot And Other Poems*
1991 *A Man Of Means*

See the table of English first editions for details of these titles.

—Appendix 9—

BOOKS ABOUT
P.G. WODEHOUSE AND HIS
WORK

First editions only.
* Literary criticism
# Reference
+ Biography

*1961 Richard Usborne, *Wodehouse At Work* (UK, Jenkins).
*1966 Richard Voorhees, *P.G. Wodehouse* (US, Twayne).
*1966 R.D.B. French, *P.G. Wodehouse* (UK, Oliver and Boyd).
*1966 R.B.D. French, *P.G. Wodehouse* (US, Barnes and Noble).
*1967 Geoffrey Jaggard, *Wooster's World* (UK, Macdonald).
*1968 Geoffrey Jaggard, *Blandings The Blest* (UK, Macdonald).
#1970 David A. Jasen, *A Bibliography And Readers' Guide To The First Editions Of P.G. Wodehouse* (US, Archon).
*1972 Herbert W. Wind, *The World of P.G. Wodehouse* (US, Praeger).
*1973 Thelma Cazalet-Keir, Ed. *Homage To P.G. Wodehouse* (UK, Barrie and Jenkins).
*1974 Robert A. Hall Jr. *The Comic Style of P.G. Wodehouse* (US, Archon).
+#1974 David A. Jasen, *P.G. Wodehouse: A Portrait Of A Master* (US, Manson and Lipscombe).
*1977 Owen Dudley Edwards, *P.G. Wodehouse* (UK, Martin Brian and O'Keefe).
*1977 Richard Usborne, *Wodehouse At Work To The End* (Revised text of *Wodehouse At Work*) (UK, Barrie and Jenkins).
*1977 Richard Usborne, *Vintage Wodehouse* (UK, Barrie and Jenkins).
+1979 Joseph Connolly, *P.G. Wodehouse: An Illustrated Biography* (UK, Orbis).
1979 C. Northcote Parkinson, *Jeeves: A Gentleman's Personal Gentleman* (UK, Macdonald). Included for completeness' sake.
#1979 David A. Jasen, *The Theatre Of P.G. Wodehouse* (UK, Batsford).
*1980 Maha Nand Sharma, *Wodehouse The Fictionist* (India, Prakashan).
*1981 J.H.C. Morris and A.D. Macintyre, *Thank You Wodehouse* (UK, Weidenfeld).
*+1981 Benny Green, *P.G. Wodehouse: A Literary Biography* (UK, Pavilion).
*1981 Richard Usborne, *A Wodehouse Companion* (UK, Elm Tree).
+#1981 Iain Sproat, *Wodehouse At War* (UK, Milner).
*+#1981 James H. Heineman and Donald Bensen, ed. *P.G. Wodehouse: A Centenary Celebration* (UK, OUP, and US, Morgan Library).

*#1981 N.T.P. Murphy, *In Search Of Blandings* (UK, privately published, also by London, Secker & Warburg, 1986 with an introduction by Tom Sharpe).
+1982 Frances Donaldson, *P.G. Wodehouse: The Authorized Biography* (UK, Weidenfeld).
#1983 Richard Usborne, *Wodehouse Nuggets* (UK, Hutchinson).
#1987 Daniel Garrison, *Who's Who In Wodehouse* (US, Peter Long).
*1991 Richard Usborne, *After Hours With P.G. Wodehouse* (UK, Hutchinson).

THE JAMES H. HEINEMAN PUBLICATIONS

Jimmy Heineman of New York, the noted Wodehouse collector, expert and enthusiast has published a number of works about P.G. Wodehouse through his eponymous company. Most of these are in finely produced limited editions published simultaneously on both sides of the Atlantic. Often they are the only such publication of the work, sometimes the first US publication.
*1978 Richard Usborne, *Doctor Sir Pelham Wodehouse Old Boy*.
*1982 Frances Donaldson and Richard Usborne, *P.G. Wodehouse 1881–1981*.
*1983 Charles E. Gould Jr. *The Toad At Harrow*.
*1983 Richard Usborne, William Douglas Home, Malcolm Muggeridge and Angus Macintyre, *Three Talks And A Few Words At A Festive Occasion In 1982*.
1983 P.G. Wodehouse, *The Great Sermon Handicap*.
*#1983 Richard Usborne, *Wodehouse Nuggets*.
1985 P.G. Wodehouse, *The Globe By The Way Book*, facsimile edition J.H.Heineman with Sceptre Press.
*#1989 Charles E. Gould Jr., *What's In Wodehouse or Jeeves Has Gone Shrimping And Bertie's In The Soup*.
1989 P. G. Wodehouse, *The Great Sermon Handicap – Rendered Into English, Latin, French, Spanish, Italian, Portuguese, Rumanian, Catalan, Rhaetoromansch and Phonetic English*.
1990 P.G. Wodehouse, *The Great Sermon Handicap – Rendered Into English, Chaucerian English, Dutch, Flemish, Afrikaans, Frisian, German, Mittelhochdeutsch, Plattdeutsch, Luxembourgian, Yiddish, Schwitzerdeutsch and Phonetic English*.
#1990 N.T.P. Murphy, *A True And Faithful Account Of The Amazing Adventures Of The Wodehouse Society On Their Pilgrimage July 1989*.
1990 *Yours Plum*, Edited by Frances Donaldson.
#1991 Eileen McIlvaine, Louise S. Sherby and James H. Heineman, *P.G. Wodehouse: A Comprehensive Bibliography and Checklist*.
*1991 Richard Usborne, *After Hours With P.G. Wodehouse*.
1991 P.G. Wodehouse, *The Great Sermon Handicap – Rendered Into English, Swedish, Norwegian, Old Norse, Icelandic, Danish, Faroese and Phonetic English*.
#+1992 Lee A. Davis, *Bolton, Wodehouse And Kern*, planned publication date, not seen by the author of this book.

—Appendix 10—

DOCTORIS IN LITTERIS
HONORIS CAUSA

The address by Dr Cyril Bailey, Public Orator of Oxford University, at the Encaenia in the Sheldonian Theatre on 21 June 1939 when presenting P.G. Wodehouse to the Vice-Chancellor of the University.

Ecce auctor magicus, quo non expertior alter delectare animos hominum risusque movere. Namque noal scaenae personas intulit et res ridiculas cuique adiunxit. Cui non bene notus dives opum iuvenis, comisque animique benigni, nec quod vult fecisse capax, nisi fidus Achates ipse doli fabricator adest vestisque decentis arbiter? Aut comes ille loquax et ventre rotundo cui patruusque neposque agnatorum et domus omnis miranda in vita – sic narrat – fata obierunt? Nobilis est etiam Clarens, fundique paterni et suis eximiae dominus, Psmintheusque 'relicta cui fac cuncta', Augustus item qui novit amores raniculus, aliusque alio sub sidere natus. Non vitia autem hominum naso suspendit adunco sed tenera pietate notat, peccataque ridet. Hoc quoque, lingua etsi repleat plebeia chartas, non incomposito patitur pede currere verba, concinnus, lepidus, puri sermonis amator.

Quid multa? Quem novere omnes, testimonio non egat. Praesento vobis festivum caput – Petroniumne dicam an Terentium nostrum? – Pelham Grenville Wodehouse, Societatis Regiae Litterarum sodalem, ut admittatur honoris causa ad gradum Doctoris in Litteris.

Dr George Gordon, Vice-Chancellor and President of Magdalen, then bestowed the degree with:

Vir lepidissime, facetissime, venustissime, iocosissime, ridibundissime, te cum turba tua Leporum, Facetiarum, Venustatum, Iocorum, Risuum, ego auctoritate mea et totius Universitatis admitto ad gradum Doctoris in Litteris honoris causa.

INDEX

1. People are listed either under the last names they used in the Wodehouse canon or under the last name by which they appear in this text.
2. People with stage or pen names are listed under that which is best known. Eric Blair refers the reader to the George Orwell entry.
3. Fictional characters are noted thus '(f)'.

325